The Handbook of
EMPLOYMENT RELATIONS,
Law & Practice

4th edition

The Handbook of EMPLOYMENT RELATIONS, Law & Practice

Edited by
Brian Towers

KOGAN
PAGE

London and Sterling, VA

First published in Great Britain in 1987 by Kogan Page Limited as *A Handbook of Industrial Relations Practice*
Second edition 1989
Third edition 1992
Fourth edition 2003 as *The Handbook of Employment Relations, Law & Practice*
Paperback edition 2004

120 Pentonville Road
London N1 9JN
United Kingdom
www.kogan-page.co.uk

22883 Quicksilver Drive
Sterling VA 20166-2012
USA

© Brian Towers, 1987, 1989, 1992, 2003

ISBN 0 7494 4208 5

British Library Cataloguing-in-Publication Data

A CIP record for this book is available from the British Library.

Library of Congress Cataloging-in-Publication Data

Towers, Brian.
  The handbook of employment relations : law and practice / Brian Towers.-- 4th ed.
    p. cm.
  Includes bibliographical references.
  ISBN 0-7494-4208-5
  1. Industrial relations--Great Britain. 2. Labor laws and legislation--Great Britain. I. Title.
KD3040.T69 2004
344.4101—dc22
                    2004001213

Typeset by Saxon Graphics Ltd, Derby
Printed and bound in Great Britain by Biddles Ltd, King's Lynn, Norfolk

For GMJ

Contents

PART IV: EMPLOYMENT RELATIONS PRACTICE

Contributors

Brian Towers, Editor of *The Handbook of Employment Relations, Law and Practice*, is Special Professor in Industrial Relations at Nottingham University Business School and Emeritus Professor at Strathclyde Business School. He is Editor-in-Chief of the *Industrial Relations Journal* which he founded in 1970, and has been an ACAS arbitrator since 1975. He has taught and researched in a number of British and North American universities and his research and publications include comparative studies of industrial relations in Britain, the United States and Europe.

Steven Anderman is Birket Long Professor of Law at the University of Essex and Advising Editor, Industrial Relations Law Reports. He has had long experience as a labour law adviser and has taken a number of 'test cases' to the Employment Appeal Tribunal. He has published widely on labour law and workers' rights including, most recently, the *Law of Unfair Dismissals*, published by Butterworth, 2001.

Chris Baldry holds the Chair of Human Resource Management in the Department of Management and Organization at the University of Stirling. He is currently Editor of the journal *New Technology, Work and Employment*. He has been writing on the subject of the interface between technology and work organization for nearly 20 years. His current research interests include new patterns of work and work–life balance, the role of the built environment in the workplace, and employee safety in the rail industry.

Brenda Barrett is Emeritus Professor of Law at Middlesex University and an Associate Tutor in Employment Law at Leicester University. She has taught employment law and the law of tort for many years and has lectured, researched and published extensively on occupational health and safety both in Britain and overseas.

Ann Blair graduated with a first class LL.B from the University of Leeds in 1993 followed by a research-based LL.M in 1995. She has been Lecturer in Law at Leeds since 1994. From

1983 to 1990, she worked as a voluntary sector advice worker. Her teaching and research interests are in Employment Law, Discrimination, Equity and Trusts and Education Law. She is an active trade unionist and voluntary sector trustee.

David Bott worked for ACAS from its inception in 1974 and from 1976 to 1980 was seconded as Secretary to the newly formed Central Arbitration Committee. He returned to ACAS and eventually retired as Director of the East Midlands Region. He is now Senior Lecturer in Employment Relations and Employment Law at Nottingham Business School.

Steve Bradley is Senior Lecturer in Economics at the University of Lancaster. Before he became an academic he spent ten years working in local government. His research and publications include the economics of education and labour and regional economics. He is the Editor of the journal *Education Economics*.

Virginia Branney is an independent employment relations consultant and trainer and a practising mediator, accredited by the Centre for Effective Dispute Resolution (CEDR), specializing in employment disputes. Formerly she was the national Deputy Head of Local Government for UNISON and is currently an associate of the TUC Partnership Institute as well as a member of the Central Arbitration Committee.

Peter Cressey is Reader in Sociology and Human Resource Management at the University of Bath. He has carried out research for the European Foundation, European Commission and the ILO. His main research and publishing interests focus largely on the EU and include the Social Dialogue, employment, industrial relations and employee participation. His other research interests are corporate strategy, corporate learning and work organization.

Ian Cunningham is Lecturer in Human Resource Management at the University of Strathclyde, Glasgow. His research interests include the management of long-term ill health and disability in the workplace, union recognition and employment relations in non-profit/voluntary organizations.

Tony Dundon is Lecturer in Industrial Relations and Human Resource Management, Department of Management, and Researcher with the Centre for Innovation and Structural Change (CISC), National University of Ireland, Galway. His research interests include employee voice, social partnership, non-union systems of industrial relations and high-performance work systems.

Lynette Harris is Associate Head of HRM at Nottingham Business School. Prior to joining the University, she was a Personnel Director having worked in the public and private sector. She is the author of publications on employment practice in both the academic and practitioner literature. She acts as an independent arbitrator for ACAS and is a member of the arbitral panel which considers unfair dismissal claims.

Jeanette Harrison worked as a management development officer before becoming a lecturer in the University of Ulster. She is currently teaching HRM and Organization Behaviour. She has researched and published in the area of management competence.

Norma Heaton worked for a public sector trade union and the Northern College, Barnsley, before joining the University of Ulster. She teaches HRM and industrial relations and has researched and published in the areas of equality in the workplace, career development and social partnership.

Phil James is Professor of Employment Relations at Middlesex University. He has researched extensively in the fields of industrial relations and occupational health and safety. His current research interests include the management of absence, the employment implications of Best Value in local government, the comparative analysis of worker compensation systems and the human resource strategies of French multinationals.

Ian Kessler is Fellow in Human Resource Management at Templeton College and Lecturer in Management Studies at the Said Business School, University of Oxford. His research interests include payment systems, particularly practices in multinational corporations, and human resource management in the public services. He has also carried out research on employee involvement and the minimum wage. He was formerly a researcher at Warwick University and the Institution of Professional Civil Servants.

Graeme Lockwood is Lecturer in Business Law at the Management Centre, Kings College, University of London. His main research interests are in Collective Labour Law.

Bob Mason started working life as a printing compositor before becoming an academic. He has taught industrial relations and HRM at the Universities of Strathclyde and Ulster. He has researched and published in the areas of trade union organization, Central and Eastern European industrial relations, workers' participation and social partnership.

Joe Morgan has worked as a personnel officer and self-employed management consultant. He is currently a doctoral student in the University of Ulster, looking at the development of workplace social partnerships. He is a part-time lecturer in HRM at the University of Ulster and Queens University Belfast.

Helen Pritchard qualified as a solicitor in 1988 and, after a career in private practice, she is now a self-employed consultant and Lecturer in Law and Management at Leeds University Business School, the Open University and the College of Law. She also sits as part-time tribunal chair for the Appeals Service.

Bob Simpson is Reader in Law specializing in labour law at the London School of Economics. His particular interests include the National Minimum Wage and he has also been involved in research into the impact of the law on industrial disputes.

Ramsumair Singh graduated from the University of Leeds with a BSc in electrical engineering and a PhD in economics. He is a Chartered Electrical Engineer and also holds an LL.B from the University of London. Currently he is an Honorary Research Fellow at Lancaster University. He has published widely and his research interests include the resolution of employment disputes. He is an ACAS arbitrator.

Jim Stewart is Professor of Human Resource Development at Nottingham Business School where he is also Joint Course Leader of the NBS Doctorate in Business Administration. An active researcher and writer, he is the author and co-editor of seven books including *Employee Development Practice* (published by Pearson); and *HRD: A Research Based Approach* (edited with Jim McGoldrick and Sandra Watson, published by Routledge. He is Chair of the UK-based University Forum for HRD.

Roger Undy is Director of the Oxford Institute for Employee Relations at Templeton College, University of Oxford. He is also Reader in the Said Business School and Fellow and Vice President of Templeton College. His research interests include trade union mergers, government and trade union relations, the practice of social partnership and employee information and consultation in the EU.

Adrian Wilkinson is Professor of Human Resource Management and Director of Research at Loughborough University Business School. A graduate of the LSE, his doctoral dissertation was a study of business strategy and labour management in financial services. He has published widely in academic journals on industrial relations and HRM and, among a number of books, his most recent (for the CIPD in 2002) is *People Management and Development: HRM at Work*.

Allan Williams is Emeritus Professor of Organizational Psychology at the City University Business School. He is a Fellow of the British Academy of Management and the British Psychological Society. He was formerly Pro-Vice Chancellor of the City University and Deputy Dean of the Business School. His wide research and publishing interests include organizational development and organizational change.

Kevin Williams is Reader in law at Sheffield Hallam University. He has researched and published widely on employment law and the law of tort and is the author of *An Introduction to Employment Law in Hong Kong* (1990), Oxford University Press.

Foreword

One of my predecessors as chair of ACAS wrote the foreword to the third edition of this handbook when it was published in 1992. In those days it was a Handbook of 'Industrial Relations' whereas now it is a Handbook of 'Employment Relations' and I think this change is significant. Even in 1992 much of the heavy industry and manufacturing in the UK had closed or was closing down. New jobs were being created but these were mainly in the service sector. Industries such as mining, shipbuilding and steelmaking, which had been strongholds of the unions, had declined and union membership was plummeting. Terms like industrial relations and industrial action already sounded old fashioned in a world where industry as we knew it was vanishing. By the mid-nineties the authors of the Workplace Employment Relations Survey (WERS) concluded that the old British adversarial system of industrial relations had largely vanished but no new system had emerged in its place. Much of the talk in the 1990s was of the rise of individualism.

Today the transformation of the workplace continues as new working patterns emerge and technology revolutionizes the way we work. We see that more and more people work in white-collar jobs where they are unlikely to be organized collectively except in the public sector. We read that people will no longer have jobs for life but 'portfolio careers'. We hear how the workplace is merging with the home as there is less and less need for workers to be present in the office as long as they have a computer link. We see a more diverse workforce with increasing numbers of women, ethnic minorities, part-timers, contract workers and many other elements. Work–life balance is seen as the solution to the UK's long-hours culture and an ageing workforce will face huge issues about retirement rights, pensions and age discrimination.

More employment legislation, more employment rights and more complaints to employment tribunals all support the view that employees are collections of individuals. But alongside this growth in individualism is a new interest in collectivism arising partly from legislation and partly from a belief that employee involvement correlates with high performance. Union membership increased by 178,000 between 1997 and 2001 alongside the introduction of a statutory right to recognition. Legislation compels employers to consult representatives of the collective workforce – whether unionized or not – on matters such as redundancies, transfers and health and safety. Works councils are now an established part of European-wide companies and the government is presently consulting on the implementation of the EC Directive to inform and consult employees in all companies with 50 or more employees.

What this means is that 'Employment Relations' is a much more complex, varied and rapidly changing discipline than the 'Industrial Relations' of previous editions of this Handbook. In addition, after years when politicians ignored industrial relations there is a growing recognition that improving employment relations is at the heart of a prosperous economy. There is more need now than ever for cogent analysis of relations between employers and employees and practical advice about how they should be conducted. The publication of this fourth edition is timely and should prove of great value to students and practitioners alike.

Rita Donaghy
Chair
Advisory, Conciliation and Arbitration Service

Introduction to the fourth edition

The first edition of this *Handbook* was published in 1987, followed by the second and third in 1989 and 1992. This fourth edition, appearing over a decade after the third, clearly warranted a major revision given the scale and pace of change in British industrial relations over that period. As in earlier editions, the *Handbook* surveys, details and analyses the current industrial and employment relations scene as well as pointing to likely future developments. However, in a book primarily concerned with the present it is still necessary to be aware of those factors which over time have been, and remain, important in explaining current developments. They include changes in the structure of the national and international economy; changes in politics, government and the law; the changing policies and actions of employers and trade unions; and changes in the structure of employment, including the education, training, skills and aspirations of workers. All of these factors continue to be important, though shifting in their relevance and closely related to each other. At the same time, there have been developments since 1992, some very recent and others of longer provenance, which are worth noting in this Introduction. The most obvious one is that there has been a change in government which, at least in 1997, could have signalled a major shift in public policy towards industrial relations. Additionally, we can identify three other important developments, though much longer in the making, which also deserve a special mention, ie the growing juridification of industrial relations, the application of information technology and the impact of globalization.

After 18 years in office the Conservatives were replaced in 1997 by Labour who were re-elected in 2001 with the prospect, at the time of writing, of a further period in government to, perhaps, 2010.

Labour's return to power and the possibility of a long tenure in government have given some respite, even succour, to the trade unions who have been losing members, in large numbers, for almost every year since 1979. The new government did indeed deliver the broad thrust of its promises to the unions – notably the statutory minimum wage and the recognition provisions in the Employment Relations Act 1999. But other items on the unions' wish list were never promised, such as some retreat from the anti-union legislation of the Thatcher government. Indeed, in most respects the Blair government maintained legislative and policy continuity with its Conservative predecessors: the Prime Minister even boasted that Britain had 'the most lightly regulated labour market of any leading economy in the world',[1] a comment reflecting the government's intention not to return to the industrial relations contexts of the 1970s and what it sees as the attendant problems of confrontational industrial relations, disruptive disputes and an under-achieving economy.

The increasing intrusion of the law into industrial relations, which had begun to accelerate in the 1960s and under all governments, continued under Labour and shows no sign of abatement. Only a part of this has been domestic in origin, such as the Employment Relations Act of 1999 and the Employment Act 2000: the greater part has arisen from British membership of the European Union. EU Directives and other forms of legislation are having an increasing influence upon its member states, most recently on human rights; to counter discrimination on religious belief, sexual orientation and age; and to introduce, EU-wide, institutions providing greater information and consultation for employees. Most of this legislation introduces or extends certain *individual* employment rights. *Collective* rights, such as through new institutions regulating and extending information and consultation at EU or member-state level are not, however, unimportant. During the 1990s and into the 2000s European Works Councils have bedded-down as familiar institutions in EU-wide enterprises. By 2008 the national-level 'works councils' will be in place. Additionally, collective bargaining, between the 'social partners' at supranational and sectoral levels through the 'Social Dialogue', is intended to replace some of the EU's formal, legal regulation of the employment relationship. So far, the Social Dialogue has made only minimal progress but its potential remains as a more flexible, voluntary alternative to legislation.

Information technology has greatly extended its reach and influence in the years since this volume's third edition. In terms of the employment relationship, IT has, for the most part, made it easier for employers to regulate, deploy, and develop their labour forces, or 'human resources' as they are now more usually called. Interestingly though, and even surprisingly, IT has also provided opportunities for trade unions to recruit new members and communicate with their existing members as well as making it easier for them to maximize and enhance their sanctions against employers. Computer databases of members allow unions to canvass opinion on specific issues and test members' willingness to support actions and campaigns. IT also makes it much easier for union members to communicate directly with each other, independently of the unions' structures, thus increasing the opportunities for debate, cooperation and even dissidence. Overall, however, IT is a tool which provides opportunities for unions at least equal to those of management and may yet prove a significant factor in the unions' attempts to revive their membership and influence.

The increasing 'globalization' of the British and other economies has, through the growth of multinational corporations, directly and indirectly influenced the nature and conduct of domestic industrial relations. Although the meaning of globalization, and the claims for its extent and impact, remain subjects of controversy and even widespread concern, it is hard to deny the significance of multinational corporations for employment and the employment relationship. Their often substantial presence within host countries provides much-welcomed employment opportunities and a stimulus to the local economy. But their employment and employee representation policies can also strongly influence industrial relations traditions and practices beyond their own factory gates, particularly the approach of other organizations – and even government – to trade union membership, trade union recognition and collective bargaining. These influences are generally not welcomed by trade unions and their members. Nor has Britain been immune from these influences, although perhaps somewhat less than other industrialized countries.

The three factors briefly discussed here have contributed, among others, to what has been termed, for the period since 1980, the 'transformation' of British Industrial Relations.[2] Additionally, the government's policies in 1997 and after, noted earlier, did not in essence depart from the approach of the Conservatives and, therefore, also contributed to this transformation.

An important feature of this transformation has been the major decline in trade union membership and the consequent contraction in coverage of collective bargaining. Both of these indicators have about halved since 1979 and continue to fall, albeit now much less dramatically. The consequence is that in substantial areas of economic activity employers have been able to implement, unilaterally, strategies and policies with minimal collective negotiation or consultation with their employees. Furthermore, both the Conservative and Labour governments have replaced old-style, voluntary collective bargaining by legal regulation which, to a large extent, has originated in the EU. This decline of an important part of the largely voluntary regulation of the employment relationship and the filling of the gap by unilateral regulation by employers and/or the law justifies the use of the term 'transformation' and the change in the *Handbook*'s title, involving the replacement of 'industrial relations' by 'employment relations'.

The structure of the book, though essentially the same as in 1992, allows for the impact of change within the individual chapters, the exclusion of some chapters and the inclusion of new chapters. The new part 'Alternatives to the Law' has two chapters reflecting the increasing interest in alternative dispute resolution and the government's attempt to divert some of the growth in unfair dismissal claims from employment tribunals to ACAS's recently introduced arbitration alternative.

As in earlier editions, though there are essential revisions of and additions to the contents to bring it up to date, this edition retains the style which was so well received in earlier editions. All the authors describe, analyse and write in an even-handed way, that is, to inform and elucidate rather than advocate. All the contributors have exceptional expertise and knowledge but they are also sensitive to, and experienced in, the practices and compromises of the workplace. The book is therefore intended to appeal to practitioners, in all their variety, as well as its substantial following, in early editions, in universities, business schools and colleges.

As before, I must thank all the contributors for the efficiency, good grace and good humour with which they have approached the task of writing and revision. I am especially grateful to Peter Cressey, Steve Bradley and Jeanette Harrison and her colleagues for contributing excellent chapters at very short notice. I must also thank Rita Donaghy, the Chair of ACAS, for providing a characteristically perceptive Foreword, as her predecessor but one, Douglas Smith, did in 1992. I am also grateful to Susan Murphy whose outstanding skills with word processing and e-mailing resolved many minor, and some major, editing crises.

Finally, for this fourth edition I did not have the advantage of the managerial and editing experience of Pam Arksey, who retired in 2000. However, Glynis Jones, her replacement as Managing Editor of the *Industrial Relations Journal*, provided the same expertise and support in the editing of a volume which though it proved to be far more arduous and protracted than its earlier editions but it has been, in the end, very worthwhile.

Brian Towers
Industrial Relations Journal
Nottingham University Business School
2003

Notes

1 This often-cited statement first appeared in the Foreword to the White Paper 'Fairness at Work' which preceded the Employment Relations Bill, CM 1998, DTI, London.

2 This judgement of the extent of the changes since 1980 is from the Workplace Industrial Relations Surveys, 1980–98. The surveys are discussed, in detail, in Chapter 1.

Part I

The background

1

Overview: the changing employment relationship

Brian Towers

INTRODUCTION

There have now been four major official surveys of British workplace employment relations since 1980, with a fifth currently under discussion. The extent and depth of the changes revealed in the surveys have been such for the authors of the most recent to discard the long-established term 'industrial relations' in favour of 'employee relations' (Cully *et al*, 1999). Furthermore, the authors of the companion volume, drawing upon all four surveys, have concluded that the totality of the developments in the workplace, since 1980, can only be described as a 'transformation':

> Our broad conclusion is that the changes we have documented in this volume can reasonably be described as a transformation. The Conservative government that came to power in 1979 confronted a system of collective employment relations that was dominant, though not universal. It pervaded the whole of the public sector, including the then extensive nationalized industries, and it covered large parts of the private sector, especially manufacturing industry and large employers generally. That system of collective relations, based on the shared values of the legitimacy of representation by independent trade unions and of joint regulation, crumbled in the intervening eighteen years to such an extent that it no longer represents a dominant model. True, the substantially reduced public sector still operates that model to a large degree. But in the far larger private sector of the economy, joint regulation is very much a minority activity. (Millward *et al*, 2000: 234)

This transformation is perhaps most clearly seen in the decline in trade union membership and the contraction of collective bargaining. In 1979, trade union membership in the UK stood at 13.3 million. By 1991 it had fallen to less than 9 million and was 7.5 million in 2001. Density, ie membership as a proportion of employees in employment, fell from well over half to 43 per cent in 1991 and, by 2001, was 29.1 per cent. Although the rate of decline slowed markedly during the 1990s and even showed a marginal increase towards the end of the decade, between 2000 and 2001 further small losses (although these are partly explained by sampling variations) were once again recorded in the official figures. The outcome is that unionization in the private sector is now as low as 19 per cent (42 per cent in 1984); although public sector density remains much higher, at 59 per cent, this is much less than just under 20 years ago when it stood at 80 per cent. The much larger public sector also then employed far more.

Table 1.1   Trade union membership density and collective bargaining coverage in Great Britain,[a] 1984–2001 (%)

Years	Union density			Collective bargaining		
	All	Private	Public	All	Private	Public
1984	47	42	80	71	52	95
1990	38	35	72	54	41	78
1993	32	23	63	49	34	76[b]
2001	29	19	59	36	22	73

[a] All years are for Great Britain except 2001 which is for the UK. Note that the data on union membership and density in Harrison *et al*, Chapter 13, p 247 is also for Great Britain and therefore differs, for 2001, from the data here. Great Britain excludes Northern Ireland, the Channel Islands and the Isle of Man.
[b] Author's estimate.

Source: Brook (2002) n 1; Towers (1997) n 7, Table 3.9

The most recent, detailed, figures do, however, reveal wide variations by industry whilst also reflecting the far-reaching changes in the economy and the structure of employment over the past 25 years. In 2001, density in the manufacturing sector was 27 per cent. In contrast, employees in public administration, education and health recorded 59, 53 and 45 per cent respectively, revealing the changing character and power bases of the trade union movement, now more strongly influenced by professional white collar unions, as the old strongholds of the manual unions have shrunk. At the same time, unionization also varies by region. Northern Ireland (40 per cent), Wales (39 per cent) and the North East (39 per cent) lead the figures, with Eastern and South East England as low as 23 per cent and 22 per cent respectively. Union membership (as WERS also confirms) is also more in evidence in large workplaces: those employing fewer than 25 in 2001 had a density of 15 per cent;

workplaces with 25 or more employees recorded 36 per cent. Women, however, are now at least as likely to be union members as men. Over the years the proportion of women in membership has grown to approach that of men, within an overall decline, so that by 2001, 30 per cent of men were union members and 28 per cent of women. Ominously, however, young people are increasingly less inclined to join unions – a trend of major concern to union leaders. In 2001 only 5 per cent of young people under 20 were unionized. These percentages increase up the age structure to 35 per cent of those 50 years and over. These statistics readily explain why union organizing campaigns increasingly target young people.

The overall, long-term decline in union membership, almost unprecedented in its extent[2], has been mirrored by the contraction in collective bargaining. In 1984, some 71 per cent of all employees (union and non-union) were covered by collective agreements on pay. By 2001 this had almost halved to 36 per cent. Again, public sector coverage remained relatively strong at 73 per cent compared with only 22 per cent in the private sector (Table 1.1). National-level bargaining, especially in local government and education, has also remained a feature of the public sector. But in the private sector, where collective bargaining survives at all, it has been almost wholly decentralized to the workplace for single employers, as multi-employer collective bargaining has virtually disappeared.

The other major feature of the transformation, and largely explained by the decline in union membership and influence, is the remarkable long-term decline in strikes and other forms of industrial action. This decline, for the 25 years from 1975, using five-year annual averages, is illustrated in Table 1.2. The peak year was 1979, the so-called 'winter of discontent', with the loss of 29.5 million working days. This was followed by the long, downwards trend, with only one exceptionally high figure in 1984, the first year of the miners' strike, when the total days lost was 27.1 million.

Table 1.2 Number of stoppages, working days lost and workers involved in the UK, 1975–99

Five-year annual averages		Thousands	
Years	Stoppages	Working days lost	Workers involved
1975–9	2,345	11,663	1,658
1980–4	1,363	10,486	1,298
1985–9	895	3,940	783
1990–4	337	824	223
1995–9	213	495	180

Source: calculated from *Employment Gazette*, **103**, July 1995, p 280, Table 2; *Labour Market Trends*, **110** (8), August 2002, p S90

These two broad parameters of change – the decline in union membership and the gradual withering away of industrial disputes – may yet prove to be transient. Long-term cycles of growth and decline in trade union membership and disputes have for long characterized British industrial relations history.[3] Union membership, and disputes, grew rapidly in the decade up to the outbreak of World War 1, and then fell just as rapidly in the depression which followed the post-war boom – as was noted earlier. There has also been recent speculation for the view that current UK strike figures and other developments are evidence of the beginning of a revival of union militancy led largely from the public sector by new, younger union leaders with members in both the public and private sectors. This prognosis will be returned to later, in the conclusions to the chapter. The next section will outline and discuss the more important contextual and causal factors which could, together, explain the 'transformation' revealed in the WIRS and WERS surveys. This will then be followed by an outline, and discussion of the transformation, drawing mainly on the surveys' findings. Finally, the chapter's conclusions will return to a brief discussion of some of the issues, partly raised earlier, concerning the future of the employment relationship in Britain.

THE CONTEXTS OF CHANGE

The contexts directly and indirectly influencing and changing the employment relationship are always in a state of flux, although, arguably, they can be said to have changed more significantly in the 1980s than at any other time in British post-war history. These contextual changes perhaps lost some of their power in the 1990s during a period of relative consolidation, although new factors became more prominent, not least the effects of the quickening pace of economic globalization and further advances in the impact of information technology on our working and non-working lives. How such changes arise and perpetuate themselves, and the extent to which they explain changes in the employment relationship, are matters of speculation and debate. Here we can do no more than outline and briefly discuss the principal contextual factors. They can be identified as political, economic and legal; technological; organizational; and changes in employment and the labour market. We shall be primarily concerned with the period since 1992, that is, since the third edition of this handbook was published.

Political, economic and legal contexts

In 1990 John Major succeeded Margaret Thatcher as Prime Minister. This was confirmed by the electorate in 1992. The new government continued the anti-union policies of its predecessors, post-1979, although more measured in its approach and with the enactment of only one major piece of legislation – the Trade Union Reform and Employment Rights Act of 1993. The government's principal preoccupation was the UK's relationship with the European Union, which had reached its high point, before the General Election, with the decision to opt out of the Social Chapter provisions of the Maastricht Treaty in 1991. But it was still nervous about the residual influence of the unions, especially given their legitimation and inclusion in the decision-making machinery of the EU as 'social partners' – a status also commonplace in most member states. The Major government echoed the Thatcherite fears, however unfounded in reality, of British unions recovering their pre-1979 power and influence 'by the back door' of the EU.[4] Hence in the 1993 Act it removed ACAS's statutory duty, dating back to 1975, to 'encourage the extension of collective bargaining…', replacing it by promoting 'the improvement of industrial relations in particular by exercising its functions in relation to the settlement of trade disputes'.[5] Additionally, in the final year of the administration legislation was being actively considered to limit, or even remove, the ability of trade unions in 'essential services' to take industrial action. This strategy would clearly not be on the new Labour government's agenda, although its approach to trade unions – not least those representing public sector workers – would be markedly different from Labour governments before 1979.

The Blair government did, however, have some debts to the trade unions. These, for 'new' Labour, had little to do with the origins and history of the two 'wings' of the labour 'movement' but owed much more to the trade unions' contributions – in manpower and money – to the landslide victory at the polls.[6] One of its first instalments was to reverse the Major opt-out of the Social Chapter of the Maastricht Treaty, followed by the setting up of the Low Pay Commission to implement the unions' strong lobby for a national minimum wage, the first time for such a measure in British history. But making history did not extend to anything near the level the unions were asking for. Nor was there any commitment to repeal the Conservatives' anti-union legislation. Despite the reintroduction of a statutory recognition procedure, in the 1999 Employment Relations Act, along lines which sensibly drew upon the two earlier failed attempts, as well as the positive experience of Canada and the negative of the United States, the outcome was still seen as flawed by the TUC and its affiliates. In their view it was too greatly influenced by the CBI and other employers' associations, particularly in the exclusion of small firms (21 or fewer employees) and the requirement, where a ballot is required, of a 40 per cent affirmative vote of all employees in the bargaining unit as well as a majority of those actually voting.

The Blair government remained unapologetic. It saw its pro-business stance as both sensible in itself and as an important ingredient in the making of its electoral success in 1997, a view it saw as confirmed by its second major victory in 2001. The government was also anxious to promote its pro-business views in the EU. The Prime Minister, in the Foreword to the 1999 Employment Relations Act, declared that despite the legislation the UK retained the 'most lightly regulated labour market of any leading economy in the world.'[7] This stance was welcomed by EU-based employers and some EU governments, notably the German, as the EU was developing its own comprehensive, flexible labour market employment strategy.[8] The British government also found allies in EU employers and among some member states in its resistance to the Working Time Directive and its ultimate dilution, in British law, allowing for extensive exclusions by listed occupations and agreements between employers and employees. This broad resistance to EU regulation was most recently seen in the British opposition to, and outcome of, the Directive on Information and Consultation which excludes firms with fewer than 50 employees and will in any case not be phased in until 2008: the original proposal was 2004.

Back in the UK the government has also developed a strong line on the public sector and its unions in its determination to maintain private sector involvement in public sector capital projects, to moderate pay demands and enhance efficiency – policies which do not differ, in their general thrust, from those of the government's Conservative predecessors. But however defensible, in terms of 'what works', such policies are naturally vulnerable to union resistance in a sector where unions still have leverage. Despite its inevitably mixed fortunes elsewhere, the Blair administration has been consistently fortunate in the progress, and/or its management, of the economy. Since 1997, although dating back earlier, inflation has been minimal as economic growth has exceeded its long-term trend rate and unemployment has progressively fallen to the levels of the 1970s. Some part of this performance is explained by global economic buoyancy, not least via the sustained boom in the United States. But whatever the explanations, the government has enjoyed the luxury of expanding public expenditure through rising tax revenues. This progress has contributed to electoral success and minimal challenge from a trade union movement which is much weaker than it was even ten years earlier (albeit less so in the public sector, as noted earlier) and yet still has gained from a government which promises at least 'fairness' if not 'favours'. However, the long-term secular trends in the economy continue to make problems for the trade unions and will continue to contribute to the 'transformation' of the employment relationship. There are also, at the time of writing, a number of storm signals in the global economy. The second biggest economy, Japan, has for some years been experiencing a reversal of its long boom as the biggest economy, the United States is beginning to experience similar problems. Nor is the EU providing any economic redress. A return to sustained economic growth, or even the avoidance of deflation, is perhaps further threatened by public policies developed in the era when the control of inflation was at the top of agendas. Furthermore, 11 September 2001 – and the policy responses to it – pose a continuing serious threat to global political and economic stability. Such developments are well beyond the capacity of trade unions to influence but have obvious negative consequences for economic well-being, employment and union membership.

A greater, though unintended 'threat' to trade unions comes from the EU. EU employment legislation mostly takes the form of individual employment law and regulation rather than collective – such as the European Works Councils' Directive and the impending Information and Consultation Directive. However, though the advance of individual employment rights is welcome to individual employees – such as those for women, part-time and temporary workers – employees generally do not need to be union members to enjoy them, or be covered by collective agreements in the workplace. This unintended negative consequence for the value and attractiveness of trade unions compounds the problems of recruitment and organization which they are already facing.[9] Some aspects of national legislation may, however, prove to be more helpful. For example, a provision of the 1999 Employment Relations Act allows for a trade union official to represent even one member in the workplace, albeit only in grievance and disciplinary procedures, even though this provision involves careful definitions of the procedures and has certain restrictions. Furthermore, though a union's ability to represent one member falls far short of the right to bargain collectively following a successful application under the statutory recognition procedure, it does offer the potential for a union to demonstrate its value to employees on important workplace issues. Additionally, the Employment Act 2002 effectively strengthens the right to be accompanied by the introduction – through later regulations – of minimum statutory procedures which employers must follow or be liable to claims for breach of contract, automatically unfair dismissal and enhanced compensation at an employment tribunal.[10] These workplace opportunities for unions may also be enhanced by ACAS's new jurisdiction for employees wishing to claim unfair dismissal. They can now do so via traditional, private arbitration rather than an employment tribunal. These industrial relations style hearings could allow union officials, representing members, further opportunities to demonstrate their skills and value. The problem, however, is that so far the take-up of cases has been very limited.[11]

Technological change

It is a truism that the extent and pace of technological development is transforming the way we work. The simplest indicator of this is the incidence of what used to be called 'new' technology in both the office and the factory. Between 1984 and 1998 the application of word processors in offices increased from 25 per cent to 90 per cent. Over the same period the automation of factory production – such as applications to machine control, handling and storage – doubled from 44 per cent of workplaces to 87 per cent (Millward *et al*, 2000: 37–8).

The automation of the factory has of course coincided with a steep decline in the total numbers employed in manufacturing and a major fall in the number of large workplaces. This has not been coincidental as technological applications have made it possible to maintain or expand output with substantially smaller numbers of employees. At the same time, the pressures of competition and innovation have led to an increasing search for a more efficient use of resources, not least labour, in the 'high performance' workplace. Academic research in this area has increasingly focused on 'bundles' of practices such as team working, information sharing, job rotation and just-in-time production.[12] However, the impact of such far-reaching innovations has had some unexpected outcomes. Issues and concerns – such as how working time is organized, its relationship to our non-working lives, and the impact of work on our physical and psychological well-being – have clearly become much more important. At the same time, more traditional concerns such as pay, fair treatment at work and job security have lost none of their salience.[13] There is also now growing concern about the appropriate age of retirement and its relationship to the level and security of occupational pensions. This growing 'industrial relations' issue has only a tenuous connection to technological applications.[14] Furthermore, whilst it has long been recognized from both research and experience that terms such as 'best practice' are from the perspective of employers, not workers, there is even some doubt that these practices necessarily lead to more efficient outcomes.[15] Another, perhaps even more unexpected outcome is that trade unions, after a slow early start, are now increasingly aware of, and developing, the potential of information technology in the recruitment, retention and mobilization of their members.[16]

Organizational change

Between 1980 and 1998, as noted earlier, large workplaces have become fewer in number although, somewhat surprisingly, as the WIRS Survey reports, there has been little change in their size. Additionally, large workplaces still dominate total employment, with those employing 500 or more accounting for 30 per cent of all employees (Millward *et al*, 2000: 25).

The continuing importance of large workplaces has well-known implications for the employment relationship. These are more likely to be associated with trade union organization, the existence of a discrete personnel function, and procedures for the orderly resolution of grievances, disciplinary issues and collective disputes. They are also therefore more likely to be those workplaces which have experienced least change in their industrial relations culture over the past 20 years: they remain as islands of relative stability in a sea of change. But they have also become more vulnerable to changes in ownership and control, perhaps especially from abroad. Between 1980 and 1998 the percentage of foreign-owned establishments in manufacturing and extraction increased from 11 to 25 per cent and in services from 5 to 11 per cent (Millward *et al*, 2000: 33). Foreign ownership, especially in firms with US origins, is more likely to be followed by attempts to challenge traditional industrial relations cultures. These enclaves of foreign ownership may also influence locally owned and controlled firms, and even governments, in their industrial relations strategies and policies.[17] But it is outside large organizations and large establishments where the pace is being set. The number of small, more recently founded workplaces – more often than not in private sector services – has increased. The significance of this development is that these workplaces have 'traditionally been characterized by less formal and more unilateral forms of management' (Millward *et al*, 2000: 36). The implications for unions and workplace representation are clear.

The changing labour force

The long-term, secular changes in the labour force responding to changing economic structure, societal change and shifts in public policy are now well documented. The progressive erosion of manufacturing employment, the rise of service sector work and the contraction of the public sector have had profound effects on the composition of employment and the nature of employment contracts. Atypical employment – part-time, temporary and forms of self-employment – has become more common as permanent, full-time work has become less so. These changes have been especially relevant to women and, for reasons of equality of treatment and the progressive removal of discrimination, have attracted the increasing attentions of EU law makers.

Between 1980 and 1998 the employment of women of working age in Britain increased from 59 to 68 per cent, with their share of all employment rising from 42 to 47 per cent. But this growth in women in the workplace has not been in full-time work. This has remained more or less constant, with almost all the expansion being confined to part-time work. Women are also more likely to be found in a limited range of private sector service occupations such as distribution, hotels, catering, repairs, finance and business services as well as in public sector education (Millward *et al*, 2000: 39–42).

The importance of women in the labour force, the industries and occupations in which they are employed and their commonly atypical employment contracts have many social and economic implications and raise numerous issues of equity and social justice. There are also implications for trade unions and collective bargaining since women are only marginally less likely to be unionized than men. This has been becoming so for some time and male and female densities are now very close.[18] There is also now clear evidence that the increasing share of women in employment and their almost equal presence, relative to men, in trade unions has been complemented by major advances in middle and senior management (Millward *et al*, 2000: 227). They have also been making significant advances in employee relations management (12 per cent in 1980 and 39 per cent in 1998) but this, as in other occupations, notably teaching, has been largely confined to the less senior roles:

By 1998 women were particularly well represented in employee relations management relative to other managerial roles. It seems that, as far as employee relations management is concerned, women are breaking through the 'glass ceiling'... However, some observers have noted that within employee relations women managers continue to be disproportionately represented in more junior jobs.[19]

THE CHANGING EMPLOYMENT RELATIONSHIP: STRUCTURE AND COMMITMENT

'In the first three decades of the post-war period, relationships between employers and employees were characterized by extensive involvement of trade unions. These voluntary collective agreements were supported by a shared commitment to joint regulation and bolstered by high levels of institutional membership on both sides. Our four surveys show a progressive disintegration of this institutional structure, facilitated by the weakening of both sides' commitment to both the structures and the values of joint regulation' (Millward *et al*, 2000: 227).

The outcomes of the breakdown of the 'institutional structure' and the retreat from 'commitment to the structures... and the values of joint regulation' are well-illustrated in the decline of trade union membership and the contraction of collective bargaining, as shown earlier in Table 1.2.

The breakdown of the institutional structure of collective bargaining – preceded and made possible by the decline of union membership – is also seen in the virtual disappearance of industry-level, single-employer and multi-employer bargaining. Falling membership is also closely linked to the processes of recognition. When membership is rising, recognition is easier to secure; but when it is falling employers naturally find it easier to press for derecognition or resist demands for recognition.[20] The WIRS 1980–1998 survey found, however, that actual derecognition has been minimal. The more common experience is that unions have been unable to gain a membership foothold in new workplaces and, in consequence, recognition could not even be claimed, let alone achieved. Furthermore, even where recognition is already in place, employers have sometimes been able to end collective bargaining or, more commonly, to reduce its scope – even in the public sector. Pay, for example, is no longer a standard ingredient of collective bargaining and may simply be set, unilaterally, by employers. Unions have also generally not replaced their role in pay determination by a more active role in joint consultation. Health and safety committees have been the exception. This must largely derive from growing EU legislation in this area. But this exceptional development confirms that, to a very large extent, union representation of workers' interests has not yet found a widespread, adequate alternative (Millward *et al*, 2000: 227–30); ie a 'representation gap' or, more graphically, a 'black hole' (Guest, 1995) has opened up and, on the evidence of the WIRS and WERS surveys, is growing.

Decentralization, workplace autonomy and employee relations management

The WIRS and WERS surveys have also confirmed the extent to which employers have been able to decentralize collective bargaining over pay in the context of weakening trade unions. Multi-employer pay bargaining with confederations of trade unions has now largely disappeared as collective bargaining has itself contracted. In 1998 only 13 per cent of workplaces with 25 or more employees had the pay of their employees set in this way. In 71 per cent of workplaces it was determined by management alone, of which 30 per cent was in the workplace (Millward *et al*, 2000: 186, Table 6.1).

One consequence of this development is the difficulty of drawing useful pay comparisons, between industries by employers and governments, in the making of policy. But it is not a development with clearly defined contours. Though the general picture is clear, many pay settlements are set, unilaterally, at head office or, where bargaining takes place, may do so only within predetermined budgetary limits. This central discipline, through cash limits, is also an abiding feature of public sector pay setting, including, in some cases, review bodies determining pay levels and structures – subject to government endorsement.

Outside pay, the currently important issue of trade union recognition is often considered too important to be left to local, workplace management. In contrast, though we have noted earlier that the HRM/Personnel/ Employee Relations function has witnessed a growth in managerial appointments, especially of women, we also noted that these appointments are rarely at senior levels. There has also been a decline in the representation of this functional specialism at board level (Millward *et al*, 2000: 227).

This apparent decline in the influence of the employee relations function contrasts with the growing numbers and expertise of those who practise it, perhaps especially because of the growth of employment law as national and EU legislation continues to grow in incidence and complexity. Practitioners have also frequently been given new job titles. According to WIRS and WERS, one-third of all specialists were engaged in 'human resource management', especially in foreign-owned companies, although in practice this often covered much the same range of activities as employee relations and the increasingly less fashionable personnel management.[21]

But if there are anomalies and contradictions within the identification of trends, what is clear, from the surveys, is that whatever the job titles of those involved, there has been a significant shift in their work away from collective to individual issues. This need not be viewed as largely arising from their preferences but as an inevitable response to the decline of unions and the contraction of collective bargaining. The consequence has been a major increase in applications to tribunals as government, and the EU, expand their jurisdictions.[22]

CONCLUSIONS AND PROSPECTS

The 'transformation' of the British workplace since 1980, recorded in the four WIRS and WERS surveys, does not yet seem to have run its course, even though the unions have some prospect that at least the long decline in their membership may soon be coming to an end. They and the TUC have also been active, from early in the 1990s, in attempts to build revival through proactive recruiting and organizing strategies. The alternative, more recent strategy, since the return to power of a Labour government in 1997, has been to look for workplace partnerships with management.[23]

Yet, so far, the impact of both strategies has been minimal in terms of membership gains and the government's view of unions is, at best, neutral. Nor is the statutory recognition procedure, though welcome to the unions despite their strong reservations concerning its design, a vehicle for substantial membership growth.[24] Furthermore, the age profile of union members is not encouraging. The age group with the lowest level of membership, as was noted earlier, is for those under 20 at 5 per cent.[25] This statistic reflects the concerns of the unions that they are still not attractive to young people despite their vigorous campaigns to recruit and retain them.[26] The unions' recruitment problems should also be seen in the context that 71 per cent of employees in the private sector and 41 per cent in the public sector are not members of trade unions. There are, of course, non-union forms of representation but, as we noted earlier from the WERS surveys, these fall far short of union representation as a form of protection for employees' interests. The authors of WERS even saw it as a 'cause for concern':

> If 'fairness at work' is to remain one of the criteria by which labour market policy is judged... then the continuing decline of union representation must be a cause for concern. No amount of 'direct participation' – management-dominated arrangements which we showed to be less durable than union representation – can be expected to encourage fair treatment for employees at work.[27]

The EU may yet alleviate some of the problems of effective representation in Britain when the Information and Consultation Directive is finally phased-in in 2008. But its limitations are evident, mainly the exclusion of organizations with fewer than 50 employees and the open question as how far it will assist or weaken union representation and collective bargaining. The government failed in its efforts to secure an effective blocking minority among EU member states against the Information and Consultation Directive. Its efforts to resist the Agency Workers' Directive – which extends directly employed workers' rights to Britain's 800,000 temporary workers – are also running into major difficulties (Turner, 2002). However, the government is moving towards eventual implementation of the EU's latest round of comprehensive legislation outlawing employee discrimination on grounds of religion, sexual orientation and age. The Directive will be implemented in stages by 2006 and will include bringing together the agencies monitoring sex, race and equality into a single body (Eaglesham, 2002).

Yet despite the government's variable approach to EU employment legislation, its domestic industrial relations and employment policies have maintained some consistency. Its well-established predilection for family-friendly policies in the workplace has given ACAS a new jurisdiction for its arbitrators. The Employment Act 2002 gives this extended role to the agency as well as effectively compelling the establishment of workplace grievance and disciplinary procedures to encourage local resolution of disputes and limit the soaring number of applications to employment tribunals. ACAS's arbitration alternative to employment tribunals is also now well into its second year. At the time of writing, the number of cases, at 21, falls far short of the number anticipated, although it has been observed that unfair dismissal applications, in the early years of the industrial tribunals, were also few and yet eventually reached almost overwhelming proportions.[28]

The government has also been consistent in its often difficult relationship with the trade unions, not least those in the public sector where pay rises have been controlled within tight spending limits. Some observers, as we noted earlier, have also detected a new militancy across the entire union movement. However, recent data on days lost, though somewhat higher than for many years, are still historically low and scanty evidence of an early return to the levels of the 1980s. Nor is the trade union movement in terms of membership, finances, solidarity – and the still strong legal constraints – able to return to the incidence and scope of the industrial battles 20 years earlier. That is of course not to say that employers in the public sector (including the government) and the private sector will be able to avoid serious confrontations with the still residually strong unions and their members. At the time of writing, this is evident in the case of the railways, London Underground and the fire service. The old concept of 'essential industries', once applied to the public utilities, may yet need to be revived in cases where the use of industrial action may be seen as too disruptive, even dangerous. But should it be given up, the corollary is that those involved should be permanently and unequivocally guaranteed the terms and conditions appropriate to 'essential' workers.

Notes

1 Brook, K (2002) Trade union membership: an analysis of data from the autumn 2001 LFS [Labour Force Survey], *Labour Market Trends*, **110** (7), pp 343–54, Table 1.1. This and other data on union membership in the introduction to this chapter are drawn from this official source.

2 One has to go back to the period between the two world wars to find a comparable decline. Between 1920 and 1933, UK membership fell from 8.3 to 4.4 million and density from 45.2 to 22.6 per cent. However, the unions then began to recover. By 1938 membership was over 6 million and density 30.5 per cent. Both statistics then continued to rise, with only minor interruptions, until 1980. See Bain, G S (1983) *Industrial Relations in Britain*, Basil Blackwell, Oxford, Table 1, p 5.

In international terms, the UK's decline in membership is far from unique. US density in the private sector, though not in the public, is now in single figures. However, in the EU, the extent of union decline in the UK in the 1990s was exceeded by only three countries – Austria, Germany and Portugal. Decline in other member states was, overall, marginal, with three – Denmark, Sweden and Finland – remaining close to or exceeding 80 per cent. See Ebbinghaus, *Industrial Relations Journal Annual Review*, **33** (5), pp 465–83.

3 An important recent theoretical and empirical contribution to explaining these recurring cycles is in Kelly, J (1998) *Rethinking Industrial Relations: Mobilization, Collectivism and Long Waves*, Routledge, London.

4 The Social Chapter was annexed to the Treaty as the Social Protocol. In Article 2 it expressly excluded industrial relations provisions, ie the Article did not apply to 'pay, the right of association, the right to strike or the right to impose lock-outs'. For a good, concise discussion, see Kessler, S and Bayliss, F (1995) *Contemporary British Industrial Relations*, 2nd edn, Macmillan Business, London.

5 For an authoritative insider discussion see Hawes, W R (2000) Setting the pace or running alongside? ACAS and the changing employment relationship, in *Employment Relations in Britain: 25 Years of the Advisory, Conciliation and Arbitration Service*, ed B Towers and W Brown, Blackwell, Oxford.

6 For the best, fairly recent contribution to the history, development and future of the relationship between Labour and the unions, see Minkin, L (1992) *The Contentious Alliance: Trade Unions and the Labour Party*, Edinburgh University Press, Edinburgh.

7 For academic appraisals of the long, arduous process towards the procedure eventually included in the 1999 Act, see Towers, B (1999) 'the most lightly regulated labour market…' the UK's third statutory recognition procedure, *Industrial Relations Journal*, **30** (2), pp 82–95; Wood, S, Moore, S and Willman, P (2002) Third time lucky for statutory recognition in the UK, *Industrial Relations Journal*, **33** (3), pp 215–33.

8 These were the four 'pillars' of employability, entrepreneurship, adaptability and equal opportunities, within the strategy for reducing unemployment. For a discussion, see Towers, B and Terry, M (1999) Editorial: unemployment and the social dialogue, *Industrial Relations Journal European Annual Review*, **32** (5), pp 1–5.

9 Trade unions have of course been sensitive to this problem for a long time. In recent years the TUC has proposed its involvement in the administration of workers' pensions and has pressed for the early inclusion of training provisions as a mandatory item (alongside the existing pay, hours and holidays) in collective agreements following statutory recognition.

10 See Chapter 16 for a full discussion of workplace procedures.

11 ACAS's voluntary alternative is described and discussed in detail in Chapter 12.

12 This research is closely associated with the work of the American academic John Paul Mac Duffie. See Mac Duffie, J P (1995), Human resource bundles and manufacturing performance: organizational logic and flexible production systems in the world auto industry', *Industrial and Labour Relations Review*, **52** (1), pp 64–81.

13 See the discussion in Chapter 4 and Chapter 17, 'Pay and Performance.'

14 Here the most recent development is the increasing resistance to the practice of large organizations abandoning their final salary pension schemes.

15 See especially Cappelli, P and Neumark, P (2001) Do high-performance work practices improve establishment-level outcomes? and Godard, J (2001) High performance and the transformation of work? The implications of alternative work practices for the experience and outcomes of work, *Industrial and Labor Relations Review*, **54** (4), pp 737–805.

16 This was also alluded to in the Introduction to the volume. For a detailed, up-to-date assessment of this development see Greene, A (ed) (forthcoming 2003) Unions and the Internet, *Industrial Relations Journal Special Issue*, **34** (3).

17 This was discussed in the Introduction to the volume. Note too that it has frequently been observed in Ireland. See, for example, Roche, W K (2001) Accounting for the trend of trade union recognition in Ireland, *Industrial Relations Journal*, **32** (1), pp 37–54.

18 Both male and female union densities have been falling for many years but for men the decline has been much faster. In 1992, for men and women they were 41 and 31 per cent respectively. In 2001, they were 30 and 28 per cent. Furthermore, again in 2001, women from ethnic minorities and those with higher education had substantially higher rates of unionization than their male counterparts. See Towers, B (1997) *The Representation Gap: Change and Reform in the British and American Workplace*, Oxford University Press, Oxford, pp 73–5; Brook (2002) op cit, pp 346–47.

19 Millward *et al* (2000: 59); see also Gooch, L and Ledwith, S (1996) Women in Personnel Management: re-visioning of a handmaiden's role?, in *Women in Organizations: Challenging Gender Politics*, ed S Ledwith and F Colgan, Macmillan, London.

20 These 'virtuous' and 'vicious' circle processes are alluded to in Millward *et al* (2000: 228), although they were perhaps first identified in relation to industrial relations – though earlier in economics – by Bain (1983), op. cit., p 33.

21 Millward *et al* (2000: 225). See also Gennard, J and Kelly, J (1997) The unimportance of labels: the diffusion of the personnel/HRM function, *Industrial Relations Journal*, **28** (1), pp 27–42.

22 For an account and analysis of the increase and the work and jurisdictions of employment tribunals see Dickens, L (2000) Doing more with less: ACAS and individual conciliation, in Towers and Brown (eds) (2000), op. cit.

23 Partnerships have been a feature of New Labour's industrial relations policy. They were prominent in the Employment Relations Act 1999, with financial assistance for joint training.

The alternative organizing strategy is not necessarily in conflict with the partnership approach, and some unions, in practice, pursue both. For a good discussion see Heery, E (2002) Partnership versus organizing: alternative futures for British trade unionism, *Industrial Relations Journal*, **33** (1), pp 20–35.

24 The procedure's clearest outcome is the encouragement of voluntary recognition, which was the intention of the statute. This has arisen through the parties taking the voluntary option available in the early stages of an application to the Central Arbitration Committee (CAC), perhaps brokered by ACAS. Additionally, ACAS has had a surge of direct approaches for voluntary assistance. The statutory procedure is also currently under review. The TUC is pressing for coverage to be extended to: organizations with fewer than 21 employees; the removal of the additional balloting requirement of a positive vote from 40 per cent of those in the bargaining unit; and for the mandatory inclusion of training to the post-statutory recognition bargaining agenda. For reviews of the statutory recognition procedure see Wood, Moore and Willman (2002) op cit, pp 215–33, and the annual reports of the CAC and ACAS: Central Arbitration Committee, *Annual Report 2001–2002*, CAC, London; Advisory, Conciliation and Arbitration Service, *Annual Report 2001–2002: Working Together*, ACAS, London.

25 See earlier data from Brook (2002) op cit, Table 2, p 346.

26 For an assessment of these campaigns see Heery, E (2000) The TUC's Organizing Academy: an assessment, *Industrial Relations Journal*, **31** (5), pp 400–15.

27 Millward *et al* (2000: 230). 'Fairness at Work' was the White Paper of the Labour government, published in 1998, which formed the initial blueprint for the Employment Relations Act of 1999.

28 See Chapter 12.

References

Cully, M, Woodland, S, O'Reilly, A and Dix, G (1999) *Britain at Work as Depicted by the 1998 Workplace Employee Relations Survey*, Routledge, London

Eaglesham, J (2002) Minister unveils "belief" discrimination rules, *Financial Times*, 23 October, p 2

Guest, D (1995) Human resource management and industrial relations, in *Human Resource Management: a Critical Text*, ed J Storey, Routledge, London

Millward, N, Bryson, A and Forth, J (2000) *All Change at Work? British employment relations as portrayed by the Workplace Industrial Relations Series*, Routledge, London

Turner, D (2002) Government dealt blow over temporary staff, *Financial Times*, 23 October, p 4

2

The influence of the European Union

Peter Cressey

INTRODUCTION

Since Britain signed the European Communities Act in 1972, there have been constant claims that the European Union – and the European Commission in particular – have had a significant impact on British domestic industrial relations (BIR). Thirty years after entry is a suitable time to take stock of that impact and to judge what realistically has been the influence of British membership on our system of employment regulation and bargaining and if a new pan-European system of employment regulation is a real possibility.

A surface appreciation would point us to enormous change and activity stemming from the EU and its various organs. Since the early 1970s there have been regular attempts to legislate in the industrial relations area. The Fifth Directive on company law was one vehicle that attempted to reorder employee representation.[1] The Vredling Proposal, and the later European Company Statute, sought to bring multinational companies within a framework of agreed rules (Carley, 1993). In addition, a number of substantive areas such as employment protection and health and safety have experienced an extensive catalogue of binding directives and regulations as well as non-binding agreements and opinions (Spyropoulos, 1990). Over the period since the early 1990s one can recount a list of initiatives and directives centred on the enhancement of employee rights, culminating in the attempt to stipulate a minimum floor of workers' rights encapsulated in the Social Protocol of the Maastricht Treaty. The New Labour government's signing of the Social Chapter and its Social Action Programme has meant a stream of well-known and discussed individual directives. These include European Works Councils, Atypical Employment, Parental Leave, and measures to protect and ensure the free movement of labour across the Union.[2] Hence, 'Co-operation on labour market policy has produced some tangible results. Part-time Work, working hours, European Works Councils, gender equality and the working environment are amongst the issues currently partially regulated on the basis of initiatives taken within the framework of the EU' (Jensen *et al*, 1999).

This process has been supplement by the fostering of what has become known as the European Social Model – a long-term approach to building regulatory institutions that are European in format and which can set the basis for a future system of European Industrial relations.[3] Within this model there are privileged social partners – employers (public and private) and trade unions who engage in the 'Social Dialogue' process that provides the main opportunity for consultation of an extensive kind. This model of Social Dialogue between peak actors has come to assume greater importance of late as it now allows those social partner consultations to result in agreements that can be formalized into Directives with European-wide effect.

Latterly one sees further evidence of European impact on employee relations with the creation of the 'Essen process'[4] where European coordination and control of employment policies in the EU has proceeded apace. This is resulting in new structures of control and monitoring for the individual member states, a process from which Britain is not opted out (Goetschy, 1999).

Given all of these initiatives, no one can say that Europe has not had a substantial impact in specific areas; the question is what is the significance of the overall European project and to what extent has it fundamentally shifted our model of industrial relations? Is it the case that the Anglo-Saxon 'voluntarist' model described by Fox (1985) in his magisterial *History and Heritage* has to be re-evaluated? Or is a European system of regulation akin to corporatism[5] being imposed in this country or, contrarily, is there evidence of a resilient domestic model with strong elements of independence and continuity?

To answer these questions means looking at recent evidence and critical judgements made by a variety of advocates. I want to contain and, to some extent, simplify the arguments by arguing that we can detect three main approaches to this question.

The first discernible one I characterize as the 'convergence approach'; those who support this view see a European industrial relations system (EIRS) as a real possibility and indicate that evidence is available to suggest the initial phases of the process have been established. In this view the impact of the EU on Britain has been high and transformative.

The second approach sees an EIRS as a misnomer in the short term but there are powerful contagion effects that will exert, and are exerting, influence upon the British system that will emerge over the medium to longer term to reshape British industrial relations (BIR) decisively.

The final approach argues that the British system and its 'voluntarist' traditions has managed a form of coexistence with what is essentially enclaves of labour market regulation emanating from Europe. In this view it is not Europe that is the engine for industrial relations change in the UK; rather we must look to other domestic and international drivers for this.

This chapter aims to look at each case in turn before assessing the arguments regarding the significance of the impact on BIR.

CONVERGENCE

This case for a convergent European Industrial Relations System should not be simply equated with the Euro-sceptic debate so loved by the British media. There are instead serious and critical questions being asked about the extent to which British traditions, institutions, rules and regulatory procedures and forms of representation have been fundamentally changed and their relevant features replaced by European mechanisms. This leads us to consider the nature of what constitutes an industrial relations system and the fundamental characteristics of the British model. Here we can go back to the founding fathers of industrial relations theory – Dunlop (1958) and Flanders (1970). They viewed an industrial relations system as made up of a number of actors who work directly on issues of industrial relations regulation, through established rules that both procedurally and substantively govern their behaviour, within institutions or legislative mechanisms that monitor and control the agreements or policies which the actors conclude. From this system there are outcomes in terms of variations in contracts, working conditions and forms of reward.

In each of the different European countries, tradition and practice have combined to render each system different. For instance, the nature of worker representation by trade unions varies by ideology (can be politically or religion based), form, level of activity and density achieved within the workforce.[6] Due et al (1991) draw out the different legal bases upon which the industrial relations systems rest. In Europe there are at least three clear models visible – the Romano-Germanic marked by high degrees of statutory intervention; the Nordic based on the provision of nationally formulated collective agreements; and the Anglo-Saxon model characterized by voluntary agreements entered into by the actors without recourse to legal jurisdiction.

The British system has been ably described by Fox. For him the British system is marked by the existence of independent social actors who are distrustful of centralism, actors who resist strongly the encroachment on their ability to create rules and agreements. It is marked by sectional and competitive collective bargaining primarily at a decentralized level, with the State largely excluded from the day-to-day regulatory processes. This 'voluntarism' is deeply rooted in the social heritage of the British industrial relations system: 'The judgement offered here is that Britain's most persistent dispositions are individualistic, both atomistic and collectivist, and the tradition of the minimal state' (Fox, 1985: 439).

Evidence from the Workplace Employment Relations Survey (Millward *et al*, 2000) and elsewhere since Fox wrote, tends to support his argument in general terms, as we see a continued decline in multi-employer bargaining and the ongoing importance of decentralized company-level bargaining.

So what are the arguments the convergence supporters put forward to prove that differing national systems are being reshaped? Jensen *et al* argue that a European IR system is indeed forming and that this resembles the features of national systems: 'At European level, parallel with the structures and mechanisms evident in the national-IR systems, it is possible to identify: a) a number of actors who "reach decisions" on labour market conditions, b) a number of rules and procedures for interaction between the actors and c) a number of "results" reached at transnational level' (Jensen *et al*, 1999: 121).

The first area mentioned is the growth and institutionalization of alternative representation structures, especially peak European levels of representation. UNICE (Union of Industrial and Employers' Confederations of Europe) for commercial employers, CEEP (*European Centre of Enterprises with Public Participation and of Enterprises of General Economic Interest*) for public sector bodies and the ETUC (European Confederation of Trade Unions) for trade unions have become critical actors capable of creating rules and reaching agreements. They are a part of the 'negotiation track' of the Social Dialogue process which can now, where agreement is reached between them, in effect enact Directives covering the whole of the European Union workforce.[7] Such a process has huge importance for European industrial relations regulation, according to Jacobi (1996). The trade unions, in particular, need to move their focus of activity from the national to the European level to counteract EMU and internationalization processes. He goes beyond seeking European bargaining at peak and recently at sectoral levels, seeing: 'Interest group policy harmonized at European level is a precondition for the unions being able to develop into worthy opponents of the ECB and play an active role in shaping the European Employment and Social Union' (Jacobi, 1996: 224).

Léonard (2001) adds another dimension to this by concentrating upon the shift towards creating new rules in the labour market through heightened coordination over employment policies. Initial evidence of this shift can be seen in the growth of the 'Essen Process' which has created a 'European Employment Strategy' that has embedded a series of specific targets within the four pillars of employability, entrepreneurship, adaptability, and equal opportunities for whose achievement member states have become responsible. Targets for labour force participation rates, youth unemployment, improved

training outcomes and measures to tackle the gender gap are closely monitored and have been assessed now for three consecutive years.[8] For Léonard,
such policy areas provide the framework for the development of new labour
market regulation at the European level. In addition to this, we also see the
creation in certain countries of Pacts for Employment and Competitiveness
(PECS) that have attempted to shape national agreements regarding pay,
flexible working and productivity. Such centralization tendencies are complemented by a decentralization of bargaining over the flexibility of working
practices across the member states. Hence Léonard's thesis is that:

> Industrial relations play an increasing role in the regulation of employment issues:
> through the impact of the European strategy for employment and through emerging
> processes of coordination and decentralization within member states, the so-called
> 'labour market' is increasingly the subject of what Reynaud (1988, 1989) calls 'joint
> regulation' with rules defined jointly by unions, employers and in some cases, public
> authorities. (Léonard, 2001)

Added to this approach, Jensen *et al* see the past five years as a crucial phase in
institution building that will underpin a European industrial relations system.
Three critical advances have made this statement possible; firstly, under the
Social Charter for the first time it was explicitly accepted that: 'The EU should
consist... of institutions regulating matters concerning industrial relations. In
that sense the adoption of the Social Charter can be seen as the starting point
of a European industrial relations system' (Jensen *et al*, 1999: 125).

The second advance came with the draft agreement about atypical work,
where a process initiated by the Commission enshrined social partner
bargaining, rather than member-state voting as the preferred route to labour
market regulation. This was then consolidated in the third phase when in the
'31st October Agreement' of 1991 the employers (UNICE) signalled their willingness to develop European IR-regulation under the 'negotiation track' of
the social dialogue (Jensen *et al*, 1999: 125).

What follows from that has been a series of outcomes in the form of social-
partner-agreed directives on Parental Leave, Part-time Work and Fixed-Term
Work and Commission-led directives on European Works Councils and
Information and Consultation Rights where there have been high inputs of
social partner consultation.

Another cardinal factor in play is European Monetary Union (EMU) with its
stringent compliance criteria which have led member states to revamp their
labour market policies and engage in new national bargaining processes as
represented by the new Social Pacts (Pochet and Fajertag, 2000). The pressures
for integration led by EMU is feeding through to new forms of cross-national
bargaining based on a convergent set of macro-economic policies determined
at the European level.

Sisson (1999) also indicates how EMU has enabled a new transparency of
costings and has reordered bargaining, especially in the automotive sector. He

also notes the growing importance of the European Central Bank macro-economic decisions for all member states and social actors both inside and outside of the euro. This, together with increased MNC activity as a result of heightened globalization of product markets and the increasing impact of the Social Action Programme, entails a profound EU effect upon employment regulation in the UK. He is less sure that this means convergence around an old-style 'corporatist' interventionist system; he argues that it displays the growing importance of introducing employment regulation via collective bargaining (as the new 'negotiation track' foreshadows). The outcome will be the creation of 'new European orthodoxy' based upon flexible frameworks of rules and 'EU-wide statutory minimum standards' (Sisson, 1999: 449).

All of these authors in their different ways indicate the formation of a new European Industrial Relations system, showing the development of significant new supra-national actors and new sources of rules and coordination bearing on member states, the social partners and the bargaining system. Novel institutional forms will also emerge to monitor and control the labour market. Finally, and importantly, there is evidence of substantive new outputs emerging from those actors and institutions. In Leonard's words: 'The EU not only define rules concerning the volume and flows of employment, they also transform the rules that regulate the "industrial relations game" itself' (Léonard, 2001: 41–2).

The upshot of this thinking is that now that the UK has lost its opt-out status from much of the social and employment legislation, a process of transformation is coming to bear on our traditional system, so much so that Sisson can say: 'It is difficult to escape the conclusion that, whatever else happens, the European connection signals the end of the "voluntarism" which has characterized UK employment relations for a century' (Sisson, 1999: 448).

In this approach it is therefore evident that there are strong views indicating a convergence around a new European industrial relations system and that this development has had significant transformative effects upon the British industrial relations system.

CONTAGION

The second approach, however, qualifies this viewpoint, being partly a critique of the convergence approach whilst retaining some elements of its thinking. In the first place the EU is seen as a source of significant influence on British industrial relations but not to the extent that there has been extensive convergence. The analysis rather stresses areas of communality and *future* possibilities of greater EU regulation in *some rather than all* areas of the industrial relations system. This critique is led by Goetschy, Hyman and, somewhat confusingly, Jensen *et al* (Goetschy, 1999; Hyman, 2001b; Jensen *et al*, 1999).

For Goetschy, the developments around the European Structural Funds, EMU and the European Employment strategy are introducing constraints and disciplines of a macro-economic kind whose long-term effect will be to legitimate EU-level activity in terms of labour market interventions. Many of the activities and initiatives post-Maastricht have had this aim, creating EU consultation spheres rather than common statutory procedures and producing EU frameworks for harmonizing national practices rather than 'highly detailed prescriptions' (Goetschy, 1999: 131). Through such mechanisms as the National Action Plans (NAPs),[9] member states enter an iterative process that ensures 'greater continuity in the relationship between the national and the Community levels' (Goetschy, 1999: 132). For Goetschy, this more incremental approach arises as a response to the 'failure' of the Commission to push through common legislative and contractual rule-making processes that might have formed the basis for a European Industrial Relations system:

> In the 1990s Germany and France joined the UK in resisting such legislative initiatives. The setbacks… focused attention upon two alternative options. The first was to encourage what Streeck calls 'neo-voluntarism', relying primarily on 'soft' forms of regulation rather than mobilizing the legislative capacity of the EU itself. … The second option for the EU was to involve member states more deeply in the pursuit of commonly defined Community Guidelines (Goetschy, 1999: 132).

This latter strategy may well mean common practices and systems of regulation in the longer term but in the short term was more indirect in industrial relations terms as the focus is on macro labour market targets and issues. For Streeck (1998), this is the difference between 'harmonization' – a process that would suspend regime competition in industrial relations and social protection – and 'coordination' which does not impose a 'single best-practice model of industrial relations' (Streeck, 1998: 437) and hence allows a great deal of diversity to remain.

Hyman confronts head-on the issue of whether the European level can constitute itself as a replica of a national industrial relations system. He answers firmly in the negative, because: 'The EU is in key respects *not* a supranational state and the European "social partners" are not authoritative nation trade unions and employers associations at a higher level' (Hyman, 2001b: 291).

He also indicates that the labour market is not merely constituted by forms of national or international regulation. In addition, there is an important role for local struggles from which emerge specific substantive *and* procedural rules that are marked by situated logics rather than macro-considerations. Because of this, at the European level there is very little capacity to get involved in the whole range of substantive outcomes that industrial relations routinely deals with. 'Even if Maastricht proves to have eased the log-jam, it seems clear that on key industrial relations issues of trade union rights, the status of collective bargaining and wage regulation the jurisdiction of the EU will scarcely apply' (Hyman, 1995). This point is also conceded by Jensen *et al*, who acknowledge that an EIRS as currently constituted 'lacks a number of central characteristics and forms/areas of regulation which are traditionally emphasized in analyses of industrial relations systems. European labour-market regulation... is not directed at issues such as pay and working hours' (Jensen *et al*, 1999: 123).

One can go further than this and say that the reality of the 'European dimension' to industrial relations diminishes the more one moves to issues of specific moment that have continuing and immediate concern to employees and employers inside enterprises. The practical reality of collective bargaining goes beyond pay and working hours, into complex reward structures, grade-specific working conditions, highly differentiated working organization, management regimes and grievance handling mechanisms. The failure of the EU to act upon the Green Paper 'Partnership for a new organization of work'[10] is a good example of the problems they face when dealing with such a detailed and multifaceted issue. The rise of the Social Pacts go only a little way to dealing with this problem but they themselves have little cross-national coherence (as Pochet and Fajertag (2000) point out), nor have any necessary degree of permanence beyond the initial phases of EMU.

Looking back over the development of 'Social Europe', Teague recognizes the vital role of the Maastricht 'Social Protocol' that defined the process and substance of European employment regulation. But he also indicates how most of the Protocol focused upon 'individual' rather than 'collective rights' and that this meant that: 'the important matters of strikes and lock-outs as well as pay determination remain outside the scope of EU action. Heavy intervention in such areas is seen as inappropriate since it may disrupt well-established and finely-tuned power relations between national employers and trade unions' (Teague, 1999: 147).

It is for these reasons that Jensen *et al* refer to the 'otherness' of the EIRS in that it is more closely linked to the 'broader pattern of EU cooperation and to the institutional logics which are dominant in this context' rather than to logics emanating from 'organizational and collective-agreement institutions'.[11] As such, the EIRS is distanced from the national industrial relations actors, processes and outcomes, being influenced more by the 'politics-based dynamics' of the EU project itself. Such a viewpoint might help to explain the curious rift between European industrial relations and national industrial relations so that the development of EU processes can proceed without major inputs from the key national actors in the field.

One exception to this rift has been the inauguration of the European Works Council. Here at least we have a European initiative that has changed enterprise behaviour, getting to what Traxler (1996) terms the micro rather than macro or meso level of industrial relations interaction. Here at least there is a cross-national perspective inaugurated within a formally constituted corporate forum for consultation between the social actors. However, even here there are few claims, if any, that these forums have gone beyond information-passing bureaux and towards incipient transnational bargaining units (Cressey, 1998a). Early analysis of 'Article 13' forums[12] showed:

> With regard to the purpose of the EWC, it was found that with one exception, every agreement explicitly stated that the function of the EWC is the provision of information and consultation. Consultation was most commonly defined in terms of 'dialogue' or an 'exchange of views'. A more 'proactive' role is provided for in 6 per cent of agreements, which were most likely to be found in Franco-Belgian companies. Clearly, the scope of involvement accorded to EWCs remains within the boundaries specified by the Directive in respect of being limited to information and consultation, with only 2 per cent of agreements allowing for negotiations on certain issues (and 4% for the EWC to make recommendations and proposals of its own). (EIRO, 1998)

Wills' (1999) study of the UK experience of EWCs mirrored this finding and said that any expectation that EWCs fostered transnational labour solidarity and cooperation was found to be wanting, with most representatives seeing the group-level issues as largely 'abstract' and unconnected to their day-to-day concerns.

Here again we see a Directive that, whilst harmonizing the basic institutional format, has done so in respect of national systems of worker representation. What this means is that managements retain the ability to indulge in Streeck's 'regime competition', able to 'threaten to relocate production to European countries with weaker participation rights, where worker representatives can be more easily persuaded to make concessions' (Streeck, 1998: 447).

In summary, this approach then views the capacity for the EU to influence British industrial relations as limited. There are indeed some mechanisms such as the European Employment Strategy's NAPs and the Social Dialogue negotiation track that are providing guidelines and directives in particular areas. However, this form of regulation is of a particular kind, hence Teague quotes Sciarra (1995) to the effect that the EU is resigned to passing 'minimal labour law' backed up by the increasing use of soft law (Teague, 1999: 150). Soft laws are described as rules of conduct that in principle have no binding force but may have practical effects. In the recent decade one finds such 'laws' increasingly used in all areas of EU social and labour market policy. Hence the influence on the British system is one that is more indirect, based upon persuasion and longer-term adaptation to politically defined aims rather than an intervention to change the institutional practices or interfere in the bargaining activities of the actors themselves.

COEXISTENCE

This viewpoint seriously questions the impact of the EU on British industrial relations. As we see above, there are valid criticisms regarding the reach and capability of any supra-national regulatory system, and the identification of specific instances of its regulatory force. The coexistence perspective also harbours further doubts as to the possibility of a strong European effect on British industrial relations.

In the first place, the strength and embedded traditions of 'voluntarism', in the UK mean that its practices, values and behaviours, may continue to isolate it from its Continental neighbours. In EU circles there was much excitement with the advent of the new Labour government and the immediate signing of the Social Chapter. However, it soon appeared clear that the new government had gone for a minimalist approach in relation to employee rights at work, the regulation of business and the involvement of trade unions in deciding and implementing policies. Deregulation was not taken off the agenda. Competitive flexibility continued to be a central plank of government policy and many of the trade union laws enacted by the previous Conservative government were kept firmly in place (Edwards *et al*, 1997). On the latter Tony Blair said in the Foreword to the White Paper 'Fairness at Work': 'There will be no going back. The days of strikes without ballots, mass picketing, closed shops and secondary action are over. *Even after the changes we propose, Britain will have the most lightly regulated labour market of any leading economy in the world*' (DTI, 1998, emphasis added).

The impact of Europe has similarly been kept at bay, with the new government firmly opposing a number of key industrial relations and labour market reforms. The most obvious has been the opposition to the extension of information and consultation rights to domestic enterprises with more than 50 employees (Gold *et al*, 2000). On this issue Blair lined up with the CBI, and with German and Portuguese employers, forcing the Commission to press the issue through outside of the negotiation track. The resulting Directive published in March 2002 for application in 2005 has been slightly amended from the original proposal and allows for a transitional period of two years before it affects the 50-employee enterprise.

This chapter of events has illustrated that whilst the actual opt-out from the Social Protocol has been rescinded, the *ideological* opt-out continues within the British government. Not that they are the only actors to respond this way: the CBI continues its root and branch opposition to statutory impositions of most kinds. Referring to the information and consultation rights Directive, they expressed themselves as extremely disappointed with the agreement, saying: 'Not only does the Directive undermine companies' freedom to manage, but it marks a step in the wrong direction for the EU – against the business-friendly trend begun at Lisbon' (CBI, 2002).

At the same time, the trade union movement is riven with conflict over the extent to which to embrace European-level policy making. The debates on EMU at the TUC Congress clearly show up the differing viewpoints that are held (Cressey, 1998b). Amongst some of the large public sector unions, the major worries regarding EMU are described by David Foden of the ETUC (Foden, 1996). These refer to problems posed for unions in achieving the tough convergence criteria. Germany and France experienced great pressure on their public spending, leading to cuts in employment, especially in the public sector. More generally, the integration of the currency could presage a possible institutionalization of monetarism at the European level. Individual national governments will have no ability to devalue or revalue currency: they will have to accept common interest rates set by the European Central Bank (ECB), which is pursuing price stability and keeping within strict convergence criteria, the interpretation of which will determine the strength of the currency. In the context of these constraints a continued campaign is being fought by some unions against the TUC's more positive view of European integration.

Secondly, and following on from the isolationist approach, there are limited interactive links between the British and European systems; this means a lack of interactions that are meaningfully changing behaviour. This occurs across virtually all of the elements of the BIR – actors, rules, institutions and outcomes.

As Hyman saw it earlier, the European 'social partners' are not authoritative and the fact that we see new actors emerging in the shape of ETUC, UNICE (and CEEP) begs the question regarding their representativeness, legitimacy and degree of interaction with British industrial relations. In many respects the 'peak' organizations are creations of the Commission needed to give credence to European activity in employment and labour market affairs. 'The Commission itself has always been, for reasons of efficiency, very much interested in dealing with one, and only one, "European organization" per side and has refused to negotiate with any purely national organization' (Keller and Bansbach, 2000).

This has led to arguments about who should be included at the European level, with UEAPME (European Association of craft and small and medium-sized enterprises) being excluded from consultation until 1998. Similarly, CEC (a body representing professional and managerial staff) has latterly been recognized and can, in conjunction with the ETUC, enter the social dialogue process. Such arguments, however, indicate both the tensions and problems of legitimacy and representation within the EU but gain little discussion in the realm of British industrial relations.

Furthermore, the extent of union merger activity within the EU can only be considered as marginal. Some activity is in evidence in the previous Deutschmark zone amongst construction workers' unions, particularly after the Doorn Agreement of June 2000 (EIRO, 2000a). There:

> construction workers' trade unions from Belgium, Germany and the Netherlands agreed a joint declaration on measures to seek harmonization of working conditions in the industry. They also signed an innovative cooperation agreement, which comes into force on 1 October 2000, providing for mutual trade union assistance and support for construction workers posted to other countries. (EIRO, 2000a)

There has been a similar move by the European Federation of Public Service Unions (EPSU), who agreed in April 2000 to put into place a framework for joint collective action, which it hopes could pave the way towards a coordinated system of collective bargaining in Europe's public services (EIRO, 2000b). The General, Municipal and Boilermakers' Union (GMB) has also established closer bi-lateral links with unions in other EU countries:

> In 1997 the GMB signed a joint membership agreement with the German chemical workers' union. The deal between the GMB and IG Chemie-Papier-Keramik means that 1.8 million workers will be entitled to joint membership. Although the two unions may not provide the same services, UK workers in Germany can expect legal advice, support from representatives, and training facilities, while German workers in the UK can expect legal advice, health and safety information and financial benefits. (EIRO, 1997c)

However, these developments are the very early stages in a long process and in the UK very little progress has been made apart from basically symbolic moves by individual unions. Talks of European Super Unions being on the horizon (EIRO, 1997b) have not as yet come to fruition.

Looking at the workplace in terms of the nature of representation inside the UK, WERS shows that the pattern of representation and bargaining is changing but not as a result of European influences; rather they are related to other dynamics. This same pattern is repeated over workplace pay and rewards, consultative mechanisms and training.

Thirdly, almost all of the academics referred to in this chapter stress that there are more influential drivers at play than those emanating from the EU Commission. The critical drivers shaping changes in British industrial relations are seen to come from the wider forces of globalization and international product market changes, with multinational company decision-making behaviour further reshaping employee relations. The complexity of this process is summed up by Streeck in this sentence: 'European integration has over more than four decades come to be firmly defined as a process of economic liberalization by international means; of the opening up of national economies through internationally negotiated expansion of markets beyond national borders' (Streeck, 1999: 429).

Associated with this has been a pattern of 'selective supranational centralization and institution building' (Streeck, 1999: 429) that enables those supranational institutions to engage in market making, whilst leaving the social regulations to the national institutions.

Hyman (2001b) picks up on the same themes of internationalization of capital as against the national rootedness of labour. The multinational 'problem' for European unions is different now than when the Vredling proposal was first mooted. Then it was a 'relatively narrow' one of trying to contain MNCs within frameworks of rules. Now, however: 'In the 1990s the problem became broader and more serious: the internationalization of "national capital" and the potential abandonment by key companies of their traditional role within a national system of "social partnership"' (Hyman, 2001b: 287–8).

The problems facing the trade unions are common but equally complex: in such periods of change, how do they enmesh capital in complementary and coherent regulatory frameworks at the micro, the meso and the macro level – achieving a form of 'multi-level governance' (Hyman, 2001b: 291)?

Fourthly, the embracing of national deregulation may be affecting other member states' industrial relations systems more than the UK because of different political trajectories in the past two decades. Streeck refers to the systems of the other member states becoming more 'voluntaristic' and less 'obligational' (Streeck, 1999: 438). As the pressure from the foregoing drivers changes, so does the nature of labour's inclusion, reordering the historic settlement that reached its stability under the conditions of 'Fordism'. Such change extends beyond the confines of labour markets and affects welfare regimes by making work and welfare intertwined, and effecting a new form of commodification that does away with the form and substance of previous social protections. One example of this set of pressures is exemplified by Tusselmann (2001) who details the impact upon the German system. He asks whether there is a discernible 'Anglo-Saxonization' at play urged on by the neo-liberal reforms. In many respects he shows that this is a clear threat: 'Disintegration of the tightly regulated and densely institutionalized German model and its convergence to the orthodox deregulated market-led Anglo-Saxon model' (Tusselmann, 2001: 544).

However, similarly to the British situation, he describes the system changes as responding to internal dynamics rather than European ones and, whilst conceding the threat of Germany pursuing a form of 'disorganized decentralism', he also puts forward evidence of a substantial continuity of institutions and representation in the social arena. This is the case even though these social actors are within the Euro-zone and subject to European Central Bank disciplines.

DISCUSSION

All three approaches display some veracity regarding the impact of the EU on British industrial relations. However, even those who are counted amongst the supporters of the convergence thesis see the difficulties involved in establishing a European industrial relations system and at the same time recognize the particularities of the British case that combine to attenuate the influence of Europe.

Britain has had a history of opting out from employment and labour market initiatives and in so doing has minimized the direct demands for change that other member states have proceeded with. The Social Chapter and its social action programme have not, until recently, been a consideration in many enterprises, the exceptions being health and safety reforms such as the Working Time Directive that avoided the need for unanimity and proceeded under qualified majority voting. The avoidance of European Monetary Union has kept the UK well away from the demands of the growth and stability pact and the subsequent need to adopt the stringent public sector spending cuts and associated labour market reforms.

The length of gestation time for many of the social and employment reforms has slowed the impact on Britain and all of the other member states as well. For instance, the drive to do something about employee representation and consultation was actually started in the early 1970s with the publication of the draft Fifth Company Directive (Gold, 1993). Labyrinthine consultation, unclear procedures and disagreements amongst the social partners has delayed progress from the initial impulse to the start of the new century before being realized in the shape of the European Company Statute and the Information and Consultation Directive.

The recent shift in emphasis from a workers' rights agenda to one animated by concern for employment has been mentioned by many (Gill *et al*, 1999; Teague, 1999). This has meant a move away from the centralization of laws, rules and procedures implicit in the European 'Corporatist' models and towards a form of flexible coordination of macro-economic policies based on guidelines and 'soft laws'. In such a shift the traditions and practices of domestic industrial relations systems have not been challenged directly.

For Britain, in particular, the forces and dynamics for system change have not been so pressing as elsewhere. That is because many of the neo-liberal reforms affecting the rest of Europe, emanating from the EES and EMU, had already been pushed through during the Thatcher administration. Then the quest for enterprise adaptability, flexibility of contracts and concession bargaining had established what Teague and Grahl (1992) called a regime based on 'competitive flexibility' as opposed to the 'constructive flexibility' found elsewhere. In part, what the past decade has seen is the ideological privileging of that competitive model inside much of EU policy thinking. Hence the lessened impact this drive for change has had upon the UK, in contradistinction to the rest of Europe.

The resilience of the UK domestic model of industrial relations in these circumstances should not surprise us, cocooned as it is in its own traditions of decentralized adversarial bargaining and politically shielded from Europe by continuing opt-outs. Though change was taking place, and the nature of those changes can be found in other chapters of this book – change emanating from Europe is less easy to quantify. Certainly there were individual areas such as part-time work where the relevant directive has had great impact. But when we ask about *system* change there is an ambivalent picture to report. There is evidence of a centralizing political will in the Commission, but the pressures from the internationalization of capital, shifting political agendas, weak social actors and untried mechanisms/institutions for regulation have made the implementation of that political will haphazard and variable.

It may be that the advocates of 'not today but tomorrow' convergence are right and the significant impact for British industrial relations is just around the corner. However, the embeddedness of custom and practice and the constructed social institutions will, as Tusselmann shows in the German context, possibly also prove resilient in the British case, mediating the impact on the system and forcing the use of guidelines and soft law over common statutes and regulations. In summing up this impact, Streeck describes the complex flows of influence succinctly: 'European industrial relations are rapidly internationalizing; internationalization, however, is not necessarily denationalization. Even as European integration accelerates, national politics and industrial relations will, for better or worse, remain the principal areas for the social regulation of work and employment in Europe' (Streeck, 1999: 429).

Notes

1 See Cressey, P (1993) Employee participation, in *The Social Dimension: Employment Policy in the European Community*, ed M Gold, Macmillan, London.
2 For a detailed account of this process, see Teague (1999).
3 For an internal Commission account of how such a process might be achieved, see European Commission (1988) *The Social Dimension of the Internal Market: Interim Report of the Inter-services Working Party*, Brussels.
4 The process was started at Essen but was continued and deepened by agreements at Vienna, Cardiff and Luxembourg. The culmination of the process was the Treaty of Amsterdam where economic stability, growth and employment targets were written into the body of the treaty. See Foden, D (1999) The role of social partners in the European employment strategy, *Transfer*, 5 (4), pp 522–41, Brussels. Also EIRO (1997a).
5 See Lehmbruch, G and Schmitter, P C (eds) (1982) *Patterns of corporatist policy-making*, Sage, London, and also Panitch, L (1976) *Social democracy and industrial militancy the labour party, the trade unions and incomes policy, 1945–1974*.
6 See, for instance, Visser, J (2002) Why fewer workers join unions in Europe: a social custom explanation of membership trends, *British Journal of Industrial Relations*, **40** (3). In this paper he shows the massive differences in Europe between the Scandinavian figures of 90 per cent and those of France where density has dropped below 10 per cent.
7 See Keller, B and Sorries (1999) Sectoral Social Dialogue: new opportunities or more impasse?, *Industrial Relations Journal*, **30** (4), pp 330–45.
8 To see all of the NAPs for the years in question, go to http://europa. eu.int/comm/employment_social/emp&esf/nap00/naps_en.html.

9 As a part of the European Employment Strategy, each member state has to report annually on the measures taken to reach the aims of that strategy.

10 The full text of the Green Paper can be found at http://europa.eu.int/comm/employment_social/soc-dial/social/green_en.htm.

11 See Jensen *et al*, 1999: 123. They borrow this term from Streeck, W and Schmitter, P C (1992) From national corporatism to transnational pluralism, *Politics and Society*, **19** (2), pp 133–64. The latter authors use it to distinguish the main actors, in addition to the State, that are necessary for an industrial system to regulate the labour market effectively.

12 These are the EWCs set up by agreement to enable the social actors to come to best-suited arrangements – rather than have a predetermined structure imposed upon them.

References

Carley, M (1993) Social Dialogue, in *The Social Dimension: Employment Policy in the European Community*, ed M Gold, Macmillan

CBI Internet site (2002) CBI press statement, July

Cressey, P (1998a) EMU and the impact on UK industrial relations, in *The Impact of EMU on Industrial Relations in European Union*, ed T Kauppinen, Finnish Industrial Relations Association, Helsinki

Cressey, P (1998b) European works councils in practice, *Human Resource Management Journal*, **8** (1), pp 67–79

Department of Trade and Industry (1998) *Fairness at Work*, HMSO, London, p I

Due, J, Madsen, J-S and Jensen, C-S (1991) The social dimension: convergence or divergence of industrial relations in the Single European Market, *Industrial Relations Journal*, **22** (2), pp 85–102

Dunlop, J (1958) *The Industrial Relations System*, Harvard University/Holt, Boston, MA

Edwards, P, Gilman, M, Hall, M, Keep, E, Lloyd, C and Sisson, K (1997) The Industrial Relations Consequences of New Labour, Warwick Papers in Industrial Relations, special Web edn, May

EIRO (1997a) Amsterdam summit agrees new draft Treaty, http://www.eiro.eurofound.ie/1997/06/inbrief/EU9706133N.html

EIRO (1997b) European super unions on the horizon? http://www.eiro.eurofound.ie/ 1997/03/inbrief/UK9703117N.html

EIRO (1997c) Joint union membership for German and UK workers, http://www.eiro.eurofound.ie/1997/03/inbrief/DE9703206N.html

EIRO (1998) European works councils: the experience so far, http://www.eiro.eurofound.ie/ 1998/03/feature/EU9803191F.html

EIRO (2000a) Belgian, Dutch and German construction unions sign cooperation agreement, http://www.eiro.eurofound.ie/2000/09/feature/BE0009327F.html

EIRO (2000b) EPSU agrees framework for coordinated action, http://www.eiro.eurofound.ie/2000/07/feature/EU0007261F.html

Flanders, A (1970) *Management and Unions*, Faber, London

Foden, D (1996) EMU, employment and social cohesion, *Transfer*, **2** (2), pp 273–86, Brussels

Fox, A (1985) *History and Heritage: The Social Origins of the British Industrial Relations System*, George Allen and Unwin, London

Gill, C, Gold, M and Cressey, P (1999) Social Europe: national initiatives and responses, *Industrial Relations Journal*, **30** (4), pp 313–29

Goetschy, J (1999) The European employment strategy: genesis and development, *European Journal of Industrial Relations*, **5** (2), pp 117–37

Gold, M (ed) (1993) *The Social Dimension. Employment Policy in the European Community*, Macmillan, London

Gold, M, Cressey P and Gill, C (2000) Employment, employment, employment: is Europe working?, *Industrial Relations Journal*, **31** (4), Autumn

Hyman, R (1995) Industrial relations in Europe: theory and practice, *European Journal of Industrial Relations*, **1** (1), pp 17–46, Sage. See p 35

Hyman, R (2001a) Some problems of partnership and dilemmas of dialogue, in *From Collective Bargaining to Social Partnerships: New Roles of the Social partners in Europe*, ed C Kjaegaard and S-A Westphalen, The Copenhagen Centre, Copenhagen, pp 39–58

Hyman, R (2001b) The Europeanization – or the erosion – of industrial relations, *Industrial Relations Journal*, **32** (4), pp 280–94

Jacobi, O (1996) European Monetary Union – a quantum leap, *Transfer*, **2** (2), ETUI, Brussels

Jensen, C S, Madsen, J S and Due, J (1999) Phases and dynamics in the development of EU industrial relations regulation, *Industrial Relations Journal*, **30** (2), p 118

Keller, B and Bansbach, M (2000) Social Dialogue: an interim report on recent results and prospects, *Industrial Relations Journal*, **3** (4), pp 291–307

Léonard, E (2001) Industrial relations and the regulation of employment in Europe, *European Journal of Industrial Relations*, **7** (1), pp 27–47, SAGE, London

Millward, N, Bryson, A and Forth, J (2000) *All Change at Work? British Employment Relations 1980–1998*, Routledge, London

Pochet, P and Fajertag, G (eds) (2000) *Social Pacts in Europe – New Dynamics*, ETUI, Brussels

Sciarra, S (1995) Social values and multiple sources of European social law, *European Law Journal*, **1** (1)

Sisson, K (1999) The 'new' European social model: the end of the search for an orthodoxy or another false dawn?, *Employee Relations*, **21** (5), pp 445–62

Spyropoulos, G (1990) Labour law and labour relations in tomorrow's social Europe, *International Labour Review*, **129** (6), pp 733–50, Geneva

Streeck, W (1999) The internationalization of industrial relations in Europe: prospects and problems, *Politics and Society*, **26** (4), pp 429–59, Sage

Teague, P (1999) *Economic Citizenship in the European Union: Employment Relations in the new Europe*, Routlege, London

Teague, P and Grahl, J (1992) *Industrial Relations and European Integration*, Lawrence & Wishart, London

Traxler, F (1996) European trade union policy and collective bargaining, *Transfer*, **2** (2), pp 287–97, ETUI, Brussels

Tusselmann, H-J (2001) The new German model of industrial relations: flexible collectivism or Anglo-Saxonization?, *International Journal of Manpower*, **22** (6), pp 544–59

Wills, J (1999) Making the best of it: managerial attitudes towards, and the experiences of, European works councils in UK-owned multi-national firms, Working Paper, University of Southampton

3

Britain in the global economy

Steve Bradley

INTRODUCTION

In this chapter we review the performance of the British economy, focusing upon the past 30 years, in the context of the so-called global economy. During this time period, there have been many changes, domestic and international, which have had, or may have, an impact on British economic performance. Domestically, there has been a 'supply-side' revolution, initiated by the Thatcher administration in 1979, including widespread deregulation of markets, privatization, the reduction in union power, reform of youth and adult training, and changes in the provision of, and systems governing, financial work incentives. We consider whether these reforms have generated an increase in wealth and a reduction in unemployment.

At an international level, Britain has become more closely integrated with the EU, but so far has been reluctant to enter the European Monetary Union (EMU). Currency crises, such as those in the EU (ie the Exchange Rate Mechanism crisis), South-East Asia, Mexico and Russia, have become more frequent and threaten global financial and monetary stability. On the political front, the Cold War has ended, resulting in the reunification of East and West Germany, and the conversion of former planned economies into market-based economies. One outcome of these changes will be eastward enlargement of the EU over the next ten years. Other changes are more pervasive, such as falling transport and communication costs, and improvements in communication and information technology, such as the Internet. These changes have led to claims of a so-called 'new economy', which may have social as well as economic and political consequences for Britain and the world economy.

In this chapter we discuss the performance of the British economy in the context of the changes described above. In the first section of the chapter, attention focuses on the medium-term economic performance of the economy in the 1990s, but also discusses its very recent performance and projections in the short term. The second section takes a long-term view of Britain's economic performance, including its growth performance over the last century, but with an emphasis on the past 30 years. Additionally, this section examines the causes of Britain's relative economic decline. The penultimate section of the chapter discusses two developments that may affect Britain's economic performance in the future. The first of these is Britain's entry to the EMU; the second is the potential impact of information and communications technology (ICT) on labour productivity and output growth. The final section of the chapter discusses the now widely accepted international consensus in policy making. Throughout the chapter, comparisons are made with economies of similar size and maturity – our main international competitors.

RECENT ECONOMIC PERFORMANCE

At the time of writing, the world economy is teetering on the brink of a recession. However, a recent OECD report states that although economic growth in OECD countries was expected to slow down in 2000, it is anticipated that the causes of weaker growth will dissipate in the latter part of 2001 (OECD, 2001). Economic growth rates are expected to drop to 2 per cent for 2001 from 4.1 per cent in 2000, but rise to 2.8 in 2002 (see Table 3.1). The reasons for this are recent reductions in interest rates in the UK and United States, falling oil prices and tax reductions in several countries, which should stimulate aggregate demand and economic growth. Furthermore, inflation is also low in most OECD economies, which leaves further scope for monetary policies that can facilitate growth.

The production sectors in Britain and elsewhere are, however, already experiencing difficulties and are close to recession. In Britain industrial production fell in the first quarter of 2001, compared to the same quarter in the previous year, but the fall was less than that of Germany and the United States. The British export sector, especially those competing in the euro area, has been struggling for some time because of the strong pound. However, other indicators of economic performance are more favourable. Although the labour market is tight, wage and earnings growth has been modest, and so the rate of inflation in Britain (2.1 per cent) is lower than that in Germany (3.1 per cent) and the United States (3.2 per cent). The rate of unemployment has fallen to levels not seen since the 1970s. In 2000 the unemployment rate in

Table 3.1 Changes in output (real GDP), 1990–2002 (percentage change on previous year)

	1990–95	1995–2000	1998	1999	2000	2001	2002
UK	1.6	2.8	2.6	2.2	3.0	2.4	2.6
France	1.0	2.4	3.2	2.9	3.2	2.5	2.3
Germany	2.0	1.8	2.1	1.6	3.1	2.2	2.2
US	2.4	4.3	4.4	4.2	5.0	1.7	3.1
Japan	1.4	1.1	–2.5	0.2	1.7	1.0	1.1
EU	1.5	2.5	2.8	2.4	3.3	2.6	2.7
Euro area	1.6	2.4	2.8	2.4	3.4	2.6	2.7
OECD	1.8	2.9	2.1	2.6	4.1	2.0	2.8
Transition economies	–6.9	1.9	–0.6	2.	5.6		
Developing economies	5.0	4.3	1.5	3.3	5.5		
World	2.0	3.1	1.9	2.7	4.0		

Notes: Projections for 2000–2 and annual averages for 1990–5 and 1995–2000.

Source: UNCTAD, 2001; OECD Economic Outlook No 69, May 2001 and National Institute Economic Review No 176, April 2001

Britain was 5.5 per cent, which compared favourably with those in France (9.5 per cent) and Germany (8.0 per cent), but was higher than the US rate (4.0 per cent). In contrast, Japan has experienced disinflation with falling prices accompanied by a rising rate of unemployment (see Table 3.2).

Table 3.2 Standardized unemployment rates (per cent)

	1998	1999	2000	2001	2002
UK	6.3	6.1	5.5	5.2	5.5
France	11.7	11.3	9.5	8.3	7.9
Germany	9.4	8.6	8.0	8.0	8.3
US	4.5	4.2	4.0	4.5	5.0
Japan	4.1	4.7	4.7	5.0	5.2
Euro area	10.9	9.9	8.9	8.5	8.3
EU	9.9	9.2	8.3	7.8	7.7
OECD	–	–	6.3	6.3	6.3

Source: OECD Economic Outlook No 69 and National Institute Economic Review No 176

Turning to the euro area economy, economic growth has been strong over the past 12 months (see Table 3.1), which suggests that it may be better able to withstand a US slowdown. However, the weakness of the euro exchange rate is still a cause for concern, and inflation has moved toward the upper end of the target band. One would have therefore expected the European Central

Bank (ECB) to raise interest rates to curb inflationary pressures; however, it has been reluctant to do so primarily because of the US economic slowdown.

The US economy has been in recession, although there are recent signs of recovery as worker productivity increased by over 8 per cent in the first quarter of 2002, which should counter the fall in corporate profits. However, the sheer size of the US economy means that events in the United States inevitably spill over to the world economy, including Britain. According to Eddie George, Governor of the Bank of England, the origin of the recession can be traced to the very high productivity gains arising from the widespread application of information and communications technology (ICT), which created strong growth (George, 2001). Strong growth, coupled with low inflation, led to expectations of higher corporate earnings growth, resulting in a rapid increase in equity prices, especially in the 'high tech' sector. Business investment and consumer demand both increased. Consequently, the private sector went into financial deficit and there was an inflow of direct and portfolio investment, causing the exchange rate to appreciate. As export growth slowed, the US economy also slowed down. Until recently, policy makers were hoping that buoyant consumer spending would help US growth to recover in so far as this would eventually stimulate business investment. However, as unemployment rises in the United States, consumer demand is likely to fall because of the fear of job loss, which will further slow the economy and may precipitate worldwide recession. The forecasts in Table 3.1 will then have to be revised.

Turning to the medium term, for the OECD area, both actual and trend growth were lower in the 1990s compared with the 1970s and 1980s, continuing the 'well documented decline in the growth rate' (Elmeskov and Scarpetta, 2000). In more recent years this trend has been reversed, especially in the United States, Australia, Ireland, the Netherlands and Norway. EU countries also witnessed a rise. The main cause of these growth rate differences, they argue, was rising labour productivity, accounting for over 50 per cent of the GDP per capita growth in most OECD countries over the 1990s. Labour productivity has risen because of improvements in human capital but also due to the impact of information and communications technology. Labour utilization (ie employment rates combined with hours worked) and demographic factors, such as the growth in the workforce, have had less of an effect. However, comparing the EU and the United States, lower labour utilization accounts for three-quarters of the gap in their levels of GDP per capita.

Economic growth in Britain has consistently been slightly lower than that in the OECD in the 1990s, but exceeded that of the euro area up until 1998. Since that time the euro area growth has been higher and this is forecast to continue in the near future. The slowdown of growth in Germany is noticeable (see Table 3.3). Unemployment has also been consistently lower in Britain in the 1990s than in either the EU or the euro area (see Table 3.2), but falling domestic demand in Britain is likely to lead to a slight increase in the unemployment rate in the next 12 months.

Table 3.3 Growth performance in OECD countries, 1970–99 (percentage change on previous year)

Country	Growth of GDP per capita				Trend growth of GDP per person employed	
	1970–80	1980–90	1990–8	1999	1980–90	1990–8
UK	1.8	2.5	1.7	1.7	1.9	1.8
France	2.7	1.8	0.9	2.5	1.9	1.4
Germany	2.6	2.0	1.0	1.4	1.6	1.9
US	2.1	2.3	2.0	3.2	1.1	1.7
Japan	3.3	3.4	1.1	0.1	2.6	1.3
EU	2.6	2.1	1.3	2.1	2.3	1.8
OECD	2.5	2.3	1.6	2.1	2.8	2.4

Source: Extracted from Table A1, Elmeskov and Scarpetta (2000)

The slowdown in the performance of the Japanese economy, apparent in Table 3.1, is well documented and there are two competing explanations (Wilson, 2000). First, the monetary perspective, or 'liquidity trap' argument, whereby conventional monetary policy, such as cutting interest rates, has little effect in stimulating the economy. A demand stimulus may therefore be required. Second, structural problems related to the 'real' side of the economy. However, Japan's economic slowdown remains a 'puzzle'. Furthermore, in combining a high dependency ratio (a measure of the proportion of a population who are dependent on those of working age), low nominal interest rates, structural problems and sluggish growth it is reminiscent of the euro area economies. The recent experience of the Japanese economy could then be regarded as a cautionary tale for EU policymakers.

A LONG-TERM PERSPECTIVE ON BRITISH ECONOMIC PERFORMANCE

International comparisons

The long-term performance of the British economy is often described as one of 'relative' economic decline. In this section, we briefly discuss the performance of the British and the world economy over the last century, and then describe in more detail trends over the last 30 years.

The leading countries in terms of growth in real GDP per person have income levels, measured in terms of purchasing power parity, that are much higher than in 1900 or 1950. For instance, in the UK income levels in 1996 were over four times those of 1900 and almost three times those of 1950. In the United States income levels in 1996 were five times greater than 1900 and over twice those of 1950. Poorer areas of the world, such as India and Africa, have experienced a growth in incomes but they have lagged behind: in 1996 income levels were nearly one-sixth of those in the UK. Growth has slowed in all countries since 1973 but is still superior to the pre-1950 period (Crafts, 1993; Bean and Crafts, 1996). Britain is regarded as having been in relative economic decline over the long term, primarily due to lower Total Factor Productivity (TFP) growth, having slipped in the ranking from having the highest real GDP per person in 1900 to fourth or fifth highest in the late 1990s, being overtaken by the United States, Germany and Japan. (Total Factor Productivity refers to output per unit of total inputs (capital and labour) used in production.)

Although there has been no convergence between the growth rates of rich and poor countries of the world, there has been some catch-up in growth rates between the leader (the United States) and other OECD countries (Crafts, 1999; Siebert, 1999). So, the picture of 20th-century economic growth is one of divergence between the rich and the poor and convergence within the OECD (rich) group. Note, however, that comparisons of growth rates ignore other factors that may affect standards of living, such as levels of education, reductions in hours worked and life expectancy. If these are included then standards of living have improved much more.

Comparing standards of living between countries over time also ignores the distribution of income within a country. Up to the late 1970s, the earnings and income distribution in Britain was becoming more equal, but since that time it has widened considerably (Atkinson, 1999). The top earners in Britain have experienced a rapid growth in earnings, whereas the growth of earnings for the less well paid has stabilized, and this polarity has given rise to concerns about social exclusion in Britain. The United States has had a similar experience, whereas many other OECD countries have not.

The post-war period up to 1973 is often referred to as the 'golden age' of economic growth, wherein the UK experienced average annual growth rates of 2.4 per cent compared to 2.5 per cent in the United States. From 1973 growth rates have, on average, at least until recently, been 1.6 per cent. Moreover, Britain's performance pales in comparison with those of West Germany and Japan over these two time periods.

Another way of looking at the long-run economic performance of Britain is to compare growth rates in labour productivity. It has been shown that labour productivity in Britain exceeded that of France and Germany until the 1960s (Crafts, 1993). However, there has been a particularly poor labour productivity performance in manufacturing in the 1960s and 1970s. Identifying the principal causes of low labour productivity in this period is a notoriously difficult exercise. These would include a 'poor' industrial relations climate and deficiencies in the training and skills of the workforce. Furthermore, though productivity improved in the 1980s, this 'productivity miracle' was largely associated with large-scale labour shedding. Table 3.4 shows that labour productivity during the 1990s has been similar to that of our main competitors, but is still below the OECD average.

Table 3.4 The changing distribution of employment

Year/Sector	UK	France	Germany	US	Japan
1970					
Agriculture	3.2	13.5	8.5	4.5	16.9
Industry	43.2	38.4	48.7	33.1	35.7
Services	53.6	48.0	42.8	62.3	4.4
Employment (000s)	24,381	20,328	26,107	78,678	50,140
1980					
Agriculture	2.6	8.5	5.2	3.6	10.1
Industry	36.2	35.1	42.9	29.3	35.1
Services	61.2	56.4	51.9	67.1	54.8
Employment (000s)	25,004	21,443	26,486	99,303	54,600
1990					
Agriculture	2.1	5.7	3.5	2.9	6.9
Industry	30.3	29.0	38.9	25.1	33.9
Services	67.6	65.3	5.6	72.0	59.2
Employment (000s)	26,818	22,082	27,952	118,93	61,710
1998					
Agriculture	1.7	4.4	2.8	2.7	5.0
Industry	26.1	24.1	33.6	22.7	31.7
Services	72.2	71.5	63.6	74.6	63.3
Employment (000s)	27,009	22,521	35,830	131,463	64,450

Notes: Figures refer to civilian employment. Unified Germany for 1998.
Source: US Department of Labour, 2001

The causes of Britain's relative economic decline

The causes of Britain's relatively poor performance with respect to economic growth, labour productivity and competitiveness have been blamed on a host of factors. Thirlwall (1979) has suggested that it arose from a balance of payments constraint, which hampered growth, whereas Bacon and Eltis (1976) put forward the view that the growth of the non-market, government, sector crowded out private sector investment, thereby reducing economic growth. Both of these approaches have been criticized by Crafts, who analyses the effect of de-industrialization (Crafts, 1993). Table 3.4 shows that Britain has experienced higher than average de-industrialization compared to the OECD, whereas Germany and Japan are the most industrialized economies. De-industrialization largely arises from changes in sectoral growth rates, shifts in the pattern of consumer demand and changes in comparative advantage. Additionally, there have been changes in world trade patterns and Britain's share of world trade in manufacturing has been in long-term decline. The de-industrialization thesis may, however, be overstated since manufacturing industry has contributed a larger share of the productivity growth over the century than its share of employment would warrant (Crafts, 1993).

Two alternative explanations of Britain's relative economic decline have been suggested by Crafts (1999). First, the problem is not that Britain has had slower economic growth rates, when compared to her main international competitors, but that the United States has experienced an acceleration of growth. The same is true of Germany and Japan. In the United States faster growth arose from technological innovations, based on an abundance of natural resources and access to a large home market. Both of these factors were unavailable in Britain. Second, Britain's ability to catch up with the United States was undermined by the nexus of institutional arrangements and incentives. Of particular importance are the systems of industrial relations and human capital accumulation, which adversely affected productivity performance. Government policy in the form of State-led industrialization, coupled with protectionist trade policies, also served to impede economic growth. Crafts therefore emphasizes 'social capability', or incentive structures, as of key importance to growth outcomes rather than technological innovation. The impact of the industrial relations system and human capital accumulation therefore need to be considered in greater depth.

Human capital accumulation and the industrial relations system

Education, training and skills

The deficiencies of Britain's vocational education and training (VET) system have been the subject of considerable research over many years. In this section we discuss the deficiencies with the VET system in Britain and explore what improvements have been made over the past 20 years as a result of changes in government policy.

Keep and Mayhew (1988) and the work of the National Institute for Economic and Social Research, summarized in Prais (1995), provide a clear assessment of the deficiencies of Britain's VET system up to the late 1980s. Compared to our major international competitors, they argued that Britain suffered from:

- A relatively poor system of compulsory education, which produced a significant proportion of unqualified school leavers who also lacked basic literacy and numeracy skills. As a result, Britain has a much higher rate of functional illiteracy (ie an inability to read simple instructions) amongst adults and youths compared to competitors such as Germany (Layard, McIntosh and Vignoles, 2000).
- A much lower staying-on rate beyond the compulsory school-leaving age, and a narrow apprenticeship system, focused almost entirely on engineering and construction trades, which have been in long-term decline.
- A lack of training for young people who did not enter apprenticeships. In comparison, the German dual apprenticeship system provided vocational

training in a wide range of occupations, including those in the service sector.

• An inadequate level of adult training, in particular management training.

In consequence, Britain suffered from having too few workers with intermediate, or craft-level, skills compared to our competitors. Britain therefore has a very high proportion of 'low'-skilled workers. For instance, in 1985 the proportion of the workforce with low skills was 65 per cent, and in 1996 this had only fallen to 52 per cent. Also, the share of low-skill workers in Britain is still considerably higher than Germany, where the proportion of low-skilled workers is only 25 per cent (Murray and Steedman, 1998). Furthermore, it is claimed that Britain is trapped in a so-called 'low-skills' equilibrium, wherein a low-skilled workforce produces low value added goods (Finegold and Soskice, 1988). Producing this type of product leaves Britain open to competition from developing and emerging economies, which have the advantage of abundant low-wage labour. The outcome of these deficiencies in the VET system for labour productivity and international competitiveness is obvious.

The election of the Conservative Government in 1979 led to a 'supply-side' revolution in economic policy making and reforms to the VET system were numerous. These included the reform of the education system, the introduction of publicly funded youth training programmes, and the devolution of control of training provision from the civil service (eg the Manpower Services Commission) to employer-led bodies (eg Training and Enterprise Councils), in an attempt to stimulate adult and youth training at the 'local' level. These reforms are discussed below with a view to evaluating their contribution to remedying the deficit in Britain's VET system:

• The Education Reform Act (1988) introduced major reforms to the secondary education sector, and sought to create a quasi-market in education. By increasing parental choice of school and stimulating competition between schools for pupils, it was hoped that educational standards would rise. Bradley *et al* (2000) show that the secondary education system does operate like a quasi-market, and that competition between schools raised performance in GCSE exams in the 1990s. Teacher productivity, measured by the number of high-grade GCSE exam passes per teacher, has also risen over the period (Bradley and Taylor, 2001). Partly as a result of the increase in exam performance, the proportion of young people staying on beyond the compulsory school-leaving age has risen to over 70 per cent of the 16–17 age group. Educational standards, when measured by success in GCSE exams, do appear to have been raised by the educational reforms. On the downside, Britain continues to lag behind Germany in terms of the number of workers with A-level equivalent qualifications and is even behind French equivalents with respect to 'good' GCSE qualifications (Layard *et al*, 2000).

• The recession of the early 1980s, which had a particularly dramatic effect on manufacturing industry in Britain, precipitated a dramatic rise in youth unemployment and the collapse of the apprenticeship system. The government response was to reform the Youth Opportunities Programme and replace it with the Youth Training Scheme (YTS). By 1983 the YTS had become a two-year programme of planned off-the-job training and work experience available for all 16–17-year-olds. Later, with the introduction of National Vocational Qualifications in 1988, the YTS offered certificated training across a wide range of occupations. The YTS has been amended several times, changing its name to Youth Training in 1990, and more recently being transformed into Modern Apprenticeships and Training for Skills. Have these programmes of youth training been a success? The consensus from micro-econometric studies of the impact of training programmes on employment and wage outcomes suggests that they have not been that successful. Participation on a youth training programme has had a small impact on employment prospects, but there is no appreciable increase in wages compared to non-participants. The quality of the training provided by government programmes is therefore questionable.

- In the area of adult training, there have been attempts to encourage employers to provide more, and better quality, training. Reforms began with the dismantling of the Industrial Training Boards, which were replaced by the Manpower Services Commission (subsequently the Training Agency), so reducing the role of the private sector. Subsequently, in recognition of the inability of the Training Agency to stimulate adult training, employer-led bodies were introduced in 1990 in the form of the Training and Enterprise Councils (TECs). Recently, the TECs have been replaced by Skills Councils, which have responsibility for work-based training and further education. According to Keep and Mayhew (1999), the most useful development in the past 20 years in the field of adult training has been the creation of 'Investors in People', a 'kitemark' signifying good practice in company training provision. Nevertheless, there is evidence that the volume of work-based adult training has remained constant (Felstead, Green and Mayhew, 1997).

The net outcome of these reforms seems to be that Britain still lags behind its main international competitors in terms of intermediate skills. 'Inadequate VET performance, as conventionally measured, is increasingly seen as the inevitable consequence and symptom of being in... [a low skills equilibrium]... rather than as a problem in its own right. Indeed, if employers continue to produce low-spec goods using Fordist production methods, clearly it would be absurd and wasteful to increase skill supply...' (Keep and Mayhew, 1999). British firms who produce such 'low-spec' goods are likely to face rising global competition because of the increasing mobility of capital, which locates and produces in low-cost labour countries and then ships output back to the home market. Britain can no longer hope that technological innovations will give it a competitive edge because such innovations diffuse quickly throughout the global economy.

For Keep and Mayhew it is poor product specification and bad job design that are at the heart of the VET problem in Britain. The remedy lies with British business, which should switch into the production of high value added goods and services. Unfortunately, British business may be hampered from doing so simply because of the inadequacies of the workforce. This 'chicken and egg' scenario suggests that changes on the demand side alone will be insufficient to remedy the problem. Consequently, further supply-side reforms may be necessary to overcome these market failures, which lead to an insufficient supply of 'skilled' workers.

Industrial relations and financial incentives

The British system of industrial relations, together with the system of work and benefit-related financial incentives, which existed up to the late 1980s, has been criticized for its contribution to the creation of an inflexible labour market. The outcomes were higher rates of inflation and rising unemployment, which reduced economic growth.

Nickell and van Ours (2000) discuss the UK experience with respect to the unemployment rate. Bertola (2000) provides a similar review of the trends in, and causes of, unemployment in Europe and the EMU. Unemployment in Britain fell below the EU average in 1993. Prior to this, the unemployment rate rose in the 1970s because of the oil price shocks, 'exploding' after the second shock in 1983. Economic growth was adversely affected. Thereafter, the unemployment rate began to decline apart from in the recession of 1991–93. Of greater importance, however, are changes in the equilibrium unemployment rate. The equilibrium unemployment rate is that rate consistent with non-accelerating inflation, and this started to rise in the 1970s. In the 1980s, after the second oil price shock, unemployment rose to 10 per cent, which was above the equilibrium rate of 7.5 per cent, and was accompanied by falling inflation and a balance of payments surplus. Since then the equilibrium unemployment rate has fallen and is now close to the actual unemployment rate.

In view of these changes, several questions arise. First, how does the system of industrial relations and financial incentives affect growth, inflation and unemployment? Second, what reforms have been introduced over the past 20 years? Third, have these reforms been successful in terms of generating less inflationary pressure, lower unemployment rates and higher economic growth?

● Union power and Britain's system of industrial relations have been criticized for raising inflation by increasing firms' costs. As costs rise, firms are forced to cut back the size of the workforce and so unemployment rises (Blanchflower, 1996). Higher rates of inflation undermine international competitiveness and constrain growth. Union density increased in the 1970s, but declined thereafter, and union coverage fell dramatically from 70 per cent in 1980 to 47 per cent in 1994. These changes are unique within the OECD and their causes remain the subject of debate (Nickell and van

Ours, 2000). This substantially reduced inflationary pressures and decreased the equilibrium unemployment rate in Britain.

• Financial work incentives also affect the equilibrium unemployment rate via their impact on labour supply. Generous benefit levels (or more specifically the replacement ratio) indefinite benefit payment and less rigorous policing of the unemployed raise the equilibrium unemployment rate because they undermine the incentive to work. The replacement ratio, that is, the proportion of income replaced by benefits if a person becomes unemployed, has fallen since the 1960s and the monitoring of the unemployed is now much tougher since the introduction of the Restart programme. Dolton and O'Neill show that the Restart programme has had positive employment effects (Dolton and O'Neill, 1996). Consequently, the equilibrium unemployment rate has fallen. However, the indefinite payment of benefits is a source of weakness for Britain and encourages long-term unemployment. To counteract long-term unemployment, the Labour government has introduced New Deal, which is a system of welfare-to-work policies. However, despite increased spending on Active Labour Market Policies (ALMPs) over the past 30 years, it appears that they have had only a small part to play in the labour market improvements of the 1990s (Nickell and van Ours, 2000; Robinson, 2000).

• Other factors have increased labour market inflexibility, such as labour taxes, excessive employment protection and skill mismatches. The latter reflects a relative demand shift in favour of skilled workers (Machin, 1996; Machin and van Reenen, 1998). Advances in technology have also contributed to an increase in demand for a more highly skilled workforce, which Britain's VET system seems unable to deliver.

Even so, there has been a very real improvement in the British labour market during the 1990s, ie, a fall in the equilibrium unemployment rate. 'This is a real phenomenon and not just a result of a statistical redistribution of non-employed workers from unemployment to other categories. In contrast with most other EU countries, there is something of a miracle here' (Nickell and van Ours, 2000). Contributing factors would include the reduction of union influence on collective bargaining outcomes and the impact of changes in financial incentives described earlier. ALMPs have been less successful.

THE FUTURE PERFORMANCE OF THE BRITISH ECONOMY

Britain and the EMU

There are two major issues related to the European Union that could impact significantly on the performance of the British economy in the future. The first is the proposed enlargement of the union to encompass a number of former Soviet bloc countries such as Hungary, Poland, Romania, Latvia and Estonia. This eastward enlargement of the EU is, however, more likely to impact on those countries that share their border, such as Germany and Austria (Read and Bradley, 2001). The second, more serious development in terms of Britain's future economic performance is the EMU.

The Labour government has promised the electorate a referendum on EMU, but only 'when the time is right' for entry. To determine whether the time is right, the Labour government has insisted on using five economic tests. First, are business cycles and economic structures sufficiently compatible so that Britain and other countries could cope with standardized, euro, interest rates? Second, should economic problems emerge, such as rising inflation or increasing unemployment in one part of the euro area, is there enough flexibility in the system to deal with them? Third, would joining EMU create better conditions for firms to invest in Britain? Fourth, what would the effect be on the competitive position of the UK financial services industry? Fifth, will joining the EMU promote higher growth, a stable macro environment and create jobs? Each of these tests is examined in the context of the pros and cons of Britain's entry to EMU. We begin, however, with a brief discussion of the mechanics of the EMU and the state of the euro area economy.

January 1999 marked a significant step toward a united Europe when 11 member countries of the European Union adopted the euro, irrevocably locking together the foreign exchange values of their currencies. Full conversion occurred in 2002. Consequently, these countries ceased to operate independent monetary policies, and responsibility for euro area monetary policy was passed to the European Central Bank (ECB). The processes leading to the creation of the EMU can be traced back to the treaty of Maastricht, signed in 1992, which stipulated the 'convergence criteria' that prospective members had to fulfil before entry would be granted. Britain, although closer to meeting the convergence criteria than many of the other applicants, decided to defer its decision on entry. Over two years have passed since the formation of the EMU and Britain is still not a member. Why?

The advantages of EMU include the removal of the uncertainty created by fluctuations in bilateral exchange rates, which serve to reduce trade and investment, and the elimination of transaction costs arising from hedging and the need to convert one currency into another. Also, given that the ECB has been modelled on the Bundesbank, which has a history of providing low and stable inflation for Germany, it is argued that the same can be delivered for the whole of the euro area.

Each of these advantages can be questioned in the case of Britain. Over 50 per cent of Britain's trade in goods and services is with countries outside the euro area, including the United States, suggesting that Britain has less to gain from joining the EMU than its present members. In terms of British investment, £1,500 billion out of a total of £2,000 billion in gross foreign assets is outside the euro area. Putting the facts about trade and investment together helps to explain why the exchange rate between the pound and the dollar is closer than with other EMU currencies (Bradley and Whittaker, 2000). Consequently, joining EMU would raise the level of exchange rate risk for British business.

The estimated saving in transaction costs of 0.4 per cent of GDP for those countries who trade within the euro area could have been achieved through reform of the banking sector rather than a single currency. De Bandt and Davis show that the level of competition between banks in the EU is much less than in the United States (De Bandt and Davis, 2000). This suggests that an increase in cross-border competition, rather than EMU *per se*, could force banks to be more 'price' competitive, so reducing transaction costs associated with trade. Also, since Britain trades less with EMU countries, the transaction cost savings would, in any case, be lower.

Inflation is low in the euro area but strong economic growth has triggered several hikes in interest rates over the past two years. However, discussion of the euro area performance masks wide disparities between countries. Clearly, the inclusion of countries like Greece, Italy and Spain, which do not have a strong record on fiscal prudence, reduced inflationary expectations. This is because EMU members are required by the Stability and Growth Pact to maintain their budget deficit within a limit of 3 per cent of GDP. This is a positive feature of EMU; however, the 'one-size-fits-all' interest rate is more contentious. Given that the countries in the EMU have different rates of inflation, and are at different stages of the business cycle, it seems unlikely that a single interest rate will simultaneously satisfy the needs of all members. The Irish case, in recent years, is the most obvious example. The combination of strong economic growth, stimulated by trade with Britain and Structural and Cohesion Fund grants, led to rising inflation and necessitated a higher rate of interest to reduce inflationary pressures. However, the fact that Irish GDP constitutes only 1 per cent of EU GDP means that policy makers at the ECB can afford to ignore these 'local' problems. Furthermore, given the reluctance of the Irish government to raise taxes to choke off inflationary pressures, eventually the cost must be a reduction in the competitiveness of Irish exports and hence lower growth.

The case of Ireland must raise alarm bells for Britain, since trading and investment links outside of the euro area mean that our business cycle is not synchronized with other EU countries. The interest rate differential between the euro area and Britain would be eliminated if we joined the EMU (at the lower rate) and this would undermine the Bank of England's work in controlling inflation in Britain. Furthermore, the Bank has established a reputation for controlling inflation, suggesting that Britain does not need the ECB to control our inflation.

Barrel and Dury evaluate Britain's membership of EMU under different policy regimes (Barrell and Dury, 2000). The regimes are the inflation-targeting approach of the Bank of England and the price stability approach adopted by the ECB. They show that the volatility of output would be greater if we became a member of the EMU, primarily because the Bank of England could no longer use interest rates to offset demand shocks. In contrast, the variability of inflation would be less and prices would be more stable in the EMU. Comparing these findings with the government's five tests for membership, the increase in the volatility of output is unlikely to lead to a lasting increase in employment, whereas the reduction in the variability of inflation and prices could promote growth and encourage inward investment. The authors argue that it is unclear at present which set of 'targets' carries more weight.

If output growth is more volatile then it implies that the economies of the EMU will not have converged adequately, and this may give rise to a balance of payments constraint on growth (Taylor and te Velde, 2001). Persistent external imbalances, which may prove difficult to finance, could be the outcome. It was thought that the elimination of exchange rate risk would facilitate the process of financing external deficits. However, cross-border financing in the EMU is still subject to 'country credit risk', which refers to widespread default by residents of a troubled member. It is argued that the perception of a member being a credit risk could develop if a weak country develops chronic payments deficits associated with low productivity, high unit labour costs, and a tendency to inflation. This would induce financial markets to impose national risk premiums when lending to residents of the deficit country, including its government. Some economies are more exposed to this kind of problem because of their intra-EU trade. Examples include Belgium, the Netherlands and Ireland – all small economies. The UK exports less, as a proportion of GDP, than these countries but is more exposed to the rest of the world than France or Spain.

Overall, the case for Britain's membership of the EMU does not look strong in the light of the arguments presented above. Entry to EMU may therefore have a detrimental impact on the future performance of the British economy.

The 'new economy'

In a recent report the OECD has argued that 'Governments today are faced with a new economic environment. ICT has emerged as a key technology with the potential to transform economic and social activity and has led to more rapid growth in countries where the conditions for macroeconomic stability are in place.' (OECD, 2001). Some commentators suggest that ICT will be as important for economic growth in the future as innovations such as electricity or the internal combustion engine were in the past.

The growth of the ICT sector, it is argued, has contributed to differences in trend growth in GDP per capita between the 1980s and 1990s. This increased in several countries, such as Australia, Ireland, the Netherlands and particularly the United States, whereas in Britain and many other European countries trend growth actually declined or stagnated.

Elmeskov and Scarpetta note that ICT can affect growth through three main channels (Elmeskov and Scarpetta, 2000). First, the acceleration of productivity in the ICT sector, which leads to it becoming more important for the entire economy. Though the ICT sector is small in most OECD countries, since 1990 labour productivity in the two sectors most heavily engaged in ICT production (office, accounting and computer equipment; and radio, television and communication) rose faster than in manufacturing at large (see Table 3.5). Second, rising growth in investment in ICT leads to capital deepening throughout the economy. Capital deepening has also been stimulated by a large fall in the quality-adjusted price of ICT equipment, which leads to the substitution of other assets for ICT and greater overall investment. The outcome is an increase in labour productivity. In Britain, for instance, investment in non-residential IT equipment rose from 5.2 per cent in 1985 to 11.7 per cent in 1996 compared to 6.3 per cent and 13.4 per cent in the United States. This growth rate has risen considerably in the United States in the latter half of the 1990s. It has been estimated that the ICT capital stock contributed 14 per cent of total output growth in the 1990s, with a surge in the latter half of the 1990s (Elmeskov and Scarpetta, 2000). It has also been estimated that the use of ICT has raised labour productivity growth in the US business sector by 0.2–0.3 percentage points between 1995 and 1999. Black and Lynch provide microeconomic evidence of the positive impact of ICT on productivity at the firm level (Black and Lynch, 1997, 2000). Third, the use of ICT creates 'spillover' effects on productivity, leading to changes in company organization, which affect the efficiency with which capital and labour are used in production. One example of the spillover effects arises from improved communication and access to information through the Internet, which gives rise to different and more efficient ways of organizing production and sales.

Table 3.5   Sectoral differences in labour productivity, 1999 (1995 = 100)

Country	Office, accounting & computer equipment	Radio, television & communications equipment	Manufacturing
UK	160	–	103
France	–	128	115
Germany	186	129	117
US	460	172	125
Japan	–	112	104
Korea	454	322	150

Source: OECD (1999), Indicators of Industrial Activity, No 4, cited in Elmeskov and Scarpetta, 2000

It would therefore appear to be the case that ICT has had a substantial effect on growth rates in a number of OECD economies and especially in the United States. However, ICT has had less of an impact in Britain, possibly because of the insufficient supply of 'knowledge intensive' workers, such as scientists, engineers and ICT specialists, or because the competitive environment is not right. Both would appear to be prerequisites for the effective utilization of ICT. Work practices are also important for the effective use of ICT, and in this respect Britain and Sweden are at the forefront. Both exhibit a greater propensity to implement new practices, such as teamwork, job rotation, employee involvement schemes and flatter management.

Thus, although there is a view that ICT has led to the creation of a 'new economy' in some countries, the impact on the British economy may only materialize in the future. The OECD argue that the growth of ICT should be encouraged and the way to achieve this is to remove barriers to new business start-ups, provide financial incentives, deregulate the telecom market and create a stable macro environment.

BRITISH ECONOMIC POLICY AND THE WORLD ECONOMY

In the final section of this chapter we briefly review the conduct of macroeconomic policy in Britain, and discuss the consensus that appears to have been reached on how to control the performance of the world economy.

The conduct of macroeconomic policy in post-war Britain is well documented (Middleton, 2000). Successive post-war governments up to 1979 regarded full employment as the main objective of macroeconomic policy, followed by price stability, a balance of payments surplus and economic growth. Fiscal policy was the main instrument for controlling the economy and the overall approach has been described as 'stop-go'. The conduct of policy changed dramatically with the election of the Conservative government in 1979, which inherited an economy where both inflation and unemployment were rising. This stimulated a change in policy objectives and policy instruments. Price stability rather than full employment was the new priority, control of which was to be achieved through monetary policy, such as control of the money supply (eg the Medium Term Financial Strategy). This was coupled with the supply-side reforms discussed earlier. This overall strategy has been continued even after the election of the Labour Government in 1997.

In fact, a consensus on the approach to macroeconomic policy was agreed in 1994, known as the Madrid Declaration. (Countries that signed the Madrid Declaration include the EU, United States, Canada, etc.) According to this Declaration, countries, including Britain, should strive for macroeconomic stability and supply-side flexibility. Furthermore, economic growth and lower unemployment cannot be achieved solely by expanding aggregate demand through expansionary fiscal and monetary policy. The underlying supply-side capacity of the economy must also be taken into account. Ignoring the supply side and simply boosting demand has led to inflation and trade deficits, which were subsequently remedied by recessions. High levels of public expenditure, financed by higher taxes, imposed a severe burden on the private sector, which was then constrained in its ability to generate jobs and wealth. It would therefore appear that lessons have been learned from the mistakes arising from the conduct of macro and microeconomic policy in the post-war period up to 1979.

In Britain, monetary policy, particularly changes in interest rates, are used to moderate the business cycle so that economic growth can occur at a rate consistent with the growth of productive potential (the supply side). Fiscal policy seeks to limit public sector borrowing and debt without increasing taxes. On the supply side, many governments favour open markets and free competition at both a domestic and international level. This is because it is believed that unfettered markets deliver global economic growth through increases in efficiency and a more effective allocation of resources. A sustained increase in the wealth of the nation will then enable the government to tackle the considerable 'social' problems that exist in Britain, such as poverty and social exclusion.

The main technical problem facing policy makers is the difficulty of predicting asset price movements. They are 'a major potential threat to financial stability, which is a necessary concomitant to monetary stability' (George, 2001). Bordo and colleagues see financial crises as a dominant feature of the 1990s. These include the ERM crisis in 1992–3, the Tequila crisis of 1994–5 and the Asian crisis of 1997–8 (Bordo et al, 2000). They analyse the causes of financial crises by comparing their frequency over 120 years. The increase in the frequency of financial crises is not the result of globalization or the conduct of international economic policy, such as flexible exchange rates and capital account liberalization. Rather, the primary causes are capital mobility and the provision of a financial safety net in the form of insurance against exchange rate risk, which is provided by a credible, pegged exchange rate policy. This encourages banks and other financial institutions to hold excessive quantities of foreign exchange, so increasing their exposure to market fluctuations.

In view of the threat to macroeconomic stability arising from financial crises, reforms have been introduced which seek to reduce the impact of volatile shifts in financial markets. These include the introduction of codes and standards of best practice, including transparency in the conduct of monetary, financial and fiscal policies.

SUMMARY AND CONCLUSIONS

In this chapter we have reviewed the economic performance of the British economy in the short, medium and long term. Comparisons have been drawn with our main international competitors. The key conclusions of the chapter are as follows:

- Economic growth in the world economy has slowed as the United States has entered recession. However, in the EU and to a lesser extent in Britain, the wider macroeconomic outlook is good and suggests that both may be able to withstand the worst effects of recession.
- Over the long term Britain has experienced relative economic decline. This has been caused, at least in part, by the problems of the industrial relations system as well as a system of financial work incentives that encourages unemployment and a poorly trained workforce.
- Policy reforms and other developments over the past 30 years have led to some improvements in Britain's relative position. The reforms have included measures partly contributing to the reduction in trade union influence in collective bargaining as well as positive improvements in the system of financial work incentives. However, the quality of Britain's VET system remains a cause for concern.
- It is possible that the future performance of the British economy may be undermined if we enter the EMU. In contrast, the ICT sector, which appears to have had a dramatic effect on the United States and other OECD economies, especially in the late 1990s, may have a favourable effect in raising British labour productivity.
- It is now widely recognized that increasing the wealth of a nation requires a stable macroeconomic environment. The consensus amongst policy makers is that this can only be achieved if growth is pursued in full recognition of capacity constraints (the supply side) in the economy.

References

Atkinson, A B (1999) The distribution of income in the UK and OECD countries in the twentieth century, *Oxford Review of Economic Policy*, **15** (4), pp 56–75

Bacon, R W and Eltis, W A (1976) *Britain's economic problem: Too few producers*, Macmillan, London

Barrell, R and Dury, K (2000) Choosing the regime: macroeconomic effects of UK entry into EMU, Working Paper, National Institute for Economic and Social Research, June

Bean, C and Crafts, N (1996) British economic growth since 1945: relative economic decline ... and renaissance?, Chapter 6 in *Economic growth in Europe since 1945*, ed N Crafts and G Toniolo, Cambridge University Press, Cambridge

Bertola, G (2000) Europe's unemployment problems, in *Economics of the European Union*, ed M Artis and F Nixson, 2nd edn, Oxford University Press, Oxford

Black, S E and Lynch, L M (1997) How to compete: The impact of workplace practices and information technology on productivity, NBER Working Paper 6120, National Bureau for Economic Research, Cambridge, MA

Black, S E and Lynch, L M (2000) What's driving the new economy: The benefits of workplace innovation, NBER Working Paper 7479, National Bureau for Economic Research, Cambridge, MA

Blanchflower, D (1996) The role and influence of trade unions in the OECD, Centre for Economic Performance Discussion Paper no 310, LSE, London

Bordo, M, Eichengreen, B, Klingebeil, D and Martinez-Peria, M S (2000) Is the crisis problem growing more severe?, *Economic Policy*, pp 53–81

Bradley, S and Taylor, J (2001) The effect of the quasi-market on the efficiency–equity trade-off in the secondary school sector, *Bulletin of Economic Research*

Bradley, S and Whittaker, J (2000) Britain, EMU and the European economy, *Industrial Relations Journal*, **31** (4), pp 261–74

Bradley, S, Crouchley, R, Millington, J and Taylor, J (2000) Testing for quasi-market forces in secondary education, *Oxford Bulletin of Economics and Statistics*, **62** (3), pp 357–90

Crafts, N (1993) *Can de-industrialization seriously damage your wealth?*, Hobart Paper 120, IEA, London

Crafts, N (1999) Economic growth in the twentieth century, *Oxford Review of Economic Policy*, **15** (4), pp 18–34

De Bandt, O and Davis, E P (2000) Competition, contestability and market structure in European banking sectors on the eve of EMU, *Journal of Banking and Finance*, **24**, pp 1045–66

Dolton, P and O'Neill, D (1996) Unemployment duration and the Restart effect: Some experimental evidence, *Economic Journal*, **106**, pp 387–400

Elmeskov, J and Scarpetta, S (2000) New sources of economic growth in Europe, paper presented at 28th Economics Conference, Oesterreichische Nationalbank, Vienna, June

Felstead, A, Green, F and Mayhew, K (1997) *Getting the measure of training*, Centre for Industrial Policy and Performance, Leeds University

Finegold, D and Soskice, D (1988) The failure of training in Britain: Analysis and prescription, *Oxford Review of Economic Policy*, **4** (3), pp 21–53

George, E (2001) International efforts to improve the functioning of the global economy, speech delivered to the Swiss Institute of International Studies, Zurich, 7 May

Keep, E and Mayhew, K (1988) The assessment: education, training and economic performance, *Oxford Review of Economic Policy*, **4** (3), pp i–xv

Keep, E and Mayhew, K (1999) The assessment: knowledge, skills and competitiveness, *Oxford Review of Economic Policy*, **15** (1), pp 1–15

Layard, R, McIntosh, S and Vignoles, A (2000) Britain's record on skills, mimeo, LSE, London

Machin, S (1996) Changes in the relative demand for skills in the UK labour market, in *Acquiring skills*, ed A Booth and D Snower, Cambridge University Press, Cambridge

Machin, S and van Reenen, J (1998) Technology and the skill structure: evidence from seven countries, *Quarterly Journal of Economics*, **113** (4), pp 1215–44

Middleton, R (2000) *The British economy since 1945*, Macmillan, London

Murray, A and Steedman, H (1998) Growing skills in Europe: the changing skills profiles of France, Germany, the Netherlands, Portugal, Sweden and the UK, LSE Centre for Economic Performance Discussion Paper No. 99, London

Nickell, S and van Ours, J (2000) Falling unemployment: The Dutch and British cases, *Economic Policy*, April, pp 137–80

OECD (2001) The new economy: beyond the hype, Final report on the OECD growth project, OECD, Paris

Prais, S J (1995) *Productivity, education and training: An international perspective*, Cambridge University Press, Cambridge

Read, R and Bradley, S (2001) The economics of eastern enlargement of the EU, *Industrial Relations Journal*, **32** (5), pp 380–400

Robinson, P (2000) Active labour market policies: a case of evidence-based policy-making?, *Oxford Review of Economic Policy*, **16** (1), pp 13–26

Siebert, H (1999) *The World Economy*, Routledge, London

Taylor, C and te Velde, D W (2001) Balance of payments prospects in EMU, Working Paper, National Institute for Economic and Social Research, January

Thirlwall, A P (1979) The balance of payments constraint as an explanation of international growth rate differences, *Banca del Lavoro Quarterly Review*, **128**, pp 44–53

Wilson, D (2000) Japan's slow-down: monetary versus real explanations, *Oxford Review of Economic Policy*, **16** (2), pp 18–33

4

Employment relations in the information society

Chris Baldry

It is now over 20 years since we first heard the phrase Information Society. The rapid development of microelectronics in the late 1970s changed the face of computing from a remote centralized process, accessible to a few initiates and affordable for only the largest organizations, to being almost a basic principle of contemporary organization with wide diffusion into a range of existing technologies and economic and social activities. What made the new technology seem to many a *transforming* technology, of the same historical importance as the steam engine or the electric motor, was firstly the combination of the processes of storage, transformation and transmission of information within a single technology, and secondly the ability to link any of the different items that now used digitized information – word processors, computer-aided design, machine tools, telecommunications – into a series of information networks which had the potential to affect almost every aspect of work and non-work life. Such was the significance of these characteristics, it was claimed, that our whole society was now characterized by the dominating importance and pervasiveness of information, and this seemed to many to hold out the prospects for a social and economic shift of the same magnitude and significance as the shift from agriculture to industrialism that transformed Europe from the late 18th century onwards.

Early debates over whether this was indeed happening, and if so what it might mean, focused initially on the technology itself, particularly in the field of work and employment. There was considerable speculation about the likely effects on aggregate levels of employment and potential changes in the skill profile, concerns which were taken up in early trade union campaigns and strategies and reflected in the short flurry of New Technology Agreements in the early 1980s. Academic research into the extent of such changes was conducted within the wider theoretical argument about whether such technologies determined our work and social behaviour or whether they were themselves determined by wider societal and economic priorities (for revues and summaries of some of these early debates see Baldry, 1988; Hyman and Streeck, 1988; Bamber and Lansbury, 1989; Beirne and Ramsay, 1992).

Twenty years on, however, much of this speculation about what the technology will bring has been made redundant by its ubiquity. Information and communications technology (ICT) is no longer new nor is it any longer the preserve of an elite of technocrats. There is now virtually no job in manufacturing or services in which the job holder will not be expected to interface with some item of ICT, whether the job involves hotel reception, selling insurance, or metal machining. And, with that pervasiveness, the focus of attention has shifted away from the technology itself to the organizational context in which it is used. For we now know that ICT seldom arrives on its own but should be seen more as the midwife of organizational change, enabling team working, Just In Time (JIT), Total Quality Management (TQM), Business Process Reengineering (BPR) and a host of other new acronyms that have accompanied contemporary changes in work organization. Many of these concepts (such as team working and JIT) pre-date the computer age but the rapid increase in their application has been contiguous with the diffusion of ICT.

The idea of a revolutionary change has not gone away, however, but has, with these organizational developments, apparently gained both momentum and some new designations on the way; at the time of writing, there is much talk in policy circles of the 'Knowledge Economy' as the latest manifestation of the Information Society. However, before we can discuss what employment relations are likely to be like in the Information Society we first need to pin down this popular but elusive concept.

THE IDEA OF THE INFORMATION SOCIETY

We have to say at the outset that, compared to previous concepts used in social and political analysis, the concept of the Information Society leaves a lot to be desired as an analytical framework for understanding the essential characteristics of society. For the past two hundred years our society has been referred to variously as capitalist, industrial or as a market economy. These labels all defined contemporary society by the fact that economic power lies in the ownership of capital (rather than land as in an agricultural society) and that materials, products and people have their prices fixed through the operation of markets, including the labour market. The term Information Society, in contrast, tells us little about the relationships between important groups in society but is all too often used as a descriptive, rather than analytical, term which seeks to define society by the content of people's jobs/economic activity and by their use of a particular technology – ICT.

Terms like capitalism or industrialism are broad-brush concepts which define and distinguish particular historical epochs. Within the capitalist or industrial period, however, we often make further historical distinctions at a slightly lower level, breaking that two hundred years into vague but recognizably different periods, usually in terms of shifts in what are called production paradigms – the ways of organizing production. So early industrialism is distinguished by craft production, the middle of the 20th century by mass production (or Fordism), and the end of the 20th and start of the 21st, perhaps, by flexible production (or post-Fordism), by the rise in service employment (Frenkel, Tam and Korczynski, 1999) or, perhaps, by the spread of ICT. Within these historical changes in the organization of production there have been both continuities and dramatic changes in employment relations.

The essential realities of employment relations have remained constant – the terms and conditions of the employment exchange between buyers and sellers of labour, that is, managers and employees, still need to be fixed by a range of mechanisms from unilateral management decision, through collective bargaining between representatives of employer and employees, to the intervention of the State. However, we recognize that, within this overarching continuity, the *patterns* of employment relations – the precise mix of these wage-fixing mechanisms, for example – have differed over time and between different societies as they have mirrored the changing contours of production and employment. In the UK, for example, trade union structures have evolved from their early origins in the craft or occupational unions to include general unions and industrial unions; they have also encompassed the rise of new sectors of employment such as white-collar work and the public sector and now, in consequence, present an extremely heterogeneous structure. Similarly, bargaining patterns have developed from early small-scale localized bargaining to the setting of national rates for whole industries, and then, more recently, have reverted to company or plant level. So we can say that employment relations remains a constant feature of capitalist or market economies but the patterns it displays are bound to vary with economic and social changes: technological change is clearly an important component here and so we should expect the widespread diffusion of ICT to contribute to such changes in the patterning of social and economic relationships.

However, if, instead of a stage in the development of capitalist industrialism, the Information Society is seen as a *replacement* for it, then the expectations about employment relations become very different. The Information Society has indeed been used as the latest in a series of societal models that have implicitly proclaimed the end of industrial capitalism. It is based on a scenario which claims to detect the beginning of the end of the machine age and the emergence of a knowledge economy, in which work is no longer about the production of tangible goods but rather focuses on the centrality of information and the manipulation of symbols (Reich, 1991).

If we accept this proposition then this, of necessity, implies that the dominant social and economic relationships that characterized industrial capitalism are also now in the process of withering away, foremost among which would be the employment relationship. Indeed, in the Industrial Society model we find frequent statements that information or knowledge workers will not only possess higher levels of skill than their industrial forebears but that they will be less and less part of conventional employment relationships – they will work for themselves or as freelance contractors. Handy (1995), for example, forecasts that we will move to a 20/80 society in which only a small proportion of us will be directly employed. The majority will be 'portfolio people' offering their skills to a variety of clients and customers. This would of course relegate employment relations as we have known them to a dwindling historical residue. Early versions of this proposition, focusing on the rise of the service sector, undoubtedly fed the 1980s rhetoric of anti-unionism: for the Thatcher governments of this period unions were not just morally bad (because they distorted the working of the market) but were in fact historical detritus, whose demise was inevitable and whose existence was being artificially prolonged.

Therefore we have to ask whether The Information Society is a useful subconcept which describes a further development in the profile of economic activity within what is still an essentially capitalist society, or whether it is a higher-level term, like Capitalism, which refers to new and distinct sets of socio-economic relationships and whose appearance therefore indicates a very significant shift in the social and economic structure. If the former, then we need to identify what the expected patterns of employment relations will be, what issues (health and safety, working hours, remuneration structures) will be thrown up by the processes of employment and what will be the responses of the labour market actors. However, if the Information Society is the latter sort of model, then it is possible that employment relations will cease to exist, as we will presumably be in other sorts of economic relationships than those of a labour market.

ICT AND HUMAN RESOURCE MANAGEMENT

The last two decades of the 20th century witnessed both the rapid diffusion of ICT and the emergence of Human Resource Management (HRM) as the new orthodoxy in employment practice. Perhaps because of this chronological correspondence, HRM is often portrayed as if it were in some way a reflection of the shift to non-adversarial work relationships in the new information-based service society: if the information society will result in information workers whose jobs are characterized by greater skill and autonomy, and whose relation to the work and organization is non-conflictual, then it could be argued that HRM represents the new way of managing these new workers. Certainly there often seems an underlying trajectory in which ICT, organizational change and HRM have gone hand in hand. For example, a company survey by Bessant in the late 1980s found that adoption of Advanced Manufacturing Technology (AMT) was directly associated with new forms of organizational design such as flatter management hierarchies, cross-functional support teams, flexible working practices and team working, mechanisms for employee involvement (particularly associated with continuous improvement and total quality systems), the redesign of reward systems, a more focused recruitment and selection policy, and higher levels of continuous training and development (Bessant, 1993).

The widely held stereotype of the information worker (and thus the prototype for the worker/citizen of the coming Information Society) certainly fits the ideal subject under an HRM regime. S/he is usually portrayed as young, personally committed to the job and the organization, prepared to work long hours in an empowered job, and with an individualistic view of their career path in which they see themselves as an autonomous 'professional' rather than a conventional employee. For this person, it is alleged, trade unions or other forms of collective representation will be perceived as irrelevant, outmoded and unnecessary. These information workers will be selected, rewarded and promoted according to individual competencies, the sharing of core values, and individual performance, rather than seniority, experience, formal skill or the rate for the job.

ICT has been frequently associated with the HRM agenda of moving employees' attitudes from 'consent to commitment' and the sub-theme of 'empowerment' – the removal of some managerial control over the work process and its replacement by limited forms of autonomy. The explanations either see the technology as a cause, in which ICT is supposed to bring about the post-bureaucratic organization in which networks displace the more traditional hierarchies and vertical supervisory relations are replaced by team-based horizontal coordination; or, alternatively, ICT is seen as an enabler which management can use to restructure work around such high-commitment work practices as empowerment and teamwork. The connection has been a reciprocal one: direct forms of communication such as company videos or videoconferencing have sometimes been used to bypass established union-based channels of communication, while the HRM techniques of consultation and employee involvement (EI) have in turn been used 'to communicate and justify programmes of technical and organizational change in order to gain the acquiescence, or better still the motivation and active support, of employees' (Beirne and Ramsay, 1992: 9).

If we are to assess the evidence for such possible changes in employment relations we must look both at the emerging information sector (for if we cannot discern new patterns of employment relations here the prospects for the Information Society look bleak), and also at the ways in which ICT may be affecting existing patterns of employment relations.

THE INFORMATION WORKERS

So who are the information or knowledge workers? Discussion of this question has been regularly confused by the way we label occupations and by a readiness to relabel existing jobs to fit a current theory. Many of the employees now counted as being part of something called the Information Sector or the Knowledge Economy are not necessarily doing anything new: journalists, academics, publishers may now be using ICT to do their work but they are not necessarily doing new *types* of work. That having been said, attempts have been made to delineate the information sector in the advanced economies and estimate its size. Using the criteria developed by the OECD, the recent survey by the European Industrial Relations Observatory (2001) makes the point that there is not one ICT sector but three – hardware and manufacturing, telecommunications, and software and services, a distinction which will be drawn on later in this chapter.

Even if we take all three sub-sectors together, the evidence for a structural shift to an Information Society, dominated by information work as the defining characteristic of economic activity, is not as yet very strong. Although employment in the information sector overall has shown continuous growth since the 1970s, it is still not a major employment sector; in the UK the sector accounts for just 5 per cent of the total workforce while the average for the EU is between 2.9 and 3.9 per cent; the rate of job growth between the three sub-sectors has also been very uneven, being fastest in software and services (until the recent downturn in the 'dot.com' economy) and slowest in manufacturing. Its economic importance, however, is substantially greater than this as in 2000 the sector accounted for 6.3 per cent of EU GDP (EIRO, 2001).

NEW TECHNOLOGY, TRADITIONAL ISSUES

After two decades of diffusion it would seem that ICT has contributed to the emergence of several new employment relations issues and to the redefinition of many existing ones. It is arguable that the individualization of the employment relationship engendered and encouraged by the US model of HRM would have not been possible without ICT. The move away from standard pay scales and grading structures to the complexities of merit pay, with its requirement for individualized appraisals and performance evaluations of each employee, was clearly facilitated by computerization and the incorporation of all individuals' information into an HRM Information System. However, recent research seems to indicate that an ICT-informed HRM strategy is often limited to those core workers of the organization whose skills are in scarce supply. For other sections of the workforce, the use of ICT to meet the demand for flexibility and competitiveness is likely to be experienced through refinements of Taylorism, the intensification of work and various forms of labour market flexibility (Warhurst and Thompson, 1998; Baldry, Bain and Taylor, 1999).

There is no doubt that ICT has enhanced management power through surveillance and measurement of employee performance. ICT makes the flow of information on workers' performance instant and incessant, leading to a transparency of effort where any failure to meet targets can, more than at any time in history, be identified with an individual worker (Sewell and Wilkinson, 1993). It is here that ICT aids the cost-conscious manager by providing a means to eliminate what the Japanese call *muda* or waste: 'wasted' time for the employer are those small parts of the task cycle where the employee can catch breath and gain a small respite and resources. Their elimination through ICT surveillance has led to a reduction in manning levels, an increase in multi-tasking and an intensification of work through the setting of ever more stringent performance targets (Bain *et al*, 2002). In the clothing industry, for example, Lloyd and Rawlinson (1992) found that increased quality standards were obtained not via an HRM programme of raised commitment but by the use of ICT to monitor individual workers' speeds, faults and waiting times. The technology allowed the tracing of faults to the offending worker and in nearly all cases the consequence was a penalty exacted via the piece rate system. Bonuses for low defect levels and penalties for high defect levels have a traditional ring to them but what was new was that the technology made the process of individual responsibility more transparent.

Intensification of work has of course long been linked to problems of occupational health such as repetitive strain injuries and occupational stress. Trade union health and safety concerns in the early 1980s concentrated on screens and keyboards and it was sustained union pressure over these issues in the UK and other industrial societies that was one of the major factors behind the inclusion of the Display Screen Regulations in the 1992 'six pack' of EU directives. However, more recent understanding of the relationship between information systems and employee health indicates that it is not necessarily a direct cause and effect model. The speed of ICT and the enhanced speed of information transaction stimulate a tendency on the part of management in a competitive environment to design jobs around the demands of market competition rather than the limitations of the human physique. This pressure of performance targets in the wider context of increased job insecurity seems likely to be a major contributor to the observed rise in occupational stress. Here, a useful theory of stress developed by Karasek and Theorell (1990) posits that it is more likely to be experienced when workload is not matched by the degree of the employee's discretion or control over the job.

Recent research on employment in the information-based sectors of call centres and software development indicates other factors contributing to problems of ill-health such as a significant extension of the hours of operation, in some cases resulting in the 24 hours a day, 7 days a week (24:7) model and a proliferation of shift patterns and (often unpaid) overtime. This in turn has contributed to an increasing 'work–life' imbalance, in which work intrudes into the non-work areas of employees' lives (Hyman *et al*, 2003). A further way in which ICT adoption can have consequences for employees' health was shown in recent work on the widely experienced but ill-understood phenomenon of the Sick Building Syndrome in offices which suggested that a major causal factor is the degree to which computerization of the built environment has been used to reduce workers' control over their physical working environment (which can be something as basic as the ability to turn on a light or open a window) (Baldry, Bain and Taylor, 1997).

These developments have taken place in a context, popularly described as globalization, in which ICT has made possible the development of extensive international supply chains and the dispersion of different stages of manufacturing processes (micro-electronics being a particularly pertinent example) among a host of different nations around the world. This international division of labour has been an undoubted factor in an increasing insecurity of employment, as labour costs in the developed world are held up for comparison against those in the developing and newly industrialized nations which, in turn, are encouraged to compete against each other. Such employment insecurity has been heightened within nation states as ICT facilitates flexible labour use and allows the boundaries of the firm to become more diffuse and blurred as functions get broken up and distributed to profit centres, franchisees and subcontractors.

ICT therefore represents both a solution and a problem for HRM: it is almost essential to the HR vision but the way organizations choose to use it can actually contribute to employees' felt insecurity. Because it enables tighter performance monitoring, this encourages a continuation and refinement of traditional techniques of scientific management and direct control which are the antithesis of HRM's goal of high-trust relationships.

It is, therefore, clear from the above that ICT continues to have significant implications for employment relations. The rapid diffusion of ICT has contributed to new forms of payment system and patterns of working time, the intensification of work, enhanced job insecurity, and issues of occupational health. It has also facilitated the direct appeal by management to individual employees which many see as a continuing threat to collective organization in the workplace. If these are some of the issues for employment relations, what have been the responses? The challenges have clearly originated from the management offensive of the past 20 years and so we would expect the industrial relations responses to be located in trade union policy and practice.

COLLECTIVE RESPONSES

The Luddites have had a bad press. These early 19th-century textile workers were faced with a cheapening of wages and prices brought about by the enhanced productivity of the new textile machinery, at a time when even forming a trade union was a criminal and political act of subversion. Their desperate resort of selectively breaking the machinery of those employers who used it to undercut standards in the trade was memorably described by Hobsbawm (1964) as 'collective bargaining by riot'. Regrettably, 'Luddism' has become synonymous with the unthinking opposition to all technological change. Despite the fact that historically 'unions have proved highly adaptable in the face of huge changes in technology or work organization' (Ackers, Smith and Smith, 1996), in the early 1980s any union attempt to question the way in which the new ICT would be used tended to be castigated as Luddism, and there were accusations that the unions simply wished to stand in the way of progress. This view was lent support by the media treatment of high-profile stoppages in the newspaper printing industry in the 1980s, in which the new technology was undoubtedly used by management to break the power of the print unions (Gall, 2000). Yet the successive Workplace Industrial and Employment Relations (WIRS/WERS) surveys have revealed the paradox that those companies that recognized trade unions were more likely to have introduced ICT, although perhaps not so likely to have introduced related organizational change (McLoughlin, 1993).

It might be useful, before we investigate the employment relations responses to the above challenges in the traditional sectors of the economy, to look at employment relations in the emerging ICT sector, as this should give us the best indicators of future patterns of an information society. As we have noted, the sector is as yet small and its growth has been somewhat erratic but is still seen as a major source of job creation; many of the companies in the sector are relatively young and thus it offers ideal circumstances to plot growing employment relations trends.

The most up-to-date data on the information sector comes from the recent review of developing trends in Europe conducted by the European Industrial Relations Observatory (2001). As we have noted above, the report identifies three sub-sectors and notes that each is characterized by a different pattern of employment relations, largely dependent on the sub-sector's history, company size and organizational country of origin.

Manufacturing and telecoms, by virtue of their evolution from existing sectors, are typified by a larger company size than software (larger in telecoms than manufacturing), and are more likely to possess elements of 'traditional' employment relations. The review concludes, however, that software and services seem, at present at any rate, very much a world apart. The companies are much smaller, they are more likely to contain 'economically dependent' workers (that is, self-employed workers who do not perceive themselves as employees of the traditional sort), and, furthermore, to overcome skill shortages in a fast-growing sector, these companies have increasingly resorted to importing non-EU labour from locations such as India. It is perhaps not surprising that, within the overall characteristics of employment relations in the ICT sector as a whole, these differences are reflected in differing employment relations patterns.

The review comments that ICT seems to act as a 'pressure cooker' or rather a magnifying glass which accentuates the prevailing characteristics of national employment relations systems. Thus for most EU member states, although there is as yet no single agreement covering the OECD-defined ICT sector, telecoms and IT manufacturing share a long tradition of sectoral bargaining, mainly encompassed by existing sectoral agreements, whereas software and services are rarely covered by collective regulation, or have only recently commenced bargaining. In countries with a voluntarist tradition, such as the UK and Ireland, there is no sectoral bargaining and relatively little collective bargaining apart from some company agreements in hardware firms (such the Korean-owned LG Electronics) or the former state-owned telecoms company BT and some plant-level agreements in such companies as EDS, CSC, Cap Gemini, ICL and (despite its former history of non-unionism) IBM. Where agreements do exist they are more likely to contain elements of time flexibility (enabling the organization to meet peaks and troughs in demand) and also more likely to contain variable pay and share option elements.

The reasons suggested for low bargaining coverage in the software and services sector include the small size of firms, their recent date of entry or start-up, attitudes of self-perceived 'professional' technology workers, and the promotion of organizational collectivism at the expense of trade union collectivism. To this we must add the hostile attitudes to collective regulation and trade unions of many of these companies, who tend to see unions as an unnecessary hindrance to the flexibility and innovativeness necessary to survive in a turbulent market. Employers in the information sector generally, particularly micro-electronics, have been noted for their hostility to trade unionism (Rigby and Smith, 1999) and these attitudes seem exacerbated when the company has its origins in the United States. This is reflected in the low and uneven spread of trade union membership and the low level of employer organization for bargaining purposes. The European evidence from EIRO shows that such attitudes are not limited to unions but extend to a reluctance to establish works councils. Again, such employers claim that these formal structures are unnecessary as they already possess high levels of employee involvement and non-hierarchical structures and cultures. The state of employers' associations in the ICT sector is very fragmented, with most employers not seeing the need for one, particularly in countries with a 'voluntarist' rather than a 'social partnership' tradition: thus in the UK there are no employers' associations involved in collective bargaining in the ICT sector.

In the UK trade union coverage in the information sectors is the same as for the service sector generally (6 per cent), while in the EU as a whole the density of union membership in the ICT sector is considerably lower than the national averages; in each case the software sector is considerably lower than the other two sub-sectors. There is no evidence in the UK that the 1999 Employment Relations Act has as yet made much impact on union recognition in ICT in general. One or two companies (such as LG Electronics) chose to recognize unions in anticipation of the Act, and in September 2000 the Manufacturing Science and Finance Union (MSF) signed the first national recognition and partnership agreement in the IT sector, covering 7,000 employees of the US-owned CSC (although not as yet for bargaining purposes).

All this could be taken as evidence in support of the dominance of the HRM culture in the emerging information economy. However, it is always dangerous to assume that variations in employment relations patterns displayed at any given moment in time are the basis for predicting the future, as this ignores the underlying continuity of the reasons and conditions that create unionism. For example, the motor industry, the leading-edge sector in the Fordist mass-production expansion of the mid-20th century, was in most industrial countries dominated by founders and corporations who were vitriolically anti-union, yet by the 1950s the auto sector had become one of the most widely unionized.

There are currently signs that the complacency which sometimes characterized these rapidly expanding growth sectors is already undergoing some shocks to the system. Referring to the sudden slump in the fortunes of the dot.com sector, the EIRO report suggests that there is evidence across Europe that in the face of economic insecurity the 'traditional' modes of representation (collective bargaining, works councils) suddenly come to seem more attractive than reliance on management-initiated employee involvement schemes. One consequence of de-layering and the fad for the 'lean' organization is that there are now fewer rungs on the internal promotional ladder and therefore the old inducements to accept one's current wages and conditions, to forego present gain for future advancement, no longer have the same appeal. The alternatives are thus to leave the organization or to organize collectively to improve terms and conditions.

There is now evidence of expanding levels of unionization in call centres (Taylor and Bain, 2001; Bain and Taylor, 2002). However, the research evidence disproves the idea that these 'new sector' knowledge workers are a predominantly young, 'Thatcher's children', generation, more likely to hold individualistic rather than collectivist attitudes and to identify with the organization and its goals rather than a perceived external agency such as a trade union.

Taking the example of call centres in the finance sector, Bain and Taylor found, firstly, that the age range is more diffuse than usually supposed, with a sizeable proportion of more experienced workers with previous trade union membership. Only a very small proportion of respondents declared opposition to trade unions on a point of principle, and a vast majority (86 per cent) saw the most important reason for joining a trade union to be 'traditional collectivist' reasons such as the necessity for workplace representation, protection and a united voice. Similarly, in identifying those issues which should be a priority for any call centre union, far and away the most frequently identified was pay and bonus levels (Bain and Taylor, 2002). The first national call centre stoppage, at BT customer services centres in 1999, provided a sharp correction to some of the prevailing stereotypes about these information workers. A significant characteristic of call centre unionization is that it is coming from a variety of directions, reflecting the efforts of the different unions already established in the particular sector from which call centres have been created: UNIFI, MSF and other banking unions in the finance sector and CWU in telecoms are good examples. This reflects the fact that technical change in general, and the emergence of a new employment sector in particular, always throws strains on existing union structures, creating potential issues of membership demarcation and recruitment as existing unions lay claim to a legitimate interest in organizing the new workforce. Thus in the UK microelectronics manufacturing has been targeted by the unions now comprising Amicus (AEEU and MSF) and by the former steel union ISTC. The policy of the latter represents the fact that as many microelectronics plants have been situated in former steel-making areas, attracted by investment grants and inducements, the ISTC has re-badged itself as a 'community union' and thus sees these workforces as legitimate recruitment targets – and with some degree of success.

A further example of the dilemma posed by a union repositioning strategy in the face of technological change and a blurring of the organizational boundaries is provided by recent trends in the graphical industry. The change from metal-to-paper printing to a digitally based process, in which the information flow can result in either a printed product or various types of electronic output, has led printing companies to relocate themselves as merely one part of large transnational information-management and media organizations. This has posed a problem for the positioning of the former printing unions. The approach taken by the British GPMU tends to assert the primacy of print on the grounds that we will always need printed products, while the German IG Medien have allied themselves with graphical designers, broadcasters and IT workers as a more broadly conceived union of media workers (Gennard *et al*, 2000).

A few as yet isolated instances of industrial action suggest that new technologies of production have the potential to engender new forms of collective action. For example, in February 2001 the WorldOnline Internet company in

Belgium saw the first 'cyber-strike' in which workers 'occupied' the company's Web site in order to tell customers about the enforced redundancies which had been announced following a merger with Tiscali, and to give up-to-date information about the strike action. All this suggests a high degree of continuity between the employment relations perspectives of a growing sector of the knowledge economy and what we know of workers in the old economy.

ICT AND EMPLOYMENT RELATIONS

In a comprehensive review of unions' own use of ICT in the United States, Fiorito *et al* (2001; Fiorito and Bass, 2000) make the point that while historically unions have taken opposition stances at key periods of technological change, this is now no longer the case with IT. Like other organizations, unions have embraced IT for the promises it holds out of heightened efficiency.

The Labour Research Department's (1998) survey of union use of the Internet found that almost two-thirds of union branches taking part in the survey were using the Internet for union work. The highest level of responses came from union branches in the education, communications and IT sectors and the lowest level from branches in manufacturing and transport. In the public sector, local government were more active users than the health service, while nine out of ten positive responses came from branches representing white-collar workers. The US survey indicates that larger unions, as perhaps one would expect, not only make greater use of a range of different information technologies but also use them across a wider range of union functions (Fiorito and Bass, 2000). The UK trade union policy discussion group Unions21 has usefully set out the different strands of union activity within which ICT could assist trade union goals (Unions21, 2000) and this can provide us with a useful framework to examine the evidence.

One of the most important uses so far has undoubtedly been for internal communications and transactions. Eighty-five per cent of union branches responding to the LRD survey found e-mail a 'very useful' tool for union work. E-mail was being used for communicating with members inside the workplace where it offered the advantages of speed, efficiency and cheapness, and ease in communicating with members who were otherwise hard to reach such as those working in different sites or remote locations. ICT clearly has the potential of overcoming the divisive nature of shiftwork for union organization. One or two cautionary comments in the LRD survey suggest that there is a recognition that the use of e-mail by reps is not a complete substitute for person-to-person communication or for 'walking about'.

The use of ICT for external communications and transactions such as gaining government information and information for bargaining was reflected by the fact that over half the LRD respondents claimed that the Web was 'very useful' while another 42 per cent thought it was 'quite useful', the feeling being that more information could be accessed and obtained faster than through more traditional routes. Where access to the Internet was through work-based computers, in almost half the cases there was an agreement with the employer which allowed this, while many other respondents reported that there was no trouble in using workplace IT.

Within the recent debates on new union organizing strategies, considerable attention has been paid to the potential offered by the technology. Around half of TUC-affiliated unions now have a Web site and an increasing number of union branches have set up their own sites. The Internet has been used both to publicize the branch and/or union and the benefits of membership and to provide pay and other bargaining information to members. In the United States Fiorito found some union organizers using laptops to customize recruitment material for particular target members and, in one of the largest union-organizing victories in two decades, use of the Internet was largely instrumental in the Machinists' Union's winning of representation rights for 19,000 airline staff in 1998 (Fiorito *et al*, 2001).

An attempt to use ICT to change traditional union structures and create almost an 'e-union', or virtual union, is reflected in the UK launch in 2001–2 of 4U@Work, promoted by, but independent of, the Engineers and Managers Association. This offers union services such as legal information or individual representation on the same basis as an insurance policy, with different grades of membership package. Supporters of the scheme claim that it is not an attempt to undercut unions but is aimed at groups who would not normally find unions attractive, such as young people, management consultants or workers in IT (Labour Research Department, 2001). This clearly reflects the observed trend towards offering more individual services and targeting individual members, particularly in 'new' and 'peripheral' areas (Bacon and Storey, 1996). Initially, attempts to do this, mainly by unions recruiting in managerial and professional grades, meant more work for union officials and more demands on time, but clearly ICT makes this strategy much more feasible. Other more conventional unions such as the banking union UNIFI have experimented with 'virtual branches' in areas where members find it difficult to get to branch meetings.

ICT has undoubtedly begun to influence the bargaining process as the enhanced speed of information flow offered enables unions to respond far more quickly to bargaining developments or employer initiatives and thus to challenge managerial prerogative even at workplace level. Unions can now monitor information on wages and working conditions, not only sectorally or nationally, but also through comparative international statistics. ICT also offers new options in the pursuit of collective action. US union Web sites have included 'hot links' that generate electronic petitions to political representatives. In the mid-1990s LabourNet hosted a site in the Liverpool dockers' dispute, the first time the Web had been used in the UK to publicize a dispute, while during the US Boeing strike in the mid-1990s union activists posted names of 'scabs' on the Web (Fiorito and Bass, 2000).

Another area which will undoubtedly expand is that of education and training, particularly for distance learning delivery, and some unions have started to launch online training programmes for members: the graphical union GPMU already offers access to its training and development handbook through its Web site

The ease of communication has, potentially, widened the scope for international cooperation, which is becoming increasingly essential in an internationalized economy. Here it must be said that the unions' use of the Internet has sometimes been outstripped by radical consumer campaigns such as those against Nike or Gap, focusing on globalization or the use of child labour. However, it must be said that at present the potential for constructive use outstrips the actuality. In their survey of union leaders' perceptions of the success of using ICT, Fiorito and his colleagues remark that: 'Essentially leaders are saying "We deserve credit for experimenting with many new practices and techniques. The fact that we have not yet seen dramatic results is a reflection of a very difficult environment"' (Fiorito *et al*, 2001).

Not all problems can be attributed to the economic and political environment. Apart from the continuing problems of lack of universal member access to Internet terminals, many unions still have not developed a coherent IT strategy. There are, in addition, issues of organizational politics. Just as the organizational literature has demonstrated the role of ICT in de-layering and disaggregating the organization, trade unions as traditional hierarchical structures are themselves not immune from such trends. The dispersal of information and thus power, which open access to information flows makes possible, may yet have consequences for conventional trade union structures that current office holders may find unpalatable.

Sometimes the reasons for failure are easy to identify. In an interview with the author, a leading official of a North American graphical union complained that when the union had proudly set up its Web site the aim of reaching the younger, more marginal entrants in the industry was undermined by the decision to have the photo of the union president on the home page: any young, female, possibly immigrant workers logging on to the site would thus have been met with a picture of an overweight, middle-aged, middle-class white man in a suit!

CONCLUSIONS

It is clear from the evidence so far that employment relations in the information age displays much more a sense of continuity rather than the radical break predicted by the Information Society prophets. If we look at what management and unions were doing before the widespread take-up of ICT, we find that they are still doing the same things, only using ICT to do them. Clearly there are differences and developments. The processes and practices of employment relations may now be undertaken a little faster, there is more opportunity for the dissemination of communication and more open access to information by employment relations participants, including workplace reps and rank and file union members. This can be both a threat and an opportunity to both labour market actors as such information may be generated by both management and union.

Employment relations are far less likely to be bounded in their horizons by the contours of national employment systems. Quite apart from transnational developments in multinational capital and the creation of bodies such as the European Union, it is now considerably easier for labour market actors to compare their situation with comparable groups in other nations, particularly Europe, to correspond electronically with such groups and even coordinate their actions accordingly. Enhanced communication made possible by ICT has contributed to growing linkages between employment relations and other issues pursued by collective groupings outside the labour market proper: for example, the ethical opposition by consumer and other critical movements to aspects of globalization overlaps with international trade union campaigns against the use of child labour.

Traditional issues of remuneration, grievance handling and job security are clearly still with us but such themes as patterns of working time, work–life balance, performance targets and style of management control, and occupational health are likely to move up the bargaining agenda. Should the unions start to recover some of the lost ground of the past few years, this may reveal that the new production paradigms are in fact more vulnerable to industrial action and therefore bargaining leverage than the old. JIT and lean production are essentially fragile systems which tolerate no disruption; in manufacturing there are now no piles of stock to draw on, no car-park full of the finished product to buffer a stoppage. The complexity and often transnational nature of contemporary production chains magnifies the effect of any stoppage in the system. In service provision the basis for competitive success is the speed and absence of delay in service delivery. To make these systems work requires either firm management control and/or the willing commitment of employees or, if these cannot be guaranteed, the negotiated consent and cooperation of the workforce, collectively arrived at. This suggests that the Information Society's obituary for industrial relations may be a little premature.

References

Ackers, P, Smith, C and Smith, P (eds) (1996) *The New Workplace and Trade Unionism*, Routledge, London, p 22

Bacon, N and Storey, J (1996) Individualism and collectivism and the changing role of trade unions, in: *The New Workplace and Trade Unionism*, ed P Ackers, C Smith and P Smith, Routledge, London, pp 41–76

Bain, P and Taylor, P (2002) Ringing the changes? Union recognition and organization in call centres in the UK finance sector, *Industrial Relations Journal*, **33** (3)

Bain, P, Watson, A, Mulvey, G and Taylor, P (2002) Taylorism, targets and the pursuit of quantity and quality by call-centre management, *New Technology Work and Employment*, **17** (3)

Baldry, C, Bain, P and Taylor, P (1997) Sick and tired?: Working in the modern office, *Work Employment and Society*, **11** (3), pp 517–39

Baldry, C, Bain, P and Taylor, P (1999) 'Bright satanic offices': intensification, control and team Taylorism, in *Workplaces of the Future*, ed P Thompson and C Warhurst, Macmillan, Basingstoke, pp 163–83

Baldry, C (1988) *Computers, Jobs and Skills*, Plenum, New York

Bamber, G and Lansbury, R (eds) (1989) *New Technology: International Perspectives on Human Resources and Industrial Relations*, Unwin Hyman, London

Beirne, M and Ramsay, H (1992) Manna or monstrous regiment? Technology, control and democracy in the workplace, in *Information Technology and Workplace Democracy*, ed M Beirne and H Ramsay, Routledge, London, pp 192–211

Bessant, J (1993) Towards Factory 2000: designing organizations for computer-integrated technologies, in *Human Resource Management and Technical Change*, ed J Clark, Sage, London, pp 192–211

European Industrial Relations Observatory On-Line (2001) *Industrial relations in the information and communications technology sector*, www.eiro.eurofound.ie

Fiorito, J and Bass, W (2000) Information technology use in national unions: an exploration, mimeo, Florida State University College of Business

Fiorito, J, Jarley, P and Delaney, J (2001) Information technology, union organizing and union effectiveness, Florida State University College of Business

Frenkel, S, Tam, M, and Korczynski, M (1999) *On the Front Line: Organization of Work in the Information Economy*, ILR/Cornell University, Ithaca, NY

Gall, G (2000) New technology, the labour process and employment relations in the provincial newspaper industry, *New Technology, Work and Employment*, **15** (2), pp 94–107

Gennard, J, Ramsay, H, Baldry, C and Newsome, K (2000) *Barriers to Cross-border Co-operation for Graphical Workers in the European Union*, Centre for European Employment Research, Department of Human Resource Management, University of Strathclyde, Glasgow

Handy, C (1995) *Beyond Certainty: the Changing Worlds of Organization*, Hutchinson, London

Hobsbawm, E (1964) The machine breakers, in *Labouring Men: Studies in the History of Labour*, ed E Hobsbawm, Weidenfeld, London, pp 5–17

Hyman, J, Baldry, C, Scholarios, D and Bunzel, D (2003) Balancing work and life: not just a matter of time flexibility, *British Journal of Industrial Relations* (2003 forthcoming)

Hyman, R and Streeck, W (eds) (1988) *New Technology and Industrial Relations*, Basil Blackwell, Oxford

Karasek, R and Theorell, T (1990) *Healthy Work: Stress, Productivity and the Reconstruction of Working Life*, Basic Books, New York

Labour Research Department (1998) *Negotiating the Net: a guide for trade unionists*, LRD Publications, London

Labour Research Department (2001) Unions make net gains in learning and links, *Labour Research*, **90** (9), September, pp 14–16

Lloyd, C and Rawlinson, M (1992) New technology and human resource management, in *Reassessing Human Resource Management*, ed P Blyton and P Turnbull, Sage, London, pp 185–98

McLoughlin, J (1993) Technical change and human resource management in the non-union firm, in *Human Resource Management and Technical Change*, ed J Clark, Sage, London, pp 175–91

Reich, R (1991) *The Work of Nations: Preparing Ourselves for 21st Century Capitalism*, Alfred A Knopf, New York

Rigby, M and Smith, R (1999) Union responses in electronics: a globalized environment, *Industrial Relations Journal*, **30** (1), pp 2–15

Sewell, G and Wilkinson, B (1993) Human resource management in 'surveillance' companies, in *Human Resource Management and Technical Change*, ed J Clark, Sage, London, pp 137–54

Taylor, P and Bain, P (2001) Trade unions, workers' rights and the frontier of control in call centres, *Economic and Industrial Democracy*, **22**, pp 39–66

Unions21 (2000) *The Creation of the E-Union: the Use of ICT by Trade Unions*, discussion document, Unions 21, London

Warhurst, C and Thompson, P (1998) Hands, hearts and minds: changing work and workers at the end of the century, in *Workplaces of the Future*, ed P Thompson and C Warhurst, Macmillan, Basingstoke, pp 1–24

Part II

The law

5

Overview: the law and the employment relationship

Steven Anderman

INTRODUCTION

Employment relations in the UK today are comprehensively regulated by two groups of statutes. The first group, *individual employment protection laws*, consists of a series of statutes which regulate the contractual relationship of employees and other workers with their employers: eg unfair dismissal, redundancy payments, health and safety, maternity and family leave, sex and race discrimination, equal pay, minimum wages and maximum hours, etc. The second group, *collective labour laws*, regulates the process by which employees are collectively represented in their dealings with employers. In recent years, it has become important to recognize that this category of legal regulation divides itself into two separate types: first, there are the historical legal rights designed to extend and maintain trade unions and collective bargaining. These include, for example, the rights to trade union membership and activity, a right of trade unions to recognition and rights of recognized trade unions to disclosure of information relating to collective bargaining. They also include laws which restrict the entitlement of trade unions and workers to organize strikes and other industrial action (see Chapter 7) and laws which regulate the internal organization of trade unions.

A second type of statute, introduced largely under the influence of European legislation, provides information and consultation rights on health and safety issues, collective redundancies, transfer of undertakings and certain pension decisions. These rights are collective representation rights, applicable to employee representative bodies established for particular purposes, but they are not limited solely to trade union organizations. In the absence of a recognized trade union, they can extend to elected workplace representatives. In more recent years, legislation has introduced a further variation on this theme, a concept of the standing works council. In 1994 the European Works Council Directive introduced the requirement of a permanent body of employee representatives to receive information and be consulted about important management decisions but this was restricted to European multinationals.[1] In 2002, a new General Framework Directive was enacted which requires by 2008 all 'undertakings' with more than 50 employees or establishments of more than 20 employees to put in place works councils with elected employee representatives for the purpose of informing and consulting with employee representatives or trade union representatives about important management decisions affecting employees' terms and conditions.[2] To understand the legal framework for employment relations today requires an examination of each of these main components as well as how they relate to one another.

The historical perspective

This extensive legislative framework for employment relations in the UK was late in coming. The dominant characteristic of labour law and collective bargaining for the latter half of the 19th century and the first 65 years of the 20th century was the relatively limited role played by statute law in shaping and regulating employers, trade unions and collective bargaining as well as individual employment relations. Apart from wartime periods, and away from specific sectors of non-unionized or weakly unionized employees in which statutory machinery under the Wage Councils Act fixed minimum wages, collective bargaining was the main source of wage rates, working time rules and many other terms and conditions of employees. This was a period of 'voluntarism' or 'collective laissez faire' in which regulatory legislation played a limited role, consisting only of the Truck Acts, regulating employers' deductions from wages, and the Factory Acts, regulating some safety issues relating to employment.

The story of the long period of 'voluntarism' from the mid-19th century to the early 1960s has been frequently told and cannot receive a detailed description here (see eg Wedderburn, 1993). The emergence of a fully developed collective bargaining system without legal support was partly a product of a strong trade union movement which opted for a wide legal immunity for strikes and a narrow base of positive statutory protection for workers and trade unions in a series of political 'settlements' with governments in 1871, 1875 and 1906 (Fox, 1985).

That there were employers antagonistic to the growth of trade unions can be seen in the landmarks of trade union history: the Taff Vale case (see eg Clegg, Fox and Thompson, 1964), the early organizing experiences of the general unions (see eg Saville, 1967) and the repeated pleas of a minority of TUC members at its AGMs for legal support for trade union recognition.[3] Throughout the formative years of UK labour relations, however, a significant number of employers were prepared to recognize trade unions and deal with them on the basis of voluntary joint disputes procedures and collective agreements (see eg Burgess, 1980).

As we now know, in the post-World War II period, the 'voluntary system' developed a propensity to wage inflation, restrictive practices and multi-unionism, owing to the growth of 'horizontal unions' such as craft and general unions, rather than vertical unions organized along industrial lines. It also included the development of the closed shop institution as a significant component of collective bargaining systems (Dunn and Gennard, 1984).

Nevertheless, collective bargaining continued to be seen by a majority of employers as useful for their purposes even in the early 1970s. Indeed, when the Heath government introduced comprehensive labour legislation in 1971, it was striking to observe that few employers made use of the legal sanctions which were placed at their disposal by the legislation and many collaborated with trade unions in avoiding the full impact of the legal framework in their collective bargaining arrangements (Weekes *et al*, 1975).

The period 1974–79 offered an experiment of a Social Contract between the Labour government and the TUC, with the government enacting an extensive range of employment protection legislation giving rights to trade unions as well as individual employees regardless of trade union membership, and rewriting the law of strikes to give a wide right to lawful industrial action, which included secondary action. After a period of cooperation on incomes policy during which a high rate of inflation was tamed, relations between the government and the TUC broke down and a rash of strikes in the late 1970s led to the fall of the Labour government and the emergence of the Conservative government with a remit to reduce the power of trade unions. From 1979 to 1997, the Conservative government attempted to dismantle many of the employment protections. It restricted the scope for legal industrial action and weakened the legal protections for trade unions and individual employees.

During that period, the sectors of established collective bargaining began to decline, as did trade union membership as a percentage of the workforce. In 1979 an estimated 53 per cent of the work force were trade union members; in 2000, the percentage had declined to 27 per cent (see eg DTI, 2000). Moreover, there was evidence of employers attempting to derecognize trade unions (see eg Claydon, 1989). Furthermore, single union agreements and 'single table' bargaining were increasingly introduced, particularly by foreign investors, suggesting a change in the attitude of employers to collective bargaining structures (Smith and Morton, 1993; Brown, 1986). Nevertheless, collective bargaining remains a method of job regulation for approximately 35 per cent of the workforce. During the 1980s and early 1990s when employers were in a position to end collective bargaining relationships, many chose not to do so, preferring instead to restructure collective bargaining to allow greater flexibility to management. Moreover, the decline in trade union membership has been arrested since 1998 (see eg Machin, 2000).

Consequently, labour legislation must be assessed with the awareness of at least two sectors in the labour market: first, an established sector of ongoing and self-regulating systems of collective bargaining perpetuated by mutual self-interest, and secondly, a sector in which trade unions are not formally recognized and many, if not all, employees are not trade union members and may be only marginally covered by collective bargaining arrangements.

The current perspective

The two main categories of labour legislation, individual employment laws and collective labour laws, may initially appear to be separate fields of legal regulation of industrial and employment relations. The reality is, however, that they are closely interconnected. Each has the capacity to reinforce the other; each has the capacity to undermine the other depending upon the form taken by the relevant statute or agreement. Thus, the contents of collective agreements determine many of the levels of benefit of individual statutory rights. And the individual rights to participate in industrial action and to be members and take part in trade union activity tend to be at the base of collective rights of trade unions. Finally, the new 'collective' representation rights have the capacity to either undermine or provide a springboard for trade unions and collective bargaining.

A major reason for the interrelationship between the different components of the legal framework is that many of the statutes in both categories are directed towards the regulation of managerial prerogatives. In particular, individual employment legislation takes the form of statutory rules imposed directly upon the employment relationship, many of which regulate management decisions to hire and fire, to promote and discipline, to grant leave or time off, to reorganize terms and conditions of employment, to establish the physical conditions of work and ultimately to close down workplaces. These statutes directly regulate the managerial prerogatives established in the individual contract of employment. Collective representation rights operate more indirectly by helping to establish structures which influence managerial decisions, either via a process of collective bargaining backed up by the potential power of industrial action or by information and consultation rights which rely on the power of persuasion of elected representatives, occasionally involving external laws, such as health and safety statutes and the Transfer of Undertaking (Protection of Employment) Regulations 1981 (TUPE), to influence management decisions.

INDIVIDUAL EMPLOYMENT LEGISLATION

Management prerogatives and the contract of employment

Underlying the huge body of individual employment legislation is the contract of employment between employer and employee, which is the legal instrument establishing management prerogatives in the employment relationship. The contract takes the form of an agreement between employer and employee but its contents help to underpin managerial prerogatives as well as to define their limits. The bargaining power of employers *vis-à-vis* employees, combined with their 'drafting power', ensures that in most cases employers retain considerable authority not only to make the initial decisions about the kind of work, place of work and hours of work to offer the employee, with little opportunity for amendment, but also to create express terms relating to disciplinary rules and flexibility and mobility clauses which create areas of unilateral discretion for management. Many jobs are offered to the employee with standard terms and conditions of work on a take it or leave it basis. Only rarely do individuals have sufficient bargaining power of their own. It takes the scarcity value of certain football players, City traders, professionals and managers to enable them to have a chance of decisively shaping the contents of their employment contract.

Once an employment starts, the contractual obligations of the employee are widened by standard terms assumed by courts and employment tribunals to be implied in all employment contracts. Thus, employees are bound by the implied terms of *fidelity* and *loyalty*. Most importantly, from the viewpoint of managerial prerogative, they are bound by the implied terms of *obedience to lawful orders* and *cooperation* which give employers considerable legal authority over the employee's conduct at work.

The contract of employment also places limits upon the prerogatives of the employer and this has three main forms: firstly, by requiring employers to adhere to the express restraints they themselves have placed upon management conduct in their disciplinary and grievance procedures; secondly, the contract of employment incorporates certain terms and conditions of employment established by collective agreements as express terms of the individual employment contract, thereby constraining the choices of management over certain types of terms and conditions; thirdly, the common law imposes on employers an implied duty of *mutual trust and confidence* which requires them not to exercise their powers, including their powers under the express terms of the contract, arbitrarily or capriciously. In case of breach by the employer of these express or implied terms, it is open to employees to attempt to enforce, mainly in the courts, their contractual rights by an action for wrongful dismissal or breach of contract, for which there is a remedy of damages or in some cases an injunction. In addition, they may also choose to claim constructive dismissal, which can lead to a statutory claim for unfair dismissal to an employment tribunal.

While this analysis of express and implied terms might suggest that contract law offers a balance between employer and employee rights, the fact is that away from collective bargaining, the contract merely serves to place limits on the extremes of unreasonable behaviour by employers. It leaves considerable discretion with the employer to decide when and whom to hire and whom and in what circumstances to dismiss or make redundant.

Individual employment protections

In principle, today, individual employment protection legislation applies across a wide front to offset the discretionary powers of the employer in the contractual employment relationship. In the first place, statutes regulate the hiring process under the sex, race and disability discrimination laws. Moreover, employers are required by statute law to give written information to employees about the terms and conditions of their employment and to provide them with a disciplinary and grievance procedure. Many of the other individual employment protections are designed to regulate employers' discretion during the course of the employment relationship. This is true, for example, of the rights to a minimum wage, maximum hours of working time, minimum holidays, equal pay, sick pay, guarantee pay, maternity leave, parental leave and protection against unlawful deductions. Still others are designed to regulate the employers' discretion upon the termination of the employment relationship. This is true of the statutes regulating unfair dismissals, redundancy payments, dismissals owing to a transfer of an under-taking and guaranteed payments to employees in the event of the insolvency of the employer (see eg Anderman, 2000; Deakin and Morris, 2000).

A further group of individual employment statutes apply to prevent the employer from discriminating between employees in terms of gender, race and disability in decisions about dismissals, discipline, training and selection for promotion.

Although these statutes are sometimes described as a 'floor of rights', such a description is somewhat misleading if it is used to suggest a 'safety net'. In practice, the statutory rules have certain qualifications and conditions which can result in different standards of protection and constraints upon employment relations for different sectors of the workforce.

Thus, many statutory rights are restricted in their scope to 'employees', ie those who work under a contract of employment, for a minimum period of continuous service. Only some of the employment protection statutes, eg the

Sex Discrimination Act, the Race Relations Act, the Health and Safety at Work Act and Part II of the Employment Rights Act 1996, apply comprehensively to self-employed as well as employed workers, part-time and full-time, temporary or permanent employment.

The legislative protections limited to 'employees' have been held not to apply to certain types of casual and temporary workers. The effect of this requirement is not only to deprive workers of individual employment protections; it also serves to undermine the statutory protections for trade unions and trade union members. In the Employment Relations Act 1999, an attempt was made to deal with this problem by deeming certain types of marginal groups as 'workers' for the purpose of certain protections, such as the right to be accompanied by a representative in disciplinary and grievance procedures. Yet this is only a partial solution to the more general problem that the use of 'employee' as the criterion for the application of employment protections combined with the requirement of certain periods of 'continuous service' creates legal protections for a selected group of employees on the labour market and denies them to more vulnerable workers.

By creating these preconditions for eligibility, statute law allows employers to retain considerable discretion to structure work relationships so as to avoid legislation,[4] both in respect of designating individuals as casual employees and by manipulating the periods of continuous service. Moreover, it allows employers to perpetuate inequalities in the incidence of protection for a workforce which is becoming increasingly hired on part-time and short-term working arrangements or accepts forms of employment viewed as self-employment.

To some extent, the legislation of the Labour government in its first and second terms has been directed towards the creation and reinforcement of 'rights' in the form of minimum standards of legislative protection, possibly in recognition of the reduction in coverage of collective agreements as a source of terms to only 35 per cent of the workforce. In this exercise, EU directives, designed to 'harmonize' legal protection for workers throughout the EU, have made an important contribution. This legislation, introduced since 1997, includes the National Minimum Wages Act 1998, the Working Time Regulations 1998 with their provision of maximum hours and minimum holiday entitlement, the Part-time Working Regulation, the Fixed Term Worker Regulation and the recent extended rights to maternity pay and leave, and rights associated with family responsibilities, including childcare responsibilities. There is also a new Act reinforcing the Race Relations Act.

Nevertheless, it would be misleading to view these newly reinforced individual employment 'rights' as 'fundamental rights' designed solely to protect workers or employees. They must also be seen as a form of regulation of employers that balances employee protection with the value of managerial efficiency. This can be demonstrated by two features of the legislation. One is the design of the laws and their interpretation. There are certain 'balancing items' in each law which require careful analysis to understand the exact scope of the legislative protection.

For example, in health and safety legislation, the requirement placed on management is to adopt measures which are *as safe as is reasonably practicable*. There is no use of the higher level of protection offered by a standard of *as safe as is technically feasible* since the costs of such a standard are thought to be too high for firms to bear. In the interpretation of the legislation, the balancing items create 'safety valves' to ensure that the legislation does not impinge too heavily upon the way managers run their businesses.

A similar type of balancing exercise is built into the various discrimination laws. This is less true of the test of *direct* race or sex discrimination in which balancing items are found in the limited defence provided by the specified 'genuine occupational qualifications'. The statutory test of *indirect* discrimination, however, includes a defence of *justification* which allows discriminatory managerial rules, collective bargaining terms and state policies, even where discriminatory, to be found to be acceptable under the discrimination legislation. The statutes apply a twofold test of whether the employer's rule (or collective term or social security policy rule) was objectively based on a legitimate need of the business or state and whether it was necessary and proportionate in order to satisfy that need.

A further, notable example is the statutory protection against unfair dismissal with its test of whether the employer's decision to dismiss *was reasonable in the circumstances taking into account equity and the substantial merits of the case*. This statutory standard of reasonableness has been interpreted to require employment tribunals not to decide for themselves whether they think that management's decision is reasonable or not but rather to ask themselves whether the employer's decision fell within or outside the 'range of reasonable responses of a reasonable employer'. In effect, the tribunals are told they must defer to reasonable managerial standards of decision making rather than deciding as industrial juries what they think is fair or unfair (Anderman, 2001).

This contrasts with the standard applied to dismissals for a protected reason such as dismissal for selection for redundancy for prohibited reasons, whistle blowing, exercising statutory rights whether individual or as an employee or trade union representative, attempting to enforce statutory rights, participation in protected industrial action, being dismissed in connection with a transfer of an undertaking, etc. In all such cases, where a dismissal fits within the statutory definition, it is automatically unfair. The relativistic test of unfair dismissal generally under ERA 1996 s.98(4) is not used and there is no balancing test between the needs of the business and employee protection. The increasing resort by legislation to categories of automatically unfair dismissals suggests that the Labour government wishes to confine the balancing exercise in s.98(4) to dismissals for prima facie fair reasons such as misconduct, incapability, ill health and reorganization. The balancing test in s.98(4) is too risky to apply to dismissals requiring protection for specific public policy reasons.

The concept of worker rights as a form of regulation of management also offers an explanation of recent government legislative policy. In the Employment Act 2002, the Labour government has introduced measures which will have the effect of reducing the scope of protection for most individual statutory protections and in particular unfair dismissals. In Parts 2 and 3 of the new Act, the government has introduced a requirement that employees must first use their employer's internal grievance procedure before being entitled to make a claim to employment tribunals for statutory protections such as race, sex and disability discrimination, equal pay, unauthorized deductions from pay and unfair dismissal.[5] The reason for this is essentially regulatory: tribunal costs have increased for the taxpayer and the costs of defending a tribunal case have risen for employers, even those who win their cases. Yet the government seem to have allowed its regulatory reformist zeal to outweigh its obligation to strike an appropriate balance between these cost concerns and the need for adequate worker protection. This is particularly true in the case of unfair dismissal claims.

It is true that the new Act initially appears to add to employee legislative protections by requiring all employers to follow minimum statutory disciplinary and dismissal and grievance procedures by compulsorily implying them into all employee contracts.[6] Yet, upon closer inspection, this requirement is a two-edged sword: it can be enforced against employees as well as employers. If either an employee or employer fails to comply with such a procedure, employment tribunals have an obligation to reduce or increase any award for compensation by a minimum of 10 per cent up to a maximum of 50 per cent.[7] Moreover, an employee can be completely barred from presenting a complaint if he or she hasn't followed the steps of the 'appropriate' grievance procedure stipulated by the statute.[8]

In the case of dismissals, the concessions made to the risk of 'regulatory burdens' created by employee rights seem excessive. It is true that if the statutory minimum procedure is not completed and this was caused by a failure by the employer to comply with its requirements, the dismissal will be automatically unfair, with the remedy for such a finding set at a minimum of four weeks' pay. However, there are serious omissions in the stipulated statutory procedure which downgrade the principles established in previous law and the ACAS Code of Disciplinary and Grievance Procedures, *inter alia*,[9] in respect of the employer's obligation to investigate the facts and its obligation to conduct a hearing in cases of summary dismissal for gross misconduct and its obligation to provide graded penalties for employee indiscipline.[10] Moreover, the new Act provides that a failure by an employer to follow an agreed procedure *more elaborate than the statutory minimum procedure* will be regarded as itself making the employer's dismissal decision unreasonable if the procedural omission would have made 'no difference' to the outcome.[11] In both cases, a concern to lighten the regulatory burden of business has resulted in a significant reduction of employee protection.

One dimension of the regulatory framework is the constant complaint from the small and medium enterprises (SME) sector that the legislation creates a burden for small businesses. The reason for this is instructive. Much of the employment protection legislation is designed not merely to protect employees but also to stimulate managers to adopt 'best practice' from a personnel and human resources management point of view. This can be seen in the emphasis placed on codes of practice which spell out how managers can best shape organizational rules to comply with the legislation. The theory behind much of the employment legislation is that managers adopting good practice will produce a managerial regime which makes employees more prepared to accept its legitimacy, because management imposes restraints on its action which reduce the risks of arbitrary action affecting individuals being taken without hearing individual representations beforehand.

The introduction of best practice managerial rules, however, comes with a price tag and while the price to be paid is sometimes seen as a good investment by larger firms, it is often viewed as too heavy a cost by smaller firms. Under the current legal framework, there are some concessions to small business in the form of exemptions from certain types of statutes. Thus, the obligation to recognize a trade union under the Employment Relations Act applies only to employers with at least 21 employees. Moreover, the test of unfair dismissal requires tribunals to take into account *the size and administrative resources of the undertaking* in determining the reasonableness of the employer's decision to dismiss. Nevertheless, there remains a continuing and non-resolvable tension between the objectives of individual employment legislation to stimulate managerial efficiency and the readiness and ability of small businesses to take on the tasks of introducing formal procedures to ensure compliance with legislative standards.

Individual employment protections and collective bargaining

A third feature of individual employment legislation is its interrelationship with collective bargaining. In the earlier period of 'voluntarism' or collective laissez faire, individual employment legislation was portrayed as 'deferring to' collective bargaining as if there was little overlap or intermingling between the two spheres. The individual employment protections were viewed as providing minimum substantive standards of protection to employees, whether trade union members or not, in the form of statutory rights to be adjudicated by employment tribunals. Collective bargaining operating alongside the legislation was supposed to produce better results for employees with good organization and bargaining power. There was provision for the extension of collective bargaining results to other more weakly organized sectors by a process of arbitration under Sch 11 to the Employment Protection Act 1975 and public sector contracting obligations under the Fair Wages Resolution. Individual employment legislation was not intended to impinge upon collective bargaining.

With the expansion of legislative employment rights in the 1970s to a more comprehensive array of statutory rights, it could no longer be supposed that the statutory protections could be isolated from collective bargaining, despite a statutory system of exclusions. The legislation's ambitions of improving and reforming collective bargaining and managerial practice were bound to impinge upon both. A good example of this is the redundancy payments legislation which provides a minimum lump sum of compensation for employees dismissed for redundancy. At first glance this legislation appeared to be concerned with compensating long-serving employees who had been dismissed through no fault of their own. However, it has given rise to collective redundancy agreements which not only increase redundancy payments to multiples of the statutory sum but also provide managerial procedures to apply rules of seniority to redundancy dismissals and inform and consult the workforce about ways of reducing the number of redundancies. Yet the statutory lump sum payment combined with the best practice rules emanating from the cases of unfair dismissal for redundancy also help managers to 'manage' redundancy more effectively and reduce collective worker resistance to managerial redundancy decisions. Similarly, the unfair dismissals provisions were designed to stimulate, and have in fact stimulated, managerial reforms of disciplinary procedures and thereby lessened collective industrial conflict over disciplinary issues. These effects can be seen either as the 'by-products' or as the results of the joint objectives of individual employment legislation.

A further point about the impact of the individual employment protections upon collective bargaining and managerial practice is that certain laws, such as the Equal Pay and Sex Discrimination and Race Relations Acts, have been quite specifically designed to override managerial practice if they violate the statutory standards. For example, section 6 of the Sex Discrimination Act 1986, as amended by s.32 of TURER 1993, gives individuals a right to a declaration that a discriminatory term of a collective agreement or employer rule is void (see eg Lester and Rose, 1991). In all such cases, the legislative policy is to ensure that the public values of the law must prevail over what are viewed as the essentially private processes of managerial practice and collective bargaining.

In the area of equal pay too, collective arrangements are not completely isolated from the individual's rights. Section 3(4) of the Equal Pay Act stipulates that where provisions in collective agreements or pay structures apply 'specifically to men only or to women only', the CAC is given powers to amend collective agreements so as to eliminate the sex discrimination in the pay structures (see eg Lester and Rose, 1991). Moreover, standards of Article

119 in respect of equal pay for work of equal value have been held to apply directly to collective agreements.[12] In these and other respects, the so-called individual employment rights have a marked interrelationship with collective bargaining and managerial practice.

Finally, the overlap between individual employment legislation and collective bargaining also results in collective norms influencing individual rights. For example, the unfair dismissals law provides that employers should dismiss employees only after ensuring that the procedure they adopt is fair – and where the disciplinary procedure provides for a right of trade union representation or a right of trade union participation in an appeal panel, these 'collective' features are given weight in the test of reasonableness built into the statute, albeit as amended by the Employment Act 2002.

In the case of redundancy law the in-built collective features are also evident. Under ERA, s.98(4), in a test of unfair redundancy, the question of whether the employer behaved with procedural propriety in consulting the trade union representative is a factor. Further, the redundancy payment provisions calculate pay on the basis of contractual payment and this is influenced by the rates established in the contract of employment by collective bargaining.

Yet, as the experience of other countries with extensive collective bargaining, such as Sweden (Anderman, 1981) and Italy,[13] suggests, the legislative integration of individual rights with collective bargaining can ensure that individual employment rights underpin rather than undermine collective labour rights and collective bargaining. One of the less obvious features of the Employment Relations Act 1999 was its introduction of a number of changes which had just such an effect. The most dramatic is the amendment to the unfair dismissal laws to ensure that employees who take part in lawful and official industrial action can be viewed as automatically unfairly dismissed if they are dismissed during at least the first eight weeks of such industrial action. This change removed the employer's former immunity from a claim of unfair dismissal for participation in industrial action in cases where the industrial action is 'official', ie authorized by the trade union and is lawful under the Trade Union and Labour Relations (Consolidation) Act 1992 (TULR(C)A). The aim of the new provisions is to align the protections against dismissals for employees who take part in official and lawful industrial action with the immunities conferred upon the leaders and organizers of 'protected' industrial action, ie the trade union officials and the trade union organizations themselves. Hence, if industrial action is official and lawful under TULR(C)A 1992, s.219 (tort immunities) and s.226(1) (secret ballots), then employees who are dismissed for participating in such 'protected' action will be treated as automatically unfairly dismissed if the industrial action ends within eight weeks, or even afterwards if the employer is at fault for not taking reasonable procedural steps.

The new provisions introduced by the 1999 Act go a long way to remove a glaring omission in the legislation that had been introduced during the 1970s and was continued during the Thatcher era. Under the previous legal framework, if employees participated in a strike, even an official and lawful one under collective labour law, they could all be dismissed and the tribunal could be deprived of jurisdiction to hear a claim of unfair dismissal. This gap in the protective legal framework was exploited by the International News Corporation in the 1980s to break its negotiations with the printers' unions and move from Fleet Street to Wapping, hiring a whole new workforce of non-unionized employees (see eg Ewing and Napier, 1986). Since all unionized employees were dismissed, none had access to employment tribunals to complain of unfair dismissal. Now, if employees take part in industrial action, which is official and lawful and therefore 'protected', they cannot be sacked *en masse* as a way of breaking the strike, or ending the relationship with the trade union, without considerable compensation by the employer.

A second relevant provision of individual employment law is s.10 of the 1999 Act which gives employees a right to be accompanied by a representative of their choice, including a trade union representative, in grievance and disciplinary procedures. This right applies to all 'workers', including those in a grade for which a trade union is not officially recognized by the employer. This statutory provision, although qualified in certain respects, may help to reduce the effect of certain judicial decisions which held that the right to representation was a procedural right which could be found to be justifiably ignored by employers under 'a range of reasonable employers' test.[14] These offer examples of how the two main components of labour legislation can and should be viewed as parts of a coherent whole rather than as two separate elements of the legal framework for employment relations.

COLLECTIVE LABOUR LAW AND COLLECTIVE REPRESENTATION

Collective labour law, which is essentially concerned with the law of collective representation, should itself be seen today as consisting of two main elements: first, there are the measures designed mainly to provide legal support for the extension of trade unionism and collective bargaining. These include the freedom of association rights which take their modern form in the rights of employees to trade union membership and trade union activities, time off etc, while still preserving the right to non-membership. These also include the legal support for trade union recognition and rights to disclosure of information for the purposes of collective bargaining, and the rights to organize strikes and other industrial action which underpin collective bargaining (see Chapter 7).

Secondly, there are the new statutory 'employee' rights to collective representation for the purposes of information and consultation which apply even where trade unions are not recognized as representatives. These information and consultation rights were introduced largely because of European Union Social Policy directives and are based on the concept of twin track employee representation rather than the single channel approach taken by the first category of laws. They are currently being reinforced by further EU Social Policy initiatives. One of the most important issues in the current UK legal framework for employment relations is how the industrial relations system will absorb this new approach to legal regulation.

Legal protections for the extension of trade unions and collective bargaining

Legal protection for the extension of trade unionism and collective bargaining was introduced quite late in Britain. Even as late as the 1960s the TUC[15] could argue that 'trade unions in Britain have succeeded through their own efforts in strengthening their organization and in obtaining recognition, not relying on the assistance of government through legislation'. However, by that time, changes in the labour market away from manual to non-manual employment and the decrease in employment in industries with high trade union densities indicated that the historical base for trade unionism in the private sector was eroding.

The first meaningful direct legal support for trade union recognition occurred during the period of the Social Contract in the form of the Employment Protection Act 1975.[16] That Act included provisions that enabled an independent trade union which was refused recognition for the purpose of collective bargaining to obtain legal support along the lines recommended by the Donovan Commission,[17] but these were repealed by the Conservative government's Employment Act 1980. The experience of the 1975 Act suggested that the legal mechanism to compel recognition had many shortcomings, but the existence of a statutory process to compel recognition coincided with an enormous increase in the number of employees covered by trade unions engaged in recognized collective bargaining relationships, particularly in the public sector.

During its 18-year tenure, the Conservative government attempted to reduce the scope and power of trade unions in other ways, in particular by restricting the scope of industrial action, the use of the closed shop and making it possible for employers to bypass trade unions on information and consultation rights. One lesson learnt from this period was the interaction between the laws of industrial action and the pattern of recognition of trade unions. With industrial action heavily circumscribed by prohibitions against secondary action, it was possible for employers to construct their companies so as to make it illegal for unions to use industrial pressure to stop de-recognition efforts.

In 1999, the Labour government enacted the Employment Relations Act which restored a right to trade unions to compulsory recognition for collective bargaining purposes in firms of 21 employees or more where the union can show support of 50 per cent of the employees in a 'bargaining unit'[18] and the majority of employees are trade union members. It also provided a procedure to determine recognition by secret ballot where the initial trade union support was below 50 per cent but amounted after the ballot to more than half of 40 per cent of the 'bargaining unit'.[19] This legislation has begun to have a noticeable effect. There have been at least five cases dealt with by the CAC concerning the issue of compulsory recognition, at least one of which survived an application for judicial review.[20] Moreover, there have been a considerable number of voluntary recognition agreements reflecting the impact of the mere existence of a recognition statute.

It is not necessary for a trade union to achieve recognition under the statutory recognition procedure to be viewed as recognized for the purposes of other statutory rights.[21] All that is required is that the trade union must be independent[22] and be found as a matter of fact to be recognized by the employer in relation to the descriptions of workers for the purposes of collective bargaining.[23]

Once recognized by the employer, trade unions have a statutory right to disclosure of information,[24] for the purposes of collective bargaining. This right is designed to ensure that trade union representatives have sufficient information about employer proposals to enable them to negotiate more effectively. Yet it is of limited use since recognized trade unions have no entitlement to see copies of original documents but must content themselves with documents specially prepared by employers for the purpose of informing them, and employers are protected by a number of exceptions, including confidentiality, which allow them to deny trade unions access to certain information. Somewhat more effective have been the laws which give trade union representatives and members an entitlement to time off work for certain trade union duties and activities.[25]

An important element of the legal structure for trade union representation consists of the indirect statutory supports to trade union activity and trade union recognition. Unlike the United States in which recognition is an all or nothing phenomenon in the sense that a trade union is either an exclusive bargaining representative or it has no rights at the workplace, current UK law, after the 1999 Act, contains various employee rights which can be viewed as possible 'stepping stones' to trade union recognition. Traditionally, the freedom of association rights, consisting of statutory rights to trade union membership and activity, has provided that type of protection. Now, however, other elements of the legal framework may perform an analogous function. In the Employment Relations Act 1999, for example, the Labour government also created a right to individuals to representation for purposes of processing grievances or disciplinary issues. Even where a trade union has not achieved full recognition, individual employees may call upon trade union representatives to represent them in grievance and disciplinary hearings. There are certain shortcomings in the actual legislative definition of this right. Strictly speaking, it is a right to be 'accompanied', not represented. Moreover, employees can select another employee rather than a trade union official to accompany them. Nevertheless, this 'individual' right may prove to be a helpful building block for collective trade union representation by influencing recruitment. Certainly, trade unions in the United States have long been lobbying for some version of representation rights short of full recognition. Moreover, some US industrial relations specialists have advocated giving trade unions rights of individual representation as part of a new workplace partnership between unions and management.

Information and consultation rights

One of the major shifts in policy in the collective sphere of employment relations in recent years has been the move from legislation requiring 'single channel' trade-union-only representation to 'twin track' employee-based representation. In the late 1990s, owing to an infringement proceeding brought by the EU against the British government's implementation of the collective redundancies and transfer of undertakings directives, much legislation has been rewritten or introduced so that it now takes a 'twin track' approach in which the representatives can either be trade union representatives or, if no trade union is recognized for that grade of employee, workplace representatives can be elected by employees for the purpose of information and consultation rights. This is true of the collective redundancies and transfer of undertakings regulations, health and safety and pension rights.

All such provisions, at least after 1997, require the employer to extend information and consultation rights to a trade union, and no other representative, if that trade union is recognized by the employer for those grades of employees. If, however, there is no 'recognized' trade union, the employer must ensure that it informs and consults with duly elected employee representatives in respect of all such matters. In all these cases, apart from health and safety, the workplace representative body is to be informed and consulted on an ad hoc basis. More recently, with the implementation of the European Works Council and the acceptance of the Directive on works councils in all EU companies with more than 50 employees, the legislation has begun to create standing committees in the form of works councils for the purpose of information and consultation about the economic planning of firms as well as the decisions which may more directly affect employees. The thinking behind this type of legislation has been spelt out in various EU documents. The idea is to ensure both that management has an input from workforce representatives in the course of planning and before specific decisions are taken that affect employees, and to ensure that employees are represented even if their employer does not recognize a trade union. Otherwise, there would be a democratic deficit at the workplace.

This category of collective labour legislation has proved to be contentious in two important respects. In the first place, the creation of legislatively sponsored workplace representatives, in particular the standing committees such as works councils and European Works Councils, have been viewed by the Labour government as too heavy a burden to business. Thus, while in principle the Labour government accepts that 'it is good practice to inform and consult employees', it also insists that its priority 'is to promote labour market flexibility and employability, and to contribute to competitiveness, without placing undue burdens or costs on British business'. Hence, it has delayed the start of the implementation of the 1998 directive on 'establishing a general framework for information and consultation in all EU companies with more than 50 employees'. Moreover, it has been extremely careful to choose a version of the European Works Council directive which 'does not impose additional requirements to those contained in the directive'.

On the other hand, from the trade union side, there is a fear that such laws may create a 'Trojan horse' in the firm in the sense of creating a substitute for trade unions and thereby preventing the evolution of genuine trade unionism. A related criticism of such elected workplace representatives is that where legislation such as the Working Time Regulation allows certain 'opt outs' from protective legislation by elected representatives in cases where the workforce is weakly organized, this would allow employers to undermine the level of protection by leaning on employee representatives.

There is a certain degree of truth in the latter argument. The Working Time Regulation was designed to create minimum standards with a view to improving protection of the health and safety of workers. All workers were to be entitled to a 48-hour week, defined rest periods and paid holiday leave. Yet the regulation implementing the Directive provides for an opt-out by individual agreement from the 48-hour maximum and an opt-out by either collective agreement or workforce agreement, where there are no recognized trade unions, for a number of other issues such as night work, daily and weekly rest periods and work breaks for adult workers. In its desire to create greater flexibility, the government has ignored the risks to minimum standards created by individual opt-outs and collective opt-outs by workforce agreement where the workforce representatives do not have any real bargaining power to resist employer initiatives.

Yet the 'Trojan horse' argument of the trade unions in the UK context is not fully convincing. It is true that employers can manipulate the information and consultation provisions to convince employees that non-union employee representation schemes are adequate to protect them. Yet for employers to do this convincingly requires a huge commitment in resources to an enlightened personnel or human resources policy.

In the meantime, there is also a case for recognizing the potential of the information and consultation laws as indirect supports for collective bargaining. In the case of the information and consultation rights in relation to collective redundancies[26] and the Transfer of Undertakings Regulation, as well as the Health and Safety representatives, it is now clear that the employer must extend sole consultation rights to recognized trade unions for the grades of employees for which they are recognized. In this sense, the consultation rights underpin existing recognition and collective bargaining arrangements rather than undermine them.

Secondly, the statutory requirement that an employer consult, before a collective redundancy decision, with trade union representatives about the reasons for a planned redundancy and ways of reducing the numbers to be made redundant can provide a stepping stone for trade unions to negotiate. It is true that the statutory obligation of the employer is only to discuss certain issues with trade unions and indeed the case law recognizes that this leaves the final decision to the employer. Nevertheless, there are no obstacles to the trade union negotiating and even using the threat of industrial action to underpin such negotiations. For, unlike the German legal system, there is nothing in the statutory rules in the UK that places a special peace obligation on the trade union as the price of engaging in consultation.

The more difficult element to assess is what happens to information and consultation rights in those categories of employees for which there is no recognized trade union. Here, we have the simple point that the laws, apart from Health and Safety Committees, stipulate only that an ad hoc committee must be formed for the purpose of the consultation exercise. As long as the law stays in this form there is little risk of creating substitutes to trade unions or much prospect that the legislation will provide an indirect support to trade union recognition.

With the implementation of the European Works Council Directive, however, there has been a change of legal policy. Now the requisite body for information and consultation rights consists of a standing committee or council capable of building up a picture of the overall economic framework for managerial decisions as well as a 'tribal memory' of previous developments in management policy. The European Works Councils are limited to information and consultation over issues at a transnational level and management decisions will generally be viewed at a European-wide level rather than a company-wide level where collective bargaining may take place. The EWCs are restricted to European companies with a Community dimension, ie companies or groups with at least 1,000 employees and at least 150 employees in at least two member states. In theory there is a possibility that the regular meetings of representatives from different subsidiaries of the same transnational company may one day encourage European-wide collective bargaining, but that day is a long way off. In any case, it seems unclear that the EWC has the capacity to produce a Trojan horse for trade union substitution in any one country.

A further issue of trade union substitution will arise with the legislation introducing works councils to firms with employees of 50 or more employees. Here, much will depend on the form taken by the implementing regulation. The problems are not likely to arise in the area where trade unions are recognized since the unions will dominate the works council *de facto* if not *de jure*. On the other hand, the creation of standing works councils for groups of employees having no trade union representatives poses certain problems. Such a legal obligation can have the effect of encouraging employers to maintain non-union works councils. Indeed, the US experience suggests that employers have used 'employee representation' schemes to break independent trade unions. Yet, if employers fail to maintain good standards of communication and treatment, works councils provide a ready-made institution to use as a springboard for trade union organization.

CONCLUSIONS

As we have seen, the relationship between the individual rights aspects of the legal framework and the collective elements is one of the most contentious features of the current legal framework for industrial relations. On the one hand, the new Labour government appears to be providing a direct measure of support for trade unions and collective bargaining in the form of a statute to compel recognition. This statute appears to have resulted in a number of orders by the CAC compelling employers to recognize trade unions as well as a considerable number of voluntary recognition agreements spurred on by the existence of a statutory procedure (see ACAS annual Report, 2001).

On the other hand, the Labour government seems to be reluctant to be seen to establish overt linkages between individual rights and collective bargaining. Thus, the right to be 'represented' in grievance and disciplinary hearings conferred by section 10 of the Employment Rights Act 1999 is cast as an individual protection, allowing a worker to choose to be accompanied by a fellow-worker or a trade union representative, and is backed up by a weak remedy of compensation of up to two weeks' pay. Moreover, in the government's proposal for new legislation for disputes resolution, it makes no mention of the section 10 right even though it seems clear that such a right will apply to grievances and disciplinary procedures applicable under the new legislation. Even if the government is loathe to portray section 10 as a possible stepping stone to collective representation, that provision offers just such a possibility to trade union representatives. Employees in any unit where a trade union representative shows skill and expertise in the task will undoubtedly be more favourably disposed towards that trade union. Whether it goes any further will depend on other circumstances but a clear opportunity to display the advantages of trade union representation is a feature of section 10 (see eg Brown, 2000).

The attitude of New Labour to the collective employee representation schemes has been even more ambivalent. It has not significantly strengthened the specific provisions for prior consultation over collective redundancies and the TUPE regulation, despite the obvious weaknesses of their existing remedies (see eg Villiers, 2000). It has, moreover, been extremely grudging in implementing the General Framework Works Council Directive, delaying its effects on firms with 50 or more employees until 2008 (see eg discussion by Bercusson, 2002). This has occurred despite its own commitment to part-nership at the workplace between trade unions and management and the trade unions' own acceptance of Works Councils as a potentially useful step in increasing workplace representation. The government seems mired in a policy of attempting to limit costs to industry without giving any weight to the potential benefits to industry of the Works Council legislation.

Whether Works Councils will in fact operate as a second stepping stone to trade union representation remains to be seen. If employers invest heavily in employment representation schemes they can sometimes convince employees that trade union representation is not needed. Yet, if there is discord on any substantive decisions by management in a situation where there is an employee representative structure, the way can be eased for trade unions to organize employees at the workplace.

Notes

1 Directive 95/45/EC.
2 Directive 2002/14/EC.
3 See TUC AGM Reports 1893–1903. Bell of the Railway Workers Union lost his motion for compulsory arbitration on several occasions.
4 Although employment protection legislation contains an express restriction against the parties contracting out of the provisions of the relevant Act (Employment Rights Act, s.203(1)) employers can achieve such a result indirectly by use of their greater bargaining and 'drafting' powers.
5 EA 2002 s.32.
6 EA 2002 s.30.
7 EA 2002 s.31.
8 EA 2002 s.32.
9 ERA 1996 s.98A(1) inserted by EA 2002 s.34(2).
10 ACAS Code 2000 paras 7, 13, 15 and 16.
11 ERA 1996 s.98A(2) inserted by EA 2002 s.34(2): see discussion by Hepple, B and Morris, G S (2002) The Employment Act 2002 and the crisis in employment rights, *International Labour Journal*, p 245.
12 See eg *Nimz v Freie und Hansestadt Hamburg*: C-184/89 [1991] ECR I-297, [1991] IRLR 222, ECJ.
13 Wedderburn, Lord (1990) The Italian workers' statute: some British reflec-tions, *International Labour Journal*, p 154. Section 238A(6) states that

employment tribunals must have regard to the following factors when deciding whether or not the employer took reasonable steps:

(a) whether the employer or a union had complied with procedures established by an applicable collective agreement;
(b) whether either employer or union had offered or agreed to resume or commence negotiations after the start of the protected industrial action;
(c) whether either party unreasonably refused a request for conciliation or mediation services to be used – the latter to help adopt a procedure to resolve the dispute.

For the purpose of this tribunal decision, the tribunal is not to take into account the underlying merits of the dispute.

14 See *Bailey v BP Oil (Kent Refinery) Ltd* [1980] IRLR 287 CA.
15 Evidence to the Royal Commission on Trade Unions and Employers' Associations London (HMSO, 1986).
16 The Industrial Relations Act 1971 introduced a statutory recognition procedure but the experience under that Act was heavily distorted by the TUC unions' unwillingness to 'register' and obtain the benefits of positive legal rights.
17 EPA, ss.11–16.
18 See TULR(C)A 1992 Schedule A1 para 22.
19 See TULR(C)A 1992 Schedule A1 para 29(3).
20 *Fullerton Computer Industries Ltd v CAC* [2001] IRLR 752.
21 In some cases, eg disclosure of information, there is a further requirement of recognition in respect of specific matters, TULR(C)A, s.181(2). See also time off for union duties, TULR(C)A, s.168(1).
22 A trade union can be found to be 'independent', if the statutory criteria are met either in fact or by certification.
23 TULR(C)A, s.178(3), 'Collective bargaining' is now defined as meaning negotiations relating to or connected with one of the matters specified in s.178(2) of TULR(C)A.
24 TULR(C)A, ss.181–5. See Gospel, H and Lockwood, G (1999) Disclosure of information for collective bargaining: The CAC Approach Revisited, *International Labour Journal*, p 233.
25 TULR(C)A, ss.168–173.
26 Part IV, Chapter II of the Trade Union and Labour Relations (Consolidation) Act 1992.

References

ACAS (2001) *Annual Report 2000–2001*, ACAS, London
Anderman, S (1981) Labour law in Sweden: a comment, in *Law and the Weaker Party*, Vol I, ed A Neal, Professional Books, Abingdon, p 193
Anderman, S (2000) *Labour Law: Management Decision and Workers Rights*, 4th edn, Butterworths, London, chs 3–6

Anderman, S (2001) *Law of Unfair Dismissal*, 3rd edn, Butterworths, London

Bercusson, B (2002) The European Social Model comes to Britain, *International Labour Journal*, p 209

Brown, W (1986) The changing role of trade unions in the management of labour, *British Journal of Industrial Relations*, **161**, p 164

Brown, W (2000) Putting partnership into practice in Britain, *British Journal of Industrial Relations*, **38**, pp 299–303

Burgess, K (1980) *The Challenge of Labour*, Croom helm, London

Claydon, (1989) Union derecognition, *British Journal of Industrial Relations*, **27**, p 214

Clegg, H A, Fox, A and Thompson, A F (1964) *A History of British Trade Unions since 1898: Vol I 1889–1910*, Clarendon Press, Oxford, ch 9

Davies, P and Freedland, M (1993) *Labour Legislation and Public Policy*, Oxford University Press, Oxford

Deakin, S and Morris, G S (2000) *Labour Law*, 3rd edn, Butterworths, London

DTI (2000) *Labour Force Survey: Great Britain, 1989–2000*, DTI, London

Dunn, S and Gennard, J (1984) *The Closed Shop in British Industry*, Macmillan, London

Ewing, K D and Napier, B W (1986) *The Wapping Dispute and Labour Law*, Cambridge Law Journal, **45**, p 285

Fox, A (1985) *History and Heritage*, Allen & Unwin, London, pp 131–37

Lester, A and Rose, D (1991) Equal value claims and sex bias in collective bargaining, *International Labour Journal*, p 163

Machin, S (2000) Union decline in Britain, *British Journal of Industrial Relations*, p 631

Saville, J (1967)Trade unions and free labour, in *Essays in Labour History*, ed A Briggs and J Saville, Macmillan, London, p 317

Smith, P and Morton, G (1993) Union exclusion and the decollectivization of industrial relations in contemporary Britain, *British Journal of Industrial Relations*, March

Villiers, C (2000) The Rover case (1) The sale of Rover Cars by BMW: the role of the works council, *International Labour Journal*, p 386

Wedderburn, Lord (1993) *The Worker and the Law*, 3rd edn, Sweet & Maxwell, London

Weekes, B, Mellish, M, Dickens, L and Lloyd, J (1975) *Industrial Relations and the Limits of Law*, Blackwell, Oxford

6

Unfair dismissal

Ann Blair

INTRODUCTION

With claims in the Employment Tribunal (ET) undergoing a threefold increase in the space of a decade, and unfair dismissal cases the largest category, the current rate of unfair dismissal represents a very significant cost to both sides of industry. Given that the remedy was introduced as long ago as 1971, one would expect that the law on this would be settled and employers would have a good idea of what the law requires of them and the scope it leaves for the exercise of discretion. Sadly, this could not be further from the truth. In recent years the law reports have groaned under the weight of new legal authority, but we are really no closer to knowing in advance whether a tribunal will consider a dismissal fair or not. The desire to limit the grounds on which a case can be appealed has led to the development of a body of rules that treats most questions the tribunal has to determine as questions of fact. These can only be appealed where the tribunal has made a mistake of law or where a decision is perverse. Instead of clear legal rules that are apt for appeal, the law is dominated by principles that allow tribunals to weigh conflicting interests. The advantage of this approach is that tribunals have a great deal of flexibility to achieve justice in the individual case; the disadvantage is the uncertainty this generates. Many employers and employees might be willing to trade some flexibility for more certainty in order to avoid or settle claims more effectively. However, for as long as these doctrines aim to keep cases out of the Employment Appeal Tribunal (EAT) it seems unlikely that the pressure on the rate of claims to the ET will be contained. The introduction of the Human

Rights Act 1998 adds to this uncertainty. However, at the time of writing, there is little sign, in the private sector at least, that the new emphasis on defending the rights in the European Convention on Human Rights is about to result in a drastic rewriting of the law on unfair dismissal.

This chapter aims to set out the elements of the claim and the remedies that are available as clearly as possible and to explain where the uncertainties arise and how tribunals deal with them. However, before turning to the question of what unfair dismissal is, it is worth emphasizing what it is not. It is not wrongful dismissal, which is a dismissal in breach of contract, and it is not redundancy. All three claims arise on termination of employment and all three overlap, but here there is only space to consider unfair dismissal.

THE ELEMENTS OF UNFAIR DISMISSAL

The law of unfair dismissal is in Part X of the Employment Rights Act 1996 (ERA).[1] There are several essential elements to a claim for unfair dismissal:

- The claimant must be an employee (section (s.) 94)
  - with sufficient qualifying service (s.108);
  - who has been dismissed (s.95);
- A fair dismissal must have been for one of a number of reasons which are defined as potentially fair (s.98(1));
- Whether the dismissal is actually fair then depends on whether the employer acted reasonably or unreasonably in treating this reason as sufficient to justify dismissal (s.98(2));
- Some reasons for dismissal are automatically unfair (ss.99–105). It is for the employee to show that the dismissal was for one of these reasons. The question of reasonableness is not relevant to these dismissals.

These elements of a claim need to be considered in turn. First, the preliminary points about qualification to bring a claim; then the nature of the potentially fair reasons and the reasonableness of the dismissal; and finally, the automatically unfair dismissals.

EMPLOYMENT STATUS AND CONTINUITY OF EMPLOYMENT

The question of employment status has been covered in an earlier chapter. This discussion is not repeated here, save to emphasize that this is an essential prerequisite for establishing a claim. If there is any doubt about status the ET can determine this as a preliminary question. In addition, all employees must have completed 12 months' continuous service with the employer to be qualified to bring a claim (s.108(1)).[2] The complications of the test of continuity of service as it used to apply to part-time workers have been swept away by the decision in *R v Secretary of State for Employment ex parte EOC*.[3] The stricter continuity requirements that used to apply to part-time workers were contrary to the Equal Treatment Directive, amounting to indirect sex discrimination, which could not be justified. The effect of the decision is now consolidated in the ERA, which makes no distinction between continuous full-time service and continuous part-time service.

Continuity is calculated on a week-by-week basis and any week in which an employee works or is under contract counts towards continuity (ss.210(3)(b) and 212(1)). Problems arise where there are breaks in service, but continuity is preserved if provisions in the ERA cover a break in the contract or a change of employer. In three sets of circumstances in s.212(3) continuity is preserved during a break in the contract. The time off work counts towards continuous service where absence is due to sickness of up to 26 weeks, 'temporary cessation of work', or by 'custom or arrangement' (case law clarifies the exact meaning of these terms). A change of employer will normally break continuity, but s.218 preserves continuity on transfer of undertakings, the death of the employer, statutory changes of employer, change in the composition of the employing partnership, and where a person moves to employment with an 'associated' employer. Associated employers are defined as: 'any two employers are treated as associated if one is a company of which the other (directly or indirectly) has control, or if both are companies of which a third person (directly or indirectly) has control' (s.231). There is detailed case law on the interpretation of this, but unfortunately there is not space to go into this here.

These continuity requirements apply to the standard unfair dismissal claim. Rights to claim that dismissal is automatically unfair accrue from day one of employment. Equally, a dismissal based on sex, race or disability discrimination can be challenged under the Sex Discrimination Act 1975, the Race Relations Act 1976 or the Disability Discrimination Act 1995 from day one.[4]

In addition to the general qualifications, there are a number of specific exclusions. These apply to persons over retirement age, either 65 or the 'normal' retiring age if different (NB: it is possible that the use of age 65 may amount to indirect sex discrimination against men, but at the moment the issue remains open[5]); share fishermen and the police; dismissals for the purpose of safeguarding national security; and where agreed disciplinary procedures are designated by the Secretary of State by Order as substituting for the statutory remedy of unfair dismissal.[6] Exclusions that used to apply to those working abroad and to those on fixed-term contracts of at least one year's duration were repealed by the Employment Relations Act 1999 (ERelA). Section 23 ErelA grants the Secretary of State the power to extend the unfair dismissal claim to groups that are currently excluded from it. This power is intended to be of potential application to groups specifically excluded from much employment protection legislation, but is wider in scope than this.[7] A final point on qualification is that a claim must be brought within three months of the date the employment ended. There is provision for this to be extended by the tribunal in some circumstances but this is rarely exercised. There is also a considerable case law on what date is the 'effective date of termination'. This is important for many reasons, but especially for setting the date from which the time limit runs and for calculating whether the employee has accrued sufficient continuity of service. There is insufficient space to go into this in detail, but employers and employees need to be aware of the consequences of getting this wrong.

DISMISSAL

Once the qualifications to bring a claim are established, it is for the employee to show that there has been a dismissal. If there is no dismissal there is no remedy, but the law recognizes three different modes of termination of the contract as dismissal (s.95):

- where the contract is terminated by the employer;
- where a contract for a fixed term expires without being renewed;
- where the employee terminates the contract in circumstances where the employer's conduct would allow termination without notice.

The first means that there is no remedy if there is an unforced resignation, or where there is termination of the contract by genuine mutual agreement, or where the contract is frustrated. Frustration occurs where the contract has become impossible to carry out because of events that the parties did not have in contemplation at the time the contract was made. Examples in the employment context are the imprisonment of the employee and the onset of long-term health problems (though it is arguable that ill-health cases are better dealt with as cases where the dismissal is for a potentially fair reason).[8] As far as the second category is concerned, employees on fixed-term contracts would seldom be able to claim unfair dismissal if the ending of a fixed-term contract by expiry of time could not count as a dismissal. However, until 1999, this was of little comfort to most employees on fixed-term contracts of more than 12 months' duration, as s.197 allowed employers to seek a written waiver of the employee's right to bring a claim. Unfair dismissal waivers were removed in 1999 (ERelA).[9] The third case covers what are known as 'constructive' dismissals. *Western Excavating v Sharp*[10] restricted claims of 'constructive' dismissal to situations where the employer's conduct amounts to 'fundamental' or 'repudiatory' breach of contract. Effectively this means that the employer's conduct must show that she or he no longer intends to be bound by one or more of the essential elements of the contract. At common law this entitles the employee to bring the relationship to an end without giving notice; following Western Excavating it is also the test of whether the employee is entitled to bring the employment to an end yet still claim that there has been a dismissal.

THE POTENTIALLY FAIR REASONS FOR DISMISSAL

Having established that there has been a dismissal, be it a 'straight' dismissal, the end of a fixed-term contract or a 'constructive' dismissal, the question now turns to the reason for that dismissal. To defend a claim the employer must show that the reason is one permitted by the ERA. The categories are not mutually exclusive, but the employer is required to show what the principal reason for the dismissal is. Tribunals will allow employers some latitude, but a 'scatter gun' approach which would allow employers freedom to plead multiple reasons, in the hope that one will suffice, is discouraged. If one of multiple reasons can't be shown to be the main reason, the employer's case will fall at the first hurdle.[11] Where industrial pressure has been brought on the employer to dismiss, the tribunal must ignore this in determining what the reason is (s.107).[12] This may leave the employer with no permissible reason. Employees with one year's continuous service have a right to a written statement of the reasons for their dismissal (s.92). If the employee disputes that the reason given is the actual reason for dismissal or if the employer refuses to provide written reasons, the ET can make a declaration as to what the real reason is.

The potentially fair reasons are found in ss.98(2) and 98(1)(b). These are:

- reasons relating to capability or qualifications;
- reasons relating to conduct;
- redundancy;
- contravention of a statutory duty or restriction; or
- some other substantial reason of a kind such as to justify the dismissal.

Where the reason is not one of the potentially fair reasons (or if the employee has shown that the reason is one of the automatically unfair reasons), the case of unfair dismissal is made out at this stage. In all other cases, once a potentially fair reason has been established it is still necessary to determine whether the dismissal was reasonable in the circumstances. This is considered below, but first it is necessary to consider the content of the permissible reasons.

Capability or qualifications

This reason 'relates to the capability or qualifications of the employee for performing work of the kind which he was employed by the employer to do' (s.98(2)(a)). 'Capability' means capability assessed by reference to skill, aptitude, health or any other physical or mental quality. 'Qualifications' means any degree, diploma or other academic, technical or professional qualification relevant to the position held (s.98(3)(a) and 98(3)(b)). The definition of capability falls into two quite different areas. First, health-based capability: employment may be ended if the employee is not in sufficiently good mental and physical health to do the work. Second, they may not have the skills and aptitude necessary to do the work. The provisions of the Disability Discrimination Act 1995 (DDA) now complicate both cases. Allowing time off for disability-related health needs might be a reasonable adjustment that the employer is required to make to enable a person with a disability to continue to participate in the workforce. Equally, adjustments such as more time or extra training might be required to accommodate a disabled person's physical or mental impairments. Thus a dismissal that would not be unfair if the employee had no disability might well be contrary to the DDA if the employee is a disabled person within the meaning of the Act.[13] A person comes under the protection of the DDA only if they have a mental or physical impairment which has a substantial and long-term adverse effect on their ability to carry out normal day-to-day activities (s.1 DDA). The duties under the DDA do not at the time of writing apply to employers with fewer than 15 employees, but this number is open to revision downwards.[14] Leaving these complications aside, because of the differences between different types of capability it is helpful to consider them separately.

Ill health

That health-related absence is a potentially fair reason for dismissal recognizes the employer's interest in having work performed. Catastrophic or long-term illness will always bring the case under this head, except where the question is avoided by the employer successfully pleading that the ill health frustrates the contract, in which case there is no dismissal and therefore no case to be heard. Dismissals for short absences are also potentially fair. Where an employee has a record of persistent absence for a number of unrelated reasons it might be conduct rather than illness that is at issue. It remains the case that it is for the employer to show what the reason was, but the rule that he or she acted reasonably in treating *this reason* as justifying dismissal may be relaxed in these circumstances in acknowledgement of the difficulties employers face in such situations.[15]

Skills and aptitude

The ability to dismiss inept employees fairly also recognizes the employer's need to have work carried out and carried out with reasonable accuracy and efficiency. This doesn't apply only to new employees; the law of unfair dismissal also recognizes that employers need to update their employees' skills. As with cases of illness, it is sometimes hard to know if poor work is the result of lack of aptitude or lack of required skills or wilful lack of application. It can be difficult to distinguish between the employee who can't and the employee who won't. As before, tribunals are willing to allow employers some latitude in specifying the reasons for dismissal in such cases.

Conduct

Dismissal for a reason that 'relates to the conduct of the employee' is potentially fair. Misconduct, quite literally, covers a multitude of sins – everything from persistent lateness or absence, through wilful failure to follow instructions, to theft, swearing, harassment and violence. If there has been such behaviour it will not usually be difficult to show that the dismissal is for one of the potentially fair reasons.

Redundancy

Dismissal where the reason 'is that the employee was redundant' is potentially fair. There is a technical definition of redundancy in s.139 and if the dismissal satisfies this definition the dismissal is potentially fair. As definitions of redundancy have been around since 1965, again one would think that the tribunals and courts, and by extension employers, would have a pretty good idea of what is a redundancy and what is not. Recent case law has only served to make it plain that what is (or is not) a redundancy is far from a self-evident truth. Whether there is a redundancy is for the tribunal to determine as a question of fact. This will resolve any uncertainty but in marginal cases this can be difficult to predict at the outset. That said, tribunals do not enquire into the business case for redundancy; this is seen as a matter for managerial discretion.[16] Many economic dismissals do not fall within the legal definition of redundancy, however, and as a result employers will sometimes argue that there is no redundancy to avoid the cost of redundancy compensation. In other cases the employer will argue that the dismissal is for redundancy and therefore not unfair dismissal which would almost certainly attract higher compensation. A fuller picture of this can only be gained once the role of dismissal for 'some other substantial reason' is explained below.

Contravention of a statutory duty or restriction

Dismissal where the reason 'is that the employee could not continue to work in the position which he held without contravention (either on his part or on that of his employer) of a duty or restriction imposed by or under an enactment' is potentially fair. This requires little in the way of further explanation. It would, for example, apply to a driver who lost his or her licence. It would also apply in some Health and Safety cases, including those that relate to foetal health.

Some other substantial reason (SOSR)

Finally, dismissal for 'some other substantial reason of a kind such as to justify the dismissal of an employee holding the position which the employee held' is also potentially fair. The content of this category is developed through case law. This includes some economic dismissals that do not fit within the narrow definition of redundancy. It would include reducing rates of pay or to reducing hours or altering overtime and shift bonuses for economic reasons.[17] In *Hollister v NFU*[18] an employee refused to agree to a variation of his rights under a contractual pensions scheme. As all other employees had agreed to join the new scheme, it was held that the dismissal was for SOSR. It was impractical for the employer to maintain pension arrangements for a single employee. As the dismissal was for SOSR (and reasonable in the circumstances), the employee was not entitled to a redundancy payment any more than he was entitled to compensation for unfair dismissal.

Vexed questions have arisen where the employer still has confidence in the employee but the employee's workmates or a client have made it clear that they are unwilling to work with this individual. In *Dobie v Burns International Security*[19] a customer's unwillingness to accept the employee onto the premises where he was a security guard was SOSR. In *Treganowan v Robert Knee & Co*[20] the difficulty was a personality clash in the workforce. In an unreported case, *Buck v Letchworth Palace*,[21] the employee's colleagues refused to work with him because he was gay and they feared he would give them AIDS. In *Saunders v Scottish National Camps Association*[22] SOSR was simply the employee's sexual orientation (but note that EU Framework Directive 2000/78 on equal treatment in employment covers age, sexual orientation and religion and will require legislation on sexual orientation by December 2003). Another example of SOSR is the expiry of a fixed-term contract.

In all of these cases the fact that the dismissal was for SOSR (or one of the other permissible reasons) did not mean that the dismissal was necessarily fair.

THE REASONABLENESS OF DISMISSAL

If the tribunal is satisfied that the reason is one of the potentially fair reasons, it will then turn to the question of whether the employer acted reasonably or unreasonably in treating this reason as sufficient to justify dismissal (s.98(4)). The burden of proof on this point is neutral. There are two main issues that underpin the whole notion of when an employer acts 'unfairly' or 'reasonably'. These need to be considered before looking at particular cases. First, the question of what degree of procedural fairness the employer must satisfy before a dismissal is fair, and second, what standard of reasonableness the tribunal must apply.

Procedural fairness

The seminal case on procedural fairness is *Polkey v Dayton Services*[23] in the House of Lords. Polkey is a case on redundancy selection, but the reasoning applies to the other permissible categories of dismissal. In essence the decision requires employers to follow procedures sufficient to enable them to reach an adequate view of the facts on which the decision is to be based and to allow the person affected by the decision a chance to put any relevant points. The main issue in Polkey was whether the employer could reach a decision to dismiss that was fair where the employee had not had an opportunity to put his or her case. An earlier decision in *British Labour Pump v Byrne*,[24] that procedures could be dispensed with if it was clear that they would make no difference, was overruled. Polkey asserts a new orthodox position that procedural fairness is fundamental, and only rarely can employers dispense with minimum procedures. In *Whitbread plc v Hall*[25] the Court of Appeal confirmed that procedural fairness is fundamental but that it is not a free-standing requirement. The overall question remains whether the employer acted reasonably given all the circumstances, including the procedures used. This position is about to be altered quite drastically; s.34 of the Employment Act 2002, which is expected to be brought into force in late 2003, will mean that procedural mistakes beyond a minimum can be disregarded if they would have made no difference to the outcome and the dismissal was otherwise fair.[26] The *quid pro quo* is that if these minimum procedures are not adhered to the dismissal will be automatically unfair.[27] So what is reasonableness?

Reasonableness

Employment Tribunals seem ideally adapted to determining the reasonableness of an employer's conduct because of their balanced composition and the fact that the 'wing persons' are chosen for their experience of industrial relations practice. However, according to the doctrine stated most clearly in *Iceland Frozen Foods v Jones*,[28] tribunals must decide if the decision to dismiss falls within a 'band of reasonable responses' that the employer might take, rather than substituting the employer's decision with their own view of what is reasonable. The aim of this seems to be to acknowledge that there is no single 'reasonable' response in the majority of employment situations and that employers should not be penalized for deciding differently than the tribunal would have in the same circumstances. This allows employers to enjoy a degree of discretion in their responses, but the test has been subject to criticism. The danger is that it is open to be interpreted as endorsing any decision to dismiss short of one that is perverse; ie, so unreasonable that it could not have been made by any reasonable employer. In *Haddon v Van Den Bergh Foods*[29] the EAT tried to address the conflict in the idea of a range of reasonable responses that did not exclude all but the perverse. The EAT reinstated the notion of the ET as an industrial jury, and that it was appropriate for the tribunal members to assess the reasonableness of the response by asking themselves what they would have done in such circumstances. An expected appeal to the Court of Appeal failed to materialize, but the question soon came before the EAT again in *Foley v Post Office*. This case rejected the notion that it was the place of the EAT to reverse established principle (albeit its own principle) and reinstated Iceland's 'band of reasonable responses', while restating that this does not amount to a perversity test. This was confirmed as the correct approach by the Court of Appeal.[30] So after an intense period of judicial activity, orthodoxy has been challenged and then reinstated. Of course the difficulties that Haddon tries to address remain, but at least it is now stated clearly in the Court of Appeal that decisions do not need to be perverse before they will fall outside the band of reasonable responses. However, deciding where to draw the line between something that is outside the band of reasonable responses, and yet not perverse, presents tribunals with an unenviable task. What does reasonableness require in each of the permissible categories of dismissal?

Capability or qualifications

Ill health

Tribunals examine a range of factors in deciding whether an employer has acted reasonably in treating illness as justifying dismissal. The essence of these is that the reasonableness or otherwise of dismissal is the balance that needs to be struck between the employer's need to have the work done and the employee's need for time off work to recover. Relevant factors will include how critical the work is and any need to make a replacement quickly and the employee's length of service. However, an assessment by the employer of how much longer it will be before the employee can return to work is essential. The employer can request a medical report or ask the employee to undergo a medical examination, but unless the contract provides for this there is no means by which the employer can compel either. Nevertheless, if the employee refuses to cooperate in providing the necessary information, it is open to the employer to draw reasonable inferences. Overall the tribunal is attempting to decide if the employer could reasonably have been expected to wait any longer for the employee to be fit to resume work.

Must the employer discuss the proposed dismissal with the employee and issue a warning that continued absence will lead to dismissal? *East Lindsey District Council v Daubney*[31] emphasized the need for consultation with the employee, to establish what the medical position is and what the prospects are for return to work before taking a decision to dismiss. However, in *Spencer v Paragon Wallpaper*[32] the employer, having established that the employee would need a further 4–6 weeks to recover, did not need to go further and warn the employee that continued absence would lead to dismissal before dismissing him. The employee had been made aware that dismissal was a possibility through discussions that had taken place earlier. *International Sports Co v Thomson*[33] involved multiple unconnected absences. Here it was accepted that the borderline between conduct and capability can become blurred, and ultimately the EAT were not prepared to displace a decision that the employer had acted reasonably in taking the view that enough was enough. The EAT was very willing to accept that employers did not need a detailed medical report that covered the likely recurrence of each minor illness.

Skills and aptitude

Here the reasonableness of dismissal will depend on the nature of the work and whether training has been offered and time given to improve. On the status of warnings in skill and aptitude cases, the situation is summed up elegantly in a quotation from *Winterhalter Gastronom Ltd v Webb*.[34] It was accepted that the employer's view that the employee was incapable of meeting sales targets and that training would not help was reasonable. Nevertheless, it was also accepted that there are 'many situations in which apparent capabilities may be stretched when [the employee] knows what is demanded; many do not know they are capable of jumping a five-barred gate until there is a bull in the field behind them'. The importance of warnings can be overstated; the overall question remains one of reasonableness. In *Alidair v Taylor*[35] the employee pilot had crash-landed one of the employer's aircraft. The employer lost confidence in him and the decision to dismiss without warning or time to improve etc was reasonable in the circumstances.

Conduct

The simplest form of defence for the employer who has dismissed an employee for misconduct is that she or he has followed the ACAS Code of Practice on Disciplinary and Grievance Procedures.[36] Although the Code has no formally binding status in law, compliance with it will usually provide good evidence that the employer has acted reasonably. The Code emphasizes the need for a staged disciplinary procedure with a system of warnings. The lower stages are appropriate for minor offences, with more serious or repeated failures dealt with at the higher levels. Each stage is accompanied by a warning, which increases in seriousness from an oral warning to a written warning to a final warning. In *Lock v Cardiff Railway*[37] the EAT held that the Code must be taken into account by the ET in any proceedings where it is relevant. A dismissal following procedures that comply with the Code of Practice should satisfy the requirements of procedural fairness laid down in the Employment Act 2002, once these are brought into force, as the proposed statutory minimum provides a lower standard than that in the Code. It is anticipated that this will result in a general watering-down of standards of procedural fairness. The implications of failing to meet this lower standard are discussed below.

When is dismissal a reasonable response to misconduct? Obviously the standards of behaviour that will be tolerated will vary from one employment to another and will depend on the precise circumstances. This means that a great deal of discretion resides in management. It will normally be appropriate to start with some sort of warning, building up to dismissal if the warnings are ineffective. If such a procedure has been followed the dismissal will usually be reasonable. Nevertheless, if an employee has been treated more harshly than others in similar circumstances, dismissal might be substantively unreasonable even if the procedures were exemplary.

The ACAS Code recognizes the common law right of the employer to dismiss summarily for fundamental breaches of the contract of employment ('gross misconduct' in industrial relations parlance). Summary dismissal for gross misconduct is normally reserved for the most serious of offences, theft or violence etc, or for a wilful refusal to obey. In *Retarded Children's Society v Day*,[38] the conduct that led to dismissal did not itself amount to gross misconduct. Nevertheless, the employer was not unreasonable in dismissing without warning because it was clear that the employee did not accept the policy behind the rules that had led to him being disciplined, or that he had done anything wrong. In less serious cases warnings are generally necessary, but it is possible for the employer to signal that breaches of a particular requirement will be grounds for instant dismissal. So, for example, a catering company could use smoking to ground an instant dismissal as long as employees were aware of the probable consequences. Although it is hard to find authority on this point, it is suggested that this idea does not go so far as to say that any breach of rules, however minor, could be grounds for dismissal without warning or notice simply because the employer chooses to make it so. If this were the case, doubtless many employers would want to make even the most minor act of disobedience grounds for instant dismissal. But if there is a clear link between the rule and the needs of the business there is little doubt that an employee can be dismissed with little ceremony for an offence that would hardly be seen as a problem for a great many other employers. However, even in cases of gross misconduct there still needs to be sufficient investigation to be sure the misconduct is attributed correctly and, subject to changes that will result from the implementation of s.34 of the Employment Act 2002, post Polkey and Burchill (discussed below), most circumstances require an opportunity for the employee to explain or ask for mitigating circumstances to be taken into account.

Violence could hardly ever not be subject to disciplinary action, given the risk that recurrence poses to the health and safety of employees or others and the potential for criminal liability and damage to the employer's reputation. Any decision that fighting amounted to gross misconduct would be difficult to displace. Equally, theft is always a serious matter and, in the case of theft of the employer's property, probably always capable of amounting to gross misconduct. Misappropriation of very minor items might be dealt with through warnings but it is unlikely that an employer who moved to dismiss summarily would be seen as acting unreasonably as long as he or she acted consistently. What about misconduct including criminal offences of violence and dishonesty that takes place outside the workplace; when does this amount to grounds for dismissal? The basic rule is that an employee is entitled to treat his or her home life as separate from work except where misconduct has a bearing on the work situation. These issues will always be difficult ones and, as with other questions of reasonableness, it is for the ET to determine this as a question of fact. Where an employee is accused of a criminal offence it is also difficult to say exactly at what point an employer can reasonably dismiss. It is unlikely that a decision to dismiss simply because an employee had been charged with an offence would be reasonable, but a conviction for an offence that makes the employee unsuitable for the type of work they are employed to do would be difficult to displace.

It is for the employer, not the courts, to decide if an offence prevents an employee from being suitable for a particular type of work.[39] Further, although it might seem unfair, the standard required is not proof of the offence according to the criminal standard of beyond reasonable doubt or even the civil standard of the balance of probabilities. Rather it requires the employer to hold an honest belief in guilt based on reasonable evidence. The leading case, *BHS v Burchill*,[40] insisted that employees must be informed of the allegations and be given an opportunity to explain themselves, but if the employer has done so and has the requisite honest belief, the dismissal will be fair. It has been said that where an employee is caught red-handed the employer can dismiss without any consultation as long as she or he believed that nothing could have been said that would have made any difference to the decision to dismiss.[41] This seems like the reintroduction of the British Labour Pump doctrine that Polkey rejected. A subtle difference is that now reasonableness depends on the employer's state of mind at the time of dismissal rather than on hindsight. Finally on this point, the fact that the standard of reasonableness is honest belief based on reasonable suspicion gives rise to one of the clearest situations where the reasonableness of the employer's response can justify dismissal even though the effect on the employee is patently unfair. In *Monie v Coral Racing Ltd* and *Parr v Whitbread Ltd*,[42] theft from the employer had been narrowed down to, respectively, one of two and one of four employees. In both cases it was found to be reasonable to dismiss all of the employees. Although clearly unfair to the innocent individuals, a thorough investigation had been unable to narrow the suspicion further and the employer had acted reasonably in balancing the prejudice to the business against the unfairness to the individuals.

Redundancy

Although redundancy is a fair reason for dismissal, such a dismissal may nevertheless be unfair, either because the procedure for selecting who was to go was flawed, or because insufficient efforts have been made to find alternative employment, or because of lack of consultation.

Tribunals recognize that employers have an interest in retaining employees who will place the business in the best position to succeed. Leading authority can be found in *Williams v Compair Maxam*,[43] which emphasizes the need for selection methods that are analytical and capable of being applied impartially. Systems based on selection methods that were not transparent have led to findings of unfair dismissal. However, without access to information about the 'score' of those the company has retained, applicants may have an impossible task showing that a selection system has been applied unfairly. Nevertheless, tribunals have refused to allow applicants to go on a 'fishing expedition' for evidence of unfairness.[44] That a company cannot dismiss for redundancy fairly without considering redeployment is set out in *Vokes v Bear*.[45] How detailed the consideration should be will depend on the circumstances. A large organization making a small number of redundancies would be expected to give the matter serious thought. In the case of mass redundancies it will often be immediately obvious that redeployment is not a realistic option. The need for consultation is shown in cases such as Polkey and *Williams v Compair Maxam*. In some cases an employer has been required to consult with the employee individually and in others consultation with the trade union has been adequate. In the case of mass redundancies there are statutory requirements to consult with the trade union if there is one or with employee representatives if there is not (s.188 Trade Union and Labour Relations (Consolidation) Act 1992 (TULR(C)A).[46] Regardless of this statutory obligation, reasonableness requires consultation with both the union and the individual in some cases.[47]

Contravention of a statutory duty or restriction

In most cases these dismissals will be reasonable. Nevertheless, the requirement of reasonableness means that an employer would be expected to redeploy to an unrestricted post if this is feasible, or to give time for the employee to acquire any permission necessary to carry out the work.

Some other substantial reason

In Saunders[48] the dismissal of a gay man was found to be within the band of reasonable responses even though his unsuitability was based on a stereotyped view of his threat to children. Even though the employee had no contact with the children at his place of work, it was felt that other reasonable employers would have acted in the same way. Equally, in *Buck v Letchworth Palace* the dismissal of an employee whose colleagues would not work with him because he was gay was reasonable because it was felt that a significant proportion of other employers at that time would have reacted in the same way. This appalling situation might now be covered by the DDA, though not at the time of writing if the man was free from HIV infection or indeed had HIV infection but his condition was asymptomatic. It is to be hoped that in the years since this decision was made social attitudes have changed and that in future tribunals would be slow to accept this kind of behaviour and employer's reaction to it. Nevertheless, the band of reasonable responses test means that if employers generally would respond in this way the tribunal will struggle to find unreasonableness, however morally repugnant they personally find the response. Since Iceland, the tribunal can only move with attitudinal change, it cannot set the standard. The fact that reasonableness is contingent should not diminish the validity of the wider point that where continued employment makes managing the workforce impossible, it is likely that tribunals will find that decisions to dismiss are reasonable. The same is true of situations where difficulties are based on customer or client views that the employer does not necessarily agree with.[49]

Dismissal arising out of the need for economic reorganization will almost always be reasonable where the employer can point to a sound business need. However, as these dismissals frequently result from the failure to force through a unilateral change in contract, it is submitted that tribunals should insist on evidence of employers having weighed business needs against the prejudice to employees' contractual rights and on employers having consulted as appropriate. Nevertheless, Hollister insisted that the question is simply one of overall reasonableness per se.

The reasonableness of the ending of a fixed-term contract seems to be unaffected by the introduction of the Fixed-Term Employees (Prevention of Less Favourable Treatment) Regulations 2002,[50] implementing the provisions of the EU Framework Directive 1999/70 on Fixed-Term Work. These regulations provide that a fixed-term employee should not be treated less favourably than a comparable 'permanent' employee as regards the terms of the contract or by being subjected to any detriment unless this is objectively justified,[51] but dismissals covered by Part X of the Employment Rights Act 1996 (the dismissals under present consideration) are expressly excluded from the scope of the regulations by regulation 6(5). Thus it remains the case that the ending of a fixed-term contract might only be reasonable if consideration has been given to other positions the employee might fill.

AUTOMATICALLY UNFAIR DISMISSAL

In all of the cases discussed so far it has been for the employer to show what the reason for the dismissal is. However, if the employee can show that the reason was one of the reasons set out in ss.99–105 then it doesn't matter how reasonable the employer was in treating the reason as sufficient to justify dismissal, the dismissal is 'automatically unfair'. The burden of proof is a disincentive for employees to bring these cases, especially if the dismissal is clearly unfair anyway, but this remains useful where the case is clear and especially where employees do not have the continuity of service necessary to bring an ordinary claim under s.98.

These reasons all have links to other employment rights: s.99 dismissal for taking pregnancy, childbirth, maternity, parental and dependants' leave; in s.100 certain health and safety-related dismissals. In s.101 dismissal for the refusal of a protected worker to work on a Sunday. S.101A covers dismissals connected to working time, s.102 trustees of occupational pension schemes; and s.103 employee representatives under various statutory representation schemes. S.103A covers dismissal for a disclosure that is protected under the 'whistle-blowing' provisions in part IVA of the Act and s.104 persons who are dismissed for asserting a number of other statutory rights, including trade union rights. S.104A applies to dismissal of an employee who is taking action to enforce rights to the national minimum wage and s.104B to an employee who is trying to secure entitlement to a tax credit. Finally, in s.105 dismissals that take the form of selection for redundancy for any of these reasons are also automatically unfair.

In addition, a dismissal for a reason relating to a business transfer that is caught by the Transfer of Undertakings (Protection of Employment) Regulations 1981 is also automatically unfair. However, in many transfer-related cases employers will be able to take advantage of the defence in regulation 8(2) which provides that the dismissal is not automatically unfair if it is for an 'economic, technical or organizational reason' entailing changes in the workforce. Rather it will fall to be considered as SOSR. It is not anticipated that changes to the regulations required by the amendment of the Acquired Rights Directive in 1998 will alter this. Transfers on insolvency and take-overs designed to take advantage of economies of scale will be particularly apt to take advantage of this defence. The most recent addition to the family of auto-matically unfair dismissals is in regulation 6 of the Fixed-Term Employees (Prevention of Less Favourable Treatment) Regulations 2002. This provides that where an employee has been dismissed for a number of grounds spec-ified in the regulations the dismissal is automatically unfair.

By way of contrast, some dismissals are by definition always potentially fair. The dismissal of an employee who was engaged to cover maternity leave or a medical suspension is always dismissed for SOSR if they are dismissed to allow the employee they replaced to return to work. This only applies where notified in writing when the employment commenced. Of course this does not alleviate the employer of the responsibility of acting reasonably in treating the reason as sufficient to justify dismissal. Dismissal of striking workers is always fair as long as all those taking part in action at the time of dismissal are dismissed and there is no selective re-engagement of workers within three months of dismissal. However, the employer is not now allowed to dismiss strikers within the first eight weeks of protected industrial action, and such a dismissal is automatically unfair.[52] However, there is no jurisdiction for the tribunal to hear a case where the action is unofficial or in breach of statutory immunities, even where there have been selective dismissals. Dismissal for trade union membership or activity continues to be automatically unfair under s.152 TULR(C)A.

ILLEGALITY

A complicating factor, which can raise insuperable problems for employees, is the question of illegality. If the contract is illegal there is no prospect of claiming employment protection rights or indeed any other such rights. In *Broaders v Kalkare Property Maintenance*,[53] defrauding the employer over pay did not make a contract itself illegal (although it was relevant to whether a dismissal was unfair or not), whereas in *Salvesen v Simons*[54] arrangements which were designed to avoid tax liability made the contract illegal and no claim based on it could be brought to the ET. Employees who have entered such contracts knowingly will be deterred from bringing a claim for unfair dismissal for fear of triggering recovery of back taxes and possible prosecution. If this situation has arisen without their knowledge and the employer seeks to avoid liability by misrepresenting the relationship as one of self-employment, this can be resolved as a preliminary issue.

REMEDIES

The remedies for unfair dismissal are damages and/or an order for reinstatement or re-engagement. These need to be considered separately.

Damages

The award is calculated in two parts, a basic award and a compensatory award. The basic award is based on a multiplier that is also used to calculate redundancy payments. This provides,[55] 0.5, 1 or 1.5 weeks' pay for each completed year of service, depending on the employee's age. The weekly amount is subject to a statutory maximum, which is uprated annually.[55] In redundancy cases the basic award is reduced by any redundancy payment. In cases of dismissal for being, or not being, a trade union member, and for some of the other reasons that give rise to automatic unfair dismissal, there is a statutory minimum basic award.

The compensatory award is based on the losses the employee has suffered as a result of the dismissal. The calculation (which is based on net pay) includes loss of earnings to the date of the hearing and an estimate of the lost value of other benefits such as the use of a company car and medical insurance etc. The employee can also recover some future loss. If the applicant is still unemployed at the date of hearing, future loss is based on the number of additional weeks of unemployment that the tribunal estimate will arise out of the dismissal. Future loss should also include an assessment of the value of loss of future pension rights. It may be that some losses that have arisen following the dismissal are not fairly attributable to it. In these cases the award can be minimal, for example where dismissal was unfair due to purely procedural defects and the dismissal would have taken place anyway. Where there is a failure to consult on redundancy and/or a failure to give time to consider redeployment, the usual approach is to award a further two weeks' compensation to represent the time that the contract would have continued while this was being considered. Where there has been a failure to consult on mass redundancy under the regulations, this will give rise to the possibility of a 'protective' award of up to an extra 90 days' wages for each affected employee. The claim must be initiated by a trade union or elected representative, but can be enforced by the employee if payment is not made (ss.189–192 TULR(C)A). Further compensation can be awarded for the loss of accrued rights such as employment protection rights, which will have to be earned from scratch with a new employer. There is no compensation for the undoubted distress that many employees suffer as a result of being dismissed unfairly, but if there is monetary loss arising out of damage to reputation caused by the manner of the dismissal this can be recovered.[56]

As the award is based on actual loss if the employee quickly finds a new job at, or close to, the same rate of pay, the compensatory award will be minimal. Nevertheless, there is no deduction for pay that the employee receives from a new employer during what would have been the statutory notice period. Since this is a windfall that can easily accrue where the contract is terminated lawfully, as a matter of policy it is not acceptable to have a rule which penalizes an employee who takes up a new post as soon as possible. However, where there has been a payment in lieu of notice or any ex gratia payment, these are deductible. These measures aim to ensure that compensation reflects actual losses, but tribunals can reduce both the basic award and the compensatory award to reflect the fact that the employee caused, or contributed in some material way to, the dismissal. The reduction is by 'such proportion as [the tribunal] considers just and equitable'. A reduction is common in cases where there has been misconduct. Following the decision in *W. Devis & Sons Ltd. v Atkins* that 'after discovered' misconduct cannot prevent the dismissal being unfair,[57] this is particularly useful where a dismissal could have been lawful if the employer had known of misconduct that was discovered later. A fixed amount of two weeks' pay is to be added or subtracted from the award where the employee was either prevented from exercising an internal right of appeal or failed to exercise a right of appeal that the employer had notified the employee of. Once the provisions of the Employment Act 2002 are brought into force, this will give employers and employees strong financial incentives to take advantage of internal disciplinary and grievance procedures of at least the new statutory minimum standard before initiating a tribunal case. Failure to use the procedures or to allow the use of procedures will result in a deduction from, or addition to, compensation of at least 10 per cent and up to a possible maximum of 50 per cent.

There is an upper limit on the total amount of compensation. Over the lifetimes of successive Conservative governments the real value was reduced to the point where, at £12,000 in 1997, even a maximum award bore hardly any restraining effect on the behaviour of many employers. The ERelA raised the global ceiling on compensation to £50,000 and the maximum amounts, including the maximum week's pay that forms the basis of the calculations, were index linked at the same time.

Reinstatement and re-engagement

The legislation sees the re-employment of the dismissed employee as the primary remedy for unfair dismissal. This can be reinstatement, where the employee is returned to the position they would have been in if the dismissal had never taken place. Or it can be re-engagement, where the employee is given a comparable position on terms and conditions as close to those that would apply on reinstatement as is reasonably practicable. In practice, however, these remedies are given in only a tiny proportion of successful cases. This reflects the reality that having gone through litigation, whatever remained of the relationship is often beyond repair, with neither the employer nor the employee having the desire to resume business as usual. If an employee wishes to be reinstated and this, or re-engagement, is ordered, it is open for the employer to refuse to take the employee back, but this will give rise to extra compensation of between 26 and 52 weeks' wages if the employee applies for it.

SOME FINAL POINTS

Informal resolution

Although it is not open to an employer to 'contract out' of employment protection legislation, many cases are concluded without the need for the matter to be heard and determined in full by the tribunal. A settlement that is negotiated with the aid of ACAS is binding on the parties and cannot in general be reopened by the employee. A settlement that is negotiated without the aid of ACAS can also be binding if it takes the form of a compromise agreement. This must be in writing, must relate to particular proceedings and the employee must have received independent advice from an approved range of advisers, particularly on the status and effect of the agreement itself. An alternative to informal resolution is a voluntary arbitration procedure created by ACAS under s.212A TULR(C)A inserted by the Employment Rights (Dispute Resolution) Act 1998. Cases can be referred for binding arbitration to an arbitrator supplied by ACAS. The referral is made as part of a voluntary settlement negotiated with the aid of an ACAS conciliator or as part of a valid compromise agreement. As yet, there is little sign that this alternative is being used widely (see Chapter 12).

As noted earlier, the Employment Act 2002 will introduce for the first time a requirement that all employers have minimum disciplinary and grievance procedures in place. This will be a statutory term of all contracts of employment. The new minimum standards for disciplinary procedures will entitle an employee to a meeting to discuss their situation prior to a decision to dismiss or the determination of a grievance and to a limited form of appeal against dismissal. Both the new emphasis on internal resolution and the availability of arbitration are designed to reduce the number of cases that need to be resolved at tribunal. Given the low rates of reinstatement and re-engagement, these initiatives will prove particularly welcome if they enable employers and employees to reconcile their differences and allow relationships that are damaged irretrievably under the current system to be rescued or revived. Whether this will prove to be the outcome is far from clear at the time of writing, however. The concern is that the new provisions are more likely to unjustifiably restrict the ability of employees to assert their rights.[58]

Costs

There is no fee to be paid to bring a claim. DTI consultation prior to the passage of the Employment Act 2002 through Parliament proposed a fee to deter unfounded claims,[59] but given the uncertainties that abound in the law of unfair dismissal it is arguable that this is as likely to put off well-founded claims as ill-founded ones. In the event, the consultation resulted in the proposals not being brought forward. In the majority of cases there is also no award of costs against the unsuccessful party. This has led to a view by some employers that it is too easy for ex-employees to bring vindictive claims that have little prospect of success but are cheaper to settle than defend. A way of trying to reduce the need for a full hearing is through the system of pre-hearings. If this shows one side has little prospect of success an order can be made that will leave that party open to the possibility of an award of the other side's costs against them if they decide to proceed regardless and lose the case. In addition to the risk of costs, the tribunal can make an order that a deposit must be paid before continuing with the application or the response.[60] Once brought into force, the Employment Act 2002 will introduce a much wider discretion in the ET (and the EAT) to award costs. The detail will be in the regulations made under these provisions, but a significant addition is the fact that the Act empowers the making of regulations to allow recovery of costs from a representative where his or her conduct of proceedings justifies this. There is no financial aid for representation at the tribunal hearing, but advice can be obtained through the Community Legal Service 'Legal Help' scheme, subject to financial eligibility. In practice, much help and advice are provided to applicants either through trade unions or through advice agencies such as Citizens Advice Bureaux. Suggestions that financial help for legal representation would improve the quality of justice in the ET have been rejected by the Report of the Leggat Review of Tribunals.[61] However, it may be that a new overriding duty in the Employment Tribunal (Constitution and Procedure) Regulations 2001, that rules of procedure are to be used to deal with cases justly, will address some of these issues. Dealing with a case justly is said to include, as far as practicable: ensuring that the parties are on an equal footing; saving expense; dealing with the case in ways which are proportionate to the complexity of the issues; and ensuring that it is dealt with expeditiously and fairly (Regulations 10(1) and 10(2)). How effective this will be in addressing the underlying issues remains to be seen.

Notes

1 All statutory references in this chapter are to the Employment Rights Act 1996 unless specified otherwise.
2 The Employment Relations Act 1998 reduced this from two years following the *Fairness at Work* White Paper cm 3968.
3 [1994] IRLR 176.
4 The other advantage of many of these claims is that the compensation regimes are less restrictive.
5 *Nash v Mash/Roe Group* [1998] IRLR 168, a decision at the level of the Employment Tribunal held that it was.
6 At the time of writing, only one scheme had received this designation; this applies to the electrical contracting industry.
7 At the time of writing, the possible use of this power is subject to DTI consultation, but it is too early to predict possible outcomes. Discussion document on employment status in relation to statutory rights: http://www.dti.gov.uk/er/individual/statusdiscuss.pdf
8 Discussed *Supra*.
9 Until 2002 redundancy waivers were still possible; this has been repealed by Para.3(15) of the Fixed-Term Employee (Prevention of Less Favourable Treatment) Regulations 2002 SI 2034/2002.
10 [1978] IRLR 27.
11 *Smith v Glasgow City Council* [1987] ICR 796.
12 It must also be ignored in determining whether the reason was sufficient to justify dismissal.
13 *Morse v Wiltshire CC* [1998] IRLR 352.

14 The EU Framework Directive 2000/78 on Equal Treatment in Employment will require this bar to be removed by December 2006.

15 See *International Sports Co. v Thomson* below.

16 *Moon v Homeworthy Furniture (Northern) Ltd* [1976] IRLR 298.

17 *Johnson v Nottinghamshire Combined Police Authority* [1974] IRLR 20.

18 [1979] IRLR 238.

19 [1984] IRLR 329.

20 [1975] IRLR 247.

21 (1986) Discussed in Pitt, G (2000) *Employment Law,* 4th edn, Sweet & Maxwell, London, where she observes that the provisions of s.107 ERA seem not to have been considered in this case.

22 [1980] IRLR 174.

23 [1987] IRLR 503.

24 [1979] IRLR 94.

25 [2001] IRLR 275.

26 The Act inserts a new s.98A to this effect into the ERA.

27 See Hepple, B and Morris, G (2002) The Employment Act 2002 and the crisis of individual employment rights, Industrial Law Journal, **31**, pp 245–69 for a stinging assault on the impact of these measures.

28 [1982] IRLR 439.

29 [2000] IRLR 288.

30 [2001] IRLR 827, and the case it was joined with in the Court of Appeal, *HSBC (formerly Midland Bank) v Madden* [2000] 2 All ER 741 (EAT).

31 [1977] ICR 506.

32 [1976]IRLR 373.

33 [1980] IRLR 340.

34 [1973] ICR 245.

35 [1978] IRLR 82.

36 A new Code of Practice came into effect in September 2000.

37 [1998] IRLR 358.

38 [1978] ICR 437.

39 *McClaren v NCB* [1988] IRLR 215.

40 As confirmed by the Court of Appeal in *Foley v Post Office*, which confirms the essential requirement of procedural fairness as laid down in *Polkey*.

41 *Duffy v Yeomans & Partners Ltd.* [1994] IRLR 642; actually a redundancy case.

42 [1980] IRLR 464 and [1990] IRLR 39.

43 [1982] IRLR 83.

44 *British Aerospace v Green* [1995] IRLR 433.

45 [1973] IRLR 363.

46 As amended by Collective Redundancies and Transfer of Undertakings (Protection of Employment)(Amendment) Regulations 1995 and 1999.

47 *Walls Meat Co Ltd. v Selby* [1989] ICR 601.

48 Op cit.

49 Subject to s.107 discussed above.
50 SI 2002/2034.
51 Reg. 3(1).
52 S.237 and 238 Trade Union and Labour relations (Consolidation) Act 1992 and S.238A (as inserted by the Employment Relations Act 1999).
53 [1990] IRLR 421.
54 [1994] IRLR 52.
55 £250 p.w. from February 2002.
56 Controversially, the House of Lords in the wrongful dismissal case *Johnson v Unisys* [2001] 2 All ER 801 used the existence of the unfair dismissal regime as a reason not to allow the common law remedy to develop to embrace damages for distress caused where the manner of the dismissal amounted to a breach of the implied term of the contract of employment of mutual trust and confidence.
57 [1977] IRLR 314, *cf. Boston Deep Sea Fishing v Ansell* (1888) 39 Ch D 339 for wrongful dismissal.
58 See Hepple and Morris *n. 27*.
59 *Routes to resolution: improving dispute resolution in Britain* http://www.dti.gov.uk/er/individual/resolution.pdf.
60 Increased to a maximum of £500 by the Employment Tribunal (Constitution and Procedure) Regulations 2001 SI 2001/1171.
61 Tribunals for Users – One System, One Service. http://www.tribunals-review.org.uk/.

7

Collective rights: recognition, representation and industrial action

Graeme Lockwood and Kevin Williams

INTRODUCTION

Between 1979 and 1997 successive Conservative governments sought to reduce the collective rights of trade unions. The Conservatives believed that trade unions had an adverse impact on labour costs, introduced restrictive practices and engaged in costly strikes disrupting economic performance. Collective labour law was accordingly subjected to scrutiny. Provisions allowing trade unions to claim recognition from employers were repealed, legal support for the closed shop removed and taking industrial action lawfully was made more difficult. However, European requirements led to some extension of consultation rights that would not otherwise have been introduced.

The election of a Labour government in 1997 marked a fresh approach to collective arrangements involving trade unions. To date, the government has accepted various aspects of European social policy, introduced a recognition procedure, amended the consultation provisions on collective redundancies and transfers of undertakings, and made minor changes to the law surrounding industrial action. Whilst these initiatives are not as far-reaching as unions might have wished, most would not have occurred at all under a Conservative government.

This chapter commences with an examination of the present legislative provisions on trade union recognition, followed by an analysis of the representation rights of recognized trade unions. In the final section, an account of the law regulating the conduct of industrial action is provided.

TRADE UNION RECOGNITION

For some years and for a variety of reasons, including industrial restructuring and other changes in the labour market, trade union membership levels and the practice of collective bargaining have been declining. Between 1990 and 1998, the Workplace Employee Relations Survey was reporting a fall in workplaces with union members from 64 to 54 per cent (Cully *et al*, 1999). However, of the 54 per cent, more than four-fifths of employers recognized one or more unions. Furthermore, because of European Union rules designed to promote consultation, even employers who recognize no unions whatsoever may find that they are legally obliged to consult their workforces about certain matters, including collective redundancies, business transfers, and health and safety.

Where recognition has been voluntarily conceded, the list of bargaining topics is usually set out in a formal agreement. Conventionally, such agreements are not normally intended as legally enforceable contracts,[1] one consequence of which is that employers are subsequently free to change their minds and de-recognize the union (Beaumont and Harris, 1995). Section 178 of the Trade Union and Labour Relations (Consolidation) Act 1992 (TULR(C)A) defines collective bargaining as 'negotiations related to or connected with' one or more matters, including terms and conditions of employment, hiring and firing, job duties and the allocation of work, discipline, facilities for union officials, and procedures for negotiation and consultation. A union can properly claim to be recognized by an employer whether it negotiates about all or only some of these bargaining topics. However, an employer who only allows a union to represent its members at disciplinary or grievance hearings is only conceding partial recognition. Nowadays, all workers have an independent statutory right to be accompanied at such hearings by a work colleague of their choice or an official of their union.[2]

Being recognized confers on a union a number of significant legal entitlements, provided it is 'independent', meaning that it is not under the domination or control of an employer nor liable to interference tending towards such control. These include the right to receive information for bargaining purposes and to be consulted about redundancy proposals and the transfer of an employer's undertaking. These matters are considered later. Additionally, members and officials of recognized unions are entitled to time off work to participate in union activities and duties, respectively.[3]

Quite apart from these legal consequences, voluntary recognition has always been a matter of great practical significance in industrial relations terms. Naturally, trade unions aspire to achieve recognition in order to represent their members' interests most effectively. In the past, disputes about recognition have been resolved without recourse to law, apart from two brief periods in the 1970s. Between 1972 and 1974 under the Industrial Relations Act 1971, and then between 1976 and 1980 under the Employment Protection Act 1975, two rather different statutory recognition procedures operated. For different reasons, neither was successful. Notwithstanding this somewhat inauspicious experience, in 1998 the new Labour administration announced its intention to provide a scheme of compulsory recognition for the 'very small minority of cases' where voluntary agreement was not forthcoming. The reasons given in the White Paper, *Fairness at Work* (DTI, 1998), included the need to offer greater protection to vulnerable workers, the desirability of providing an alternative to disruptive industrial action, and the claim that businesses that ignore the wishes of a substantial group of workers for union representation would be unlikely to establish the kind of successful partnerships necessary to cope with market-led demands (DTI, 1998: para 4.12). The necessary legislation was enacted in 1999.

The statutory recognition procedure

The Employment Relations Act 1999, by inserting a new Schedule A1 into TULR(C)A 1992, created a procedure for compulsory recognition with effect from 6 June 2000. Broadly, this highly technical scheme of 172 paragraphs allows one or more independent trade unions to seek recognition over 'pay, hours and holidays' or such other matters as the parties may agree (para 3). Only employers (and 'associated' employers) with 21 or more workers are caught (para 7). This threshold requirement probably excludes some eight million people (about 30 per cent of the total workforce) but was justified by government on the basis that compulsory recognition might be harmful to the management of very small businesses.[4] Voluntary recognition by such employers is rare.

The scheme is designed to encourage the parties to settle their differences amicably (with the help of ACAS if necessary). According to the preceding White Paper (para 4.10), voluntary agreements 'are most likely to be successful and suited to the needs of the enterprise'. In default, a union must make a written request for recognition to the employer, indicating the 'bargaining unit' it wishes to represent (para 4). Tight time limits are laid down for every stage of the process. If no acceptance is forthcoming, the union then applies to the Central Arbitration Committee (CAC)[5] to decide whether the proposed (or some other) bargaining unit is appropriate (paras 11 and 12). Unless the CAC is able 'to help the parties' reach agreement on this critical question, the Committee must settle the issue, taking into account above all 'the need for the unit to be compatible with effective management'.

The CAC may also have regard to the views of the parties, existing bargaining arrangements, and the desirability of avoiding small fragmented bargaining units, as well as the characteristics and location of workers in the proposed bargaining unit or elsewhere (paras 18 and 19). In order to keep out speculative bids for recognition, the CAC must be satisfied that the applicant union's members constitute at least 10 per cent of the workers in the bargaining unit. Moreover, a majority in the unit must 'be likely to favour recognition', though quite how the CAC is to establish this is not made clear (paras 14 and 36). Seemingly it may draw on survey evidence as well as the industrial experience of its panel members. The CAC cannot proceed with an application where another union already has negotiating rights in respect of some workers in the proposed bargaining unit, even if that union lacks a certificate of independence (para 35), opening up the opportunity for blocking 'sweetheart' deals.[6]

Thereafter, the degree of worker support, as demonstrated in a secret ballot, is the key to success. The ballot, which need not be postal and is funded jointly by the employer and the union, must be conducted by a 'qualified independent person' asking the workers whether they want the applicant union to bargain on their behalf. Where the union already has a majority of workers in the bargaining unit in membership, the CAC must ordinarily make a declaration in favour of recognition without resort to a ballot, unless any one of three 'qualifying conditions' is fulfilled. These are that it is 'in the interests of good industrial relations' that a ballot should be held, alternatively that a 'significant number' of members have told the CAC that they do not want to be represented by their union (which seems unlikely) or, thirdly, that there is other evidence raising doubts about the wishes of the workforce (para 22). In order to be successful in the ballot, a majority of those voting, *and* at least 40 per cent of those eligible to vote, must vote for recognition (para 29). Abstentions accordingly count against the union. If a ballot is lost, the union cannot reapply to the CAC to represent substantially the same bargaining unit for a further three years.

In an attempt to ensure that the process runs smoothly and with the maximum degree of participation, employers are required to cooperate generally in the conduct of the ballot. In particular, they must supply workers' details to the CAC and allow the union reasonable access to staff in order to canvas support (para 26 and the *Code of Practice on Access to Workers during Recognition or De-recognition Ballots*). The CAC may sanction an employer's failure to cooperate by declaring that the applicant union is recognized without the need for a ballot (para 27). It was the absence of any comparable duty on employers that proved to be one of the fatal flaws in the recognition scheme introduced by the 1975 Act and which led to its repeal.[7] Employers who put improper pressure on workers because of their participation in the recognition process (as by voting, etc) risk tribunal proceedings claiming detrimental treatment or automatically unfair dismissal, though the latter remedy is open only to those contracted to work as employees (paras 156–164).

Where a ballot is won by the special majority vote, the CAC must declare the union recognized. If the two sides are unable to agree how to implement the declaration, the CAC may impose a 'method by which they are to conduct collective bargaining'.[8] This takes effect 'as if it were contained in a legally enforceable contract made by the parties' (para 31). The duty so created is only to meet and talk, and only then about 'pay, hours and holidays', rather than the full range of issues identified in the definition of collective bargaining in s.178 of the 1992 Act.[9] There is no duty to bargain in good faith (as there is in the United States), much less to reach agreement, and neither ACAS nor CAC have power to compel the arbitration of any disputed issue. Failure to conduct talks according to the prescribed method entitles the union to apply to a court for an order that the employer 'specifically perform' his or her obligations. No damages are available. Specific performance is declared to be the 'only remedy', though a continued failure might be sanctioned as a contempt of court.

A declaration of recognition ordinarily lasts for three years, and no employer can withdraw unilaterally. However, in defined circumstances, an employer (or dissatisfied workers in the bargaining unit) may invoke a de-recognition procedure by making an application to the CAC.

It is too soon to say with any certainty what will be the long-term effects of legislating in this manner. The early survey evidence suggests that there was a marked increase in voluntary recognition immediately prior to, and during the first year of, the statutory scheme (IDS Report 836, 2001). Most deals were struck at local level, usually conferring full recognition on a single union. Publishing, transport and electronics were especially active. Only 80 applications were received by the CAC in the first year, fewer than many had expected. The complexity of the statutory scheme appears to have persuaded many employers and unions to favour the voluntary route.[10] There is some evidence that the slide in union membership had been halted prior to, and independently of, the introduction of the statutory procedure (Hicks, 2000), though it may also be that an increased awareness of the benefits of recognition and the possibility of legal enforcement have persuaded more recruits to join. It is also possible that the mere existence of the statutory procedure will discourage hostile employers from pursuing de-recognition strategies or moving to so-called individual bargaining. To date, fears that such employers would resort to US-style 'union-busting' lawyers and tactics appear to have been unfounded, though resort to judicial review to challenge unwelcome or contentious decisions by the CAC remains a possibility.[11] The government committed itself to revising the procedure should that prove to be necessary, and in July 2002 the DTI announced an intention to review its operation. It remains to be seen whether the statutory recognition scheme will prove to be a turning point in the fortunes of trade unions.

TRADE UNION REPRESENTATION RIGHTS

As mentioned earlier, recognized unions have certain rights. These are considered below.

Disclosure of information for collective bargaining

Provision for legally based disclosure of information for collective bargaining was first outlined in Labour's 1968 White Paper, *In Place of Strife*, but was enacted in the Conservatives' Industrial Relations Act 1971. These provisions, only marginally amended, were re-enacted in 1975, backed up by a Code of Practice from ACAS. Despite a proposal from the Conservatives to repeal the legislation in 1996 (DTI, 1996), the law survived and is now contained in ss.181–185 of TULR(C)A 1992.

Under s.181 (2), an employer is obliged to disclose information (a) without which a union would be materially impeded in collective bargaining and (b) which it would be in accordance with good industrial relations practice to disclose. However, a precondition has to be satisfied. Bargaining must be about matters and in relation to workers in respect of which the union is recognized by the employer. Employers are exempted under section 182 (1) from supplying certain types of information. There need be no disclosure which (a) would be against the interests of national security, (b) illegal, (c) a breach of confidence, (d) relates specifically to an individual, (e) would cause substantial injury to an employer's undertaking for reasons other than its effect on collective bargaining or (f) relates to legal proceedings. There are two further restrictions on union rights under s.182 (2) (a) and (b). First, employers need not disclose information, the compilation of which would involve a disproportionate amount of work. Second, they need not provide documents other than those specifically prepared for the purpose of providing the information.

The Act is supplemented by an ACAS Code of Practice. This lists items which might be relevant to collective bargaining under the headings of pay and benefits, conditions of service, manpower, and performance and financial matters. A second list contains items which might cause substantial injury to the employers, such as cost information on individual products, detailed analyses of proposed investment, sales, or prices, and quotes on the make-up of tender prices. The Code states that substantial injury may occur if customers or suppliers would be lost (ACAS, 1977).

If a union considers that an employer has failed to meet the statutory requirements, it may complain to the CAC. If the complaint cannot be settled by conciliation, the Committee must hear it and declare whether the complaint is well founded. If it is, the Committee must specify the information that should be provided and a timetable for disclosure. If the employer still fails to disclose, the union may bring a further complaint, which again may issue a declaration.[12] On a further failure, the union may ask the CAC to incorporate certain improvements in terms and conditions into the contracts of relevant employees.[13] The CAC may make an award, either for the improvements desired by the union or such other terms and conditions as it considers appropriate.[14] This then becomes an implied term in each individual employee's contract of employment.[15]

A significant weakness of the statutory provisions is that the tests and exemptions are extensive, restrictive and somewhat unbalanced. They inhibit union claims for information and provide employers with too wide a range of arguments against disclosure.

Consultation on redundancies and business transfers

In response to European Directives, domestic law obliges employers to disclose information to recognized unions (or to employee representatives) in the event of redundancies and business transfers. These obligations are the result of the Collective Redundancies Directive (75/129/EEC) and the Acquired Rights Directive (77/187/EEC as amended by 98/50/EC). The former was originally enacted into UK law by the Employment Protection Act 1975 and the latter by the Transfer of Undertaking (Protection of Employment) Regulations 1981 (TUPE). The original provisions have been amended several times since. The current provisions are contained in the Trade Union and Labour Relations (Consolidation) Act 1992. TULR(C)A 1992 specifies the information to be disclosed: the reasons for the redundancies, the number to be dismissed, the methods of selection and implementation, and the calculation of redundancy payments.[16] The legislation requires the employer to give a reasoned reply to any representations that might be made. If an employer fails to consult and disclose, the trade union can present a collective complaint to an employment tribunal, which can make a 'protective award'.[17]

In relation to redundancy consultation, s.188 of TULR(C)A requires an employer who is *proposing* to make 20 or more employees redundant within a 90-day period to consult with trade unions or employee representatives in good time, before the dismissals take effect. Section 188 TULR(C)A is intended to enact the EC Collective Redundancies Directive. Article 2 (1) of the directive states that if an employer is *contemplating* redundancies, consultation must begin in good time. This raises the question of what is the difference between contemplating and proposing redundancies.

In the case of *MSF v Refuge Assurance* [2002] IRLR 324, it was held that an employer 'contemplates' collective redundancies when it first envisages the possibility that redundancies may have to be made. However, a 'proposal' relates to a state of mind much more certain and further along the decision-making process. UK law is therefore incompatible with the Directive, since it currently permits consultation to begin at a later stage than the Directive would allow.

However, in *Middlesbrough Borough Council* v *TGWU* [2002] IRLR 332 the Employment Appeal Tribunal (EAT) made it clear that an employer must not have made a firm decision on the proposed redundancies when consultation begins, since this would give rise to a claim for compensation for failure to inform and/or consult. In the Middlesbrough Council case, the employer decided that the only answer to its significant financial problems was to make redundancies. The union was notified of this and consulted on proposed redundancies. However, no consultation took place on the decision to implement the redundancy programme affecting 352 staff. The EAT held that this was a breach of the requirement under both the Directive and UK law to consult about ways of avoiding the dismissals. It was no defence for the employer to state that redundancies were inevitable and that consultation would make no difference. The duties to consult are mandatory.

The disclosure obligations relating to business transfers provide that, before a relevant transfer, the employer should inform appropriate representatives of the following matters: the reasons for the transfer and its timing; the legal, economic and social implications for the employees concerned; measures the employer might take in relation to the affected employees; and measures which the transferor envisages the transferee might take in relation to the employees.[18] The duty to furnish information is activated when a transfer is proposed, and the obligation to give information applies to all the above issues.[19] If an employer fails to inform or consult, the union or affected employee may present a complaint to an employment tribunal.[20]

For the obligation to consult to arise, the employer must have formulated some definite plan or proposal on which it is intended to act as opposed to mere projections or forecasts. It has also been stated that in a developing situation, for reasons beyond an employer's control, measures might only be envisaged at a late stage. In that situation, if there was insufficient time for effective consultation to take place before the transfer, the employer could not be criticized. Furthermore, the obligation to consult is restricted to the subject matter of the proposed measures and not the other heads listed in Regulation 10 (2) TUPE 1981.[21] These restrictions on information disclosure may result in the employer unnecessarily withholding highly relevant information that would be of value to employees and their representatives.

In the case of both collective redundancy and business transfers, the law was amended in response to the 1994 European Court of Justice decision that the UK had, by restricting consultation to recognized trade unions, failed properly to implement the Directives.[22] That decision led to the Collective Redundancies and Transfer of Undertakings (Protection of Employment) (Amendment) Regulations 1995.[23] The 1995 regulations amended the consultation provisions in TULR(C)A and in the TUPE Regulations. They provided that employers must consult either a recognized trade union *or* employee representatives elected in advance or ad hoc. The 1995 regulations were, however, thought to have several significant shortcomings. First, in relation to the timing of disclosure, they provided that employers 'shall consult in good time', rather than at the earliest opportunity. Second, they were framed in a way that jeopardized the position of recognized trade unions. Employers could bypass such unions and instead choose to inform and consult only worker representatives who had been elected via a process which the employer might potentially influence. Furthermore, the 1995 Regulations introduced the provision that employers need not disclose information or consult if fewer than 20 people were to be made redundant at any one establishment. Whilst this is consistent with the threshold contained in the Collective Redundancies Directive, it represents a retrograde step since UK law had originally required consultation regardless of the number of dismissals.

As the result of criticism of the 1995 regulations, the Labour government introduced new rules concerning employers' obligations. They are contained in the Collective Redundancies and Transfer of Undertakings (Protection of Employment) (Amendment) Regulations 1999, which clarify what needs to be done by employers to undertake genuine consultation. First, in relation to redundancies, the representatives of all employees who might be affected need to be consulted and not just those to be made redundant. This enlarges the scope of consultation since employers must now consult over the consequential impact on 'survivor' employees on matters such as work organization and workload (Hall and Edwards, 1999). Second, employers who recognize a trade union must now consult that union and cannot bypass it by consulting other representatives instead. This provision applies to both redundancies and business transfers. Third, it is made clear that consultation may take place exclusively with other representatives only in cases where there is no recognized union. In such circumstances, the regulations prescribe specific requirements for the election of employee representatives. Employers are responsible for operating fair elections. Employees who believe that an election does not accord with the legal requirements can complain to an employment tribunal. Fourth, the regulations provide employee representatives with specific rights for time off for training. Finally, where employers fail to comply with the regulations, the remedies are simplified and strengthened.

However, these changes have not remedied all of the previous weaknesses. Employers are still only required to consult 'in good time' (not 'at the earliest opportunity'), and only then if the redundancy proposals affect 20 or more workers.[24]

Consultation over health and safety

Under the Health and Safety at Work etc Act 1974 and related regulations (many derived from European Directives), employers are under a general duty to consult safety representatives appointed by recognized trade unions.[25] As part of this process, employers must disclose specified inf͟ mation and in this case non-compliance may, in theory, result in fines.

Disclosure of information on pensions

Pensions law[26] requires the disclosure of basic information to members of contracted-out schemes and their trade unions. However, the provisions are very specific and do not constitute a significant extension of information rights. Comprehensive information and consultation rights are especially important in this domain if trade unions and employee representatives are to be in a position to safeguard the interests of their members.

Information and consultation on training

Section 5 of the Employment Relations Act 1999 entitles a recognized trade union that meets certain qualifying conditions to be consulted on training. In particular, trade union representatives should be consulted about the employer's policy and forthcoming plans as well as being informed about training previously provided.

The European dimension

Trade unions may also benefit from European Union rules that have the stated aim of improving information and consultation rights for workers. These provisions may represent a significant new route to increased cooperation in multinational companies as well as an opportunity for trade unions to indirectly influence the strategic decision making of corporations.

The Transnational Information and Consultation of Employees Regulations 1999[27] implement the European Works Council (EWC) Directive (94/45/EC). Undertakings or groups of undertakings with at least 1,000 employees, and with at least 150 employees in establishments in two different member states, must establish an EWC or an alternative employee information and consultation procedure. Central management must meet at least once a year with the EWC for the purposes of consultation and the provision of information on the basis of a report drawn up by management. Additionally, in exceptional circumstances such as the closure of an establishment, there should be extra *ad hoc* information disclosure and consultation meetings as soon as is possible.

In March 2002, an Information and Consultation Directive (2002/14/EC) concerning companies operating in only one member state became effective. It has yet to be transposed into domestic law and, in fact, the UK will be able to apply the Directive in three delayed stages. In the first instance, undertakings with 150 or more employees must be covered by March 2005. After a further two years, it will extend to undertakings with 100 or more, and by March 2009 to all those with more than 50 employees. The Directive gives employees in these undertakings a right to be informed about the undertaking's economic situation, and to be informed and consulted about employment prospects and decisions that are likely to lead to substantial changes in the organization of work or contractual relations. The transposition of the Directive into UK law will depend on political circumstances, and the debate will be along a spectrum of what Wedderburn (1997) has described as 'soft' and 'strong' rights.

The existing law on disclosure seems to have had a small, but positive impact on the flow of information in both collective bargaining and joint consultation. There is, however, a continuing tension between the traditional UK approach to disclosure and representation based on collective bargaining with recognized unions, and the alternative approach derived largely from European Union approaches to consultation (Hall, 1996). Indeed, there is a possibility that the one may displace the other. The two approaches are often portrayed as dichotomous. In practice, unions may view them as complementary and seek to utilize both to produce a comprehensive framework of information, bargaining, and consultation rights for employees and their representatives.

The potential strength of disclosure for collective bargaining to recognized trade unions is that, being continuing associations that are independent of employers with expertise and resources beyond the particular workplace, they have the organizational capability to use the information most effectively. However, given the shrinkage of collective bargaining and the growth of non-union workplaces, consultation with ad hoc workers' representatives has become more important in recent years. The legal framework should aim to provide disclosure of worthwhile information for collective bargaining wherever possible and, where this is not possible, the provision of information for joint consultation (Gospel, Lockwood and Willman, 2000).

INDUSTRIAL ACTION

Industrial action can manifest itself in various forms, including the all-out strike, the overtime ban, go-slow, work-to-rule, and picketing. Historically, it was almost impossible for industrial action to be organized without infringing some common law rule. Most forms of industrial action constitute a breach of contract on the part of the worker, while organizing it constitutes one or more of the economic torts, such as inducing breach of contract, intimidation, and conspiracy. Picketing may involve trespass or nuisance as well as crimes such as obstructing the highway or a police officer in the execution of his or her duty.

The Conspiracy and Protection of Property Act 1875 gave trade union members some protection by removing criminal liability for conspiracy from those who participated in a trade dispute. However, this did not protect trade unions themselves or their members from civil law actions, thus putting union funds in jeopardy.[28] The Trade Disputes Act 1906 attempted to rectify this by giving those who organized or took part in industrial action a limited immunity in tort where action was taken 'in contemplation or furtherance of a trade dispute' (the so-called 'golden formula'). The Industrial Relations Act 1971 restricted this immunity, though it was subsequently restored by the Labour government's Trade Union Labour and Relations Acts of 1974 and 1976.

When the Conservatives took office in 1979, after the events of the so-called 'winter of discontent', the trade union movement was portrayed as too powerful, out of control, and acting contrary to the national interest. The new government, therefore, embarked on a step-by-step process of legal reform substantially restricting the trade unions' ability to engage in lawful industrial action. A total of five statutes in ten years removed the immunity of unions from suit, narrowed the definition of a trade dispute, mandated strike ballots, and made all secondary action unlawful. With the passing of so much legislation, there was considerable scope for a rationalization and the law was eventually consolidated in TULR(C)A 1992, which was itself amended in 1993 and 1999.

The current Labour government has made it apparent that it has no intention of reversing much of its predecessor's legislation on strikes. The basic tenets of the Conservative legal reforms remain.

Trade dispute

The scope of the 'golden formula' immunity protecting actions by individuals or trade unions was narrowed in 1982 and is currently contained in s.219 TULR(C)A 1992. The immunity now covers only disputes 'between workers and their employer', rather than disputes between workers, or between workers and employers generally, or between a trade union and an employer independent of employee support. The dispute must relate 'wholly or mainly to' (and not merely be connected with) one or more of the industrial relations issues listed in s.244 of TULR(C)A 1992, such as pay and conditions, jobs, allocation of work, discipline, negotiating machinery or trade union membership. The significance of this change was demonstrated in *Mercury Communications Ltd v Scott-Garner* [1984] Ch 37, where an injunction was granted against BT workers for refusing to link up a new competitor to the telephone network. The union pleaded it was campaigning against privatization and loss of jobs. The court held that its actions did not relate 'wholly or mainly to' the loss of jobs but was primarily a political objection to liberalization and (eventual) privatization and was, therefore, outside the protection.

Acting in 'contemplation or furtherance' of a trade dispute requires a dispute which is 'impending or likely to occur'.[29] Anticipating a dispute as a mere possibility is not sufficient. In *Bent's Brewery Co Ltd v Hogan* [1945] 2 All ER 570, a union asked its members, who were employed as pub managers, to provide financial details concerning the income and expenditure of the establishments they managed. The company said that the request constituted an inducement to breach contracts since the pub managers were obliged not to disclose confidential information. The union claimed statutory immunity on the ground that they were collecting the information to help prepare a pay claim and thus were acting in contemplation of a trade dispute. The court rejected this argument since no demand had been made for either better conditions or increased wages. A dispute cannot exist until there is a difference of opinion between the parties as to some matter. There was no evidence that a dispute already existed or was likely.

Even acts properly done in contemplation of a trade dispute may be unlawful. A union will lose its statutory immunity if it fails to hold a properly conducted strike ballot, fails to provide the required notice of industrial action to the employer or engages in secondary action or unlawful picketing.

The introduction in 1984 of the requirement to hold secret ballots in connection with official industrial action marked a significant stage in the Conservative government's attempt to control the activities of trade unions. The requirement to show majority support among those workers likely to be involved was intended to moderate calls for industrial action. Failure to hold a properly conducted secret postal ballot leads to a loss of immunity. The detailed and technical requirements of the legislation ensure that this is a fertile source of litigation. The legal requirements are now contained in ss.226–235 TULR(C)A 1992. The ballot paper must specify the persons authorized to call on members to take part in industrial action. All industrial action ballots must have an independent scrutineer, and the name and details of the scrutineer must be given on every voting paper (unless fewer than 50 members are entitled to vote). The ballot paper must warn voters that by striking they may be in breach of their contract of employment. A trade union must also give notice of a ballot (and the result) to the employer. A union must take reasonable steps to ensure that not less than seven days before the opening day of the ballot, the employer receives a written notice stating the union's intention to hold a ballot, specifying the opening date of the ballot, and details of the employees entitled to vote.

The Labour government introduced some limited reforms in an attempt to make the law slightly less burdensome for trade unions.[30] First, it is no longer necessary for the union to identify all individuals being balloted, although it must provide 'such information… as would help the employer to make plans and bring information to the attention of those employees'. Second, the fact that a union has overlooked one or more members during the balloting process will not invalidate the final result, if the omission of these individuals was inadvertent and on a scale unlikely to affect the outcome. Third, a union is relieved of the requirement to conduct separate ballots at different workplaces in specific circumstances. Fourth, the period a ballot can remain effective was extended to a maximum of eight weeks where the union and employer agree. Finally, the Labour government also introduced a new revised Code of Practice, which provides guidance on desirable practices in the conduct of industrial action ballots (Simpson, 2001).

The evidence is that such ballots have become an accepted part of union practice, although their moderating influence is less evident than their use as a negotiating tactic in disputes. The majority of ballots result in support for the proposed industrial action (ACAS, 1997).

In order for a union to be protected in legal proceedings, s.234A requires the employer to be given at least seven days' notice of any proposed industrial action, whether action is to be continuous or discontinuous, and the date(s) it is to take place.

What is now s.224 TULR(C)A 1992 removes legal protection from all secondary action. Secondary action occurs where industrial action is taken against anyone who is not party to the dispute, such as a supplier or customer of the primary employer with whom the union is in dispute. It is usually taken with the aim of exerting additional indirect pressure on the primary employer and is sometimes referred to as 'sympathy' or 'solidarity' action.

Section 220 of the 1992 Act declares that it shall be lawful to 'attend at or near' one's own place of work 'for the purpose only of peacefully obtaining or communicating information, or peacefully persuading any person to... abstain from working'. Attendance is restricted to one's normal work premises and does not extend to other sites (even where there is a common dispute across sites), much less to the premises of another employer. There are limited exceptions in favour of mobile workers or those who find it impracticable to picket their place of work: they may picket any premises from which they work or from which their work is administered. Union officials may accompany members they represent: workers dismissed in connection with a trade dispute may picket their former place of work.

Guidelines on the conduct of picketing are contained in a Code of Practice, originally issued by the Secretary of State for Employment in 1980 and revised in 1992. This suggests that six pickets at any one entrance is a reasonable number, a figure stressed in some of the cases arising from the miners' and subsequent disputes. In practice, the control of picketing is largely a matter for the discretion of the police.

Trade union liability

Where a trade union engages in unlawful industrial action, a party affected by it may seek an injunction from the courts and/or damages. Traditionally employers have sought injunctions rather than damages, employers' prime concern being either to have industrial action stopped or to prevent it taking place initially. Furthermore, prior to 1982, it was unusual to sue for damages because legal action could only be taken against individual union officials since trade unions themselves were immune from suit. Section 15 of the Employment Act 1982 (now section 20, 1992 Act) removed that immunity.

This change has been particularly important because, by this means, litigants and the courts have been able to avoid 'martyring' individual officials, although suing individuals is still the only option in the event of unofficial action not 'authorized or endorsed' by the union. However, the amount of damages awarded is subject to specified limits, which depend on the membership size of the union. For a union with fewer than 5,000 members the maximum is £10,000; £50,000 if it has between 5,000 and 24,999 members; £125,000 if it has between 25,000 and 99,999; and £250,000 if it has 100,000 or more members.[31]

The law also gives an individual the right to bring 'cease and desist' applications, seeking an injunction to restrain unlawful industrial action which affects the supply of goods or services to that individual.[32] Any union disobeying a court order can find itself liable to penalties for contempt of court, which, unlike the limits on damages, are not capped. In the case of repeated disobedience, not only could the fines multiply but sequestration of union assets follow.

Dismissal of employees taking industrial action

Fairness at Work (para 4.21) declared that it was 'anomalous' that employees who take lawful industrial action risked dismissal. Accordingly, the Employment Relations Act 1999 enables employees to claim unfair dismissal where they participate in 'protected industrial action', that is, action which is *both* official *and* lawful within s.219 TULR(C)A 1992. It is automatically unfair to dismiss an employee for this reason (regardless of their length of service) if their dismissal takes place within eight weeks of them starting to take part in the action. Dismissals which take place after eight weeks may also be unfair, depending on whether the employer had taken proper steps to try to resolve the dispute.[33] In more limited circumstances, a claim of unfair dismissal can be made by those participating in what is merely 'official' industrial action. However, they must have a year's service and be able to show that they were dismissed when others were not, or that if all were sacked some were re-engaged within three months.[34] Employees taking 'unofficial' industrial action will not generally be able to claim unfair dismissal, regardless of the circumstances.[35]

The impact of industrial action law

An assessment of the impact of legal change is often problematic since it can be difficult to know whether it is the law or other related changes that have produced an observed result. Secret strike ballots have increased the financial costs to unions and have had several burdensome effects upon union organization. Because the ballot procedures are extremely complex and cumbersome, it has been difficult for unions to ensure that they always act within the law. However, unions have used industrial action ballots as ammunition in their bargaining strategy. They provide opportunities to mobilize support amongst members and a credible strike threat to test an employer's final offer (Martin *et al*, 1995).

Furthermore, whilst the laws introduced by successive Conservative governments between 1979 and 1993 may have contributed to the significant fall in the number of working days lost, industrial disputes have not been completely consigned to the history books. Indeed, the last two ACAS annual reports show ACAS as having conciliated in almost 1,500 collective disputes, a significant increase over previous years (ACAS, 2001). ACAS also reports a significant increase in the number of disputes concerning trade union recognition, which may reflect a positive trend for the future development of union density.

Despite the Workplace Employee Relations Survey 1998 charting a new low in the numbers of union members, improved relationships with a more sympathetic Labour government since 1997, and new legislation on individual rights, have helped to increase optimism within trade unions. However, there remains consternation amongst some trade unionists that the Labour government has made only minimal reforms to the law surrounding collective action. Whilst further significant change seems unlikely, a union 'wish list' might have on it the creation of a positive right to strike, secondary action legitimated in defined circumstances, and removal of some of the restrictions on disciplining union members who refuse to accept majority collective decisions to engage in lawful industrial action.

Notes

1 *Ford Motor Co v AEF* [1969] 2 QB 303 and s.179 TULR(C)A 1992.
2 ss.10–13 Employment Relations Act 1999 and ACAS Code of Practice on Disciplinary and Grievance Procedures.
3 ss.168–173 TULR(C)A 1992 and the ACAS Code of Practice No 3, Time off for Trade Union Duties and Activities.
4 Lord McIntosh, HL Deb, Vol. 603, col. 1045, 8th July 1999.
5 For an evaluation of the eighty year life of the CAC (including its recognition jurisdiction), see Rideout, R W (2002) What shall we do with the CAC?, *Industrial Law Journal*, **31**, pp 1–34.
6 Ewing, K (2000) Trade union recognition and staff associations – a breach of international labour standards?, *Industrial Law Journal*, **29**, pp 267–73 claims para 35 violates the right to organize and bargain in ILO Convention 98. Part V1 of Schedule A1 provides a procedure for de-recognizing non-independent unions.

7 See *Grunwick Processing Laboratories Ltd v ACAS* [1978] AC 655 and Simpson, R C (1979) Judicial Control of ACAS, *Industrial Law Journal*, **8**, pp 69–84.

8 The CAC must adopt the model method (patterned on a Joint Negotiating Body) set out in the Trade Union Recognition (Method of Collective Bargaining) Order 2000, SI 2000/1300, unless satisfied it is not appropriate. The union and employer can subsequently vary the imposed method by written agreement.

9 In *UNIFI v Union Bank of Nigeria plc* [2001] IRLR 726 the CAC declared that the obligation to negotiate over 'pay' includes employer's contributions to a pension scheme.

10 The preference for voluntary solutions is shown by an 80 per cent increase in requests to ACAS for conciliation assistance in 2000–01. Two-thirds of the 264 completed cases resulted in full recognition compared to 37 per cent the previous year. Recognition now forms over a fifth of the collective caseload of ACAS. See ACAS, *Annual Report 2000–2001*, pp 8 and 24. Furthermore, a number of formal applications to the CAC are withdrawn with a view to concluding a voluntary agreement, see CAC, *Annual Report 2000–2001*, pp 16 and 19–22.

11 According to Simpson, B (2000) Trade union recognition and the law, a new approach, etc, *Industrial Law Journal*, **29**, pp 193–222 at 219, the opportunities for judicial review may be 'considerable'. However, by October 2002 only two (unsuccessful) challenges had been reported. They suggest that courts may not be easily persuaded to intervene in determinations by the CAC. See *Fullarton Computer Industries Ltd v CAC* [2001] IRLR 752 (CAC's discretion to order recognition without a ballot open to challenge only if exercised irrationally) and *R v CAC ex parte Kwik-Fit(GB) Ltd* [2002] IRLR 395 (CAC's task is to determine whether the bargaining unit proposed by the union is appropriate, not whether there might be one that is more appropriate).

12 s.184 TULR(C)A 1992.

13 s.185 TULR(C)A 1992.

14 The terms and conditions may reflect the improvements which the union could have expected to gain through collective bargaining if the employer had not withheld the information.

15 The final part of the procedure does not envisage disclosure of the contested information by its incorporation into the contracts of relevant employees. However, it could be argued that this view does not accord with the approach taken by the CAC in the case of Holokrome Limited and Association of Scientific, Technical and Managerial Staffs (Award No 79/451).

16 s.188 (4) TULR(C)A 1992.

17 s.189 (3) TULR(C)A 1992.

18 Regulation 10 (2) TUPE 1981.

19 *Banking Insurance and Finance Union v Barclays Bank plc* [1987] ICR 495.
20 If the complaint is upheld, the employment tribunal may award appropriate compensation of no more than 13 weeks' pay to each affected employee. Regulation 11, TUPE.
21 *IPCS v Secretary of State for Defence* [1987] IRLR 373, per Millet J.
22 *EC Commission v UK* [1994] ICR 664.
23 SI 1995 No 2587.
24 In 2000, the failure of BMW to inform and consult before the break up of the Rover group and General Motors' announcement of the closure of the Vauxhall plant at Luton suggest that the UK's provisions on information and consultation are inadequate.
25 The Health and Safety (Consultation with Employees) Regulations 1996 SI 1996/1513 require employers to consult employees not covered by safety representatives appointed by a recognized trade union.
26 See generally the Occupational Pension Scheme (Contracting Out) Regulations 1996, SI 1996/1655 as amended.
27 SI 1999 No 3323.
28 *Taff Vale Rly Co v Amalgamated Society of Railway Servants* [1901] AC 426.
29 *Lord Loreburn, Conway v Wade* [1909] AC 506 at 512.
30 s.4 and Schedule 3, Employment Relations Act 1999.
31 s.22 (2) TULR(C)A 1992.
32 See s.235A TULR(C)A.
33 s.238A TULR(C)A 1992.
34 s.238 TULR(C)A 1992.
35 s.237 TULR(C)A.

References

ACAS (1997) *Annual Report*, p 43
ACAS (2001) *Annual Report 2000–2001*, pp 22–24
ACAS (1977) *Code of Practice on Disclosure of Information to Trade Unions for Collective Bargaining Purposes*, ACAS, London, paras. 11 and 15
Beaumont, P B and Harris, R (1995) Union de-recognition and declining union density in Britain, *Industrial and Labor Relations Review*, **48**, pp 389–402
Cully, M *et al* (1999) *Britain at Work as Depicted by the 1998 Workplace Employee Relations Survey*, Routledge, London, pp 234–41
Department of Trade and Industry (1998) *Fairness at Work*, Cm 3968, London
Department of Trade and Industry (1996) *Industrial Action and Trade Unions*, Cm 3470, London
Gospel, H, Lockwood, G and Willman, P (2000) *The Right to Know: Disclosure of Information for Collective Bargaining and Joint Consultation*, Discussion Paper, Centre for Economic Performance, London
Hall, M (1996) Beyond Recognition? Employee representation and EU law, *Industrial Law Journal*, **25**, pp 15–27

Hall, M and Edwards, P (1999) Reforming the statutory redundancy consultation procedure, *Industrial Law Journal*, **28**, pp 299–318

Hicks, S (2000) Trade union membership: an analysis of data from the Certification Officer and the Labour Force Survey, *Labour Market Trends*, **108** (7), pp 329–37

IDS Report 836 (2001) *Trade Union Recognition Widens*, Incomes Data Services, London

Martin, R *et al* (1995) The legislative reform of union government 1979–1994, *Industrial Relations Journal*, **26**, pp 146–55

Simpson, B (2001) Code of Practice on industrial action ballots and notice to employers 2000, *Industrial Law Journal*, **30**, pp 194–98

Wedderburn, W (1997) Consultation and collective bargaining in Europe: success or ideology? *Industrial Law Journal*, **26** (1), pp 1–34

8

Discrimination in employment

Helen Pritchard

INTRODUCTION

It is unlawful to discriminate in employment against workers or employees on the grounds of race, sex, marital status or disability. There are also provisions making it unlawful to discriminate against persons undergoing gender reassignment, persons engaged on part-time or fixed-term contracts, and those engaged in trade union activity. This applies not only to the recruitment and selection of employees, but also to the opportunities and rewards that they receive after the commencement of their employment. In short, the rules are designed to ensure fairness and equal treatment throughout the people management process, from the decision to place a recruitment advertisement to the termination of the contract.

Discrimination in this context can be seen as unfavourable treatment based on prejudice, but it is an objective test and there is no requirement that the person who acts in a discriminatory manner should intend to inflict upon the claimant any harm or detriment. To this extent, a tribunal will look at the acts taking place and will not try to determine the reasons or motives behind those acts.

This chapter will firstly look at the general principles of the anti-discrimination legislation, and will go on to examine the rules in more detail as they apply to each potentially disadvantaged group. Precise definitions and examples are given under the relevant subject headings below.

GENERAL PRINCIPLES

The appropriate comparison

By its very nature, a complaint of discrimination involves making a comparison between the types of treatment meted out to the complainant and to others in a similar position. In situations of race discrimination it is a relatively straightforward matter to compare the treatment of a member of one race or ethnic group with another. The major difficulties in this area are concerned with determining what characteristics define a separate race or ethnic group and are discussed more specifically below. In cases of sex discrimination, the appropriate comparator is a man in similar circumstances to a female complainant, or vice versa.

The dismissal of a pregnant woman is automatically unfair under the provisions of the Employment Rights Act 1996; however, whereas compensation for unfair dismissal is limited to £50,000, there is no upper limit on the level of damages for sex discrimination. Although the two legal schemes are separate, the situation can often arise where a woman has a potential claim for both unfair dismissal and sex discrimination. In the case of *Webb v EMO Cargo (No. 2)*[1] the court decided that, in line with European law, no comparison is necessary where the treatment of a pregnant woman is under consideration and discrimination in such circumstances is automatic. When considering discrimination against a person with a disability, there is no requirement to find a comparator to determine whether discrimination has taken place.[2]

What amounts to 'employment'?

In order to bring a complaint for discrimination in employment under the Sex Discrimination Act 1975 (SDA), Race Relations Act 1976 (RRA) or Disability Discrimination Act 1995 (DDA), the complainant must be employed in Great Britain. 'Employment' requires that there be a contract of service and such contract may be either written or oral. The definition of employment also includes a 'contract personally to execute any work or labour'[3] and the case of *Quinnen v Hovells*[4] held that this phrase was intended to have a wider meaning than strict employment and could, on occasions, include self-employment.

There appears to be a gap in the protection from discrimination offered to ex-employees. Whilst the European Court of Justice[5] has held that national laws should protect workers from discrimination by former employers, the Court of Appeal has recently stated that an employment tribunal does not have jurisdiction under the discrimination legislation to consider a complaint in respect of acts or events which occurred after the employment is terminated, unless the claim is for victimization.[6] Thus, a former employee whose prospects of future work are blighted by a former employer's refusal to provide references was not successful in her discrimination claim.

Vicarious liability

Employers should note that they are liable **as well as** the individual who discriminates. It is no defence that the employer neither knew, nor approved, of the discrimination taking place.[7] Employers should also be aware that they can be liable for acts which are unauthorized and unconnected with the employee's work.[8] Liability can extend to acts of discrimination occurring at a social gathering. A tribunal, when faced with such a claim, must consider the following factors:

- whether the person was still on duty;
- whether the incident took place on the employer's premises;
- whether the gathering was organized by or on behalf of the employer;
- whether the incident took place immediately after work.[9]

Indeed, an employer's only defence is that he took all such steps as were 'reasonably practicable' to prevent the employee's discriminatory behaviour.[10] For example, an employer might successfully defend himself if he can show that he had a proper system of supervision, that he had published an equal opportunities policy and that he was unaware of the acts complained of.[11] For the employer's vicarious liability to arise, the discriminatory act must have been done in the course of the discriminator's employment. In determining whether an employee's wrongful act has been committed in the course of his employment, the court must concentrate on the relative closeness of the connection between the nature of the employment and the employee's wrongdoing. Thus in *Lister v Helsey Hall Ltd*[12] a boarding school was held liable in damages to former pupils who had been subject to sexual abuse by the school warden, even though such activity was clearly not authorized by the employing school.

The role of the commissions

The government has established commissions as independent bodies to help secure and promote civil rights for disadvantaged groups. The Commission for Racial Equality, Disability Rights Commission and Equal Opportunities Commission share comparable statutory duties to work to eliminate discrimination, promote equal opportunities, encourage good practice and advise the government on the workings of the relevant legislation. They have powers to investigate complaints and to take enforcement action against persons or organizations which persistently act in a discriminatory manner. The commissions also issue Codes of Practice which give practical guidance to employers and others on how to stay within the law. Courts and tribunals must have regard to the Codes of Practice when deciding discrimination cases.

SEX AND RACE DISCRIMINATION

The legislative framework follows a similar pattern for both sex and race discrimination. The Sex Discrimination Act 1975 (SDA) prohibits discrimination against any person (male or female) on the ground of their sex, and legislates against discrimination in employment against people who are married. In 1999 the Act was amended to afford protection against direct discrimination to those undergoing gender reassignment (transsexuals). The Race Relations Act 1976 (RRA) prohibits discrimination on grounds of race and defines this as including colour, race, nationality or ethnic or national origins.[13] Note that 'national origins' can mean citizenship and it is therefore unlawful to discriminate against nationals of other countries even if they are not of a different race. The term 'ethnic' was held by the House of Lords to be wider than 'race'. In the case of *Mandla v Dowell Lee*,[14] which involved Sikhs, the court ruled that for a group to establish itself as an ethnic group for the purposes of the Act, it must have certain characteristics and regard itself as a distinct community. These characteristics include a long shared history and cultural tradition.

The RRA is modelled on the SDA, and decisions of courts or tribunals on the basis of one Act may be used when considering the meaning of the other. Both types of discrimination may arise directly, indirectly or by way of victimization.

Direct discrimination[15]

Direct discrimination occurs when a person is treated 'less favourably' than someone of the opposite sex or of a different colour or racial group. The appropriate question to determine whether or not direct discrimination has occurred is 'would the complainant have received the same treatment from the defendant but for his or her sex?'[16] In the leading case on sex discrimination, Mr and Mrs James, both aged 61, were in regular attendance at their local swimming pool. The borough council, which owned and operated the pool, introduced a policy offering free swimming to children under three years old and to people over pensionable age. All other swimmers had to pay a 75p fee. Mr James complained of discrimination on the grounds of his sex as he had to pay the admission fee, whereas his wife did not. The case went eventually to the House of Lords where the finding that the borough council had discriminated against Mr James was upheld.

It must be possible to compare the treatment of the complainant with the treatment, in similar circumstances, of a member of the opposite sex. The comparison need not be actual, but can be a hypothetical comparison with how someone of the opposite sex *would have* been treated. Sexual harassment can also be direct sex discrimination, as decided in *Strathclyde Regional Council v Porcelli*.[17] In that case a female laboratory technician felt obliged to transfer to another place of work after suffering incidents in which two other (male) technicians deliberately brushed against her and made sexually suggestive remarks. The court held that she had been subject to unlawful discrimination as she had received treatment of a sexual nature to which a man would not have been vulnerable.

In cases of direct racial discrimination, the test is that a person treats the complainant less favourably than he would treat someone else, on racial grounds. Provided that the discrimination is based on racial grounds, the actual race of the person discriminated against does not matter. This is well illustrated by the case of *Wilson v TB Steelworks*[18] in which a white woman's job offer was withdrawn when she revealed that her husband was black. This action was held to be unlawful discrimination by the company. The Act specifically states that a person is treated less favourably if he is segregated on the ground of his race.[19] There can be no defence of justification to a situation of direct discrimination.

Indirect discrimination[20]

Indirect discrimination occurs when a 'requirement or condition' is imposed which, although applying to both sexes (or all races), has a discriminatory effect. It is intended to ensure that 'practices that are fair in form, but discriminatory in operation'[21] are prohibited. To determine whether or not a particular requirement will offend the provisions against indirect discrimination, the following questions must be asked:

- Is the proportion of one group able to comply 'considerably smaller' than the other?
- Can the requirement or condition be justified?
- Has the complainant suffered a detriment because of his or her inability to comply?

In order to decide whether or not the condition or requirement can be justified, the tribunal must follow the justification test set out in *Hampson v Department of Education and Science*:[22]

- Does the employer have a genuine operational need for the imposition of the condition or requirement?
- Does the requirement or condition meet that operational need?
- Is it reasonably necessary to impose the condition in order to meet the need – or might there be other ways of meeting it?

If the answer to each of these three questions is yes, then the proportionality principle must be applied in which the tribunal seeks to balance the employer's reasonable needs against the discriminatory impact of the condition on the complainant. For example, in *Panesaar v Nestle & Co Limited*[23] the Court of Appeal decided that a factory rule prohibiting beards and long hair was indirect discrimination against the Sikh complainant, but that it was justified in the interests of safety and hygiene.

Remember that the complainant must be able to show that he has suffered a detriment – an unjustified sense of grievance does not amount to less favourable treatment and therefore an employee who is treated differently (but not less generously) than employees in a different racial group, for sound reasons, will not succeed in a claim under the Act.[24] The Court of Appeal case of *De Souza v Automobile Association*[25] held that a racial insult, by itself, amounted to a detriment.

Victimization – a form of discrimination[26]

It is unlawful to treat a person less favourably because he has taken proceedings under the anti-discrimination legislation, because he has assisted another person in doing so or because he has made allegations of discrimination against another person. Such activities amount to victimization and are prohibited.

Lawful discrimination on grounds of sex

Generally, 'positive' discrimination, designed to give priority to persons of a particular sex, is not permitted.[27] However, it is permissible to discriminate if the sex of the person is a genuine occupational qualification for the job.[28] Such situations are narrowly interpreted by the courts and fit into the following specific categories:

- The essential nature of the job calls for authentic male or female character-istics. This must not include physical strength or stamina.
- The job needs to be held by a person of a particular sex to preserve decency or privacy.
- The employer provides premises, in which the employee is required to live, but such premises are not equipped with separate sleeping and sanitary facilities, *and* it is not reasonable to expect the employer to provide such separate facilities.
- The place of employment is a hospital, prison, or similar establishment and all the residents are persons of one sex *and* it is reasonable that a person of a particular sex should hold the job.
- The employee provides personal services promoting the welfare or education of individuals, where this can most effectively be done by one sex.
- The job is likely to involve duties outside the United Kingdom in a country with laws or customs which mean that a woman could not effectively perform those duties. (See *O'Conner v Kontiki Travel*[29] below).
- A married couple is required.

The case of *O'Conner v Kontiki Travel* illustrates the strict approach of the courts. This involved a female coach driver who was refused employment on the ground that she would have to drive through Muslim countries. On examination, it was found that the only Muslim country on the itinerary was Turkey, and the travel company could produce no evidence of objection to women drivers there. The refusal to appoint the female coach driver amounted to unlawful discrimination.

Lawful discrimination on racial grounds

It is similarly permissible to discriminate where membership of a particular racial group is a genuine occupational qualification for the job.[30] The provisions are more restrictive than those in the Sex Discrimination Act 1975 as there are only four situations in which discrimination is permitted:

- where the job involves performing in drama or entertainment and a person of a particular racial group is required for reasons of authenticity;
- where the job involves modelling work and a person of a particular racial group is required for reasons of authenticity;
- where the job involves work in a place where food and drink are provided to members of the public in a particular setting and a person of a particular racial group is required for reasons of authenticity (for example, in a Thai restaurant);
- where the jobholder provides persons of a particular racial group with personal services promoting their welfare and those services can be most effectively provided by a person of the same racial group.

Race Relations (Amendment) Act 2000

Under the provisions of the RRA, employers were made vicariously liable for the discriminatory acts of their employees; however, certain categories of worker were excluded from these provisions, notably police officers who are defined as office holders rather than employees. This meant that chief officers of police could not be held vicariously liable for acts of race discrimination perpetrated by their officers. The 2000 Act was passed in response to the findings of the Macpherson report and extends the provisions of the RRA in relation to public authorities and outlaws race discrimination in functions that were previously not covered. Furthermore, it places a general positive duty on specified public authorities to work towards the elimination of unlawful discrimination, promote equality of opportunity and good relations between persons of different racial groups. Further developments in legislation against race discrimination are inevitable, as there is a European Race Directive which is due for implementation in the UK by July 2003. Although many of the provisions are already enacted in domestic law, some commentators argue that the evidential requirements to prove indirect discrimination are less stringent under the Directive and that this will require new legislation.

DISCRIMINATION ON THE GROUNDS OF DISABILITY

Introduction

Protection from discrimination for people with disabilities is provided by the Disability Discrimination Act 1995 (DDA). The DDA differs significantly from the SDA and RRA:

- Discrimination is defined as less favourable treatment 'for a reason which relates to the disabled person's disability'[31] – there is no prohibition of indirect discrimination.
- Discrimination is not unlawful if the employer can show that the less favourable treatment is 'justifiable'.[32]
- There is no equivalent of the SDA and RRA requirement to find a person with whom to compare in determining whether or not discrimination has occurred.[33]

The DDA imposes a duty upon employers to make reasonable adjustments to accommodate the needs of disabled employees. Businesses employing fewer than 15 people are currently exempt from the provisions of the DDA, but will be required to comply by 2004.

Who is disabled?

A person is classed as disabled for the purposes of the Act if he or she has a physical or mental impairment that has a substantial and long-term adverse effect on his or her ability to carry out normal day-to-day activities.[34] The duty is on the complainant to establish that he or she has a disability. It is important to understand that the Act covers both people who are already disabled when they begin work and those people who become disabled during the course of their employment – for example, after an accident or illness. A functional approach is taken which means that the complainant must demonstrate two things: the existence of a disability, and actual, substantial impairment to normal day-to-day activities.

The question of what activities are 'normal' and when the effect on them is 'substantial' are issues to be determined by the tribunal on the facts of the individual case. 'Long-term' is defined as lasting at least 12 months or likely to last for the rest of the complainant's life. It is not necessary for the impediment to be constant and unrelenting as the tribunal can regard it as being continuous if it is likely to recur.

In determining the extent of the disablement suffered, the tribunal should disregard the effect of any medication used to treat the condition. The only exception to this is where spectacles or contact lenses are used to correct defective vision. This applies even if the medical treatment results in the effects of the disability being completely under control or not at all apparent.[35] Schedule 1 to the Act gives practical examples, including: where a person with a hearing impairment wears a hearing aid, the question of substantial adverse effect is to be decided by reference to the hearing level without the hearing aid; in a person with diabetes, the tribunal should look at the effect of the condition as if he was not taking medication.

Case law has established that persons with illnesses such as repetitive strain injury, chronic fatigue syndrome (ME) and depression can have substantial and long-term effects on their ability to carry out normal day-to-day activities as required by the Act. In each case, the decision will turn on the specific circumstances of the individual complainant. The tribunal is bound to take into account the provisions of the Disability Discrimination Code of Practice, which contains what it describes as 'general advice to help employers avoid discrimination'. It gives numerous examples of less favourable treatment to be avoided and reasonable adjustments that employers could make.

The duty to make reasonable adjustments

Sections 5(2) and 6(1) of the DDA impose this duty, which only arises when a person with a disability is placed at a 'substantial disadvantage', as a job applicant, by the arrangements made for selection, or, as an employee, by the working conditions or physical features of the workplace. The Disability Discrimination (Employment) Regulations 1996 give additional guidance by defining the physical features of the workplace as those arising from:

- the design or construction of buildings;
- access and exits to buildings;
- fixtures, fittings, furnishings, equipment or materials;
- any other physical element or quality of land or buildings.

It should be noted that where an employer is under a duty to make reasonable adjustments to premises, it is no defence to say that the business is being run from rented premises and the lease precludes alterations to the fabric of the building by the tenant. The DDA implies a contractual term into the lease to the effect that the lessor should not unreasonably withhold his consent to the making of the required alterations.[36]

The appropriate test for the application of the duty to make reasonable adjustments was set out in *Morse v Wiltshire County Council*[37] which held that the tribunal must ask firstly if there is a duty on the employer to make any adjustment; secondly, has the employer taken such steps as are reasonable to make such an adjustment; and thirdly, is any failure on the part of an employer to take such steps justified? In determining the kind of action an employer might have to take, it is worth referring to the examples contained in section 6(1) of the Act:

(a) making adjustments to premises
(b) allocating some of the disabled person's duties to another person
(c) transferring him to fill an existing vacancy
(d) altering his working hours
(e) assigning him to a different place of work
(f) allowing him to be absent during working hours for rehabilitation, assessment or treatment
(g) giving, or arranging to give, training
(h) acquiring or modifying equipment
(i) modifying instructions or reference manuals
(j) modifying procedures for testing or assessment
(k) providing a reader or interpreter
(l) providing supervision.

The Disability Discrimination Code of Practice provides more concrete examples of the sort of steps which might be required under each heading – for example, 'adjustments to premises' might include 'widening a doorway, providing a ramp or moving furniture'. A number of factors will be taken into account to determine whether it is reasonable for any particular employer to take a certain step to comply with section 6(1).[38] The tribunal shall have regard to factors such as:

(a) the extent to which taking the step would prevent the effect in question
(b) the practicability, and
(c) the costs and disruption associated with taking the steps, as well as
(d) the employer's resources, and
(e) any financial or other assistance available.

Thus, it may be seen that the expectations of a large multinational company to adjust for and accommodate its disabled employees appropriately may be far greater than the requirements placed on a small, local employer.

The case of *London Borough of Hillingdon v Morgan*[39] illustrates the practical effects, as it held that the employer had failed in its duty under section 6 by failing to consider, at least in the short term, whether an applicant who suffered from ME could have been provided with work at home, and by applying to her the normal rules governing redeployment of those on long-term sick leave or facing redundancy.

Justification

As we have seen, discrimination under the DDA can occur in two ways – either by less favourable treatment or by failing to make reasonable adjustments. Such acts will only amount to discrimination if the employer cannot demonstrate that the differential treatment or failure to adjust was 'justified'. Under section 5(3), treatment is justified if, but only if, the reason for it is both material to the circumstances of the case and substantial. In the case of *Clark v TDG Ltd (t/a Novacold)*[40] both the Employment Appeal Tribunal and the Court of Appeal emphasized the importance of being guided by the Disability Discrimination Code of Practice. This addresses the issue of justification by asserting that less favourable treatment will be justified only if the reason for it relates to the individual circumstances in question and is not just a trivial or minor matter. The question of justification is one of fact for the tribunal to decide, subject to taking into account the relevant provisions of the Code of Practice.

PRE-EMPLOYMENT AND SELECTION ISSUES

All three Acts make it unlawful to discriminate in recruitment and selection practices.[41]

Job advertisements

These must be drafted so as to ensure that job opportunities are available to all, irrespective of sex or race.[42] Where issues of sex or race discrimination arise, an individual does not have the power to challenge the advertisement – this may only be done by the Commission for Racial Equality or the Equal Opportunities Commission. The Disability Rights Commission has enforcement powers for the DDA but it is open to employers to demonstrate that a condition of employment, which has a discriminatory effect against a person with a disability, is justified. The use of an advertisement, which indicates that a person's disability may preclude him from successfully applying for the job, gives rise to a rebuttable presumption that the employer's attitude is discriminatory. The onus would then be on the employer to demonstrate that the discrimination was, in fact, justified. It follows, therefore, that there may be circumstances in which an employer can openly say in a recruitment advert that the nature of the job is such that it will not be possible to accommodate applicants with certain forms of disability.

Recruitment and selection procedures

An employer must not discriminate in the arrangements made for determining who should be offered employment. The Acts make it unlawful to discriminate against potential employees.[43] A situation involving sex or race discrimination may be either direct or indirect (as defined above), where conditions are imposed which have an adverse effect on the number of women or minority group members who are able to apply (for example, the requirement for a beard or for blonde hair).

The Codes of Practice for the SDA and the RRA contain valuable advice for employers to help them avoid discriminatory practices in recruitment, selection and interviews. The Commission for Racial Equality Code, for example, gives advice which demonstrates how easy it is for the well-intentioned but ill-informed employer to fall foul of the provisions: 'it is recommended that employers should not confine recruitment unjustifiably to those agencies, job centres, careers offices and schools which, because of their particular source of applicants, provide only or mainly applicants of a particular racial group'.[44]

This Code goes further, recommending that employers do not rely on word-of-mouth recruitment, and this must lead to questions about the advisability of the 'head-hunting' approach to acquiring staff. The Code is keen to ensure that short listing and interviewing is done by more than one person to reduce the risk of bias, although ensuring diversity in such panels may prove difficult for those working in very small organizations. The Equal Opportunities Commission Code of Practice states that interview questions should relate only to the requirements of the job, and not include questions about marriage or family plans that may indicate a bias against women.

Offers of employment

The employer must not discriminate in the arrangements made to determine who should be offered employment.[45] It is no defence for the employer to say that the arrangements were not made with an intention to discriminate. If, when the arrangements are put into operation, the effect is discriminatory then the selection arrangements are unlawful. The Employment Appeal Tribunal considered this in the case of *Brennan v Dewhurst*[46] in which Miss Brennan applied for a job as a butcher's assistant. She was interviewed by the branch manager who stated clearly that he had no intention of appointing a female to the post. It was not the branch manager, but the district manager who had the responsibility to make the final appointment and he ultimately concluded that there was no need to fill the vacancy. It was held that the manager had discriminated against Miss Brennan even though that was not the company's intention.

It is unlawful to assume that any particular job is appropriate only to one gender and that appointment of someone of a different gender or race would fail because the person recruited does not 'fit in' with the rest of the workforce.[47] An example is the case of *Croyston v Texas Homecare Limited*[48] in which a man failed to secure a post as a personnel assistant in a company where almost all of the mangers were female. It was held that he had been discriminated against, as the manager to whom he made his application told him that her staff would be extremely surprised if a man were to be appointed.

Opportunities for training and promotion

It is unlawful for employers to discriminate in the way in which they afford access to opportunities for promotion, transfer or training.[49] Promotion systems must be open to all groups equally, irrespective of gender or race. The Equal Opportunities Code recommends the regular review of promotion and career development patterns – particularly if employees of one sex are concentrated in a section of the workforce from which it is difficult to rise through the ranks. In *Francis v British Airways Engine Overhaul Limited*[50] the Employment Appeal Tribunal recommended that where there are no promotion opportunities from a certain grade which is predominantly made up of women (or minorities) then an indirect discrimination claim could be formulated.

REDUNDANCY

When employers find it necessary to reduce the size of their workforce, they must not discriminate on grounds of sex, race or disability when it comes to selecting those employees whose positions are to be made redundant.[51] Redundancy selections are often, in practice, done on a last-in-first-out (LIFO) basis or by dismissing part-time workers before full-time workers. Both of these practices may amount to indirect discrimination. In *Clarke and Powell v Eley (IMI Kynoch) Limited*[52] the Employment Appeal Tribunal held that the selection of part-timers first was grossly discriminatory in its effects and that selection according to LIFO had a lesser discriminatory effect which might be more easily capable of justification.

HARASSMENT

Harassment is a particular type of detriment under the discrimination Acts.[53] It is not specifically defined in domestic law, but the European Commission Recommendation on The Protection of the Dignity of Men and Women at Work[54] states that conduct of a sexual nature or other conduct based on sex affecting the dignity of women and men at work is unacceptable if it is:

1   unwanted, unreasonable and offensive to the recipient;
2   used as a basis for employment decisions, such as promotion, or is
3   such as to create an intimidating, hostile or humiliating work environment for the recipient.

The Recommendation is accompanied by a Code of Practice which expands the definition of sexual harassment as including 'unwelcome physical, verbal or non-verbal conduct' and suggests measures to combat such behaviour. It makes it clear that it is for individuals to decide for themselves what kind of behaviour is acceptable to them. Sexual attentions become sexual harassment if they persist after it has been made clear that the behaviour is both unwelcome and unacceptable. The Employment Appeal Tribunal in *Wadman v Carpenter Farrer Partnership*[55] commended both the European Recommendation and the Code of Practice to tribunals and they are now commonly used to set the standard by which the conduct of the parties and the employer's actions to combat the behaviour may be judged. The racial harassment case of *De Souza v Automobile Association*[56] held that the appropriate test was 'that the court must find that by reason of the acts complained of a reasonable worker would or might take the view that he had thereby been disadvantaged in the circumstances in which he had thereafter to work'. When judging the standard of behaviour which could amount to racial or sexual harassment, the actions must be considered from the victim's point of view – did the conduct in question create an intimidating, hostile or humiliating work environment? Where potentially harassing behaviour is directed towards a number of individuals, the effect upon each person must be considered separately. In the case of *Wileman v Minilec Engineering Limited*[57] a director's secretary who complained of some four years of sexual harassment from her boss was not permitted to bring forth evidence from other women who had allegedly been harassed by the director. Sexual harassment may be regarded as either direct or indirect discrimination. The test is whether the woman has been treated less favourably on the grounds of her sex than a comparable man would have been treated and that she has thereby suffered detriment. In *Bracebridge Engineering Limited v Darby*[58] a woman was subject to an indecent assault by her charge hand and the works manager. The Employment Appeal Tribunal held that a single incident of sexual harassment can be a sufficient detriment to result in a successful discrimination claim, provided the incident complained of is serious enough.

REMEDIES

The complainant must apply to an employment tribunal within three months of the date upon which the discrimination occurred.[59] Where discrimination is ongoing, the three-month time limit does not start to run until the discrimination stops.[60] The tribunal has power to make a declaration of rights, recommend that the respondent takes a particular action, and to award compensation. There is no upper limit on the amount of compensation and interest is payable from the date on which the discrimination took place. The tribunal is free to assess the amount of compensation and takes into account: the loss sustained (for example, for not being promoted), and injury to feelings. This second category may include an element for the anger and distress caused by the discriminatory act and for loss of a chosen career path.

To succeed in obtaining this part of the compensatory award, the complainant must have been aware of the discrimination and must be able to prove that his or her feelings were injured in some way.

EQUAL PAY

Introduction

The Equal Pay Act 1970 (EPA) was introduced with the objective of eliminating discrimination in terms and conditions of employment which exists only because of the sex of the person employed. The Act and related regulations must be interpreted in line with relevant decisions of the European Court of Justice, and the Equal Pay Directive. Where conflict arises between domestic and European law, or where there are differences of interpretation, the European law will prevail. It should be noted that although under UK law, it is the responsibility of the complainant to demonstrate that she is not receiving equal pay, the European Court has ruled that where pay systems manifestly produce inequalities between the sexes, the burden shifts to the employer to prove that the system giving rise to those inequalities is not discriminatory.[61] The EPA and SDA complement each other and should be construed together as one single comprehensive code.[62]

The fundamentals of the EPA

Firstly, to raise the issue of equal pay, the relevant men and women must be employed 'in the same employment' which means at the same establishment or at different establishments where common terms and conditions of employment are observed.[63] The Act works by implying an equality clause into the contract of employment of any woman who is:

1 engaged in like work with a man[64]
2 engaged in work rated as equivalent to that of a man[65]
3 engaged in work to which equal value is attributed.[66]

The equality clause has the effect of modifying any term of the woman's contract which is less favourable than a term of a similar kind in a man's contract so that it is not less favourable, and also treating more beneficial terms from the man's contract as similarly being applied to the woman. The Act is applicable to women of all ages working at an establishment in Great Britain under a contract of service. The equality clause applies to men as well as women, with the exception of contractual terms under which women are afforded special conditions in connection with pregnancy and childbirth.

In order for the equality clause to operate, there must be an existing contractual term relating to the issue that is under dispute[67] and each individual term of the contract may be examined separately for equality. Any term seeking to exclude the operation of the EPA (or indeed the SDA) is unenforceable.[68]

What is 'like work'?

To qualify as 'like work' the activities must be the same or broadly similar and any differences between them must be of no practical importance. For example, in the case of *Capper Pass Limited v Lawton*[69] a woman was employed as a cook for the company directors' dining room preparing lunches for between 10 and 20 people per day without supervision. She claimed equal pay with two assistant chefs who worked in the factory canteen preparing 350 meals per day under the supervision of the head chef. The Employment Appeal Tribunal held that she was entitled to equal pay as the work did not have to be the same, it was sufficient for it to be broadly similar. The tribunal must consider any differences between the work done and ask if these are significant enough that it would be reasonable to expect to see them reflected in different wage settlements. Case law has categorized differences into three groups that are more likely to be of practical importance:

1 Different duties – these must be both required by the contract of employment and actually performed by the individual to a significant extent if different pay rates are to be justified.[70]
2 It is appropriate to vary basic rates of pay between different groups of employees according to the hours worked, provided that the payment of differential rates has nothing to do with the sex of the person undertaking the work.[71]
3 Where men and women are employed on like work, but have different responsibilities, it may be possible to justify differences in remuneration.[72]

What is 'work rated as equivalent'?

This is work that has been examined by a properly conducted job evaluation scheme taking into account such issues as the amount of effort, skill, and decision making required of the employee. The scheme must be both thorough in analysis and impartial in application.[73] It is not sufficient to apply subjective criteria such as what 'feels fair'.[74]

What is work of 'equal value'?

A claim for equal value must be made to an employment tribunal to decide whether or not the issue can be dealt with under 'like work' or 'work rated as equivalent'. If these options are inappropriate, the tribunal can either:

1 decide that there are no reasonable grounds for making the claim;
2 decide the question of equal value itself; or
3 refer the claim to an expert for the preparation of a job evaluation study.

If the tribunal chooses the third option, it will not be able to decide the case until the expert's report is available, and even then it is not bound by the recommendations.

The employer's defence

Where a woman successfully satisfies the requirement that she is employed on like work or work of equal value as described above, the employer may still justify a differential in pay on the basis that it is 'genuinely due to a material factor which is not the difference of sex'.[75] Such factors must not be based on any difference in the actual work done, as this is considered when looking at 'like work' etc. The sort of factors which could amount to material differences include long-service increments, extra pay for additional qualifications, additional responsibility allowances or a genuine mistake in putting an employee in the wrong salary bracket. Pay differentials may also be justified where an employee's pay is protected through 'red circling'. This arises, for example, where a redundant employee is moved to work of a lower grade but remains on the level of pay appropriate to his or her previous position. Economic factors, such as the need to pay a higher rate to attract staff from the private to the public sector, may also allow pay differentials to continue.[76]

Remedies under the EPA

Claims made to the employment tribunal can include a claim for arrears of pay or for damages. The claimant may choose a male employee with whom she wishes to be compared and therefore a woman who is receiving pay which is equal to that of certain male employees can still claim equal pay with a man earning a higher rate if their work is the same or broadly similar.[77] Claims can be made for a period up to two years preceding the date of claim and the tribunal has power to order interest to be paid on any award made. It should be noted that there is general concern about the delays and complexities that accompany many equal pay cases and that procedural reform is likely in the near future.

A NOTE ON PART-TIME WORKERS

The Part-time Workers (Prevention of Less Favourable Treatment) Regulations[78] came into force on 1 October 2002 and implemented the European Directive on Part-time Work. These regulations apply to any worker contracted for fewer hours than would normally be regarded as full time in that particular type of employment and protect such workers from discrimination. Part-time employees therefore have the right to receive the same benefits as a comparable full-time employee, but calculated pro rata. If the benefit is such that it is not possible to fractionalize it, then the employer may exclude a part-time worker from receiving it, but the burden of proving that such exclusion is justified lies with the employer. Such justification may include, for example, a disproportionate cost to the organization in providing the benefit. As a last resort, an employer may consider converting the benefit into a cash payment. The regulations do not confer a statutory right to work part-time but employers who fail to properly consider an employee's request to work part-time run the risk of facing a claim for indirect sex discrimination or unfair dismissal. If employers wish to refuse a request for part-time work from an employee then they must be able to show that they have fully investigated whether part-time work was possible, which would include assessing whether the post was an appropriate one for job sharing.

A NOTE ON FIXED-TERM WORKERS

The Fixed-Term Employees (Prevention of Less Favourable Treatment) Regulations,[79] which came into force on 1 October 2002, make it unlawful to discriminate against fixed-term employees as required by the European Directive on Fixed-Term Work and limits the use of successive fixed-term contracts.

TRADE UNION MEMBERSHIP

It is unlawful to refuse to employ a person, or to cause him or her any detriment short of dismissal, because he or she is or is not a member of a trade union.[80] The aim of the legislation is to prevent any form of discrimination on the grounds of trade union membership. An employer may still refuse to employ a notoriously militant worker, provided the decision was based on his or her disruptive conduct in previous employment and not on trade union membership *per se*.[81] This will be a question of fact to be decided by the tribunal in each case. Any dismissal of an employee which was principally because of his or her part in union activities, or because of his or her membership or non-membership, will be an unfair dismissal.[82]

HUMAN RIGHTS OVERLAP

Article 14 of the European Convention on Human Rights (ECHR) contains a general prohibition of discrimination on grounds of race, religion, sex, political views or other status, unless this can be justified objectively. Article 9 protects an individual's right to freedom of conscience and religion. The

Human Rights Act 1998 (HRA) allows the provisions of the ECHR to be enforced in the UK courts. Prior to this Act, enforcement was only possible via the European Court of Human Rights in Strasbourg. The extent to which the HRA will extend the boundaries of anti-discrimination law is not yet clear. All domestic legislation must be interpreted in a manner consistent with the articles of the ECHR. This will have a bearing on the existing anti-discrimination legislation. However, even decisions of the European Court of Human Rights have been relatively conservative in applying the articles of the ECHR to situations of discrimination in employment. For example, where a Christian employee was dismissed for working on a Sunday, she claimed that this was a breach of Article 9 of the ECRH, which protects an individual's right to religious observance. The European Court of Human Rights dismissed the claim and found that the employee had been dismissed for failing to comply with the terms of her contract of employment.[83]

FUTURE DEVELOPMENTS

Further extensions to anti-discrimination legislation are virtually guaranteed as the UK is required to implement the European Union Equal Treatment Directive over the next few years. Although the provisions making it unlawful to discriminate on grounds of race, sex and disability are already enacted in national law, some commentators argue that further provisions and amendments will be necessary to fully comply with the Directive.

Legislation must be enacted to make discrimination unlawful in the following areas by the dates shown:

- Religious beliefs   2003
- Sexual orientation   2003
- Age   2006

The usual rule in discrimination cases is that it is the duty of the complainant to prove the claim. On 12 October 2001, new regulations[84] came into force that shift the burden of proof from employee to employer in sex discrimination cases, making it generally easier for claimants to succeed.

Notes

1 [1995] IRLR 645.
2 *Clark v TDG Ltd (t/a Novacold)* [1999] IRLR 318 CA.
3 RRA s.78(1), SDA s.82(1), DDA s.68(1).
4 [1984] IRLR 227.
5 *Coote v Granada Hospitality Ltd* [1998] IRLR 656 ECJ.
6 *Rhys-Harper v Relaxion Group plc* [2001] IRLR 460.
7 SDA s.41, RRA s.32, DDA s.58.

8 *Jones v Tower Boot Co. Ltd.* [1997] IRLR 168.
9 *Chief Constable of Lincolnshire v Stubbs* [1999] IRLR 81.
10 SDA s.41(3).
11 *Balgobin v Tower Hamlets LBC* [1987] IRLR 401.
12 *Lister v Hesley Hall Ltd* [2001] IRLR 472.
13 RRA s.3.
14 [1983] 2 AC 548.
15 SDA s.1(1)(a) RRA s.1(1)(a).
16 *Per Lord Goff* in *James v Eastleigh Borough Council* [1990] 2 AC 751.
17 [1986] IRLR 134, Ct of Sess.
18 IDS Brief 150.
19 RRA s.1(2).
20 SDA s.1(1)(b), RRA s.1(1)(b).
21 Per Chief Justice Burger *Griggs v Duke Power Co* (1971) 401 US 424.
22 [1991] 1AC 171.
23 [1980] IRLR 64.
24 *Barclays Bank plc v Kapur* [1991] 1 All ER 748.
25 [1986] IRLR 103.
26 SDA s.4, RRA s2.
27 SDA s.48.
28 SDA s.7.
29 IDS Brief 98.
30 RRA s.5.
31 DDA s.5(1)(b).
32 DDA s.1 (b).
33 *Clark v TDG Ltd (t/a Novacold)* [1999] IRLR 318 CA.
34 DDA s.1(1).
35 DDA 1995, Schedule 1 Para A12.
36 DDA s.16.
37 [1998] IRLR 352.
38 DDA s.6(4).
39 EAT/493/98.
40 [1999] IRLR 318 CA.
41 RRA s.4(1)(a), SDA s.6(1)(a), DDA s.4(1)(a).
42 RRA s.29(1), SDA s.38(1).
43 RRA s.4(1)(a), SDA s.6(1)(a), DDA s.4(1)(a).
44 Commission For Racial Equality Code of Practice Paragraph 1(9).
45 RRA s.4(1)(a), SDA s.6(1)(a), DDA s.4(1)(a).
46 [1983] IRLR 357.
47 RRA s.4(1)(c), SDA s.6(1)(c).
48 Case Number 63658/94.
49 RRA s.4(2)(b), SDA s.6(2)(a).
50 [1982] IRLR 10.
51 RRA s.4(1)(c), SDA s.6(1)(c), DDA s.4(1)(c).

52 [1982] IRLR 482.
53 RRA s4(2)(c), SDA s6(2)(b), DDA s4(2)(d).
54 [1992] O.J. C27/4.
55 [1993] IRLR 374.
56 [1986] IRLR 134.
57 [1988] IRLR 145.
58 [1990] IRLR 3.
59 SDA ss.63 & 76.
60 *Barclays Bank plc v Kapur* [1991] 1 All ER 748.
61 *Handels v Dansk Arbejdsgiverforening* [1991 ICR 74.
62 Per *Bridge L J Shields v E Coomes (Holdings) Ltd* [1987] ICR 1159 CA at 1178.
63 *British Coal Corporation v Smith* [1994] IRLR 342.
64 EPA s.1(2)(a).
65 EPA s.1(2)(b).
66 EPA s.1(2)(c).
67 *Pointon v University of Sussex* [1979] IRLR 119 CA.
68 SDA s.77(3) unless it falls within the exceptions in s.77(4).
69 [1977] QB 852.
70 *Electrolux v Hutchinson* [1977] ICR 579.
71 *Kerr v Lister & Co Ltd* [1977] IRLR 259.
72 *Eaton Ltd v Nuttall* [1977] IRLR 71.
73 *Eaton Ltd v Nuttall.*
74 *Bromley v H & J Quick Ltd* [1988] IRLR 249 CA.
75 EPA s.1(3).
76 *Rainey v Greater Glasgow Health Board* [1987] IRLR 26.
77 *Ainsworth v Glass Tubes and Components* [1977] IRLR 74.
78 Part-time Workers (Prevention of Less Favourable Treatment) Regulations 2002/2035.
79 Fixed-Term Employees (Prevention of Less Favourable Treatment) Regulations 2002/2034.
80 Trade Union and Labour Relations (Consolidation) Act 1992 s.137 (as amended).
81 *Birmingham District Council v Beyer* [1978] 1 All ER 910.
82 Trade Union and Labour Relations (Consolidation) Act 1992 ss.152, 153.
83 *Stedman v UK* 2000 IDS Brief 671; ECHR.
84 Sex Discrimination (Indirect Discrimination and Burden of Proof) Regulations 2001/2660.

9

Pay, working time and individual employment rights

Bob Simpson

For the majority of workers, the legal basis of the employment relationship with their employer is a contract.[1] Most workers have the legal status of 'employees' and they are employed under 'contracts of employment',[2] which were once famously described as the 'cornerstone of the edifice' of labour law.[3] An increasing minority of the labour force do not, however, have the legal status of 'employee', although most of these do fall within the category of 'worker' as defined in current employment legislation.[4] Their employment contracts are generally known as 'contracts for services'. The first place to look for the employment rights of both workers and their employers is therefore the employment contract, whether it is a contract of employment or contract for services. The contractual rights and corresponding obligations of the parties are 'terms' of the contract.

The terms of a contract may be either 'express' or 'implied'. Express terms may be agreed on an individual basis. The limited bargaining power of most, though by no means all, workers means that most express terms which are 'agreed' in this way are generally the employer's terms. Workers whose terms of employment are determined by collective bargaining may have more 'say', albeit indirectly through trade unions, in the terms on which they work and thereby their rights and obligations *vis-à-vis* their employer, since relevant terms of collective agreements can be expressly incorporated into their employment contracts by reference. Such incorporation may also be implied where it is not expressed.

Implied terms are an important source of employment rights and obliga-tions for most workers. They can be divided into two groups. First, there are those implied terms which are peculiar to the particular job or employer. As well as terms impliedly incorporated into the employment contract from collective agreements, the courts may find that provisions in 'works rules', 'staff handbooks' or the like have become implied terms of individual employment contracts. Through implied terms, external documents and even unwritten custom and practice, which may reflect a degree of *de facto* control exercised by the workers, can therefore become a source of legal rights. The other group of implied terms comprises those implied 'by law'. Acts of Parliament may imply terms into the employment contract. The Equal Pay Act 1970, for example, implies an 'equality clause' into all the employment contracts to which it applies[5] and the National Minimum Wage Act 1998 simi-larly implies a contractual right for workers to be paid at least the rate of the national minimum wage (see below). Equally important are those terms which have been implied into employment contracts by the courts in the form of duties imposed on the employer, the employee or both. The courts have been particularly active in formulating new employment rights and corre-sponding obligations in this way in recent years.

The first section of this chapter looks at the 'employment rights' of general application which have come about in this way, together with some of the related body of statutory 'employment protection' rights which has been steadily built up since the 1960s.[6] Statutory employment rights are frequently intended to provide only a floor which can be built on by agreement – indi-vidual or collective – in ways appropriate to particular jobs or workplaces. This is true of the extensive body of statutory regulation concerning pay, which is arguably the most important issue to be covered by employment rights. Rights relating to pay, including the national minimum wage, are discussed in the following section while those relating to working time are the subject of the third section of the chapter.

RIGHTS DERIVED FROM TERMS OF THE EMPLOYMENT CONTRACT

Most of the rights which derive from decisions of the courts are normally expressed in legal terms as obligations or 'duties' which are owed by the other party. Adopting this legal frame of reference, it is possible to identify a number of duties which are owed by the employer, duties which are owed by the employee and an area of mutual duties of cooperation, trust and confidence which employer and employee owe to each other.[7] This section concludes with an analysis of an employee's statutory right to be given by his or her employer a written 'section 1'statement which sets out specified terms of the employment.

Duties owed by the employer

Until recently, the duties imposed by the law on employers in respect of all employment were quite limited in scope, though of central importance. The employer's duty to pay – and therefore the worker's right to receive – the agreed wage, salary or other remuneration is discussed in the next section of this chapter. Although there is no general duty on an employer to provide employees with work,[8] a duty to provide work may be implied as a term of the employment contract in certain circumstances. Where a worker's pay is calculated by reference to some measure of output, the courts have held that the employer is under a duty to provide a reasonable amount of work. This again is discussed more fully in the next section.

An uncertain issue of potentially wider importance is whether the courts are prepared to imply a more general 'right to work' into the terms of an employment contract and if so, in what circumstances. It attracted some judicial comment in the 1970s in two different contexts. The first, the rights of non-unionists employed in work which is covered by a closed shop is of little contemporary relevance.[9] The second concerned the rights of workers to exercise skills, update knowledge or maintain contacts in order to retain a competitive position in the labour market. This is clearly an issue of considerable importance and a decision of the Employment Appeal Tribunal in 1976 provides support for the view that it is a breach of contract for an employer to deny an employee these opportunities by providing no work to do; an employee who left his or her job in these circumstances could, therefore, claim that this was a case of constructive dismissal.[10]

One of the most important duties which the law has imposed on employers is the duty to take reasonable care for the health and safety of their workforce. Health and safety at work are discussed separately in Chapter 10 of this book. It may be noted in this context, however, that although most claims for breach of the duty are made in the law of tort, the duty also exists as an implied term in the contract of employment.[11] This was a significant feature of a major development of workers' rights in relation to working time, which is discussed in the third section of this chapter.

Another area in which there has been a significant recent advance in employment rights concerns references provided by employers for their employees or former employees. There is no general legal 'right to a reference' from an employer, so that a refusal by an employer to provide a reference does not necessarily give rise to any sort of legal remedy for the worker concerned. In 1994, however, in *Spring v Guardian Assurance*, the House of Lords held that in the ordinary case, an employer who provided a reference for one of its employees to a prospective future employer owed a duty of care to the employee.[12] While that duty was imposed as part of the tort of negligence, it was recognized that it could equally be expressed as an implied term in the contract of employment and as such it continued to apply after the employee concerned had left the employment of the person providing the reference. The duty is a duty to exercise reasonable care and skill in ensuring the accuracy of facts which either were communicated to the recipient of the reference and from which an adverse opinion of the employee could be formed, or were the basis of an adverse opinion about the employee expressed as part of the reference. While it would not of itself be a breach of this duty for an employer to express an adverse opinion about a current or former employee's abilities in a reference, if it causes the employee loss, the opinion could be an actionable breach of duty if the employer is unable to point to any facts on which it could reasonably be based.

Duties owed by the employee

The courts have imposed a wide range of obligations on employees by way of implied terms in the contract of employment. Perhaps the most basic obligation of an employee is to obey lawful orders given by the employer. This can be construed to include a duty to turn up for work at the time and place which have been agreed as part of the employment contract. Disputes over the employer's 'right' to require an employee to be flexible between different jobs or tasks, or prepared to work at different times or different places, which have arisen frequently in the context of claims for redundancy payments or unfair dismissal, have generally been resolved by reference to the express terms of the particular contract of employment and terms implied 'in fact' in relation to that contract. The general duty to obey lawful orders is, however, important in that an employee's refusal to do so can provide the grounds for a lawful 'summary' dismissal without the due notice that would otherwise be required.

The employee's duty not to commit misconduct also has a very broad ambit. While the House of Lords has held that employees do not owe a separate duty to disclose their own misconduct to their employer, an employee may be under a duty to disclose the misconduct of other, fellow employees even if the employee thereby incriminates him- or herself. This duty is more likely to exist where the employee has some managerial responsibilities.[13] A similar quasi-fiduciary obligation may arise under the implied duty of fidelity which all employees owe to their employer. What this duty to provide 'faithful service' actually means depends on the nature and circumstances of the job. It seems clear, however, that the unauthorized disclosure of confidential information, or use of that information for the employee's personal benefit rather than to advance the employer's interests, will normally amount to breach of the duty of fidelity which the employer can usually prevent or stop by seeking an injunction in the courts. Moreover, an employee may be restrained from using some confidential information acquired while in a particular job even after the employment has come to an end. It should be noted, however, that it is not always easy to identify which information is confidential and which is not.[14]

It is also well established that there is an implied term in contracts of employment that the employee will exercise due skill and care.[15] The level of skill which the employee can be expected to show depends in the first place on what abilities the employee professed to have when he or she started the job. But employees can be expected to show a progressive increase in their abilities as they gain more experience. While rare, it is not unknown for employers to seek damages for breach of this duty where an employee's unacceptable shortcomings have caused the employer loss.[16] An important extension of the logic underlying the duty of skill and care may be seen in the case of *Cresswell v Board of Inland Revenue*.[17] In this case staff at the Inland Revenue unsuccessfully sought a declaration from the court that they could not be required to perform tasks or discharge functions other than those expressly stipulated in the terms of their employment, habitually carried out by custom and practice, or other tasks and functions which were necessarily or reasonably incidental thereto. To the contrary the judge found that it was an implied term in the employment contract that the employee would be expected to adapt to new methods and techniques introduced in the course of the employment. On the facts, the Revenue staff could therefore, as a matter of their contractual duties, be required to change from carrying out tasks manually to doing the same tasks on computers. This effective 'duty of adaptability' has potentially far-reaching implications in terms of the 'right' of employers to expect their employees to acquire new skills, subject to the correlative obligation to facilitate employees developing the skills in question.

Mutual duties of cooperation, trust and confidence

One of the most recent important developments in employment law has been the evolution of an implied term in the employment contract which recognizes the need for continuing 'trust and confidence' between employer and employee. The main beneficiaries of this term as recorded in reported cases have been employees, but it is clear that the duty is a mutual one and not just a duty owed by the employer.[18] The existence of this implied term was confirmed by the House of Lords in *Mahmud v BCCI* in 1997, a decision which allowed former employees of BCCI to proceed with claims for damages against the Bank's liquidators for losses alleged to flow from the 'stigma' of having worked for BCCI now that it had been exposed as having carried out its operations in a corrupt and dishonest manner.[19]

However, the House of Lords subsequently imposed an important limit on the circumstances in which employees can rely on a breach of the 'trust and confidence' duty against their employer. In *Johnson v Unisys Ltd* 20 a former employee's claim for damages for wrongful dismissal alleged that the manner of his dismissal was a breach of the implied duty of trust and confidence because the employers were aware that he had psychological problems and after his dismissal he suffered major psychiatric illness. A majority of the Law Lords, however, held that it would not be appropriate to extend the rights which the duty of trust and confidence conferred on the employee that far, for two reasons. First, the express terms of the contract gave the employer the right to terminate the contract at any time by giving due notice and an implied term could not qualify that right. Second, they considered the substance of the claim to be one for unfair dismissal for which legislation had provided a separate remedy (and for which Johnson had in fact received the maximum compensation attainable). It was not considered appropriate for the courts to devise a separate remedy for the same wrong. The employee's rights based on an alleged breach of the mutual duty of trust and confidence do not therefore extend to a remedy for the detrimental consequences of dismissal beyond those provided by the common law action for wrongful dismissal or the statutory claim for unfair dismissal (see Chapter 8).

The employee's right to a statement of employment particulars

There is no requirement for employment contracts to be in writing,[21] but section 1 of the Employment Rights Act 1996 (ERA 1996) requires employers to give a written statement of particulars of employment to all employees within two months of the beginning of their employment. This does not apply to employees whose continuous employment lasts for less than a month. The content of the statement may be subdivided into three parts. First, it must identify the employer and the employee, state when the employment began and the date when the employee's period of continuous employment began. Continuous employment is a statutory concept, the details of which are in sections 210–219 of the 1996 Act. The point here is that for the purposes of some statutory employment rights an employee's 'period of continuous employment' may include the time that he or she was employed by a previous employer, for example if the current employer took over a previous employer's business. This is an issue that has given rise to a considerable volume of contested litigation and section 1 would appear to require employers to be aware of the circumstances in which, as a matter of law, any of their employees can 'count' a period of employment with a previous employer as part of their continuous employment.

Second, that statement must contain 'particulars' of certain terms of the employment. Particulars of pay (rate, scale or method of calculating pay), the intervals at which the employee is paid, notice which each party has to give, job title and place of work or, where the employee is required or permitted to work at different places, the employer's address, must be given. Certain other particulars must be given if there are 'any' terms and conditions:

relating to hours, including normal working hours, entitlement to holidays, including public holidays and holiday pay, incapacity due to sickness or injury, including sick pay, pensions and pension schemes (unless the employee's pension rights are under a scheme in respect of which legislation requires the employee to be given information about pension rights), and any collective agreements which directly affect the terms and conditions of employment (if the employer is not a party to the collective agreement, the particulars must state who the parties are). If the employment is not intended to be permanent, the statement should identify the period for which it is intended to continue (and if it is a fixed-term contract the date when it ends). Where the employee is required to work outside the United Kingdom (UK) for more than a month, the particulars must include the period for which the employee is to work outside the UK, currency in which he or she will be paid, any additional pay or benefits provided, and any terms and conditions relating to the employee's return to the UK. For the required information on sickness and pensions the statement may refer to another reasonably accessible document and for the particulars on notice it may refer to the law – for example, the statutory minimum notice periods in section 86 of the 1996 Act – or a collective agreement. Subject to this, all the information must be in a single document.

Third, the statement must include a 'note' containing information on disciplinary rules and procedures and grievance procedures.[22] As far as procedures are concerned, the note must specify the person to whom the employee can apply if dissatisfied with a disciplinary decision or in order to raise a grievance, and either set out – or refer to a reasonably accessible document which sets out – the procedures that will apply. Changes to any of the particulars which the statement has to contain should be notified to the employee in a separate statement within a month of their taking effect.

Under section 11 of the 1996 Act an employee can make a claim to an employment tribunal (ET) that no statement has been provided, that not all the required 'particulars' have been given, or that some of the particulars given are wrong. The tribunal can confirm, amend or substitute particulars, but it probably cannot imply terms on those matters, for example working time, on which the legislation contemplates that there may be no provision.[23]

A 'section 1 statement' is not the same as a written contract and it cannot override express provisions in documents which do form part of the employment contract, as may be the case with a letter of appointment, for example.[24] In practice, however, employers frequently treat statements of 'written particulars' as if they were the contract and may well describe them as such. While this is a natural response to the legal requirement, it can give rise to confusion, particularly where there are other written documents like letters of appointment, which the courts are likely to treat as having overriding contractual force where they contain conflicting information.

PAY

Rights under the employment contract

In most contracts pay is, in legal terms, the 'consideration' provided by the employer in return for the work done by the worker.[25] The worker's 'right to be paid' the agreed amount is one of the fundamental terms of the contract such that in the case of both a total failure to pay and a unilateral reduction of pay by the employer, the entire foundation of the contract is undermined. Where this occurs, the worker can always claim damages for breach of contract and may be able to sue for the pay due.[26] Since the breach is, in legal terms, repudiatory, the workers can also treat the contract as at an end and will then be immediately free to accept alternative employment.[27] It follows from these principles that unless there is an express term in the contract which entitles the employer to do so, the employer cannot impose a pay cut without the worker's agreement.[28]

Pay is the one aspect of employment rights that has long been subject to a degree of statutory regulation. In addition to the legislation discussed in the remainder of this section and the following section on working time, two other aspects of the law may be briefly noted. First, the expanding body of parental rights includes provision for maternity pay for women who are on maternity leave and from April 2003 provides for a short period of paid paternity leave. Second, there is now an important body of case law in which workers have sought – almost invariably without success – to establish a right to some pay where they were taking part in a form of industrial action short of a strike and were, therefore, performing at least some of their normal contractual duties.[29]

Protective legislation

The Wages Act 1986 replaced earlier legislation in the Truck Acts concerning deductions from the pay of manual workers and shop assistants with a new body of protective legislation which regulates the right of employers to make deductions from the pay of all workers. These provisions are now in Part II of the ERA 1996. For employees, but not workers who are not employees, they complement the right to an itemized pay statement, originally enacted in 1975 and now in sections 8–10 of the 1996 Act. This is a straightforward right, the purpose of which is to ensure that all employees are made aware of their gross pay for each pay period, details of the deductions made and the resulting net pay. Subject to one qualification, all this information must be set out in a statement given to the employee each time that he or she is paid. The qualification is that in respect of 'fixed deductions', details need not be set out in each pay statement as long as the employee is given a statement of fixed deductions at least once a year. The right to an itemized pay statement is enforceable by way of complaint to an employment tribunal which can determine the information that should have been included in a pay statement and may order the employer to repay unnotified deductions which can go back up to 13 weeks before the employee initiated tribunal proceedings.[30]

Part II of the 1996 Act gives effect to one of the most important rights for workers in modern employment law: the right to receive full pay subject only to deductions which are authorized by legislation, such as income tax and national insurance contributions, or have previously been 'agreed' by the employer and worker concerned. This 'agreement' must either be a term of the worker's contract, in which case the worker must either have a copy of the contract or be notified in writing before any deduction which it authorized has been made, or evidenced by separate prior written agreement or consent to the deduction (ERA 1996 s.13). To this general rule there are six exceptions in section 14: reimbursement of an overpayment of wages or expenses incurred by the worker; deductions made in accordance with any disciplinary proceedings held under a statute; statutorily authorized deductions of sums paid over to a public authority; deductions which are paid, in accordance with the worker's written agreement, to a third party;[31] deductions made on account of the worker having taken part in industrial action;[32] and deductions made, with the worker's written agreement, in order to satisfy a court order requiring the worker to pay that amount to the employer.

These provisions cannot be avoided by imposing an obligation on the worker to make payments to the employer in place of rights for the employer to make deductions from pay. Sections 15 and 16 of the 1996 Act contain parallel provisions to sections 13 and 14 in respect of payments to the employer. In the mid-1980s publicity was given to the practice of some retailers of making deductions from the pay of their workers to make good stock shortages or till deficiencies at the end of their shifts. To address this particular issue, sections 17–22 of the 1996 Act impose additional constraints on employers in respect of deductions from the pay of 'retail workers' on account of any 'cash shortages' – deficits in amounts received in connection with retail transactions – or 'stock deficiency' arising in the course of retail transactions. They must not exceed 10 per cent of the gross wages due for that pay period[33] and they must relate to shortages or deficiencies established (or which the employer ought reasonably to have established) in the immediately preceding 12 months. But this 10 per cent limit does not apply to any deduction made from the final instalment of wages made on termination of the worker's employment.

These rights are enforceable in ETs and in recent years only the number of unfair dismissal claims has exceeded those made under these provisions.[34] In the leading case, *Delaney v Staples*, the Court of Appeal held in 1991 that any shortfall in pay amounted to a 'deduction' and therefore had to comply with the requirements now in section 13 of the 1996 Act. In the same case in the House of Lords a year later, however, it was held that with one exception 'pay in lieu of notice' was not wages for the purposes of this body of law so that workers could not use it to challenge any alleged shortfall in the sum received. The one exception, where a worker is given 'garden leave', that is, paid for the notice period which the employer is required to give but not required to work during that period, occurs most frequently in relation to highly paid executive posts in respect of which disputes that give rise to litigation are more likely to focus on details on each party's contractual obligations and take place in the High Court.[35] Part II of the 1996 Act was also given a restrictive construction by the Court of Appeal in *New Century Cleaning v Church*,[36] where a majority held that it could not be used to challenge an alleged underpayment of a team of workers where the employer agreed only the total amount due to the team and acted on the advice of the team leader in making payments to individual team members.

Guarantee pay

There is no universally implied term in employment contracts which gives the employer a right to lay workers off, or put them on short time, when there is a shortage of work for them to do. It is possible for a term to this effect to be implied on the basis of established custom in relation to particular jobs. Equally, a term which gives the employer the right to impose lay-offs or short-time working may be incorporated into individual workers' contracts from collective agreements, but where this occurs the employer will only be able to rely on the right if all the conditions attached to it – for example, the agreement of local union officials – are complied with.[37] The thinking behind collectively agreed 'guaranteed week agreements' is evident in the statutory right which is now in sections 28–35 of the ERA 1996. This provides employees who have normal working hours and have been employed for at least a month with a right to guarantee pay for up to five 'workless' days in any three-month period. A 'workless day' is one on which an employee is not provided with any work, except where this is due to industrial action involving any employee of the employer, or an unreasonable refusal by the employee either of suitable alternative work or to comply with any reasonable requirements imposed by the employer for ensuring that the employee's services are available. The amount of the payment is, in principle, calculated by reference to the employee's 'week's pay' which in turn is computed in accordance with sections 220–229 of the 1996 Act. But it is subject to a maximum which is, from February 2002, £17 per day.[38] The statutory right to guarantee pay is subject to exemption orders in favour of collective agreements providing for guarantee pay. Twenty-four exemption orders were in force in 2000.

Sick pay

As already noted, the 'section 1 statement' which employers are required to give to their employees should include particulars of 'any terms and conditions relating to incapacity for work due to sickness or injury, including any provision for sick pay' (ERA 1996 s.1(4)(d)(ii)). Whether a worker has a right to be paid while off work because of sickness or injury depends in the first place on the terms of the employment contract. Most contracts make express provision on this issue. Where there is no express term, the courts can imply a term and in so doing, the Court of Appeal has held that they can have regard to what had happened in practice since the contract was made as one of the relevant facts and circumstances. Thus if no employee doing a particular type of work ever asked for or received pay while off sick, that would support an implied term that there was no right to receive any pay while off sick.[39]

In 1983, the social security entitlement to sickness benefit was replaced by 'statutory sick pay' (SSP). After several modifications, the Social Security (Contributions and Benefits) Act 1992 now requires employers to pay SSP to all employees whose average weekly earnings are at or above the 'lower earnings limit' (from April 2002 £72 per week).[40] No SSP is payable for the first three days of absence, but absences within an eight-week period can be combined for this purpose. SSP is payable for up to 28 weeks and the rate, which is revised annually, was £63.25 from April 2002. Only 'small' employers whose total national insurance contributions fall below a prescribed threshold are now entitled to a rebate from the State of the amount of SSP paid. While the detail of SSP entitlements can only be understood by reference to constantly changing regulations, one important general provision is that payment of sick pay under the terms of a worker's employment contract counts towards meeting an employer's SSP obligations. Most contractual sick pay arrangements provide for a level of payment above the rate of SSP, at least during the early weeks of a period of absence due to sickness.

Right to pay on an employer's insolvency

When an employer becomes insolvent, employees can claim up to four months' arrears of pay due (up to a maximum of £800) and accrued holiday pay as preferred creditors. In most circumstances the right to claim certain unpaid items from the State, technically the Secretary of State for Trade and Industry, will be more valuable. This claim can cover up to eight weeks' arrears of pay, pay in lieu of the statutory minimum notice entitlement in section 86 of the 1996 Act, six weeks' arrears of holiday pay and, where a former employee has been awarded compensation for unfair dismissal, the 'basic award' part of that compensation (see Chapter 6). The maximum amount of a week's pay for these purposes, £240 as from February 2002, is index-linked under section 34 of the Employment Relations Act 1999 and is adjusted annually in line with the Retail Prices Index.

The national minimum wage

When the National Minimum Wage Act 1998 (NMWA) came into force in April 1999, it marked a major departure from previous practice in setting a legally backed minimum rate of pay which was applicable across the whole labour force. Although the tripartite wages councils which fixed minimum pay rates on a sectoral basis were abolished in 1993, the structurally similar Agricultural Wages Boards are still in existence. Their power to fix minimum pay rates for agricultural workers is now subject to the caveat that the rates which they set must not be lower than the applicable national minimum wage (NMW) rate. Although the concept of a minimum rate of pay for all workers is a straightforward one, the legislative detail is of some complexity.

The NMW is expressed as an hourly rate of pay. This was increased to £4.20 in October 2002, implementing the recommendation of the Low Pay Commission (LPC) in its Third Report.[41] The government has, however, made use of its powers in sections 3 and 4 of the NMWA to exclude some workers from the right to the minimum wage and provide lower rates for others. Young workers aged 16 or 17 are currently excluded from the right to any NMW. So too are apprentices under the age of 19 or, if aged 19–26, during the first year of their apprenticeship. Workers aged 18 to 21 inclusive[42] qualify for a lower rate (often called the 'development' rate) which was set at £3.60 in October 2002. Since June 2000 this rate for young workers has been the same as the 'training' rate which applies to workers of any age during the first six months of their employment if, during that time, they are receiving at least 26 days' 'accredited training' as defined in regulation 13 of the NMW Regulations.[43] All these provisions for exclusions and lower rates have been controversial. It should be noted, however, that subject to these provisions the NMWA is drafted so as to cover virtually all sections of the labour force, whatever the legal nature of the employment relationship between worker and employer.[44]

The most difficult issues raised by a legally binding NMW are defining the 'wage' and the working time for which it has to be paid. The NMW is expressed as an hourly rate, but compliance with the law is measured not by reference to each hour worked but to a 'pay reference period' (PRP) which is either a month or the shorter period by reference to which a worker is paid, for example a week. All payments made 'in respect of' a PRP count, even if they are paid in the following PRP or later where the reason that they were not paid earlier was the worker's failure to submit a required record of work such as a time sheet. Subject to one qualification, the 'pay' that counts is limited to money payments for standard work: all money payments made by the employer to the worker for a PRP count, subject to 'reductions' to exclude overtime premiums, allowances (such as shift premiums or London allowances) and tips or gratuities which are not distributed through the payroll. The only benefit in kind that counts towards an employer's NMW obligations is the provision of accommodation, a declining practice which is most common in the hospitality sector. Since October 2001 employers have been able to count the lesser of 57p for each hour worked in the PRP or £2.85 for each day in the PRP for which accommodation was provided towards meeting their obligation to pay the NMW.

The most difficult issues raised in drafting legislation which translates the concept of a minimum wage into a meaningful legal entitlement concern identification of the working time for which the NMW must be paid. All work is assigned to one of four categories. 'Time work' is the most straightforward; it includes not only work paid solely by reference to the time worked but also work paid partly by reference to time and partly by reference to output, for example piece work subject to a guaranteed minimum for a fixed number of hours worked. 'Salaried hours work' is work which entitles the worker to an annual salary for a basic number of annual hours, paid in equal weekly or monthly instalments[45] even though the amount of work done may fluctuate – for example, with seasonal demand or as between school terms and holidays. 'Output work' is work paid by reference to some measure of output such as pieces made or sales processed. All other work is 'unmeasured work'.

Time 'on call' counts as either time work or salaried hours work unless the worker is entitled to spend the time at home 'at or near the place of work', a provision intended to address the abusive practice of 'zero hours contracts'. 'Sleepover time' can only be excluded from time for which the NMW must be paid if suitable facilities for sleeping are provided at or near the place of work and even then the time when the worker is awake for the purpose of working is time for which the NMW must be paid. Travelling time, except for travel between home and work, counts as part of working time. So too does the time when the worker is receiving training or travelling between the workplace and the place where training is provided.

Subject to these points, a worker is *prima facie* entitled to be paid at least the NMW for all hours worked on time work, output work or unmeasured work. For output work or unmeasured work, however, this may be displaced by an agreement between the worker and employer on hours worked. For unmeasured work, the regulations require any 'daily average' agreement on hours worked to be 'realistic'. The worker's NMW entitlement is then calculated on the basis that the worker worked this number of hours on each day in the PRP. For 'output work' a 'fair estimate agreement' can only displace actual hours where the employer does not in practice determine or control the hours worked. The estimated number of hours must also be at least 80 per cent of the hours which an 'ordinary' worker would spend on the job to produce the same output.[46]

For salaried hours work, it is assumed that the worker works an equal number of hours in each PRP – one-twelfth of the annual hours where the

PRP is a month. Where pay is reduced because of absence from work, the number of hours which the worker is deemed to have worked is correspondingly reduced. If and when the number of hours worked in a year exceeds the basic annual hours, the worker is entitled to the NMW for the extra hours actually worked as well as for the contracted annual hours.

A worker does not have the right to be paid the NMW for periods of absence from work.[47] The 20-minute break which all workers are entitled to take after six hours' work under regulation 12 of the Working Time Regulations (see below) therefore does not have to be paid. However, the right to four weeks' paid holiday under regulation 13 of those regulations, for which pay is calculated by reference to the statutory provisions on a 'week's pay' in sections 220–229 of the Employment Rights Act 1996, will in practice give most workers the right to be paid at least the NMW rate for the period of the holiday.

There are two strands to the procedures for enforcing the NMW. First, workers can enforce their right to be paid the NMW in one of two ways. They can make a claim in the County Court for breach of contract, since section 17 of the NMWA gives them a contractual right to the amount of any underpayment below their NMW entitlement. Second, this amount is treated as an unlawful deduction for the purposes of Part II of the Employment Rights Act 1996, so that the right to be paid the NMW can be enforced in employment tribunals. Workers are also given the right to make tribunal claims against their employer when they are subjected to any 'detriment' for taking action to enforce the right to be paid the NMW. A dismissal of an employee for this reason is automatically unfair.[48]

The NMWA makes additional provision for the enforcement of the NMW by 'officers' and the Inland Revenue has been given this task. Employers are required to keep records sufficient to establish that workers are being paid at least the NMW and the designated Revenue officers have a right of access to those. Workers also have the right of access to records which relate to them and to be accompanied by another person when inspecting the records. An employer who fails to comply with a request for access can be taken to an employment tribunal and if the claim is upheld, an award of 80 times the then current main NMW rate is automatic. Inland Revenue officers can initiate proceedings on behalf of workers to enforce their right to be paid the NMW (though they cannot take cases of alleged detriment or unfair dismissal on behalf of individual workers).

The main coercive power which Revenue officers have is the right to serve an enforcement notice on an employer which requires the payment of arrears due to specified workers. Employers can appeal against an enforcement notice to an employment tribunal, which can rescind or modify the notice if it upholds the appeal. Subject to this, non-compliance with an enforcement notice can result in the Revenue serving a penalty notice imposing the penalty of a payment of twice the then current NMW rate for workers per day of non-compliance. This is also subject to a right of appeal to an employment tribunal.

WORKING TIME

As with pay, the starting point when looking for employment rights relating to working time is the individual worker's employment contract. For workers whose terms and conditions are determined to any extent by collective bargaining, working time and holiday entitlement are two issues on which at least some aspects of their employment rights are likely to be incorporated from collective agreements. While the 'section 1 statement' to which employees are entitled should include particulars of 'any' terms and conditions on hours of work and holidays, this clearly contemplates that in some jobs there will be no provision on these issues. Working time is a matter on which the nature and extent of contractually binding terms varies considerably.

Most of the patchwork of statutory regulation of working time which had been built up over the 19th and 20th centuries was repealed in the late 1980s and in 1994 a further step was taken in this 'deregulation' process when the Sunday Trading Act repealed the Shops Act 1950 and replaced the general regulation of shop opening hours by a more permissive legal regime. The removal of the very restricted scope for Sunday opening (which had been widely ignored) was accompanied by a limited degree of protection for workers with regard to Sunday working which is now part of the ERA 1996.

As far as working time generally was concerned, however, the deregulation policy was forced into reverse by two European Community Directives on Working Time in 1993 and Young People at Work in 1994. The United Kingdom implemented most of these Directives in 1998. The Working Time Regulations have, however, been subsequently amended in 1999 in response to employers' concerns, and in 2001 to remedy the defective implementation of the right to a paid holiday. Within the next few years steps will have to be taken to extend the scope of the regulation of working time to cover new workgroups who have been brought within the ambit of European Community regulation by subsequent Directives.[49]

Working time and the common law

Where employment contracts do make provision about working time, this may give rise to difficult issues of construction. In *Ali v Christian Salvesen Ltd*, for example, the courts had to resolve a dispute over entitlement to overtime pay under annualized hour agreements between the employer and trade unions.[50] These provided for pay at time and a half only when the agreed annual hours of each worker, 1,824, were exceeded in any year. The year for this purpose ran from June to May and workers worked more than the notional standard 40-hour week in the early months of this year; they normally worked shorter hours thereafter. Workers who were dismissed in November 1992 had therefore worked many hours in excess of 40 a week since the previous June without receiving any overtime premium. The Court of Appeal held that they were not entitled to any overtime premium for any of the weeks in which they had worked more than 40 hours, as a matter of construction of the annualized hours agreement. The potential advantage to employers of an agreement on working time of this type is clear.

By contrast the implications of the well-publicized Court of Appeal decision in *Johnstone v Bloomsbury Health Authority* in 1991, while far from clear, were rather more favourable to workers whose employment contracts could require them to work long weekly hours.[51] In that case, a junior hospital doctor challenged the right of his employer to require him to work the long hours that the express terms of his contract required: 40 a week plus 'on average' a further 48 hours a week 'on call'. The Court of Appeal could not agree on the difficult issue of how to reconcile these express terms of the contract with the employer's implied duty to take reasonable care for the doctor's health. There was a majority support for the view that the express terms on hours at most narrowed, but did not override, the implied duty, which became a duty to take only such care for the doctor's health as was consistent with his working on the specified high-risk tasks. As is noted in footnote 49, the particular issue of the hours of work of doctors in training has now been addressed at European Community level.

Statutory rights to time off work

Statutory rights to time off work now form a substantial body of law. Some of them carry a right to pay during time off; others do not. A majority of them are functionally linked to other rights. Thus the right of employees who are under notice of dismissal for redundancy to take time off to look for alternative work or training can appropriately be seen as part of a wider body of rights for redundant employees, including the right to redundancy pay. The right to pay during time off for this reason is limited to a maximum of two-fifths of a week's pay for all the time off taken. Similarly, the right of pregnant employees to a reasonable amount of time off – paid at the normal rate – for antenatal care is part of a wider package of maternity rights for working women. The right of employees who are pension fund trustees to paid time off for their functions as trustees or undergoing relevant training was introduced as part of the mid-1990s legislation on pensions. Officials of independent recognized unions have been entitled to paid time off for specified 'trade union duties' since the 1970s and members of these unions have the right to unpaid time off to take part in trade union activities. These rights are being extended by the Employment Act 2002 to include paid time off for union learning representatives and unpaid time off for members to have access to these representatives. When the obligation for employers to inform and consult workforce representatives in advance of redundancies and business transfers was extended to workgroups for whom there was no recognized union in 1995, a similar right to paid time off was extended to 'employee representatives' elected for this purpose and candidates for election as employee representatives.

There are three other rights to time off work which are not functionally linked to any other legal rights. Employees have a right to a reasonable amount of unpaid time off for 'public duties' as a member of one of a range of specified public bodies. Sixteen- and seventeen-year-old employees whose educational achievements fall below prescribed standards are entitled to paid time off to study for certain specified qualifications. Finally, one of the rights introduced under the 'family-friendly policies' umbrella in 1999 was the right of an employee to unpaid time off to take action necessary to deal with one of a specified list of matters concerning dependants, including illness, injury, death and unexpected disruption of care arrangements.

Working Time Regulations

Like the NMWA, the Working Time Regulations 1998 (WTR) provide employment rights in relation to working time and holidays for 'workers' rather than the narrower category of 'employees' to which many statutory employment rights are confined. However, several 'significant' workgroups are at present excluded from the rights provided by the WTR. These include all workers in the air, road, rail, sea, inland waterway and lake transport sectors, sea fishermen, mariners and doctors in training (regulation 18). As already noted, though, European Community Directives have now extended the regulation of working hours to those sectors, in each case subject to some sector-specific modifications or permitted derogations (see note 49). Further domestic regulations will have to be introduced in the near future in order to implement these extensions. Other more limited exclusions from WTR rights can best be explained in the context of analysis of the rights or entitlements to which they relate.

The two core provisions of the WTR are regulation 4(1) which states that a worker's working time shall not exceed an average of 48 hours a week and regulation 6(1) which provides that a night worker's normal hours shall not exceed an average of eight for each 24 hours. Just as compliance with the hourly rate of the NMW is assessed over a pay reference period of normally a week or a month, so too compliance with the 48-hour week is determined over a reference period. This is normally 17 weeks, but in relation to particular workgroups this may be replaced by a different period, not exceeding 52 weeks, established by a collective agreement or 'workforce agreement'.[52] More controversially, it is possible for individual workers to opt out of the 48-hour week by written agreement. The procedure for individual opt-outs was simplified by the 1999 Amendment Regulations. They must be agreed in writing and can be withdrawn by the workers on an agreed period of notice of at least seven days but not more than three months.[53] Employers must keep up-to-date records of workers who have opted out.

A night worker is defined as a worker who normally works at least three hours during night time. This is an agreed period of seven hours including the period from midnight to 5 am; in default of agreement it is the period from 11 pm to 6 am. Again, the reference period against which compliance with the average eight hours maximum is assessed is 17 weeks. Workers must be offered the opportunity of a free health assessment before they are assigned to night work. Young workers under the age of 18 must not be assigned to any work between 10 pm and 6 am unless they have had this opportunity and, if they do night work, must have the opportunity for free health assessments at regular intervals.

Subject to express qualifications, these provisions on weekly hours and night work are mandatory limits on working time, reflecting the health and safety basis of the Regulations. By contrast the provisions on rest periods are expressed as 'entitlements'. Regulation 8 imposes a general obligation on employers to ensure that a worker is given adequate rest breaks where the work pattern puts his or her health and safety at risk 'in particular because the work is monotonous or the work rate is predetermined'. But the specific provisions on 'daily rest', 11 hours (12 for young workers) in 24; 'weekly rest', 24 hours in 7 days or 48 hours in 14 days (48 in 7 days for young workers, reduceable to 36 for technical organizational reasons); and a rest break of 20 minutes after 6 hours' work (30 minutes after 4½ hours for young workers) are 'entitlements' which workers can choose not to take.

None of these rights apply to 'managing executives or other persons with autonomous decision-taking powers' where 'on account of the specific characteristics of the activity in which he is engaged, the duration of his working time is not measured or predetermined or can be determined by the worker himself' (reg.20(1)). More controversially, where part of a worker's work is measured, predetermined or cannot be determined by the worker, but the worker may also do other work 'the duration of which is not measured or predetermined but can be determined by the worker himself', the limits on maximum weekly hours and night work only apply to the measured or predetermined part of their work (reg.29(2)). While the complexity of this exception for 'unmeasured working time' may be helpfully unravelled to some extent by the illustrations in the DTI Guide to the WTR, it clearly increases the uncertainty as to the circumstances in which the core regulations do not apply. Other exceptions from the limits on night work and the entitlements to breaks, daily and weekly rest are made in relation to specified work where there is a need for continuity of service or production, foreseeable increases in activity in agriculture, tourism and postal services and to take account of exceptional or unforeseen circumstances (reg.21).

The WTR provide for enforcement of the main limits on weekly working hours and night work by the Health and Safety Executive in accordance with the procedures in the Health and Safety at Work Act 1974 (regs.28 and 29). Under regulation 30, the entitlements to rest breaks, daily and weekly rest are enforceable by individual workers in employment tribunals. The WTR also provide for workers to seek a remedy in employment tribunals when they are subjected to any detriment for asserting their rights or claiming their entitlements: the dismissal of an employee on these grounds is automatically unfair. In an important decision in *Barber v RJB Mining* in 1999 it was held that regulation 4 gives a worker a contractual right not to work more than an average 48 hours a week over the reference period. Where the working time required exceeded this, the worker was entitled to a declaration that he or she could not be required to work until sufficient time had elapsed to bring the weekly average hours back below 48.[54] The background to this litigation was unresolved negotiations between the worker's trade union and the employer over working time. Consistent with the objectives of the legislation, agreements on working time reached against the background of the WTR remain the most appropriate way of securing the effective regulation of working time.

Holidays

Before the WTR came into force in 1998, a worker's holiday entitlement, and the right to be paid while on holiday, depended almost exclusively on the terms of the employment contract. The Agricultural Wages Boards still fix minimum holiday entitlements for agricultural workers, but now this cannot be less than their entitlement under the WTR. Contrary, perhaps, to popular belief, there is no general legal right to take any of the six bank holidays or Christmas Day and Good Friday (which are customary holidays) as holiday. However, all or any of these public holidays may be part of a worker's contractual holiday entitlement by virtue of an applicable collective agreement.[55] Premium rates of pay for working on public holidays and/or time off in lieu are frequently agreed for particular jobs on either a collective or individual basis.

Regulation 13 of the WTR provides that all workers are entitled to four weeks' annual leave and regulation 16 requires this to be paid at at least the rate of a 'week's pay' as calculated under sections 221–224 of the ERA 1996. A worker's 'leave year' begins on the date agreed in a collective or workforce agreement; where there is no such agreement it begins on 1 October or the anniversary of the date on which the worker started work. Where workers leave employment before they have taken all or any of their annual leave entitlement for the current leave year, they are entitled to compensation for the proportionate part of untaken leave.[56] Many workers do, of course, have rights to paid holidays under the terms of their employment contracts. Regulation 17 of the WTR provides that where this is so, the worker can take advantage of whichever right – the contract right or the right under regulation 13 – is, in any particular respect, the more favourable.[57] In 2001 the WTR were amended in response to a decision of the European Court of Justice so that the right to four weeks' paid annual leave now accrues at the rate of one-twelfth per month worked.[58]

Notes

1 There has been much debate over whether those in Crown employment – civil servants – have contracts with the Crown, or whether their employment is solely a matter of status.

2 Lawyers and legislation still use the older term 'contract of service'. For all practical purposes this means a contract of employment.

3 Kahn-Freund, O (1954) Labour law, in *The System of Industrial Relations in Great Britain*, ed Flanders and Clegg, Blackwell, Oxford, p 45.

4 Section 230 of the Employment Rights Act 1996, the main source of statutory employment rights, defines a worker as an individual who works under a contract of employment or 'any other contract... whereby the individual undertakes to do or perform personally any work or services for another party to the contract whose status is not by virtue of that contract that of a client or customer of any profession or business carried on by the individual'.

5 Equal pay for men and women is discussed in Chapter 8 of this book.

6 The most important of these are discussed elsewhere in this book – eg Chapter 6 on unfair dismissal and Chapter 8 on discrimination.

7 These duties have evolved in cases concerning contracts of employment between employer and employee. It is uncertain to what extent they exist as a matter of law between employers and workers who are not their employees but with whom they have contracts for the workers to provide services.

8 *Turner v Sawdon & Co* [1901] 2 KB 653 CA.

9 *Langston v AUEW* [1974] ICR 180.

10 *Breach v Epsylon Industries* [1976] ICR 316 EAT.

11 See *Wilsons & Clyde Coal Co Ltd v English* [1938] AC 57 HL.

12 [1994] ICR 596 HL; see too the earlier High Court decision *Lawton v BOC Transhield Ltd* [1987] ICR 7 and the later decisions *Batholomew v London Borough of Hackney* [1997] IRLR 246 CA, *Kidd v Axa Equity & Law Life Assurance Society* [2000] IRLR 301, and *Cox v Sun Alliance* [2001] IRLR 448 CA.

13 *Bell v Lever Brothers* [1936] AC 161 HL; *Sybron v Rochem* [1983] ICR 801 CA.

14 See *Marshall Ltd v Guinle* [1979] Ch 227 and *Faccenda Chicken v Fowler* [1986] ICR 297 CA. The legal protection of confidential information and the legal remedies for 'breach of confidence' are separate areas of the law. In some circumstances, the disclosure of confidential information may be a

protected disclosure under the Public Interest (Disclosure) Act 1998, which provides some legal protection for 'whistleblowers'.

15 *Lister v Romford Ice and Cold Storage Co.* [1957] AC 555 HL.

16 Eg *Janata Bank v Ahmed* [1981] ICR 791 CA.

17 [1984] ICR 508. See too the earlier decision in *North Riding Garages v Butterwick* [1967] 2 QB 56 DC.

18 See eg Lord Millett in *Johnson v Unisys* [2001] ICR 480, 505 para. 78.

19 *Mahmud v Bank of Credit and Commerce International SA* [1997] ICR 606 HL. The claims that were litigated as test cases failed because the former employees were unable to prove that the alleged 'stigma' had adversely affected their attempts to find new employment: *BCCI v Ali (No.2)* [2000] ICR 1354.

20 [2001] ICR 480 HL.

21 There are exceptions, notably a contract of (traditional) apprenticeship.

22 The note should also state whether there is a certificate in force certifying that the employment is 'contracted-out' for the purposes of the Pensions Schemes Act 1993.

23 The Court of Appeal has expressed different views on this point: *Mears v Safecar Security Ltd* [1982] ICR 626 cf *Eagland v British Telecommunication plc* [1993] ICR 644.

24 See in particular *Robertson v British Gas Corporation* [1983] OCR 351 CA.

25 There are exceptions, notably with voluntary workers, on whose employment rights see Debra Morris (1999) 28 ILJ 249.

26 The distinction is important. A claim for damages is subject to the worker's duty to mitigate his or her loss by seeking alternative employment. On when a claim can be made for the remuneration due see *Abrahams v Performing Rights Society* [1995] ICR 1028 CA and *Cerberus Software v Rowley* [2001] ICR 376 CA.

27 *Cantor Fitzgerald v Callaghan* [1999] ICR 858 CA, where the general principles in this area of the law are fully discussed.

28 *Burdett-Coutts v Hertfordshire County Council* [1984] IRLR 91; *Rigby v Ferodo Ltd* [1988] ICR 20 HL.

29 See Ewing, K D (1991) *The Right to Strike*, Oxford University Press, Oxford, ch 4, and *British Telecommunications plc. v Ticehurst* [1992] ICR 383 CA.

30 See *Scott v Creager* [1979] ICR 493 EAT; *Coales v John Wood* [1986] ICR 71 EAT.

31 The 'check off' of trade union subscriptions from pay is an example of this. The legality of the check off also turns on compliance with sections 68 and 68A of the Trade Union and Labour Relations (Consolidation) Act 1992.

32 It appears that an ET claim under Part II of the 1996 Act cannot therefore be used to challenge the amount of such deduction: *Sunderland Polytechnic v Evans* [1993] ICR 392 EAT.

33 Parallel provisions in section 19 cover arrangements whereby pay is calculated by reference to the extent of cash shortages or stock deficiencies, rather than a 'deduction' being made on account of these.

34 In 2001–2, 37, 591 claims under Part II of the 1996 Act were referred to the Advisory Conciliation and Arbitration Service (ACAS) for conciliation compared with 52,000 unfair dismissal cases: ACAS *Annual Report 2000–2001* Appendix 1 Table 8.

35 *Delaney v Staples* [1991] ICR 331 CA; [1992] ICR 483 HL. Disputes that could be brought before ETs under Part II of the 1996 Act may be taken to the High Court as breach of contract claims in appropriate cases: *Rickard v PB Glass Supplies* [1990] ICR 150 CA.

36 [2000] IRLR 27 CA.

37 See *Neads v CAV Ltd* [1983] IRLR 360; *Miller v Hamworthy Engineering* [1986] ICR 846 CA.

38 This sum is index-linked under section 34 of the Employment Relations Act 1999 and is adjusted annually in line with the Retail Price Index.

39 *Mears v Safecard Security Ltd* [1982] ICR 626 CA.

40 This may include workers who are employed on a daily basis since their employment is deemed to be for an indefinite period after they have in fact worked for more than three months. See *Brown v Chief Adjudication Officer* [1997] ICR 266 CA.

41 The Low Pay Commission is a tripartite body which was originally established in 1997 to advise on the rate(s) which at the NMW should be introduced. It is now a statutory body which reports to the Secretary of State on any issue relating to the NMW which is referred to it. See ss.5–8 of the NMWA.

42 The LPC has consistently recommended in its first three reports that workers who are aged 21 should receive the full adult rate, but the government has yet to agree to this.

43 SI 1999 No. 584.

44 Not only does the right to the NMW apply to all workers and not just employees, but express provision is made to ensure that agency workers and homeworkers or other outworkers are covered. NMWA ss.34 and 35.

45 The amount of each payment may vary as long as the total amount paid in each quarter is the same.

46 Where a 'fair estimate agreement' exists, the worker's NMW entitlement is determined by calculating the 'daily average' hours a worker is likely to work and multiplying that by the number of days on which the worker actually worked in the PRP.

47 Times when the worker is taking part in industrial action are treated as absence from work even though, where this is action short of strike, the worker may be doing some work. See regulations 15(6), 17(2) and 18(2) of the NMW Regulations.

48 This right applies to all employees; the normal qualifying period of one year's employment and the exclusion of claims by workers over the normal retiring age do not apply.

49 The Horizontal Amending Directive 2001 has extended the provision of the Working Time Directive, with modifications in relation to several

particular types of worker, to most workers in the transport sectors – air, rail, road, sea, inland waterway and lake transport, fishing and other work at sea, and doctors in training. Most of the workers must be covered by new regulations by 2002 or 2003. The 48-hour working week for doctors in training may, however, be phased in over a period ending in 2012. In addition, the Aviation Directive and Seafarers Directive make further provision for mobile workers in those sectors.

50 [1997] ICR 25 CA, reversing [1996] ICR 1 EAT.

51 [1991] ICR 269 CA.

52 A 'workforce agreement' is an agreement with elected representatives of a particular group within the workforce (or if that group consists of 20 or fewer workers with a majority of those workers). See Schedule 1 to WTR.

53 The DTI *Guide to the Working Time Regulations* contains a model opt-out agreement: p.6.

54 [1999] ICR 679.

55 See eg *Tucker v British Leyland* [1978] IRLR 493.

56 Cf the refusal of the Court of Appeal to imply a term to this effect into the contract of employment in the pre-WTR case of *Morley v Heritage* [1993] IRLR 400.

57 The same is true of the worker's 'entitlements' to rest, daily and weekly breaks under the WTR.

58 Working Time (Amendment) Regulations 2001, SI 2001 No.3256 responding to the decision in *R (BECTU) v Secretary of State for Trade and Industry* [2001] ICR 1152 ECJ.

10

Health and safety

Brenda Barrett

The principal objective of occupational health and safety law needs to be the prevention of accidents and work-related illnesses. However, it is also necessary to provide compensation for those who are injured. In recognition of the primary importance of the protection of the workforce, this account is mainly concerned with the legislation and systems for the prevention of work-related accidents and ill health. It only briefly reviews compensation law.

PREVENTION OF OCCUPATIONAL INJURIES

For 200 years Britain has had regulatory legislation imposing sanctions on employers failing to achieve satisfactory standards of health and safety. The present statutory framework dates from the 1970s. In 1970 Parliament appointed a Select Committee to review the then existing law. That Committee reported in 1972 and the Health and Safety at Work Act 1974 closely followed its recommendations. The 1974 Act remains the principal legislation. It now supports many European directives. Whether it provides a suitable framework for the 21st century has been questioned,[1] but there are no firm proposals to replace it.

The Select Committee of 1970

The Select Committee on Safety and Health at Work (under Lord Robens's chairmanship) was appointed in 1970 with very wide terms of reference. It was required: 'To review the provision made for the safety and health of persons at work... and consider whether any changes are needed...'. The Committee reported[2] that then existing 'legislation is badly structured...'.[3] It recommended: 'The existing statutory provisions should be replaced by a comprehensive and orderly set of revised provisions under a new enabling Act. The new Act should contain a clear statement of the basic principles of safety responsibility... .'[4]

The Committee urged Parliament to entrust management with the implementation of broad general duties. It stressed that: 'The promotion of safety and health is not only a function of good management, but it is, or ought to be, a normal management function – just as production or marketing is a normal function.'[5] However it believed that: 'In this context more than most, real progress is impossible without the full cooperation and commitment of all employees... We believe that if workpeople are to accept their full share of responsibility... they must be able to participate fully in the making and monitoring of arrangements for safety and health at their place of work.'

What came to be called 'the Robens philosophy'[6] can, with hindsight, be criticized. The proposal to shift from a checklist of narrow specification standards to a broad systems approach that depended on management initiative to achieve performance standards was a cultural change that large organizations might welcome but few smaller firms would appreciate.[7] There was also a naiveté in the Committee's belief that health and safety need only be a matter of consultation between management and employees because both had an equal interest in ensuring that workplaces were safe. The assumption that safety was not a matter for negotiation was questionable.[8] However, there were comparable contemporary developments in a large part of the Western world. For example, the American Safety and Health at Work Act 1970 and the Norwegian Worker Protection and Working Environment Act 1977 demonstrated the same approach. Research funded by the EEC's Foundation for the Improvement of Living and Working Conditions in the late 1970s indicated similar activities in much of the EEC.[9] The Robens Report has also influenced Australian occupational health and safety law.

The Health and Safety at Work Act 1974

A Health and Safety at Work Bill was introduced by a Conservative government early in 1974. In the same year a Labour government enacted a very similar Bill. Both parties were agreed that legislation was necessary. It is possible that had there been less urgency the Labour government might have further modified the Conservatives' Bill.

There are four Parts and 10 Schedules to the Act. For present purposes Part I is the most important, for it contains both the general duties and the system for administering and enforcing the Act. Part II provides for the maintenance of the existing Employment Medical Advisory Service and Part III, Building Regulations and Amendment of Building (Scotland) Act is barely relevant to the general purposes of the Act. Part IV entitled 'Miscellaneous and General' includes some relevant provisions. For example, s.84(1) provides that the Act does not apply to Northern Ireland and s.84(3)[10] provides that parts of the Act may, by Order in Council, be extended, as necessary, to situations outside Great Britain. Section 84(3) has enabled provisions of the Act, and regulations made under it, to be extended to offshore installations in the North Sea.

Purposes of the Act

The Act was somewhat unusual for its time in that in s.1(1) it set out its intentions. These were:

(a) securing the health, safety and welfare of persons at work;
(b) protecting persons other than persons at work against risks to health or safety arising out of or in connection with the activities of persons at work;
(c) controlling the keeping and use of explosives or highly flammable or otherwise dangerous substances, and generally preventing the unlawful acquisition, possession and use of such substances;
(d) controlling the emission into the atmosphere of noxious or offensive substances from premises of any class prescribed for the purposes of this paragraph.

The remarkably wide scope of the Act is noteworthy even now, and was exceptional in 1974. The following matters are particularly significant:

● The statutory protection is not confined, as was the case in earlier legislation, such as the Factories Act 1961, to workers classified as employees. The expression 'persons at work' must be read together with s.52 which states:

  (a) 'work' means work as an employee or as a self-employed person;
  (b) an employee is at work throughout the time when he [throughout this Act, as is common in legislation, the word 'he' includes 'she'] is in the course of his employment, but not otherwise; and
  (c) a self-employed person is at work throughout such time as he devotes to work as a self-employed person;...

In 1974 this extension to the self-employed was very unusual. In more recent years it usefully complies with the broad approach to worker protection required by European directives. By subsequent regulations 'at work' has been extended for certain specific situations. Offshore workers are deemed to be 'at work' throughout the time they are on the installation[11] and certain activities involving the consignment, storage or use of biological agents are now included.[12]

- The Act covers not only workers but also members of the public. The inclusion of public protection is particularly significant in relation to premises such as hospitals, theatres and sports' stadia, but its full impact can be seen in *R v Board of Trustees of the Science Museum*.[13] The Museum was convicted under s.3 of the Act because its faulty air conditioning plant put the public at risk by allowing the escape on to the highway of bacteria *capable* of causing legionnaire's disease.
- S.1(1)(d), covering emission of noxious substances into the atmosphere, was intended to embrace legislation such as the Alkali etc Works Regulation Act 1906, but subsequently the boundary between occupational health and safety and environmental protection was more clearly defined when the Environment Protection Act 1990 repealed s.1(1)(d).

The 1974 Act repealed very little of the existing legislation but s.1(2) authorized its replacement by regulations and approved codes of practice intended to maintain and improve standards. Over time most of the legislation predating the Act has been repealed, though not always without controversy. Notably, mineworkers challenged whether broad-based regulations gave the same protection as the detailed regulations they replaced.[14] The Deregulation and Contracting Out Act 1994, ss.1(1) and 37, enables the removal without replacement of pre-1974 legislation that cannot usefully be updated.

General duties

The rules of substantive law are in ss.2–7 of the Act, in the form of broad general duties. They bring into legislation the concept of 'safe system of work' which underlies compensation law.[15] These sections identify, and place responsibilities on, each category of person likely to be playing a role at the workplace; the employer (s.2), the contractor (s.3), the occupier of premises (s.4), the manufacturer/supplier (s.6) and the employee (s.7). Section 5 (emissions into the atmosphere) has ceased to be important since the Environment Protection Act 1990.

Section 2

Section 2(1) imposes on the employer the duty 'to ensure, so far as is reasonably practicable, the health, safety and welfare at work of all his employees'. The phrase 'to ensure, so far as is reasonably practicable...' is reiterated in most of the other general duties. It has been held that duties so expressed are absolute ones, entailing liability for even the 'unforeseeable', subject only to what is 'reasonably practicable'.[16] Section 40 imposes on the defendant the burden of showing that it was 'not reasonably practicable to do more than was in fact done to satisfy the duty or requirement'. It is generally supposed that the judgment of Asquith LJ in *Edwards v National Coal Board*[17] provides an appropriate formula for determining what is reasonably practicable: 'a computation must be made… in which the quantum of risk is placed on one scale and the sacrifice involved in the measure necessary for averting the risk (whether in money, time or trouble) is placed in the other;…'. However, there does not appear to be any recent authority to support this view.[18]

It has been argued that such general duties are too imprecise to support enforcement[19] but there have been a number of convictions that refute that argument.[20] Section 2(2) paragraphs (a) to (e) spell out matters to which the duty extends, but the list is intended to be illustrative rather than exhaustive:

(a) the provision and maintenance of plant and systems of work that are, so far as reasonably practicable, safe and without risks to health;

(b) arrangements for ensuring, so far as is reasonably practicable, safety and absence of risks to health in connection with the use, handling, storage and transport of articles and substances;

(c) the provision of such information, instruction, training and supervision as is necessary to ensure, so far as is reasonably practicable, the health and safety at work of his employees;

(d) so far as is reasonably practicable as regards any place of work under the employer's control, the maintenance of it in a condition that is safe and without risks to health and the provision and maintenance of means of access to and egress from it that are safe and without such risks;

(e) the provision and maintenance of a working environment for his employees that is, so far as is reasonably practicable, safe, without risks to health, and adequate as regards facilities and arrangements for their welfare at work.

The following matters are noteworthy:

- S.2(2)(a) is broken if the plant is unsafe, whether or nor workers are present.[21]
- S.2(2)(b) must be read in conjunction with s.6, which imposes duties on the manufacturer and supplier of articles and substances, and with specific regulations covering matters such as the packaging[22] and carriage of goods.[23]
- S.2(2)(c) goes to the heart of the legislation, and is spelt out in other regulations.[24] Moreover, it was held in *R v Swan Hunter Shipbuilders Ltd and Telemeter* (1981)[25] that circumstances may require that an employer instruct workers who are not its own employees in order to ensure that their behaviour does not put its own employees at risk.
- S.2(2)(d) is spelt out in regulations, particularly the Workplace (Health, Safety and Welfare) Regulations 1992.[26]
- S.2(2)(e) is one of the few occasions that this legislation specifically mentions 'welfare'. This can be compared with the Factories Act 1961, Part III, Welfare (General Provisions) which covered drinking water, washing facilities, seating facilities and first aid. These matters are now spelt out in the Workplace (Health, Safety and Welfare) Regulations 1992 and the Health and Safety (First-Aid) Regulations 1981.[27]

Section 2(3) requires every employer[28] to have a written safety policy and to bring it to the notice of its employees. The employer has to state where safety responsibilities lie within its organization and also the arrangements for carrying out the policy. This provision should be read in conjunction with the risk assessment requirements in regulation 3 of the Management of Health and Safety at Work Regulations.

Section 2 (4)–(7) provide for regulations to enable worker participation. These will be explained later in the chapter.

Section 3

The general duty in s.3 (1) imposed an entirely new obligation on employers and has done much to develop the concept of safe systems of work. It provides: 'It shall be the duty of every employer to conduct his undertaking in such a way as to ensure, so far as is reasonably practicable, that persons not in his employment who may be affected thereby are not thereby exposed to risks to their health or safety.'

Section 3 (1) is wide enough to encompass both workers and the general public[29] and has been the subject of a number of important appeal cases. It has been held that an organization may be in the course of its undertaking even when no one is actually at work: so cleaning contractors were liable when, on their day off, one of their client's employees was electrocuted while using their machine.[30] Similarly, in *R v Associated Octel Co Ltd*.[31] the House of Lords held that work being carried out for Octel, by contractors, was conducted in the course of Octel's undertaking,. Thus Octel was liable when one of the visiting workers was badly burnt while cleaning out a tank during Octel's annual shutdown. It could be argued that this was because Octel's premises were a major hazard installation,[32] and they had failed to ensure that the visiting workers followed the work procedures which were part of Octel's safety case. However, Lord Hoffmann's opinion, delivered on behalf of the House, suggests a much broader reasoning. He said: 'If, therefore, the employer engages an independent contractor to do work which forms part of the conduct of the employer's undertaking, he must stipulate for whatever conditions are needed to avoid those risks and are reasonably practicable. He cannot, having omitted to do so, say that he was not in a position to exercise any control.' His Lordship rejected the argument that employers were not vicariously liable for the wrongdoings of persons other than employees,[33] and appeared to take the view that this was Octel's personal wrongdoing in that they had failed to set up and enforce a safe system of work.

In *R v British Steel plc*[34] the defendants were found liable for the death of a visiting worker engaged by them to move a heavy steel platform under the supervision of British Steel's own engineer. There was dispute as to whether the workers had ignored the directions of the engineer or whether he had given inadequate instructions. Before the Court of Appeal the defendants submitted that even if their engineer had been at fault they should not be liable following the House of Lords' decision in *Tesco Supermarket Ltd v Nattrass*.[35] *Nattrass* had held that an employer should not be criminally liable for the wrongdoing of an employee who was not of sufficient seniority to be the 'directing mind' of the defendant. The court distinguished *Nattrass* because it concerned liability under different legislation[36] and upheld the decision of the trial court. Steyn LJ said:

> If it be accepted that Parliament considered it necessary for the protection of public health and safety to impose, subject to the defence of reasonable practicability, absolute criminal liability, it would drive a juggernaut through the legislative scheme if corporate employers could avoid criminal liability where the potentially harmful event is committed by someone who is not the directing mind of the company. ... s.3(1) is framed to achieve a result, namely that persons not employed are not exposed to risks to their health and safety by the conduct of the undertaking. If we accept British Steel's submission, it would be particularly easy for large industrial companies, engaged in multifarious hazardous operations, to escape liability on the basis that the company through its 'directing mind' or senior management was not involved.

Regulation 21 of the Management of Health and Safety at Work Regulations 1999 now provides that in criminal proceedings it is no defence for an employer that the wrongdoing was that of an employee.[37]

Section 4

The intention of s.4 is to impose responsibility on every controller of premises for the safety of those who are not its employees. The section acknowledges that two or more persons may simultaneously have some control over, and therefore be deemed to be in some degree responsible for, premises.[38] It requires each occupier to do what it is *reasonable* for a person in its position to do to ensure *so far as is reasonably practicable* the safety of the premises and any plant and substances which visitors may use there. Domestic premises are exempt but it has been held that the common parts of a block of flats, eg the entrance hall and lift, are within the section.[39] The leading case on the interpretation of s.4 is *Mailer v Austin Rover Group plc.*[40]

The facts of the Austin Rover case are very similar to those of Octel. In both, an accident involved a visiting workman cleaning a booth when the defendant's plant was closed. In the Austin Rover case the defendants had instructed the visiting workers that they must not use the paint thinner that was on tap, they must use a special lamp and no one should work in the sump while someone was working above. Austin Rover did not take the simple precaution of cutting off the supply of thinner. The visitors ignored all three stipulations, there was a flash fire and a fatality occurred. Austin Rover successfully argued that in imposing conditions in the contract they had done all that it was reasonable to expect them to do under s.4 in their capacity of controller of the premises.

It may be significant that subsequent cases, such as Octel, involving contractual relationships between employer and contractor have been prosecuted under s.3, where there is no concept of shared responsibility.

Section 6

Section 6 (1) imposes a general duty on the designer, manufacturer, importer and supplier of articles for use at work. Section 6 (4) imposes a similar duty in relation to substances. The principal object is to ensure that articles and substances are as safe for use at work as is reasonably practicable. This section, for the protection of employees, parallels the protection given to the general public under the Consumer Protection Act 1987, which was enacted to implement the EC Product Liability Directive.[41] There is little case law on the interpretation of this section.

This section knits in with the employer's duty under s.2. In the discharge of its duty the employer must ensure that instructions provided with articles and substances are properly conveyed to the employees who use them, and compliance with them is monitored and enforced. Section 6 is underpinned by regulations concerning the supply of articles[42] and substances and the circumstances in which employees may use them.[43]

Section 7

It is the duty of every employee while at work:

(a) to take reasonable care for the health and safety of himself and of other persons who may be affected by his acts or omissions at work; and

(b) as regards any duty or requirement imposed on his employer or any other person by or under any of the relevant statutory provisions, to cooperate with him so far as is necessary to enable that duty or requirement to be performed or complied with.

The inspectorate rarely invokes this section, not least because it is often the case that where there is misconduct by an employee, there is an element of fault on the part of the employer. The employer should have in place systems that require employees to conduct themselves safely and in cases where the employee's conduct has been unsafe investigation may reveal a failure on the part of the employer to enforce a safe system.

Again the general duty in the Act is underpinned by the Management of Health and Safety at Work Regulations, particularly regulation 14. Other regulations similarly impose specific duties on employees personally. One example is the Gas Safety (Installation and Use) Regulations 1994.[44] Another example is the Personal Protective Equipment at Work Regulations 1992, regulation 10(2) of which states: 'Every employee shall use any personal protective equipment provided to him by virtue of these Regulations in accordance both with any training in the use of the personal protective equipment concerned which has been received by him and the instructions respecting that use which have been provided to him ... .'

Administration, enforcement, offences and penalties

Section 10 of the Act created two bodies corporate; namely the Health and Safety Commission (HSC) and the Health and Safety Executive (HSE). The Commission, which consists of a Chair and no more than nine members (representing employers, employees and other bodies, such as local authorities) is the policy-making unit. Management lies with the Executive which is primarily responsible for the appointment of inspectors (s.18 (7)). In practice, inspection of many workplaces is by inspectors employed by local authorities.[45]

Section 15 and Schedule 3 of the Act confer wide powers to make regulations. Regulations so made, and the general duties in the Act, are 'relevant statutory provisions' enforceable by inspectors appointed under the Act. Since 1974 offshore installations and railways have been brought largely within the jurisdiction of the inspectorate. Road traffic is separately controlled, except that certain regulations concerning the carriage of goods are enforceable by HSE inspectors. Virtually all the regulations cited in this chapter are relevant statutory provisions. Many of them have been made to implement EC directives.[46] Notably, the EC Framework Directive,[47] and five subordinate directives closely related to it, were implemented in Britain in the so-called 'Six Pack'.[48] Controversially the Working Time Regulations 1998[49] are also relevant statutory provisions. The Schedules to the Control of Substances Hazardous to Health Regulations are the medium through which many EC directives are implemented and the output of these directives necessitates the constant updating of the British regulations.

Section 16 empowers HSC to approve and issue codes of practice for 'the purpose of providing practical guidance with respect to the requirements' of the relevant statutory provisions. Several of the regulations in the six pack are accompanied by codes of practice. For example, there is a code with the Management of Health and Safety at Work Regulations. Following review, in 1995, of the use of codes, HSC agreed criteria for their use. These include: '(a) there is clear evidence of a widespread or significant problem; ... (d) the alternative... is likely to be more prescriptive regulation.'[50]

It is noticeable that when the management regulations were reissued in 1999 the revised code was shorter than the original one and, following a Discussion Document,[51] HSC decided mental stress was not a suitable subject for a code. Failing to comply with a Code of Practice is not an offence, but the code may be called in evidence in a prosecution. In recent years HSC/E has tended to issue guidance rather than codes. Guidance has no legal status but provides valuable interpretations of how to comply with the law.

A major part of the work of HSC/E is in raising awareness of hazards encountered at work. It regularly conducts campaigns addressing particular problems. One addressed back injuries, another, *Good Health is Good Business*, was 'successful in raising the profile of occupational health and how to manage it'.[52] Currently the focus is on stress. Research suggests there is little hard evidence of the effectiveness of HSC/E in improving the incidence of harm.[53]

Where education and persuasion fail, HSE has to enforce the law. The 1974 Act gave inspectors the then novel powers to issue improvement and prosecution notices, requiring that unlawful situations be rectified (ss.21–22). An improvement notice relates to a specific statutory provision and requires the duty holder to comply with it within a given time. A prohibition notice need not specify breach of a particular law: it may be served whenever, in the opinion of an inspector, there is a 'risk of serious personal injury'.[54] An 'immediate' prohibition requires that the dangerous activity is stopped at once and thereafter work may not take place while the danger is present. Failure to comply with a notice is a serious criminal offence. No compensation can be claimed for economic loss caused by negligently serving an unwarranted prohibition notice.[55]

Section 38 empowers inspectors to prosecute where statutory provisions are broken. Most offences are tried in magistrates' courts, but serious ones may be heard in the crown court. Penalties vary according to the offence, but the maximum fine in the magistrates' court is £20,000: there is no limit in the crown court. A few offences may lead to imprisonment (s.33 – eg contravention of a prohibition or improvement notice). Sections 36–37 enable prosecutions to be brought against individuals rather than the corporate body, where an individual, such as a director, is the real wrongdoer. There is no provision for a homicide charge to be brought under the 1974 Act and the general criminal law has proved unable to deal effectively with corporate manslaughter.[56]

The management of Health and Safety at Work Regulations (MHSWR)

While it is not possible to provide here details of the numerous regulations now underpinning the 1974 Act, it is necessary to single out MHSWR. These regulations are the principal means by which the EC's Framework directive was implemented in Britain. Today they occupy a somewhat uneasy position between the 1974 Act and other regulations made under that Act. They develop the general duties by, for example, spelling out the employer's responsibility in selection and training of, and providing information to, employees. In many instances, however, the general provisions of these regulations are reiterated in other, problem-specific regulations. In their revised form they address other European directives; namely the protection of young people at work,[57] the protection of new or expectant mothers,[58] fire precautions[59] and temporary workers.

Regulations 3 to 6 encapsulate the whole philosophy of current British health and safety legislation. Regulation 3(1) requires every employer to:

> make a suitable and sufficient assessment of –
> (a) the risks to the health and safety of his employees to which they are exposed whilst they are at work; and
> (b) the risks to the health and safety of persons not in his employment arising out of or in connection with the conduct by him of his undertaking, for the purpose of identifying the measures he needs to take to comply with the requirements and prohibitions imposed upon him by or under the relevant statutory provisions...

Regulation 4 stipulates that where an employer implements any 'preventive and protective measures' it shall do so on the basis of the principles specified in Schedule 1 of the regulations. Schedule 1 sets out Article 6(2) of the Framework Directive. Thus the Schedule seeks to ensure British law has properly incorporated the directive. Regulation 5 requires the employer to 'make and give effect to such arrangements as are appropriate, ... for the effective planning, organization, control, monitoring and review of the preventive and protective measures'. Where the employer employs more than five, these arrangements must be recorded.

Regulation 6 requires health surveillance where the risks of the employment make this appropriate.

These provisions relating to risk assessment should be considered together with the safety policy requirement of s.2 (3) of the Act.

Worker participation

Section 2 (4)–(7) of the 1974 Act responded to the Robens recommendation that employers consult with employees on health and safety matters. Section 2 (4) authorized the making of regulations to empower recognized trade unions to appoint safety representatives. Section 2 (5) made similar provision for the election of safety representatives where there was no recognized trade union. Section 2 (6) required employers to consult with appointed safety representatives and s.2 (7) required the employer to set up a safety committee in certain cases.

Section 2 (5) was repealed by the Employment Protection Act 1975 by a government committed to encouraging trade union representation. The Safety Representatives and Safety Committees Regulations 1977 implemented s.2 (4), (6) and (7).[60] They enable recognized trade unions to appoint safety representatives and provide that when the employer has been notified of their appointment they may carry out the functions set out in regulation 4. Such representatives may consult with their employer on safety matters. In addition, their functions include investigating hazards and complaints by employees, inspecting the workplace, consulting with, and receiving information from, HSE inspectors at the workplace and attending safety committee meetings. They are entitled to paid time off for training and for carrying out their functions. The regulations do not require a system of safety representation in unionized workplaces, nor, if there is such a system, does it have to follow the scheme of the regulations. The regulations are a floor of rights that an employer cannot withhold.

By the 1990s it was apparent that these regulations made insufficient provision for worker participation. With the decline in trade union membership they were available to a smaller proportion of the workforce and arguably they failed to satisfy the EU's expectation that workers must be in a position 'to contribute, by means of balanced participation... to seeing that the necessary protective measures are taken'.[61] The 1977 regulations were amended to give unionized employees extended rights of consultation.[62] The shortcomings of the safety representative system were but an aspect of the general failure of the British 'corporatist' approach to meet European requirements on worker participation.[63]

An attempt to rectify the situation was made through the Health and Safety (Consultation with Employees) Regulations 1996.[64] They impose on employers a duty to consult employees who are not represented under the 1997 regulations. They require the employer to consult with employees either directly or through elected representatives. However, they give lesser rights to non-unionized workplaces than those granted to unionized employees by the 1977 Regulations. For example, in the 1996 Regulations there is no right to inspect the workplace.

The 1996 Regulations should have ensured that all employees had the opportunity to be consulted by their employers about health and safety matters. In fact the combined effect of the two sets of regulations remained unsatisfactory. In 1999 HSC issued a discussion document *Employee Consultation and Involvement in Health and Safety* and the debate this generated led them to announce a package of measures to improve consultation.[65] Work has begun on drafting new regulations to harmonize consultation arrangements based on the 1977 Regulations. The proposal is to empower employees in non-unionized workplaces to decide whether they wish to be consulted directly or through elected representatives, and specify the functions of elected representatives. In addition, a pilot scheme will test allowing workers' safety advisers in workplaces where there is little or no employee representation but safety performance is poor.

In the meanwhile the revision of the Treaty Establishing the European Community gives the social partnership a much greater role in the development of health and safety standards. Health and safety are now dealt with in the chapter entitled 'Social provisions'. Not only may individual member states entrust management and labour with the implementation of directives,[66] but further, should management and labour so desire, their dialogue at community level may lead to contractual relations enforceable at member state level without legislation.[67] It has yet to be seen whether these provisions will be invoked in respect of health and safety. It is difficult to envisage safety standards being enforced in Britain through collective bargaining. Nor is it clear that HSE would be empowered to enforce collective agreements as if they were rules of law.[68]

The future of health and safety law

The initiative in the making of health and safety standards has passed from HSC/HSE to the EU and it appears that the European framework is now in place. In July 1999 HSC published a consultation document, *Revitalising Health and Safety*, to encourage debate about how a new impetus could be created for the further improvement of national performance. This was followed in June 2000 by a *Strategic Statement* with targets for reducing accidents and ill health. It specifically proposed new provisions relating to manslaughter and to employee involvement. The *Strategic Plan for 2001–4* sets out how HSC/E will contribute to meeting the targets, through:

- taking action in priority areas where significant improvements are required;
- effective regulation of the major hazards sectors;
- carrying out its responsibility to secure compliance with the law;
- carrying out its mandate to modernize and simplify the regulatory framework; provide information and advice; promote risk assessment and technical knowledge; and operate statutory schemes.

COMPENSATION FOR INJURY AND ILL HEALTH

In the 19th century it was judicially recognized, in litigation by victims of industrial injury, that employers owed a duty to take reasonable care for the health and safety of employees.[69] However, until well into the 20th century it was difficult to impose civil liability for industrial injuries on employers. The courts rarely found the employer had been negligent and the doctrine of common employment protected them from vicarious liability if an injury could be attributed to the fault of a fellow-employee of the victim. At the end of the 19th century some income maintenance became available under the Workmen's Compensation Acts, the forerunner of the National Insurance (Industrial Injuries) Scheme.

It was only in the middle of the 20th century, following the recognition of a general liability for negligent conduct,[70] that common law litigation for employers' liability became more frequent. *Wilsons & Clyde Coal Company v English*[71] is regarded as the foundation of the modern law. In that case the House of Lords held that employers have a personal legal duty to provide a safe system of work. Their Lordships referred to the need for competent staff, safe plant and effective supervision.[72] Liability is incurred if the duty is broken by negligent conduct.

The Occupiers' Liability Act 1957 was important both because it clarified the occupier's duty to lawful visitors and because of its wider influence on the development of liability for negligent conduct. Section 2 (2) provides that the occupier has a duty: 'to take such care as in all the circumstances of the case is reasonable to see that the visitor will be reasonably safe in using the premises for the purposes for which he is invited or permitted by the occupier to be there'. This undoubtedly clarified that the employer owes a duty of care not only to employees but also to visiting workers. This is so even though s.2 (3) (b) qualifies the duty by providing that the occupier may expect that a person 'in the exercise of his calling' will appreciate and guard against any risks ordinarily incident to it.[73]

The wider significance of the 1957 Act was that it encouraged a major advance towards a general duty owed by persons of whatsoever status to take reasonable care not to cause foreseeable personal injury to their 'neighbours'.[74] This development shifted the focus of litigation from whether the defendant owes a duty of care to the claimant to whether the defendant had broken the duty by negligent conduct.[75] The tendency today is to expect conduct of a high standard. To establish liability it is also necessary for the claimant to prove that the defendant's conduct has caused the claimant to suffer personal injury for which damage may be claimed.[76] These changes in focus mean that cases are more likely to be decided according to their facts than on the law. Therefore there are relatively few precedents created today.

While developments in the law of negligence have largely whittled away the distinction between an employer's liability to employees and its liability to other workers, there remain significant differences. Firstly, as a matter of fact the employer may have to do more to take care of its own employees, for example select a suitable person for the job and provide instruction and training. It is also significant that it is in the narrow context of employers' liability that the frontiers of liability for work-related ill health are being challenged. In a series of cases employees have claimed for repetitive strain injury,[77] and through *Walker v Northumberland CC*[78] it has been established that an employer can be liable to an employee who suffers foreseeable stress-related mental illness.[79]

In some cases[80] an employer may be liable to a worker who suffers injury or illness as a result of breach by the employer of a statutory duty imposed on the employer for the protection of the worker. In former times, when common law liability for negligence was less well recognized, those disabled by work found this form of action very valuable.[81] In effect the claimant seeking compensation through the civil courts relies on a rule intended for use in the criminal courts to prevent injury. In order to succeed, the claimant has to show that the rule imposes a duty on the defendant for the protection of the claimant, that the duty has been broken and the breach has caused the claimant's injury. Section 47 of the Health and Safety at Work Act provides that the general duties in ss.2–7 of that Act may not be relied on in this way, but creates a presumption that regulations made under the Act may be so used. While there have been relatively few reported cases in recent years, *Stark v Post Office*[82] is an important exception. The claim was in respect of injury sustained by the failure of the frame of a bicycle. The Court of Appeal found for the claimant, holding that regulation 6 (1) of the Provision and Use of Work Equipment Regulations 1992 imposed an absolute obligation on employers to ensure that work equipment was maintained in an efficient state, in efficient working order and in good repair. Interpretations of a regulation in the civil courts can have significance for subsequent enforcement of that regulation in the criminal courts.

In civil litigation a finding that the claimant's own negligence has contributed either to causing the injury or the extent of the damage suffered frequently reduces the defendant's liability.[83] Further, the statutory provisions for recoupment of social security benefits received make it unrewarding to sue for other than major injuries.[84] In addition, the majority of personal injury cases are either settled out of court or heard in county courts. The result of this combination of factors is that only a small number of employers' liability cases are formally reported today.

A remaining significant difference between employers' liability and other civil liability of organizations is that the employer is required by the Employers' Liability (Compulsory Insurance) Act 1969 to have a statutory minimum level of insurance to cover injuries suffered by its employees. There is no similar comprehensive obligation to have public liability insurance.[85]

CONCLUSION

The Robens expectation that management should accept responsibility for operating a safe system of work is now largely fulfilled in both the criminal and the civil law. Indeed judicial activity in both the interpretation of the statutory provisions and the common law of negligence has moved towards imposing strict, even absolute, liability on organizations. However, there are unresolved problems concerning the extent of worker participation in setting up, monitoring and maintaining safe systems. Tackling the problem of limited worker participation and the, possibly related, incidence of work-related stress will be challenging, particularly in the prevailing climate of short-term employment and job insecurity. Moreover, it is not sufficient to empower workers to participate, it is also necessary to educate and persuade them to exercise their powers.

Notes

1 Eg Alters, D and James, P (1998) *Robens Revisited: the Case for a Review of Occupational Health and Safety Legislation. An Interim Report from the Institute of Employment Rights*, June.
2 Safety and Health at Work Report of the Committee 1970–72 (1972) (HMSO) (Cmnd 5034).
3 Ibid at para 29.
4 Ibid at para 469.
5 Ibid at para 47.
6 Eg Howells, R and Barrett, B (1975) *The Health and Safety at Work Act: A Guide for Managers*, Institute of Personnel Management, London, p 5 et seq.
7 The author remembers speaking at a seminar at the launch of the Report where representatives of the oil companies welcomed what they perceived as recognition that they had more expertise than the inspectorate. On the other hand, in subsequent research, a works director at a relatively small workplace commented that 'it is a bit like asking management to climb Everest without guidance as to how it should be done'. (Management Responsibilities under the Health and Safety at Work Act 1974 (1980), prepared at Middlesex Polytechnic under Health and Safety Executive Research Agreement 1591.)
8 'The TU movement should insist that safety, like any other subject, is a fit one for the negotiating table.' David Lewis (1974) Worker Participation in Safety II: An Industrial Relations Approach, *Industrial Law Journal*, **3**, p 95.
9 National reports were presented at a seminar held at the Foundation's premises in Dublin on 29th and 30th March 1979.
10 There is similar provision in Northern Ireland.
11 The Management of Health and Safety at Work Regulations 1999 (SI 1999/3242), regulation 23(2).
12 The Control of Substances Hazardous to Health Regulations 1999 (SI 1999/437, regulation 19.
13 [1993] 1 WLR 1171.
14 *R v Secretary of State for Employment Ex p National Association of Colliery Overmen, Deputies and Shotfirers* (1993) Co/2576/93. See Geoffrey Holgate (1994) in *Industrial Law Journal*, **23**, p 246.
15 This was judicially recognized when in the criminal prosecution *R v Swan Hunter Shipbuilders Ltd and Telemeter* [1981] IRLR 403 the Court of Appeal relied on *McArdle v Andmac Roofing Co and Others* [1967] 1 All ER 583 (a compensation case).
16 Eg per Lord Goff in *Mailer v Austin Rover Group plc* [1989] 2 All ER 1087 at 1090.
17 [1949] 1 KB 704 at 712–3.
18 In *R v Nelson Group Services Ltd (Maintenance)* [1998] 4 All ER 331 the Court of Appeal set aside a conviction because the judge in the lower court had

failed to properly direct the jury as to the defence, but did not itself interpret the words.

19 Eg *West Bromwich Building Society Ltd v Townsend* [1983] ICR 257.

20 Eg *R v Swan Hunter Shipbuilders Ltd and Telemeter* [1981] IRLR 403.

21 *Bolton Metropolitan Borough Council v Malrod Insulations Ltd* [1993] IRLR 274.

22 Eg Chemicals (Hazard Information and Packaging for Supply) Regulations 1999 (SI 1999/197).

23 Eg Carriage of Dangerous Goods by Road (Driver Training) Regulations 1996 (SI 1996/2094).

24 Eg Management of Health and Safety at Work Regulations 1999, regulation 13.

25 Supra at note 18.

26 SI 1992/3004. See also Fire Precautions (Workplace) Regulations 1997 (SI 1997/1840).

27 SI 1981/917.

28 Small organizations are exempted by Employers' Health and Safety Policy Statement (Exceptions) Regulations 1975 (SI 1975/1584); for an interpretation see *Osborne v Bill Taylor of Huyton Ltd* [1982] IRLR 17.

29 See the Science Museum case, supra.

30 *R v Mara* [1987] IRLR 154.

31 [1996] 1 WLR 1543.

32 Subject to the regime set out in the Control of Major Accident Hazards Regulations, now SI 1999 No.743.

33 On the doctrine of vicarious liability, see employer's liability infra.

34 [1995] IRLR 310.

35 [1972] AC 153.

36 The Trade Descriptions Act 1968.

37 This confirms *R v British Steel plc* [1995] IRLR 301 and impliedly overrules *R v Nelson* (supra).

38 Established by the House of Lords in the civil case, *Wheat v Lacon Co Ltd* [1966] 1 All ER 582.

39 *Westminster City Council v Select Managements Ltd* [1985] 1 All ER 897.

40 [1989] 2 All ER 1087.

41 85/373/EEC.

42 CEN approval of articles is relevant.

43 Eg Control of Substances Hazardous to Health Regulations 1999 (SI 1999/437), Chemicals (Hazard Information and Packaging for Supply) Regulations 1999 (SI 1999/197), Health and Safety (Display Screen Equipment) Regulations 1992 (SI 1992/2792), Provision and Use of Work Equipment Regulations 1998 (SI 1992/2306 and Personal Protective Equipment at Work Regulations 1992 (SI 1992/2966).

44 SI 1994/1886. See *R v Nelson Group Services Ltd (Maintenance)* [1998] 4 All ER 331.

45 See Health and Safety (Enforcing Authority) Regulations 1998 (SI 1998/494), Schedule 1.

46 HSE is represented in relevant law formulating committees in Europe.

47 89/391/EEC.

48 Management of Health and Safety at Work Regulations 1999, Workplace (Health and Safety and Welfare) Regulations 1992, Health and Safety (Display Screen Equipment) Regulations 1992, Provision and Use of Work Equipment Regulations 1998, Personal Protective Equipment at Work Regulations 1992 and Manual Handling Operations Regulations 1992.

49 SI 1998/1833.

50 Cited in *Managing stress at work*, Discussion Document 1999 (HSC).

51 Supra.

52 Ibid at paragraph 32.

53 The Impact of HSC/E (200). A review carried out for HSC/E by the Institute of Employment Studies together with Middlesex University.

54 S.22(2).

55 *Harris v Evans and HSE* [1998] 1 WLR 1285.

56 Eg P&O European Ferries (Dover) Ltd (1991) 93 Cr App R 72.

57 94/33/EC.

58 92/85/EEC.

59 Fire precautions are specifically referred to in the 1999 regulations because they should have been covered to comply with the Framework directive, but were omitted in the 1992 edition of the regulations because they were not in the British system 'relevant statutory provisions' under the 1974 Act.

60 SI 1977/500.

61 Preamble to Framework Directive.

62 MHSW Regulations 1992.

63 *UK v EU Council* [1996] All ER (EC) 877.

64 SI 1996/1513.

65 HSE Press Release C072:00 – 15 December 2000.

66 Article 137 (4).

67 Article 139.

68 Possibly compliance with collective arrangements might be regarded as 'reasonably practicable' and therefore within the ambit of general duties.

69 Eg *Priestley v Fowler* (1837) 3 M&W 1; Smith v Baker [1891] AC 325.

70 *Donoghue v Stevenson* [1932] AC 564.

71 [1938] AC 57.

72 Ibid at p 78 per Lord Wright.

73 See *Roles v Nathan* [1963] 1 WLR 1117.

74 The expression used by Lord Atkin in *Donoghue v Stevenson* (a product liability case).

75 In respect of employer's liability see *Qualcast v Haynes* [1959] AC 7433.

76 Eg *McWilliams v Arroll* [1962] 1WLR 295; McKew v Holland [1969] 3 All ER 1621. For the special rules concerning industrial diseases see *Bonnington Castings v Wardlaw* [1956] AC 613.

77 Eg *Mughal v Reuters Ltd* [1993] IRLR 571.

78 [1995] IRLR 35.
79 In *Sutherland v Hatton, Somerset County Council v Barber, Sandwell Metropolitan Borough Council v Jones,* and *Baker Refractories Ltd v Bishop* [2002] EWCA Civ 76 the Court of Appeal considered four cases of work-related stress and laid down guidelines for employer's liability.
80 While the 1974 Act s.47(2) creates a presumption that breach of regulations is actionable some regulations, eg the Management of Health and Safety at Work Regulations, 1999, reg.22, exclude civil liability, but this particular exclusion is likely to be removed in response to EC requirements.
81 The concept can be trace to *Groves v Wimborne* [1898] 2 QB 402.
82 [2000] ICR 1013.
83 See Law Reform (Contributory Negligence) Act 1945.
84 Social Security Administration Act 1992, s.82.
85 There may be particular circumstances where public liability insurance is necessary: the requirement for driver insurance under the Road Traffic Acts is an obvious example.

Part III

Alternatives to the law

11

Alternative dispute resolution

Virginia Branney

DEFINING ALTERNATIVE DISPUTE RESOLUTION

Dispute resolution methods can range from unilateral action, where the protagonist has control over the process and outcome, to litigation, where both the process and the outcome are determined by a third party. Within this range, alternative dispute resolution (ADR) describes methods of resolving disputes that do not involve the imposition of a legally binding outcome on the parties (Mackie, Miles and Marsh, 1995). In turn, an 'ADR spectrum' can start with negotiation as the 'least invasive' approach, in which the parties have the most control over the process and outcome, and end with the 'most invasive' methods, including arbitration, which allow the parties the least control over the process and outcome (Costantino and Sickles Merchant, 1996).

Applying this concept to UK employment disputes,[1] an ADR spectrum would include:

- unilateral action (such as uncontested dismissal, employee resignations, successful industrial action);
- negotiation (from one-to-one to transnational level);
- internal investigatory, grievance and disciplinary procedures;
- sector or industry procedures to resolve collective disputes;
- conciliation and mediation;
- advisory mediation and joint problem solving;
- arbitration.

In theory, ADR can include all methods of dispute resolution apart from recourse to the employment tribunal and the courts, but this is often not what ADR practitioners mean when they use the term. Typically, the ADR spectrum is defined more narrowly, excluding methods where there is no intervention by a neutral third party (Mackie *et al*, 1995). This chapter confines itself to forms of ADR where there is such intervention, while noting that even ADR experts acknowledge that definitions of ADR 'are not watertight or conclusive' (Mackie *et al*, 1995: 7). Arguably, for employers, workers and their respective representatives, definitions matter less than understanding what the main ADR methods entail and their appropriateness or otherwise for resolving a particular dispute.

Arbitration

Before leaving the matter of the definition of ADR in employment, it is necessary to briefly mention arbitration. The inclusion of arbitration as alternative dispute resolution can cause confusion. For example, in commercial dispute resolution, arbitration is not considered to be ADR because of its closeness in process and outcome to litigation (Mackie *et al*, 1995). In contrast, arbitration of employment cases (whether involving individuals' complaints or trade disputes) does not operate as a quasi-legal process and in general arbitrators' awards have been considered to be binding by virtue of the parties' consent to participate or the terms of a collective agreement. But can the Advisory, Conciliation and Arbitration Service (ACAS) arbitration scheme for the resolution of unfair dismissal claims (launched in May 2001) be described as ADR? Certainly the scheme is intended as an alternative to tribunal proceedings and is promoted as ADR. Participation is voluntary and the process is informal, having been designed to avoid the legalism of the employment tribunal. However, the arbitrator's award is legally enforceable and grounds for appeal are extremely limited. On this basis, it could be claimed that the scheme does not qualify as ADR. Notwithstanding, the scheme is much more akin to ADR methods than litigation. Technically, it might be best described as a 'hybrid'.

The following chapter covers arbitration in detail. This chapter will concentrate on the different types of mediation and conciliation as applied to employment disputes. Together, they are the most common UK forms of ADR involving the intervention of a neutral third party.

MEDIATION AND CONCILIATION

Broadly, mediation and conciliation describe a voluntary, non-binding, private dispute resolution process, in which an independent, neutral person helps the parties to reach a negotiated settlement. Mediation is sometimes used as a generic term incorporating conciliation. However, in the employment context, conciliation and mediation are commonly understood to mean different processes. To complicate matters, they are defined differently by different ADR organizations and there are different models of mediation and conciliation. The distinctions can be important in that employment relations practitioners need to be clear precisely what is meant by the term being used; and debates about the merits or otherwise of these forms of ADR can be marred when the same terms are used to mean different things. This chapter will focus on the definitions and principal models that apply in the field of employment dispute resolution in the UK.

Key principles

As a starting point, it is useful to outline the key principles that distinguish mediation and conciliation from litigation. As mentioned above, participation is voluntary. If any prospective party declines to participate, they cannot be ordered to do so. In these circumstances, the mediation or conciliation will not happen, unless the principal parties are willing to go ahead and it is agreed that the unwilling party or parties are extraneous to the dispute. Any party or the neutral third party (the mediator or conciliator) can terminate the process at any time.

Conciliators and mediators do not act as arbitrators and have no authority to impose decisions on the issues in dispute. They do not give professional advice to the parties, individually or collectively. They must act impartially and preserve their impartiality at all times. Their primary role is to facilitate negotiations between the parties, with a view to achieving an outcome which is acceptable to them. The neutral third party aims to assist the parties to reach an agreed outcome that is appropriate to the circumstances of the particular dispute. This allows the parties to explore a wider range of options for settlement and explains why mediation and conciliation are seen by their proponents as more creative dispute resolution processes than litigation. It is not the task of the mediator/conciliator to ensure that the outcome is just or fair. The assumption is that provided the process itself operates fairly (for which the mediator/conciliator has a large measure of responsibility) the parties will only agree an outcome that they find acceptable or satisfactory.

Mediation and conciliation are informal procedures. The meetings are not 'hearings' in the legal sense. Depending on the number of parties attending, a typical mediation or conciliation will be conducted by one or two third-party neutrals. A pair may act as 'co-mediators' or co-conciliators, or as lead and assistant. The informality of mediation and conciliation derives from the fact that they are not adjudicatory processes. There are comparatively few procedural strictures. The process is non-adversarial. It is managed by the mediator/conciliator with the consent of the parties.

Unlike tribunal and court proceedings, mediation and conciliation are conducted in private. Apart from what is already in the public domain and what the parties agree to disclose, all discussions and any shared documentation are confidential.[2] If the mediator/conciliator has separate discussions with parties in the course of the mediation/conciliation, those discussions are confidential as well, and the mediator/conciliator must not disclose anything to another party without explicit permission. The outcome is also private and confidential, apart from what the parties themselves agree to disclose.[3] In conciliation of trade disputes, it is common for a draft agreement to be reached, subject to ratification by one or both side's constituents.

Mediation and conciliation are regarded as privileged and without prejudice. Agreements reached by the parties are informal unless they take a legally binding form, as a compromise agreement or a COT3 agreement. COT3 agreements constitute a general and final settlement; whereas compromise agreements are limited to a particular claim, so that there remains a possibility of residual legal action. In the UK, by law individuals cannot be required to waive their statutory rights as a precondition for participating in mediation. Nor can they be deemed to have waived their statutory rights by taking part or even by concluding an informal agreement. On one hand, this may encourage workers to participate in mediation, in that they have nothing to lose, provided that the relevant time limits for lodging claims are observed. On the other hand, employers in particular may be discouraged by the knowledge that an agreement reached in mediation in good faith does not settle the matter irrevocably in legal terms. However, this problem can be overcome if the parties agree to formalize their settlement as a compromise agreement or a 'COT3' as appropriate. In practice, the transition should not be difficult, provided it is well managed. There may be a fear that things could unravel once lawyers (and others) enter the frame, if they were not directly involved with the mediation. But it can also be argued that the limits on waiving statutory rights are an important protection for unrepresented parties who might otherwise conclude unfair or disadvantageous agreements in ignorance.[4]

Mediation and conciliation models

There are many different models of mediation and conciliation. Broadly, they may be categorized as transformative, facilitative and evaluative.

The transformative model is the least interventionist. In brief, it is based on 'transformational theory', which sees conflict not as dysfunctional but as a vital social function. The goal in transformational or transformative mediation is 'to move beyond solutions to transforming relationships'. The neutral third party does not set out to achieve an agreement or settlement, but 'to influence the interaction patterns' between the parties (Isenhart and Spangle, 2000).

Other goals in mediation are considered important but secondary. The transformative model is practised more widely in the United States but it has informed the practice of many UK mediators, particularly those trained in community mediation.

The facilitative model also allows for a flexible process but it is more structured. The neutral third party will guide the parties through the process and actively encourage them to reach a mutually acceptable outcome which may be a list of agreed action points or an oral or written agreement, as the parties (not the mediator or conciliator) determine. This is the most commonly applied model in employment ADR in the UK. For example, ACAS conciliation and workplace mediation are mainly facilitative processes.

The evaluative model is more interventionist. The neutral third party may give their opinion on the merits of the case (for example, the chances for success at court) and make non-binding recommendations as a basis for settlement. For example, ACAS 'dispute mediation' is evaluative in that the mediator can make non-binding recommendations as a basis for settlement; however, it also encompasses elements of the facilitative model. Another variation is 'med-arb' (mediation-arbitration), where the parties will agree that any remaining unresolved issues from the mediation will be arbitrated upon by the mediator; or where an arbitrator attempts to narrow the issues for arbitration by seeking to achieve some agreements through mediation first. (Med-arb in employment disputes is not commonly undertaken in the UK.)

The key principles of mediation and conciliation are common to the three models. They influence mediators' and conciliators' practice, but not to the extent that the processes involved become rigid and inflexible. The very flexibility of ADR is one of its key advantages over highly formalized procedures such as tribunal hearings. However, flexibility can be unnerving for potential participants and organizations who will want a reasonably clear idea what the different ADR options entail. Aside from ACAS conciliation, employment relations practitioners may not be very familiar with other forms of ADR and other providers. Certainly most individual workers (and many employers) taking part in conciliation or mediation will not have experienced it before. In addition to general information provided in advance, more specific information is often set out in an agreement to mediate (in the case of externally provided workplace mediation) or the organization's staff handbook. In any event, in opening a mediation or conciliation, the neutral third party will explain their role, the process, the proposed structure (in so far as there may be a structure) and any ground rules that the parties are requested to agree (or want to propose).

ADR providers

ACAS

In England, Wales and Scotland, the independent statutory agency ACAS is the main provider of ADR services. Its dispute resolution services are largely free of charge (a fact that most users probably take for granted). The Northern Ireland Labour Relations Agency has an equivalent role.[5]

ACAS is the only body sanctioned by the State to carry out *external* conciliation and mediation of 'trade disputes', as defined by s.218, Trade Union and Labour Relations (Consolidation) Act 1992. ACAS assistance may include:

- collective conciliation;
- advisory mediation;
- dispute mediation; and
- arbitration.

In the case of disputes between individuals and their employer, ACAS conciliators have a statutory duty to promote settlements of a wide range of employment rights complaints which have been *or* could be made to an employment tribunal. (See the Employment Tribunals Act 1996 s.18.) In practice, ACAS conciliation officers deal mostly with complaints already lodged with the Employment Tribunal Service.

Private providers

Some ADR services are available from specialist ADR organizations (including training in mediation and related skills) and legal firms. In commercial mediations, usually the provider's fees are paid by the parties. However, it is common for the employer to pay for the mediation in workplace disputes, other than those cases where the complainant is a former employee who is legally represented. In commercial mediations, the parties include their legal costs in their claims. In reaching a settlement, reimbursement of costs is a matter for negotiation. For example, one side may agree to pay the other side's costs in part or in full; or they agree to meet their own costs. Currently, this is not an issue in respect of most employment mediations (apart from some county or sheriff court claims).

Trade disputes

ACAS collective conciliation

The role of the conciliator is to be 'a creative force in dispute resolution, assisting the parties to identify and explore ways of settling their differences' (ACAS, 1999). Participation is voluntary, with no preconditions requiring the parties to accept any particular outcome. It can be requested by either or both parties, and on occasion may be initiated following an invitation from ACAS. Most commonly, conciliation is triggered when external conciliation is the agreed next stage in the dispute resolution procedures (internal procedures having been exhausted), or when direct negotiations become deadlocked. The majority of cases concern disputes over pay and conditions of employment.

The conciliation process entails one or two conciliators holding a series of separate or joint meetings (or combination of the two) with the parties, to facilitate further negotiation and discussion. The parties may spend much of the time in separate meetings while the conciliator shuttles between them. The conciliator aims to establish common ground, identify and clarify barriers to progress and assist the parties to develop possible solutions. But responsibility for deciding the outcome and ownership of any agreement reached rests with the parties. Conciliators do not recommend settlement terms, nor propose solutions in any formal sense, although they may air possible ideas for discussion and, from their impartial position, test the viability of the parties' options for settlement with them.

Central Arbitration Committee mediation

The Central Arbitration Committee (CAC) is not an ADR provider, but it may offer mediation under the statutory provisions for trade union recognition (see Schedule A1 of the Trade Union and Labour Relations (Consolidation) Act 1992). The Schedule does not refer specifically to mediation, but if the CAC accepts an application from a union (or unions) 'it must try to help' the union and employer 'to reach… an agreement as to what the appropriate bargaining unit is' (para 18(1)). And where the parties make an agreement for recognition, the CAC 'must try to help the parties to reach… an agreement on a method by which they are to conduct collective bargaining' (para 31 (2)). The parties are under no obligation to agree to mediation or ACAS conciliation. But failing agreement between the parties (with or without third-party intervention), the CAC is required to decide the appropriate bargaining unit and, where relevant, to specify a method of collective bargaining. This could be described as a form of 'med-arb' by the CAC. Because the CAC may have to adjudicate on the application, what is said in any mediation session enjoys only qualified confidentiality, as it may have to be revealed to ensure any formal hearing is fair. In contrast, discussions with an ACAS conciliator remain confidential.

In 2000–1, CAC panels undertook little mediation (CAC, 2001) while ACAS received 384 requests for assistance over union recognition – an 80 per cent increase on the previous year. However, most of these cases were not within the statutory recognition procedures. ACAS reported that 'over 70 per cent' were 'leading to voluntary recognition' (ACAS, 2001: 3).

Advisory mediation

'Advisory mediation' describes a service provided by ACAS which is designed to prevent disputes as well as resolve them. Working with employers, employees and their representatives, ACAS staff encourage and support cooperative and joint problem-solving approaches to tackling issues that confront them. In

1998–2000, the predominant subjects of ACAS projects were 'communication, consultation and employee involvement'; and 'organization effectiveness and enabling change' (ACAS, 2000: 51). In practice, advisory mediation entails the setting up of a non-negotiating forum, such as joint workshops and/or a joint working party. Joint participation is a prerequisite. Discussions are facilitated by ACAS staff and typically joint working parties are chaired by them. The process of working together has much in common with the facilitative model of mediation in that the neutral 'advisory mediator' will guide the parties through a structured problem-solving process, helping them to define the problems, gather and consider information, generate and evaluate options, agree solutions and implement them. Advisory mediation is a hybrid of facilitation and mediation. It would normally take place over a longer timescale than a one-off mediation and involve more people, particularly in the early stages of gathering information (which may involve focus groups and a series of meetings with staff groups). ACAS (but not necessarily the advisory mediator) may also have an ongoing role, for example in conducting a ballot on a proposed agreement. As chair of a joint working party, the advisory mediator may have more of a hands-on role than would typically be the case in a facilitative mediation session, and may be more proactive in making suggestions to the parties, although they are under no obligation to accept them.

Advisory mediation is solely an ACAS service. However, some ADR organizations and consultancies specializing in organizational development and human resources management offer 'conflict management' services, such as system design and facilitated problem solving. The work of the TUC Partnership Institute also embraces these services.[6]

ACAS dispute mediation

Dispute mediation differs from collective conciliation in that the neutral third party 'offers the parties… positive recommendations for resolving their differences, while allowing them to achieve the final solution through direct negotiation' (ACAS, 2000: 26). Normally, ACAS will agree to arrange dispute mediation or arbitration only when it has not been possible to produce a conciliated settlement. For these purposes, ACAS maintains a panel of independent mediators and arbitrators. Between 1998 and 2002, only 19 cases were referred to dispute mediation, compared with 227 referrals to arbitration and 5,645 requests for collective conciliation (ACAS, 2000: 50, 52; 2002: 24, 25).

Disputes concerning individual workers

ACAS conciliation

Conciliation of complaints by individual workers is by far the most predominant form of ADR provided by ACAS owing to its statutory duty to attempt to conciliate in most types of complaints which can be taken to the employment tribunal, with a view to promoting settlement. In 2001–02, ACAS conciliation officers dealt with 165,093 complaints (ACAS, 2002: 11). Taking a common scenario as an example, the process can be summarized as follows: the Employment Tribunal Service informs ACAS that a formal complaint has been lodged; or, one of the parties (or their representative) informs ACAS that a formal complaint could be made and no voluntary settlement has been reached. Within short prescribed timescales, ACAS contacts the parties and their representatives by telephone or letter to provide information about the conciliation process and to offer conciliation. The conciliator may then 'take prompt action' if requested by either party, or on their own initiative, 'when it is useful to do so' (ACAS, 1999: 115). The parties are to be kept informed about the options open to them and their possible consequences, but the conciliator should not express an opinion on the merits of a case. In unfair dismissal complaints, the conciliator must seek to promote reinstatement or re-engagement *before* any other form of settlement (normally a compensatory payment). Information shared with the conciliator in confidence is not disclosed to the other party unless the conciliator is obliged to disclose it by law. The parties will be encouraged to consider the consequences of proposed settlement terms and to seek further advice if necessary. If an agreement is arrived at, the conciliator will encourage it to be recorded as quickly as possible as a 'COT3' to settle the claim.

Conciliation by other statutory bodies

The Equal Opportunities Commission and the Commission for Racial Equality have statutory powers to assist in achieving settlements of tribunal proceedings or prospective proceedings but 'settlements procured solely through their offices do not exclude the tribunal's jurisdiction and an ACAS COT3 is still required' (Nicholls and Ball, 1995: 46). The Disability Rights Commission has powers to conciliate but not in respect of employment cases.

Workplace mediation

Workplace mediation is distinct from ACAS dispute mediation and it differs from ACAS conciliation in a number of ways. Most workplace mediation involves disputes between an employer (typically a line manager) and an employee or between a small group or team of employees. In the main, those involved are employed, as opposed to having been dismissed. While ACAS conciliators do deal with such cases, they constitute a small proportion of their overall caseload. Workplace mediation is mainly provided by private ADR organizations, while a small number of organizations (mainly public and voluntary sector) have set up in-house schemes. Some law firms and ADR organizations, such as the Centre for Effective Dispute Resolution (CEDR), also provide 'workplace' or employment mediation in respect of tribunal and court claims.

In general, UK workplace mediation (as distinct from ACAS dispute mediation) follows the facilitative model. Evaluative mediation is not practised, in that mediators do not offer advice or their opinions on the merits of the case. However, particularly in workplace disputes involving actual tribunal claims or county/sheriff court actions, the mediator is likely to ask probing questions of the parties' legal representatives (in private sessions) as to the viability of their side's claims or proposals and their realistic chances of success at law if agreement is not reached. In a one-to-one dispute between a line manager and employee where the working relationship is the key issue, the mediator may draw on elements from the transformative model to help the parties focus on creating the basis for an improved relationship. Because of the inherent flexibility of mediation, it is impossible to be definitive in describing how mediators work. The influencing factors include the ethos of the mediator's organization and code of conduct, the terms of reference of an agreement to mediate; practical issues such as the number of parties at the mediation; the nature of the dispute and whether the parties are represented or not; and the mediator's personal style, training, experience and background.

Does workplace mediation differ from ACAS conciliation in respect of individual disputes? While both processes are basically facilitative, there are significant differences. Unlike the workplace mediator, the conciliation officer is under a statutory duty to promote settlements. Unlike most conciliations of individuals' complaints, workplace mediation always involves meeting with the parties to the dispute. Depending on the nature of the dispute, the parties may attend unaccompanied or with their union and/or legal representative, or a colleague. (The danger of imbalance in representation is addressed before the mediation takes place to the extent that there should be agreement as to who will be present at the mediation meeting.) The mediation meeting will typically involve a joint opening session with all the parties in the room. In mediations involving two unrepresented individuals, the mediator may work with the parties together for the duration of the meeting. Or the mediator may intersperse the joint discussions with short separate discussions with each party. Then again, one or both parties may only participate on the basis that they are apart from the other side for most or all of the mediation. For example, this may occur in cases of harassment and bullying where the complainant does not feel safe or able to engage face to face with the alleged harasser. In these cases, the mediator conducts the process by shuttling between the parties. They may remain apart for the whole session, or they may agree to come together at any point. Particularly where the parties are legally represented, it is common for the mediator to hold separate meetings (sometimes called caucuses) with both sides, usually after the opening session. Normally the parties come together at the end of the mediation to conclude negotiations and draw up the heads of agreement.

In-house workplace mediation

Workplace mediation can also be conducted in-house, by internally appointed mediators. A small number of UK employers, mostly in the public and voluntary sectors, have set up their own schemes, often prompted by a positive experience of mediation in other sectors (such as community mediation) or by the belief that their existing dispute resolution procedures are not best suited to deal effectively with a range of workplace conflicts. Typically, mediation is on offer as an option to supplement rather than replace existing investigatory, disciplinary and grievance procedures. In most cases, the mediation scheme stands apart from those procedures – it has not yet been 'written into' disciplinary and grievance procedures set out in the collective agreement (where unions are recognized) or the company's procedures.[7]

The issues in dispute often involve communication breakdown, personality clashes, the employee's or manager's performance and difficult or inappropriate behaviour. They may also concern allegations or complaints of harassment, bullying or discrimination which are currently outwith the grievance or disciplinary procedures, either because (at this stage) the employer does not favour disciplinary action, or the complainant does not want to pursue the other avenues open to her/him. In-house mediation can also be used to address dysfunctional working within and between teams and departments.

The main advantages of using in-house mediators are that they know the organization and its culture; mediation may be quicker to set up and conduct; and it will probably cost less than using external providers other than ACAS. (However, ACAS does not have the capacity to provide this type of mediation on any scale.) The chief disadvantage is that the parties do not perceive in-house mediators to be as neutral and impartial as external mediators who have no other association with them or the organization. Seasoned external mediators are also likely to have a greater breadth and depth of mediation experience. Some organizations have developed a hybrid model whereby they provide a bespoke in-house mediation scheme using external mediators. For example, the Department of Work and Pensions mediation scheme uses CEDR registered mediators.

THE BENEFITS OF ADR

The benefits claimed for ADR are usually cited as advantages over litigation, including lower cost, speediness, higher success rates, potential for more creative solutions and greater user satisfaction. The main reservations about the use of ADR in employment cluster around issues of appropriateness, power imbalances and justice. This section draws on additional sources from the United States, because there seems to be comparatively more data available on the outcomes of employment-related ADR than in the UK (excluding ACAS activity).

Internationally, there is evidence that in general ADR costs less than litigation, including some evidence in the employment field (Dewar, 2001; Hunter and Leonard, 1997). In Great Britain, the Survey of Employment Tribunals 1998 (SETA 98) found that 42 per cent of all employers incurred legal costs when handling a tribunal case (DTI, 2001a). Excluding cases where no legal costs were incurred by respondents, the mean legal cost of settling privately or via ACAS was £1,363 as compared with £2,504 where cases were heard by the tribunal (1996–7 prices). Although more than 40 per cent of applicants had no representation at the full hearing (compared with 15 per cent of employers), just over 20 per cent had legal representation (DTI, 2001a: 8, 10). This incurs a cost – if not to the applicant, to their trade union or other service provider. Trade union officials and advice workers spend considerable time in preparing for tribunals even where they do not directly represent applicants at full hearings. An indication of the management time saved by settlement prior to tribunal is given by SETA 98, quoted in *Dispute Resolution in Britain – a background paper*, issued by the Department of Trade and Industry (DTI, 2001a: 10). It showed that median senior management time spent on cases settled privately or via ACAS was 16 hours compared with 27 hours where cases went to tribunal.

Experience from commercial cases suggests that even where unresolved disputes proceed to litigation, the extra cost of privately provided mediation may be offset where the mediation has narrowed the issues in dispute or resolved some aspects of it. If the wider use of ADR can reduce the number of cases going to a full hearing, significant public savings stand to be incurred given that 'the public cost of running the Employment Tribunal Service is currently £51.7 million' (DTI, 2001b).

Another benefit claimed for ADR is the relative speediness with which claims can be resolved. With mediation, once the parties have decided on this option, it can take as little as a week to a month to arrange and conclude. Based on their studies of mediation in US sex discrimination cases, Hunter and Leonard concluded that 'it seems likely that mediated settlements could, on average, be achieved more quickly than tribunal decisions' and this 'would apply even more strongly to cases that would otherwise go to the County Court' (Hunter and Leonard, 1997: 304). ADR dispenses with elaborate case preparation, because it is not an adjudicatory procedure. Mediation or conciliation sessions in individual cases rarely last longer than a day or two.

Hunter and Leonard observed that the speedy resolution of claims is particularly important where the complainant is still employed, as it 'can prevent deterioration or even termination of the employment relationship' (Hunter and Leonard, 1997: 304). It may increase the possibilities of reinstatement where termination has occurred. The time it takes to resolve an unfair dismissal case in the tribunal can in itself render reinstatement or re-engagement untenable. In fact, the remedies of reinstatement and re-engagement are rarely applied in the employment tribunal – in only 0.3 per cent of all hearings is such an order made (DTI, 2001a: 9).

The Institute of Employment Studies Awareness Survey 2000, quoted in *Dispute Resolution in Britain – A background paper*, reported that 44 per cent of individuals who had experienced problems in the workplace eventually left their employer (DTI, 2001a: 10). Had their problems been more effectively dealt with at an early stage by management, and possibly by mediation where appropriate, it is reasonable to assume that at least a proportion would have decided to remain with their employer. While a 'parting of the ways' is sometimes agreed to be the best outcome, it is expensive to replace staff who leave or are dismissed. It has been estimated that the cost of recruiting a replacement was an average of £3,500 per employee in 2000(DTI, 2001a: 11). For the parties, ADR processes offer informality and privacy, unlike the tribunal and courts. In sex discrimination cases in Great Britain, for example, research has shown that applicants found the tribunal 'panel or the process itself formal, off-putting, intimidating and/or extremely stressful'. Hunter and Leonard contrast this with the 'overwhelmingly positive' reaction of participants in a US Equal Employment Opportunities Commission (EEOC) pilot mediation scheme, 'largely regardless of the outcome of the mediation' (Hunter and Leonard, 1997: 303). Similarly, the US Postal Service (USPS) REDRESS program has reported high levels of user satisfaction with the mediation process. For example, one exit survey of participants recorded that 83 to 97 per cent of employees and 84 to 99 per cent of supervisors were 'satisfied' or 'highly satisfied' with various aspects of the process. This is considerably higher than US satisfaction rates cited for litigation (Dewar, 2001: 28).

Probably the major advantage claimed for mediation and conciliation over adjudication is their potential to enable the parties to work out a mutually acceptable solution for themselves as opposed to having a decision imposed on them which normally results in a 'winner and a loser'. Terms of settlement or outcomes from mediation and also conciliation can include apologies, provision of references, agreement to amend the organization's policies and practices, compensation, dropping legal action, provision of training, transfer to a different position, changes in working arrangements, a voluntary departure package and reconsideration for a position. Hunter and Leonard cite a more extensive list of settlements agreed in the US EEOC mediation pilot program and the Australian conciliation of sex discrimination complaints (Hunter and Leonard, 1997: 305).

What about the 'success rates' of mediation and conciliation measured in terms of settlements achieved? Overall, the US Postal Service reported a 70 per cent settlement rate for the first two and a half years of the REDRESS program (Dewar, 2001: 29). In the UK, 75 per cent of the employment disputes mediated by CEDR result in settlement (CEDR, 2002). In a news release dated 24 October 2000, ACAS claimed to have 'resolved 76 per cent [of individual complaints] before they reached the more costly and time consuming tribunal system'. (This figure included cases which are withdrawn as well as those settled by conciliation.) In 2001–02, the ACAS Annual Report recorded that 42 per cent of individual complaints were settled in conciliation, 33 per cent were withdrawn and 25 per cent proceeded to the tribunal (ACAS, 2002: 27).

The precise role played by the intervention of ACAS in achieving this level of success cannot be gauged purely from the figures, but given that conciliation is offered largely when individuals' complaints or disputes are at an advanced stage, it has been suggested that there is potentiality for conciliation to achieve higher settlement levels through earlier intervention, as in US workplace mediation. Measures of the parties' satisfaction with outcomes are perhaps more illuminating. For example, under the USPS REDRESS program, 62 per cent of employees and 67 per cent of supervisors were satisfied or highly satisfied that the dispute was partially or fully resolved (Dewar, 2001: 29). As yet, there is little comparable data available publicly on the outcomes of UK workplace mediation, including in-house schemes.

APPROPRIATENESS OF ADR

ADR is not appropriate for every employment dispute. It is difficult to be definitive about when not to use ADR, but as a guide, CEDR considers that it is most likely to be inappropriate in cases where:

- a legal precedent is sought;
- a party or parties want the case to be heard in public;
- one or both parties want judgment on the issues in dispute;
- an injunction is needed to preserve rights;
- participation would be involuntary;
- issues of social justice should be aired publicly;
- the other party has no genuine interest in settlement;
- legal action needs to be started or continued to get the other side to the negotiating table. (CEDR, 1998: 7)

This is not an exhaustive list. In the specific context of employment, other types of cases or disputes might be considered inappropriate for ADR as a first approach or altogether. For example, in the workplace, gross misconduct or serious breaches of disciplinary rules should not be dealt with through mediation. In this respect, unions have expressed fears that mediation may be used by employers to avoid taking responsibility for dealing with breaches of rules and policies. Thus the TUC cautioned against the danger of mediation 'letting, say, a serial harasser off the hook' (*The Independent on Sunday*, 2000). It has also been noted that tribunal claims that 'turn on how the law applies to a set of circumstances which are not in dispute… do not often result in settlement' at conciliation. In 2001, this led the government to propose removing the duty on ACAS to offer conciliation in disputes over 'pay, breach of contract and redundancy payments', to enable conciliators to focus on more complex cases (DTI, 2001b: 23). (Following consultation, the government dropped this proposal.)

In Great Britain, in 1999–2000 ACAS achieved a conciliated settlement rate of 50 per cent in respect of individuals' claims under the Sex Discrimination Act and 57 per cent under the Equal Pay Act. The settlement rate for claims under the Disability Discrimination Act was 48 per cent. The significantly lower 38 per cent rate in respect of claims under the Race Relations Act prompted ACAS to consider options to increase settlement rates including 'mediation-style strategies for resolving disputes' but little detail was publicly available on outcomes.

Based on studies of mediation of sex discrimination cases in Australia and the United States in the 1990s, Hunter and Leonard noted 'a number of advantages that might be gained by a move to mediation' in such cases; but they also drew attention to 'several well-recognized drawbacks of, or grounds for scepticism… which would need to be overcome before mediation could be wholeheartedly endorsed'. Drawing on the Australian experience of conciliation in particular, these were identified as 'privacy, power imbalance between the parties and lack of attention to legal rights' (Hunter and Leonard, 1997: 305, 307). If a system of mediation was to become an option for sex discrimination cases in Great Britain, Hunter and Leonard argued that it should be a publicly funded, 'rights-based or evaluative model' which 'must have as its primary objective the promotion and enforcement of the Sex Discrimination Act'. In brief, this would place 'primary responsibility with mediators to ensure that the parties were adequately informed of their rights and that the objectives of the SDA were met through mediation'. For example, the mediator would have responsibility for 'explaining the legal implications of the various issues in dispute' to the parties, and for 'ensuring that the provisions of the SDA were not breached by the terms of a settlement'. The mediator might also advise the parties to seek further legal advice or representation. Hunter and Leonard also suggested that mediated settlements should be a matter of public record (unless agreed otherwise by the parties), enforceable by the tribunal or county court (Hunter and Leonard, 1997: 311–14).

Without these safeguards, it is argued that the outcome of mediations will be 'a product of power relations rather than of… free agreement of each party', apart from when there is more or less equal power between the parties (Hunter and Leonard, 1997: 307). This seemed to be borne out by Hunter and Leonard's study of conciliation of sex discrimination cases in Australia. Similar concerns have been raised about ACAS conciliation, in that conciliators do not give advice on the merits of proposed settlements. A counter-argument is that competent mediators will be aware of power imbalances and act to mitigate them, while not intervening to give advice to one or both parties. Ideally, applicants, in particular, should have access to support and independent legal advice where appropriate. (This is relevant to tribunal proceedings as well as ADR.) In reality, many do not have representation because it is not affordable nor widely available on a *pro bono* basis. Only members can call upon unions for assistance.

In 2000, the role of ADR in discrimination cases was examined by an independent review of the enforcement of UK anti-discrimination laws. The report of the review noted that ACAS had 'signalled a reluctance to attempt a more proactive approach at reaching settlements which promote equal opportunities. They believe this would undermine their neutrality' (Hepple, Coussey and Choudhury, 2000), a concern which many other ADR practitioners would share. The review recommended that a pilot project for mediation in sexual harassment cases, and subsequently in other discrimination cases, should be supported. In 2001, a pilot project was being run in a local authority in respect of discrimination cases. This offered facilitative mediation, not an evaluative 'rights-based' model. However, the accredited mediators were lawyers and consultants experienced in anti-discrimination law and/or practice, trained in equality awareness. (At the time of writing, the pilot Workplace Mediation Project had not been completed and evaluated.)

Extending the debate to employment cases in general, the Industrial Society (now the Work Foundation) has argued that 'ADR does not guarantee fairness or consistency in outcomes'. With reference to the ACAS arbitration scheme, its policy paper, *Courts or Compromise? Routes to Resolving Disputes*, highlighted 'dangers where there is no appeal process, in lack of precedent and where confidentiality is unjustifiable' (Bennion and Rogers, 2001). It also pointed to the risk that compensation awarded through ADR may be less than in a tribunal or court. On the other hand, the Industrial Society acknowledged that mediation 'can take better account of both parties' views and relative positions of power' compared with judicial processes (The Industrial Society, 2001a).

The Industrial Society contended that 'much of the interest in ADR is based on a preconception which is 'difficult to support', namely that there were 'increasingly large numbers of "vexatious" claims and people using the tribunal system simply to extract money from employers' (The Industrial Society, 2001b). Certainly the rise in the number of claims to tribunals (trebling between 1990 and 2000) and 'worrying evidence that employees are increasingly resorting to litigation to sort out workplace disputes' led in 2001 to a government review of dispute resolution with the aim of achieving 'better dispute handling in the workplace and a greater focus on conciliation, ahead of litigation' (DTI, 2001b: 3, 5).

Proposals included 'enabling other organizations to provide conciliation services alongside ACAS' and 'modernizing employment tribunals'. On one hand, the review marked a recognition of the valuable role to be played by ADR, particularly conciliation and mediation, in resolving many employment disputes. On the other hand, the drive to reduce tribunal claims raised concerns about access to justice. There is a danger that cases could be channelled into ADR expediently, undermining its core principle of voluntary participation. There is also a fear that ADR participants may not pursue (or may relinquish) their statutory rights when this would not be in their best interests nor the public interest. There are issues about the affordability of privately provided ADR.

Responses to the consultation showed a 'lack of interest in the proposal to change the law to allow other organizations to provide conciliation services on the same basis as ACAS'. Few respondents commented on proposals to promote ADR; however, the government remained keen to 'encourage projects to develop good practice in ADR and mediation' (DTI, 2001c: 29). The Employment Act 2002 does not explicitly enable the expansion of mediation and conciliation, but the government has adopted two taskforces' recommendations to promote the use of ADR and mediation in particular. In 2002, the Better Regulation Taskforce recommended that ACAS should pilot a mediation service for businesses with fewer than fifty employees.[8] The Employment Tribunal System Task Force dealt in more depth with ADR. It recommended that mediation pilots should be run by ACAS, and possibly a commercial organization; research should be undertaken to determine when it may be appropriate to use mediation to settle employment disputes and the types of cases which may benefit from this; and that additional resources should be given to ACAS to undertake further preventative work and promote good practice. The ETS Taskforce also called for ADR in the workplace to be encouraged, including through in-house procedures; and for information about ADR to be included in guidance to parties, for example in Codes of Practice and best practice booklets. It recommended that generally ADR techniques for the resolution of employment disputes should be encouraged by the dissemination of best practice, training and research into 'how mediation may be used to better effect while the employment relationship is still subsisting' (*Report of the Employment Tribunal System Taskforce*, 2002, p18). If these recommendations are acted upon, ADR is likely to become a more familiar feature of the employment relations landscape.

Notes

1 The term 'employment disputes' is used to mean disputes involving individuals' complaints or rights and disputes between the employer/s and groups of workers, or disputes between workers.

2 Anything communicated to an ACAS conciliator is not admissible in any proceedings before an employment tribunal, except with the consent of the person who communicated it to the conciliator (Employment Tribunals Act 1996 s.18 (7)). Mediators seek the same protection by requiring the parties to sign a legally binding agreement to that effect.

230 I Alternatives to the law

3 An agreement to settle an actual or potential claim to the tribunal with the assistance of an ACAS conciliation officer is called a 'COT3' (after the form on which it is recorded). COT3 agreements are notified to the employment tribunal. Some tribunals publish the settlement schedule while others do not. However, parties wishing to keep a settlement private and confidential may record it as a separate schedule with the 'COT3' recording simply that 'the parties have settled on terms agreed'. See Nichols and Ball (1995: 44).
4 There is no requirement for parties to be legally represented when participating in mediation or conciliation. However, lawyers (or other statutorily authorized persons) must be involved where parties wish to formalize an agreement reached in mediation as a compromise agreement. Among neutral third parties, only ACAS conciliation officers have authority to record COT3 agreements to settle statutory claims.
5 For information on the Northern Ireland Labour Relations Agency, see Web site http://www.lra.org.uk.
6 The TUC Partnership Institute is explicit in its purpose 'to help unions and employers develop effective working relationships' by offering 'practical support in establishing partnerships at work' through its training and advisory services. TUC Partnership Institute (2000) *Partners for Progress: Winning at Work*, TUC, London, p 31.
7 Mediation can take place before, during or after these procedures. For example, the *ACAS Code of Practice on Disciplinary and Grievance Procedures* refers to the option of ADR 'during the grievance procedure'. Once invoked, the procedure in question may need to be suspended to allow for mediation. If mediation forms part of these procedures (at any stage), care must be taken to preserve its voluntary, confidential and without prejudice status. ACAS (2000) *Code of Practice on Disciplinary and Grievance Procedures*, HMSO, London, p 17.
8 See the Report of the Better Regulation Taskforce (2002) *Employment Regulation: striking a balance*, www.cabinet-office.gov.uk/regulation/taskforce/2002/EmploymentRegulation.pdf

References

ACAS (1999) *Annual Report 1998*, ACAS, London, p 39
ACAS (2000) *Annual Report 1999–2000*, ACAS, London, p 51
ACAS (2001) *Annual Report 2000–2001*, ACAS, London, p 3
ACAS (2002) *Annual Report 2001–2002*, ACAS, London, p 24
Bennion, Y and Rogers, A (2001) *Courts or Compromise? Routes to resolving disputes*, Industrial Society Policy Paper www.indsoc.co.uk/policy/polpapers4.htm August
Central Arbitration Committee (2001) *Annual Report 2000/01*, London
Centre for Dispute Resolution (1998) *ADR Route Map: an introduction and practical guide for managers and professionals on using ADR*, CEDR, London, p 7

Centre for Effective Dispute Resolution (2001) *CEDR Mediation in Employment: Seminar Paper*, www.cedr.co.uk/index/php?location=/library/articles/employmentseminar.htm, March

Costantino, C and Sickles Merchant, C (1996) *Designing Conflict Management Systems*, Jossey-Bass Inc, San Francisco, p 37

Department of Trade and Industry (2001a) *Dispute Resolution in Britain – a Background Paper*, p 10 www.dti.gov.uk/er/individual/resolution.pdf 22 June

Department of Trade and Industry (2001b) *Routes to Resolution: Improving Dispute Resolution in Britain*, p 12, www.dti.gov.uk/er/individual/resolution.pdf July

Department of Trade and Industry (2001c) *Routes to Resolution: Improving Dispute Resolution in Britain Government Response* www. dti.gov.uk/er individual/response.et.htm November

Dewar, N (2001) Responding effectively to conflict in the workplace: the systematic use of ADR in the USA, *Journal of ADR, Mediation & Negotiation*, April, pp 23–32

Hepple, B, Coussey, M and Choudhury, T (2000) *Equality: A New Framework – Report of the independent review of the enforcement of UK anti-discrimination law*, Hart Publishing, London, p 112

Hunter, R and Leonard, A (1997) Sex Discrimination and Alternative Dispute Resolution: British proposals in light of international experience, reprinted from *Public Law*, Summer, pp 298–314 (cited in this chapter as 'Hunter and Leonard')

Isenhart, M W and Spangle, M (2000) *Collaborative Approaches to Resolving Conflict*, Sage Publications Inc, p 10

Mackie, K, Miles, D and Marsh, W (1995) *Commercial Dispute Resolution: An ADR Practice Guide*, Butterworths, p 7 (cited in this chapter as 'Miles, Mackie and Marsh')

Nicholls, P and Ball, P (1995) *Tolley's Discrimination Law Handbook*, 2nd edn, Tolley Publishing Company Limited, London

The Independent on Sunday (2000) An easier way to solve workplace disputes, 30 April

The Industrial Society (2001a) *Government plans to stem number of employment tribunals could disappoint employers say IS report*, Policy Web site Press Releases www.indsoc.co.uk/policy/press7.htm August

The Industrial Society (2001b) *Policy Brief: Alternative Dispute Resolution*, www.indsoc.co.uk/policy/polbriefs4.htm August

Report of the Employment Tribunal System Taskforce (2002) DTI, p 18

12

Arbitration and unfair dismissal: the ACAS Scheme

Ramsumair Singh

The settlement of employment disputes presents one of the more pressing problems faced in many countries. In Britain, the new structures and processes recently introduced for the settlement of such disputes are a curious mixture of old and new and, in many cases, the old procedures continue to exist alongside the new (Smith and Thomas, 2000; see also Bowers, 2000). Furthermore, although alternative dispute resolution (ADR) methods – conciliation, mediation and arbitration – have been used over a very long period, dating back at least to the 19th century, it is only under the new ACAS scheme of May 2001 that arbitration can be used for unfair dismissal cases as an alternative to Employment Tribunals (ETs) (Rees, 2001a, 2001b). However, ETs still remain overwhelmingly the principal way of resolving unfair dismissal claims.

Employment Tribunals were established under the Industrial Training Act 1964. They started life as 'Industrial Tribunals' but were renamed in 1998 as 'Employment Tribunals'. The greater part of employment and industrial relations litigation is determined by Employment Tribunals. In 2001/2002 the Employment Tribunal System disposed of well over 100,000 cases.[1]

The Employment Tribunals determine those disputes which relate mainly to individual employment rights. They have jurisdiction to determine over 50 types of complaints, including complaints of unfair dismissal, race, sex and disability discrimination, unlawful deduction of wages, breach of contract, and redundancy pay. The majority of cases involve disputes between individual parties. There are also some cases which can be brought against the

Secretary of State for Trade and Industry, such as, for example, an application for redundancy pay where an employer is insolvent (Leggatt, 2001).

Appeals on points of law, against decisions of ETs, are to the Employment Appeal Tribunal (EAT). This is the main function of the EAT as a superior court of record. It also deals with appeals on questions of law and fact issuing from certain proceedings of the Certification Office for Trade Unions and Employers' Associations.

Over the years, the proceedings and decisions of tribunals have become more legalistic and expensive, with long delays before a case is heard by a tribunal. Attention has also been drawn to the fact that there is an over-whelming consensus that cases referred to ETs are becoming progressively more difficult for those without legal representation, including the impracticability of preparing or presenting most cases involving allegations of discrimination or on points of European law. There are also cases, in particular those including unfair dismissal, where it is unreasonable to expect unrepresented parties to maintain the detachment required of an advocate presenting such a case.[2] Operating in an area of jurisprudence as legally complex as that of employment, in which disputes are primarily adversarial, ETs are bound to be inherently complex and legalistic institutions. Indeed, the increase and spread of legalism in employment tribunals has been viewed as a disease infecting them (Smith and Thomas, 2000: 402; for a defence of the tribunal system see McMullan, 1999), and concomitantly, a cure is therefore urgently necessary.

Employment Tribunals, when they were first established, were designed as an easily accessible, informal, speedy and inexpensive alternative to the ordinary courts for dealing with employment disputes (Royal Commission on the Trade Unions and Employees' Associations, 1968). However, it has been widely recognized for a number of years that not only have Employment Tribunals departed from their laudable aims but also that those aims cannot in practice be realized. This is perhaps especially serious in the case of unfair dismissal, given the volume of such claims in case law and in references to employment tribunals. Table 12.1 illustrates the distribution of unfair dismissal cases as a proportion of all cases for the years 1997 to 2002.

Not surprisingly, given the criticisms of tribunals, alternative ways of resolving disputes, not least unfair dismissal, have been widely discussed. These can be subsumed under alternative dispute resolution (ADR). In essence, ADR describes the range of processes other than litigation used to settle disputes. Many of the developing ADR processes are, in fact, being incorporated into court procedures or accepted by legislation as adjuncts to settlement mechanisms.

The Leggatt Review of Tribunals reported that there was widespread support for alternative dispute resolution in the area of employment, and in particular for the need to support and extend the role of ACAS. Leggatt noted that many cases are diverted to ACAS from the tribunal system. A more

Table 12.1 Distribution of Employment Tribunal unfair dismissal cases over the period 1997–2002

Year	Number of cases registered	Number of unfair dismissal claims	Unfair dismissal claims as % of all cases
1997/98	80,435	37,366	46.5
1998/99	91,913	37,034	40.3
1999/2000	103,935	51,270	49.3
2000/01	130,408	49,401	37.9
2001/02	112,227	51,512	45.9

Sources: Employment Tribunals Service and Labour Market Trends/Employment Gazette

positive and constructive view is often achieved by a reference to ACAS than is possible for a tribunal. Even if no settlement results, at least the issues can be clarified (Leggatt, 2001).

ARBITRATION AS AN ALTERNATIVE TO EMPLOYMENT TRIBUNALS

The potential benefits of arbitration as an alternative to employment tribunals were under active consideration from the early 1990s.[3] The Conservative government at the time favoured introducing arbitration in the context of growing employment tribunal caseloads. Subsequently, the Labour government adopted the idea and introduced the Employment Rights (Dispute Resolution) Act 1998[4] into the statute book. The arbitration alternative has been supported by the Confederation of British Industry (CBI), as a means of reducing the number of tribunal cases, and the Trade Union Congress (TUC), as a way of tackling undue legalism in unfair dismissal cases. The ACAS Arbitration Scheme can be viewed as part of an ongoing programme of reforms to stem the growth in employment tribunal cases.

The ACAS Arbitration Scheme owes much to the work of Roy Lewis and Jon Clark and in particular their seminal monograph published by the Institute of Employment Rights in 1993 (Lewis and Clark, 1993). They compared the Employment Tribunals with arbitration for the resolution of employment disputes, and argued strongly for the adoption of ADR – arbitration – in this field. All this is not to deny that arbitration has long been considered as an appropriate method to resolve dismissal cases. What the Lewis and Clark monograph did, as noted by Ian Smith, was to put the whole issue of ADR back on the map for consideration by successive governments.[5]

THE ACAS SCHEME

After the introduction of the Employment Rights (Dispute Resolution) Act 1998, ACAS issued a consultative draft of the Scheme and submitted revised proposals to the Department of Trade and Industry for approval in the autumn of 1998.

The Scheme was initially scheduled to come into operation in early 2000, but the introduction of the Scheme was delayed, reportedly due to the heavy programme of other employment legislation and the need to make its provisions consistent with those of the Human Rights Act 1998. The ACAS Arbitration Scheme for the resolution of unfair dismissal disputes was finally introduced in England and Wales on 21 May 2001.[6]

The Scheme is designed to overcome the widely made criticisms of employment tribunals in that they are too slow, expensive, legalistic and formalistic. In sharp contrast, the ACAS Scheme is intended to be 'speedy, informal, confidential and non-legalistic'. Interestingly, it embodies some of the aims of the employment tribunals when they were initially introduced.

KEY FEATURES OF THE SCHEME

There are significant differences between the ACAS Arbitration Scheme and the conventional tribunal process. These can be summarized as follows:

(a) The scheme is entirely voluntary and is available only in respect of unfair dismissal claims. It can be used only where both the parties agree to opt for it and to waive certain legal rights they would have had at an employment tribunal. The scheme is not intended to deal with complex legal issues.

(b) Hearings are held in private, for example in an ACAS office or a hotel, and will normally be completed in one day or less. Each party is invited to submit a written statement of their case in advance of the hearing.

(c) The case is heard by an ACAS Arbitrator, chosen by ACAS, not by the parties themselves. Legal representatives may be used by the parties but will be given no special status.

(d) There is no set format for the hearing. Arbitrators have a general duty to act fairly and impartially between the parties, giving each party a reasonable opportunity of putting its case and responding to that of the other party. The process is intended to be 'inquisitorial' or 'investigative' rather than adversarial, the opposite from tribunal hearings. The arbitrator will question the parties and witnesses informally but he will not cross-examine them.

(e) Each party meets its own costs in attending the hearing. However, if a dismissal is found to be unfair, the arbitrator can include in the calculation of any compensation a sum to cover the costs incurred by the dismissed employee in attending the hearing.

(f) Arbitrators are required to apply EC law and the Human Rights Acts 1998 (regarding which a legal adviser may be appointed, if required, to provide guidance). Otherwise, instead of applying strict legal tests and case law, the arbitrator's decision will have regard to the 'general principles of fairness and good conduct in employment relations'. These principles include those set out in the ACAS Code of Practice and Discipline and Grievance Procedures, and the ACAS Handbook on Discipline at Work.

(g) As with unfair dismissal cases determined by an Employment Tribunal, reinstatement, re-engagement and compensation are the available remedies if the dismissal is not upheld. Unlike the award in tribunal cases, however, here the award is confidential to ACAS and the parties. Furthermore, the arbitrator's decision will be final and binding. The Award itself will state the reasons for the dismissal and whether it was fair or unfair, and will refer to the main considerations taken into account. There is only limited scope for appealing (on questions of EC law and the Human Rights Act 1998) or challenging the arbitrator's award (eg on grounds of 'serious irregularity').

Source: Compiled from *ACAS, the ACAS Arbitration Scheme for the resolution of unfair dismissal disputes: a guide to the scheme*

Table 12.2, largely based on the work of Clark and Lewis, compares and contrasts the main characteristics of the ACAS Scheme with those of Employment Tribunals. The Lewis and Clark 'model' also appears in their monograph *Employment Rights, Industrial Tribunals and Arbitration: The Case for Alternative Dispute Resolution*, IER, 1993, p 16.

There is a separation of roles between ACAS and arbitrators under the Scheme. ACAS acts as the 'administrator' of the Scheme, whilst the arbitrator performs the 'judicial function' of the decision-making process. ACAS has no power to order the arbitrator as to how a case is decided: the arbitrator has the sole responsibility for this. He or she alone is empowered to determine the rights and obligations of the parties. The importance of the role of ACAS, however, should not be underrated. When an award is ready, before it is sent out, ACAS scrutinize it and refer clerical or similar errors back to the arbitrator for corrections. ACAS sends out the award to the parties. Arbitrators are appointed by ACAS to a panel from which members are selected to arbitrate the individual cases under the Scheme.

When the new Scheme was introduced, ACAS had to appoint new arbitrators. These newcomers supplement the arbitrators already on the existing panel who had opted to serve on the new scheme. All arbitrators under the scheme received specialized training in various aspects of the Scheme. At the time of writing, there were 93 arbitrators appointed under the Scheme: 62 were new arbitrators and 31 were from the existing panel.[7] A small number of

Table 12.2 Employment tribunals and ACAS arbitration: a comparison

Unfair dismissal/ key process areas	Employment tribunal	Arbitration
Decision (fair or unfair dismissal) based on:	Statute and case law/ 'test of reasonableness'	ACAS Code of Practice and Handbook and general principles of fairness and good conduct in employment relations
Hearing	Application by claimant	By agreement of both parties
Those hearing the case	Legally qualified chairman and side members	Single ACAS arbitrator with knowledge/experience of employment relations
Location of hearing	Employment Tribunal office	By agreement at a hotel/ACAS office/the workplace/representatives' premises or other
Completion of case	Within three months of entering scheme	Several weeks/months
Length of hearing	Normally at least one day to several weeks	Normally within one day
Presentation of evidence	Cross-examination of 'witnesses' on oath	Informal presentation, no oaths or cross-examination by parties but questioning by arbitrator
Availability of 'witnesses' and documents	'Witness' orders, orders for discovery/inspection or production by 'witnesses' of documents	No powers in scheme to make orders, but failure of parties to cooperate can count against them when decision is made
Expenses to attend hearing/Loss of earnings	Tribunal can reimburse expenses and losses for parties, 'witnesses' and some representatives	No expenses paid by ACAS, but compensation for unfair dismissals may include a sum for cost of attending hearing
Remedies/Awards	Statutory provision/ Interim relief available	ACAS Scheme/Interim relief not available
Publicity: Presentation of case	Public hearing/ adversarial/ public award	Private hearing/inquisitorial/ confidential award
Decisions/awards	Normally within three weeks of hearing	Several weeks/months
Appeal/Challenge	Can be made to EAT and Appellate courts	No appeal on point of law or fact (other than EC law or Human Rights Act issues); challenge only for jurisdiction and serious irregularity

Sources: Adapted from *The ACAS Arbitration Scheme for the resolution of unfair dismissal disputes* (2001). The table was itself adapted by ACAS from Jon Clark and Roy Lewis (1992) Arbitration as an option for unfair dismissal claimants, *Personnel Management*, pp 36–9

arbitrators on the existing panel did not join the new scheme. In total, ACAS have some 103 arbitrators in 'new' and 'old' schemes. It is important to note that ACAS arbitrators are largely drawn from the academic profession and a wide range of disciplines, including engineering, law, economics and the social sciences. As might be expected, they all need to have experience in industrial relations, and fulfil the stringent conditions for appointment to the ACAS panel by open competition.

THE SCHEME IN PRACTICE

Before a person can use the ACAS Scheme, certain conditions have to be met. First, they must have made a complaint of unfair dismissal to an employment tribunal or have claimed that they have grounds for doing so. An ACAS 'conciliator' (industrial relations officer) will then contact both parties to see whether the issue can be resolved without any sort of hearing. If not, the conciliator will then explore with both parties to see whether the case is a suitable one for arbitration under the Scheme. Although the conciliator will explain the procedure to both parties, he or she is not allowed to recommend which option, as between the ACAS scheme and an Industrial Tribunal hearing, they should choose.

The conditions that must be satisfied before a dismissed employee can have referral to the ACAS Scheme can be briefly summarized as follows:

- The employee must have a complaint which is solely for unfair dismissal – allied claims of unlawful deduction of wages, breach of contract or discrimination will either have to be settled separately or proceed to an Employment Tribunal.
- There are no jurisdiction issues relating to the unfair dismissal, such as whether it actually occurred, whether the employee has sufficient continuity of service to bring a claim, or whether the period allowed for bringing a claim has elapsed.
- The case is relatively straightforward and does not raise any complicated legal issues, especially relating to jurisdiction.
- Both the employer and the dismissed employee voluntarily agree to choose the ACAS Arbitration Scheme.
- The dismissed employee works in England and Wales.

Source: Compiled from the *ACAS Arbitration Scheme for the resolution of unfair dismissal disputes: a guide to the scheme*

THE ARBITRATION AGREEMENT

Access to ACAS arbitration schemes will be through an 'arbitration agreement' arrived at by both parties. The 'arbitration agreement' can be concluded in either of two ways: a 'conciliated agreement' reached with the assistance of an ACAS conciliator (under S18 of the Employment Tribunals Act 1996 (ETA)), or a 'compromise agreement' reached with the assistance of the parties' independent advisers. (Conditions regulating such agreements are regulated by the Employment Relations Act 1996 (ETA)).

It is the responsibility of both parties or their advisers to ensure that a valid arbitration agreement is concluded. Appendix 2 of the ACAS guide to the Scheme suggested the following wording for the 'arbitration agreement': 'The parties hereby agree to submit the dispute concerning the alleged unfair dismissal of [employee's name] to arbitration in accordance with the ACAS Arbitration Scheme having effect by virtue of the ACAS Arbitration Scheme (England and Wales) Order (SI2001 No 1185).'

This agreement should be a separate document, especially where, within the conciliation agreement or compromise agreement, the parties are settling other issues which fall outside the ambit of the ACAS Scheme. Once the arbitration agreement is signed the claim can no longer proceed to an Employment Tribunal for determination.

All arbitration agreements must be notified to ACAS within six weeks of their conclusion, and the responsibility for this rests with the parties or their advisers. An arbitration agreement must be accompanied by a completed waiver form (also set out in the ACAS guide to the Scheme). In essence, both parties sign a waiver and agree to forego certain rights.

These foregone rights include the following:

- a public hearing;
- having the decision published;
- the cross-examination of witnesses;
- appeal;
- having the case decided in accordance with strict law, except on points of EC Law or under the HRA 1998.

The safeguards inherent in, and inseparable from, the arbitration agreement ensure that the parties are not under any misapprehension about the terms on which the case is proceeding to arbitration under the ACAS Scheme.

THE APPOINTMENT OF THE ARBITRATOR

Once ACAS Head Office has accepted the agreement to go to arbitration under the Scheme, an arbitrator will be appointed by ACAS. The parties do not choose the arbitrator. The arbitrator needs to confirm, in writing, on a special ACAS form, that there is no conflict of interest between the arbitrator and any of the parties.

The arbitrator, moreover, after being appointed and until the arbitration is concluded, has a continuing responsibility to inform ACAS and the parties of any conflicts of interest that may arise. Arbitrators must be mindful of the need on their part to avoid any possible perception or appearance or bias in the eyes of the parties. The need for impartiality in 'judicial' decisions cannot be over-emphasized, especially since the Pinochet case.[8] Lord Hoffman, a leading Law Lord, did not disclose his association with Amnesty International in the General Pinochet extradition case on which he sat in the House of Lords. As is well known, the entire Pinochet case had to be reheard by the House of Lords. Relevant here is the maxim 'if in doubt, disclose'. The parties can waive a disclosed circumstance if they so wish. In this case the arbitrator can proceed or continue to sit, in the particular case. The parties are entitled to expect that an arbitrator will be impartial at all times.

Once an arbitrator has been appointed, a hearing must be arranged as soon as reasonably practicable, with the assistance of the ACAS Arbitration Section. It will be dependent on the availability of the parties involved, but it usually takes place within two months. The hearing is held at a location convenient for both parties or it can be held at one of ACAS's own premises, or at a hotel. The costs are borne by ACAS.

Prior to the hearing, both parties are required to submit a written statement of the case to the arbitrator through the ACAS Arbitration Section. Statements of case are also exchanged between the parties. They normally include: the contract of employment, staff handbook policy and procedures; time sheets; correspondence between employer and dismissed employee, eg disciplinary letters; and evidence of attempts to gain new employment or earnings in new employment.

THE HEARING

There is no set format for the hearing, but all ACAS arbitrators have been trained, and generally adopt the same procedure for hearings. All parties will be given an opportunity to state their cases, and the arbitrator will help if either party has difficulty in presenting its case. The hearing will not follow a legal procedure so there will be no swearing on oath or cross-examination. The hearings are 'inquisitorial' rather than 'adversarial' in nature. Importantly, the arbitrator will not take into account any strict statute or case law unless the case involves European law or the Human Rights Act 1998.

Both parties can bring persons of their own choosing to represent their cases, but no special status will be given to legally qualified representatives. Parties will be liable for their own representative's fees, travelling or other expenses. Before the hearing is concluded the arbitrator will ensure that all parties to the hearing are given the opportunity to say what he or she believes to be relevant. No more evidence can be submitted following the hearing.

The parties can withdraw their cases at any time before or during an arbitration hearing. If a settlement is reached the arbitrator can make an 'award by consent' under the Scheme.

THE AWARD

The arbitrator's decision is termed an 'award'. On reaching a decision as to whether the dismissal was fair or not, the arbitrator will take account of:

- the ACAS Code of Practice on Disciplinary and Grievance Procedures, and the ACAS Advisory Handbook Discipline at Work;
- their knowledge and experience of good employment relations;
- the evidence presented.[9]

If the arbitrator finds the dismissal was unfair he or she can order reinstatement, re-employment or compensation. As in an Employment Tribunal, in coming to a decision the arbitrator will take into account the views of the parties and his or her own view as to what is practicable and just. Any compensation will be calculated in a similar way to that used by Employment Tribunals. The decision will not be made or announced at the hearing, but will be sent in writing to the parties through ACAS. It is normally forwarded to the parties within three weeks of the hearing.

The award is final and binding with no right of appeal on a point of law or fact, although serious irregularities can be challenged. It is private and confidential to the parties; and is enforceable by the courts in England and Wales.

EVALUATING THE ACAS SCHEME

Prior to the introduction of the Scheme, ACAS estimated that around 1,000 cases would be dealt with during its first year. This estimate represented only a fraction of the number of unfair dismissal cases (over 50,000 in 2001–2, of which about 10,000 went on to an employment tribunal hearing).[10]

The impact of the new Scheme, in terms of volume of cases determined, has been minimal. In the first year of operations only 13 cases were determined; and from its inception on 21 May 2001 to 14 September 2002 there were 20 cases in all.[11] ACAS, however, noted that although business has been less brisk than was anticipated, there is now a steadily growing caseload. Moreover, informal feedback has been favourable, with parties expressing the view 'that the less formal, non-adversarial approach at an Arbitration hearing is preferable to that of the Employment Tribunal System'.[12]

The reasons for this slow and limited take-up of the scheme are by no means clear, but various reasons have been advanced. Lawyers, in particular, are uncertain as to the merits and likely attractiveness of the new Scheme. Some have expressed concern that because the criteria for arbitrators' decisions (general principles of fairness and good conduct in employment relations) differ from the statutory tests applied by the tribunals, a two-tier system of justice may develop. It has also been suggested that the ACAS Arbitration Scheme offers employers and dismissed employees less certainty of outcome, and that the confidentiality of awards may mask variable standards within the scheme.

Some lawyers also take the view that the confidentiality of proceedings under the Arbitration Scheme favours the employer, anxious to avoid the damaging publicity sometimes associated with tribunal cases. Conversely, however, for dismissed employees, others are of the view that the fact that the process is private may be a disincentive in considering the arbitration route, it being arguable that to do so would forego the 'embarrassment value' (for employers) of the prospect of public hearings which might lead to favourable out-of-court settlements for dismissed employees. Limitations on the grounds for appealing against the arbitrator's decision are also seen as particularly unattractive to employers. It may likewise be a disadvantage to both parties. The cost efficiency cited as one of the driving forces behind the Arbitration Scheme may not be very 'cost efficient' since parties lose out on the recent rule changes at Tribunals which can now award costs of up to £10,000.[13]

It has also been argued that parties opting for arbitration lose the help of the 'industrial jury' that you get at Employment Tribunals. In reaching a decision the arbitrator will not, with some exceptions, take account of strict law or case law. The arbitration route may not only provide less certainty of outcome for both employers and dismissed employees but they would also be unable to access the procedure set by similar cases.

Whilst Employment Tribunals are still struggling to cope with increasing claims, those unfair dismissal cases which are suitable for ACAS arbitration are likely to be set down relatively quickly, and determined within three months. Yet the parties seem to prefer to stay with the tried and tested tribunal system, even if it does take much longer and is more expensive than the ACAS Scheme. They may just prefer the greater perceived consistency of going to an Employment Tribunal or perhaps to 'have their day in court' as a catharsis!

The author has discussed the ACAS Scheme with a number of employment lawyers. With few exceptions, they were not supportive of the Scheme, for the reasons discussed above. Some, however, were not fully conversant with the Scheme or, indeed, with arbitration as a means of resolving employment disputes. There can be little debate, however, that the fees earned by lawyers for tribunal work far exceed the remuneration of arbitrators in an arbitration case! The view has been put forward, based on the principles of negligence law, that it should be professional negligence not to mention the Scheme to a client as a realistic option in a dismissal case.[14]

In any assessment of the ACAS Scheme it must be borne in mind that arbitration as a means of resolving employment disputes has never been a popular option. It has always been a last resort. It would therefore seem that some of the traditional approaches to arbitration have inevitably become associated with the new Scheme. Whilst initially slow to become established, the new Scheme may nevertheless yet gain a secure foothold.

It is difficult to make proposals for reform of the new Scheme without detailed research, and a systematic review of policy options in the light of it. Even so, it is reasonable to suggest that Employment Tribunals themselves should be required to put forward the advantages the ACAS Scheme offers in straightforward unfair dismissal cases. There would be no new principle involved. Lord Woolf in his report *Access to Justice* (Woolf, 1996) noted that 'the Lord Chancellor and the Court Service should treat it as one of their responsibilities to make the public aware of the possibilities which the ADR offers'. In a booklet entitled *Resolving Disputes without going to Court* the Lord Chancellor's Department reminded potential litigants that 'Going to court is not the only way to resolve a dispute. There are other options' (Lord Chancellor's Department, 1998). The fact that ADR processes have not been used to resolve a wide range of disputes and unfair dismissal cases should be no exception. The ACAS Scheme is, however, undoubtedly the 'sleeping giant' for the resolution of such cases (Singh, 1996).

Whilst it is too early to make a thorough assessment of the Scheme for the resolution of unfair dismissal cases, all the indications, apart from the very limited volume of cases, is that the Scheme is successful as a process, ie it is an easily accessible, informal, speedy and inexpensive alternative to Employment Tribunals for dealing with unfair dismissal cases.

Notes

1 Employment Tribunal Sources, Annual Report and Accounts, 2001–2002.
2 This point was stressed by Sir Andrew Leggatt in his Report.
3 However, arbitration in the resolution of unfair dismissal cases had long been established procedure in some industries, notably electricity supply.
4 Employment Relations Act (Dispute Resolution Act) 1998.
5 Ian Smith, NJL Practitioner, May 25 2001.
6 ACAS Arbitration Scheme (England and Wales) Order 2001.
7 Information Supplied by ACAS Arbitration Section.
8 *R v Bow Street Metropolitan Stipendiary Magistrate and Others ex parte Pinochet Ugarte HL* (2000) I AC147.
9 ACAS, the ACAS Arbitration Scheme for the resolution of unfair dismissal disputes. See also ACAS, *An Introduction to the ACAS Arbitration Scheme* and *ACAS, Choosing our Arbitration Scheme*.
10 ETS, Annual reports and Accounts, 2001–2002.
11 Information Supplied by ACAS Arbitration Section.
12 ACAS, Arbitrators Bulletin, Summer 2002. This is the view of an ACAS Arbitrator.
13 See also *Kovacs and Queen Mary College and Another CA* (2002) IRLR 414.
14 Ian Smith, NJL Practitioner, May 25 2001.

References

Bowers, J (2000) *Employment Law*, London: Blackstone Press, London
Leggatt, Sir Andrew (2001) *Tribunals for Users of One System, One Service, Report of the Review of Tribunals*, March, Lord Chancellor's Department, London

Lewis, R and Clark, J (1993) *Employment Rights, Industrial Tribunals and Arbitration, the Case for Alternative Dispute Resolution*, The Institute of Employment Rights, London

Lord Chancellor's Department (1998) *Civil Justice: Resolving and Avoiding Disputes in the Information Age*, London

McMullan, (1999) Employment tribunals: philosophies and practicalities, *International Labour Journal*, **28**, p 33

Rees, W M (2001a) A new role for ACAS: The ACAS arbitral alternative for unfair dismissal cases in the employment ADR context – part one, *Journal of ADR, Mediation and Negotiation*, **1** (3)

Rees, W M (2001b) A new role for ACAS: The ACAS arbitral alternative for unfair dismissal cases in the employment ADR context – part two, *Journal of ADR, Mediation and Negotiation*, **1** (4)

Royal Commission on the Trade Unions and Employees Associations (1968) Cmnd. 3623

Singh, R (1996) Alternative dispute resolution: a gift to charities, *The Charities Law and Practice Review*, **14**, June, pp 73–82

Smith, I T and Thomas, G (2000) *Industrial Law*, Butterworth, London, ch 8

Woolf, Lord (1996) *Access to Justice Final Report to the Lord Chancellor on the Civil Justice System (England and Wales)*, Stationery Office, London

ACKNOWLEDGEMENTS

I wish to thank the ACAS Arbitration Section for providing me with information relating to the Arbitration Scheme. The help received from the Employment Tribunal Office in Manchester is likewise acknowledged. Dr Damon Berridge kindly assisted me with the statistical analyses. Thanks are also due to Mr Michael Dunne, Law Librarian of Lancaster University, for assistance in locating documents. Comments on the chapter by Professor Brian Towers, Mr Alan Airth and Dr Catherine Singh are also gratefully acknowledged.

Part IV

Employment relations practice

13

Overview: approaches to managing the employment relationship

Jeanette Harrison, Norma Heaton, Bob Mason and Joe Morgan

INTRODUCTION

In this chapter, we trace the growing plurality of approaches to the employment relationship, focusing on the changing character of relationships between employers, managers, workers and their trade unions in contemporary organizational settings. In order to explore this complex picture, the chapter is structured in the following way. First, we overview changes in the institutional environment and the structures of collective representation, concentrating on the period since 1997. We trace the fortunes of trade unions in the UK through this period, noting that in quantitative terms, whilst both union membership and density (the percentage of the workforce belonging to a trade union) have appeared to stabilize in recent years (following a linear decline since the early 1980s), non-unionism remains a significant feature of the employment relations scene in the UK. We then go on to discuss the various ways in which the changing approaches to managing people have created a diverse picture in terms of both collective and non-union employment relations in the workplace.

In exploring these themes, we note that the new environment is creating the potential for a stronger institutional basis on which collective employment relations may develop, in particular with the advent of the union recognition law and the European Works Council Directive. Moreover, the continuing need for employers to seek performance and productivity improvements indirectly creates possibilities for collective employment relations, most noticeably in the guise of workplace social partnerships. However, whilst the institutional basis for trade unions appears more favourable than for many years, it is uncertain to what extent the potential of these changing factors will be realized in practice. There is, for example, no direct imperative on the part of employers to seek strategic alliances with trade unions, and as we note in the final part of this chapter, non-union employment relations are likely to continue to be a major characteristic in the UK economy for the foreseeable future.

A number of abstract models have been constructed to shed light on the plurality of employment relations, which attempt to characterize both collective and non-collective forms of employment relations. Hyman (1997), for instance, offers an elegant summation of these trends, with two outcomes denoted for 'union inclusion' approaches, namely social partnership and the more traditional UK industrial relations approach, labelled the 'regulated market' by Hyman; and for employment relations that exclude unions, the soft (possibly strategic) human resource management (HRM) approach is contrasted with the 'bleak house' regime, in which a black hole has appeared where neither employee-friendly HR practices nor trade union protection are to be found. These potential outcomes are explored in detail below.

However, even the terms 'exclusion' and 'inclusion' might imply a relatively conscious, clear-cut strategic approach to the employment relationship, a view we question in this chapter. If the employment relationship remains a 'frontier of control' (Goodrich, 1920), then it is a frontier that is characterized by inconsistency, experimentation, opportunism and U-turns on the part of both employers and unions. As our empirical evidence[1] will demonstrate, even where organizations flirt with social partnership, this is just as likely to reflect an unsustainable short-term survival strategy as it is a long-term sustainable strategic alliance between the employer and one or more trade unions. In this respect, what might be seen as the main rationale underpinning various partnership and direct employee involvement strategies, that is, aligning senior management's strategic knowledge affecting the long-term prosperity of the organization with the workforce's (including line management) operational knowledge, there are nevertheless a number of possible scenarios emanating from this. In terms of collective employment relations, organizations might attempt to develop a strategic partnership between senior management and trade unions in order for both parties to realize the potential advantages of this alignment. Alternatively, it is equally likely that neither party will be prepared to take the risks that social partnerships entail, and will therefore be unwilling to seek the potential advantages of this approach. Somewhere in between, we have the organization that may flirt with partnership, but in an ad hoc way, attempting to make gains, but never fully committing itself to the risk that a more sustainable strategy would entail. Similarly diverse approaches are likely in the non-union organization, ranging from a strategic direct employee involvement strategy to a total lack of awareness of the potential advantages of a strategic alliance between workforce and senior management, *inter alia* a feature of the 'bleak house' employment relations organization. We attempt to shed empirical light on these theoretical scenarios throughout this chapter, noting that very often, delineating model employment relations practices is a highly problematic exercise.

NEW INSTITUTIONS AND STRUCTURES OF EMPLOYMENT RELATIONS

It is worth remembering that just a decade ago the terminal decline of collective employment relations and, by implication, trade unionism seemed imminent, with non-unionism and the non-union enterprise placed firmly on the employment agenda. Purcell summed up the perceptions emanating out of the 1980s thus:

> The latest workplace industrial relations survey has begun to show what happens when institutional support is withdrawn. There is little doubt that we are seeing the progressive decline in institutional industrial relations. What evidence we have points to the emergence of a free, unregulated labour market of the sort that predated the birth of collective bargaining 100 years ago. (Purcell, 1993)

Since then, however, the UK has experienced further change in the environment and institutional framework underpinning employment relations; changes that have potentially created a new and more positive framework for the re-establishment of collective forms of industrial relations. The return of a Labour government to office in 1997 triggered a number of institutional reforms potentially beneficial to collective employment relations, both at European and national levels. In the context of the European Union, the government's ending of the opt-out from the Social Chapter (of the Maastricht Treaty) meant the UK committing itself to introducing legislation on a raft of social and employment issues, including the European Works Council (EWC) Directive, to which the UK became a signatory on 15 December 1997. This Directive covers organizations operating in at least two member states, employing a minimum of 1,000 workers, with at least 150 employees in each country, and came into force in the UK in December 1999. Reflecting the Directive's stated objective, nearly all existing agreements state that their essential purpose is to provide an effective channel for information provision and consultation of employees (although only about 10 per cent of agreements define consultation in terms of 'negotiation'). Its potential influence on managerial approaches to employment relations is significant, in that it has been estimated that 114 UK-based companies had established EWCs prior to September 1996 (the deadline set for EU states other than the UK), and of these 58 were UK owned. Moreover, another 125 UK-owned and UK-based non-European Economic Area foreign-owned companies with their headquarters in the UK were covered by the Directive by the end of the 1990s (EFILWC, 2000; Weber, Foster and Egriboz, 2000).

The government has also introduced national-based legislation, noticeably the Employment Relations Act (1999), which has strengthened union representation by, in particular, reintroducing a statutory procedure for union recognition. As detailed in Chapter 7, the statutory right to trade union recognition came into force in June 2000, and companies are now no longer able to ignore or de-recognize a trade union that a majority of its employees support. The government has attempted to foster a new culture of partnership in the workplace, encouraging 'understanding and cooperation', and the legislation has been designed to emphasize the benefits of a voluntaristic approach to this issue. For instance, voluntary recognition agreements are likely to be quicker and less conflictual, and give the employer greater control over the content of the agreements than its statutory counterpart (Wood and Godard, 1999; Smith and Morton, 2001). Preliminary evidence points to the relative popularity of the voluntary approach, with the TUC reporting 234 new recognition deals signed between 1999 and 2000 (prior to the legislation coming into force), with the Central Arbitration Committee (CAC) (the body charged with overseeing the recognition legislation) receiving 80 applications in the year to June 2001. Of these, only five cases had progressed through the entire CAC recognition procedure (Incomes Data report, 2001).

Whilst there has been a strong current of scepticism regarding the likely influence of this new institutional basis for collective employment relations, particularly given the disaggregation trends divorcing workplace employment regimes from both national and European industrial relations systems (Streeck, 1992), we would caution against the view. As we illustrate below, managerial approaches to employment relations tend to be characterized by inconsistency, and strategies 'emerge' through experimentation, opportunism and negotiation, rather than through a linear top-down process. This presents opportunities for the collective interests of workers to be represented, although it should be noted that trade union approaches to the changes in employment relations can be equally as inconsistent as management's.

Partly reflecting this new institutional basis, trade unions have experienced a slow reversal in their declining fortunes, at least measured quantitatively in terms of aggregate membership and union density, as shown in Table 13.1.

Whilst in broad terms the decline in trade union membership has been stemmed in recent years, the extent of non-union employment relations remain significant. The most reliable source of information about the size and

Table 13.1 Trade union membership and density 1990–2000

Year	No. members	% change from previous year	Union density
1990	8,835,000		33.9
1991	8,602,000	–2.6	33.6
1992	7,956,000	–7.5	32.2
1993	7,767,000	–2.4	31.5
1994	7,530,000	–3.0	30.1
1995	7,309,000	–2.9	28.8
1996	7,244,000	–0.9	28.2
1997	7,154,000	–1.2	27.3
1998	7,152,000	0.0	26.9
1999	7,257,000	1.5	27.0
2000	7,321,000	0.9	27.0
2001	7,295,000	–0.4	26.5

Source: Brook (2002)

characteristics of the non-union sector is the series of Workplace Industrial (now Employee) Relations Surveys (WERS), first carried out in 1980 and most recently conducted in 1998. Using the presence of one or more union members as an indicator of whether a workplace has employee representation based on trade unions, Cully *et al* (1999) have estimated that there was no union presence in 30 per cent of workplaces in 1980 and in 1984, but that this proportion rose to 39 per cent in 1990 and then to 47 per cent in 1998. The latest WERS figures show that in private manufacturing the proportion of workplaces with no union presence rose from 33 per cent in 1980 to reach 58 per cent in 1998, while in the private services sector the relevant proportions were 50 per cent in 1980 and 65 per cent in 1998. Union recognition in the public sector, however, has remained the norm; in the relatively small number of public sector workplaces where unions are not recognized for bargaining, this is largely because pay is determined by review bodies rather than direct bargaining (in the Armed Services and nursing professions, for example).

Within the private sector, almost all types of workplace showed a lower incidence of union recognition in 1998 than in 1980, the exceptions being the energy and water supply industries. Overall, in 1998, nearly two-thirds of private sector workplaces were without a trade union presence, while only one in four recognized a trade union. Table 13.2 shows that recognition is associated with workplace size, with recognition a minority phenomenon for those workplaces with fewer than 200 employees. Furthermore, the age of the workplace has a significant bearing on recognition. Disney, Gosling and Machin (1995) showed that the rate of recognition among new workplaces was lower in the 1980s than in earlier decades. This lower rate of recognition in workplaces less than 10 years old continued through the 1990s.

Table 13.2 Trade union recognition in private sector workplaces in 1998

Workplace size	% of workplaces
25–49 employees	16
50–99 employees	23
100–199 employees	39
200–499 employees	54
500 or more employees	64
Workplace age	
Less than 10 years	18
10–24 years	22
25 or more years	32

Source: Cully et al, op cit, p.240.

Views on (de)recognition trends have varied over the past decade. On the one hand, a fairly pessimistic picture emerges from Machin's (2000) analysis, which argues that most critically for membership levels, unions have consistently failed to organize new establishments set up over the past 20 years or so. Going on to examine the extent to which unions have been able to gain recognition, Machin points to a 'collapse' in establishments set up after 1980 in private sector manufacturing, with a sharp fall also in private services. Reflecting these structural shifts, the number and proportion of employees whose pay and conditions were determined by collective bargaining arrangements declined during the 1980s and 1990s, falling from 70 per cent of all employees in 1984 to 54 per cent in 1990 and 41 per cent in 1998 (Cully *et al*, 1999). For some, this indicates concerted employer attempts to bypass or marginalize trade unions and to unilaterally impose new terms and conditions of employment (Kelly, 1998).

A different view is offered by Gall and McKay (1994, 1999, 2001) who have studied a range of data sets to unravel the changes in both de-recognition and recognition. They point to the following overall trends. After a period of stability in the early to mid-1980s, the number of recognition agreements and the number of workers covered by them fell markedly from the late 1980s until the mid-1990s. Also between 1988 and 1994, incidences of de-recognition increased from relatively small levels to become significantly greater than many commentators had anticipated. However, figures for the later part of the 1990s reveal that the annual rate of de-recognition actually peaked in the early 1990s and declined thereafter, while the annual rate of new recognition agreements roughly matched those of de-recognition from 1989 to 1992 and then increased towards the end of the 1990s. In fact, taking the period of 1989 to 1998 as a whole, Gall and McKay show that the number of reported cases of new recognition agreements exceeded those of actual de-recognition by some two hundred.

The analyses by Gall and McKay also point to the changing relative importance of reasons given for de-recognition. While the early part of the 1990s saw the most commonly cited reasons as 'low or falling levels of union membership', 'move to single union/fewer unions', 'resulting from privatization/deregulation' and 'part of a wider dispute', in the later part of the decade 'change in ownership' and 'relocation or re-organization' were more prominent. Overall, Gall and McKay tend to downplay the significance of derecognition, suggesting that the number of companies likely to de-recognize is becoming fewer so the pool of 'de-recognizers' has reduced over time. Also, the notion of employers working with unions in partnership is becoming more widespread, indicating that a pragmatic pluralism may be experiencing a revival. A multi-sectoral study, for example, found that of 748 recognition deals listed since 1995, about 150 are described as 'partnership' agreements (Gall, 2000). Furthermore, once it became clear that the Labour government would introduce some statutory mechanism for trade union recognition, the climate of industrial relations began to change. Finally, many unions have put relatively more resources into trade union membership and recognition campaigns, and Gall and McKay argue that 'it is increasingly the case that persistent and bold union campaigns can secure recognition from unwilling employers', though Wood et al (2002) have suggested that any reversal in union decline will involve unions venturing beyond their conventional territories (Gall and McKay, 1999).

Despite this, however, the picture from the 1998 WERS data is one where almost half of workplaces had no union members and two-thirds had no union or other representatives. These were mostly small workplaces and were disproportionately found in certain industries, including construction, hotels and restaurants, and wholesale and retailing. Not surprisingly, the managers in these workplaces held the least favourable views towards unions, with only 2 per cent in favour of union membership compared with 42 per cent in all other workplaces (Cully et al, 1999). Whilst this may reflect generalized views towards trade unions, in the rest of this chapter we explore the complexities towards managing employment relations often hidden in the broad structural picture.

DEFINING THE MANAGEMENT OF EMPLOYMENT RELATIONS

Whilst the institutional and structural changes outlined above offer some hope for trade union revival, perhaps more importantly we need to assess the influence that managerial approaches towards the employment relationship may have on shaping both collective and non-union employment relations. We have noted Hyman's schema identifying four ideal-type scenarios, which in a number of ways echo Fox (1966) who made the distinction between two contrasting views of the employment relationship. In essence, he identified 'unitary' views as those where trade unions are seen as an unwelcome intrusion, and 'pluralist' views as those where unions are seen as the legitimate representatives of workers.

In a development of Fox's work, Purcell and Sisson (1983) proposed a typology that was based on two broad categories: individualism and collectivism. Here, individualism means a focus on the feelings and sentiments of each employee, with policies based on the belief on the right of the individual to advancement and fulfilment at work. Collectivism, on the other hand, is the recognition by the organization of the collective interests of employees in decision making. Purcell and Sisson identified five different styles or approaches, of which two are based on the unitary approach and have a particular non-union (low collectivism) stance: these are the *traditionalist* and the *sophisticated HR* styles. The *traditionalist* style would be characterized by exploitation of labour, with opposition to and often vilification of trade unions. An example here would be McDonald's, whose first restaurant opened in the UK in 1974, although it was not until the early 1980s that they had a significant number of employees. By that time, trade unions were finding things difficult under the Thatcher government, so the McDonald's way of operating in the United States, that is a strictly non-union policy, was not problematic in the UK. Despite recruitment attempts by the three main trade unions in the UK fast-food industry (USDAW, TGWU and GMB), they have had no success in organizing McDonald's workers in the UK. This *traditionalist* approach is characterized by an ex-personnel chief in the UK, who stated in 1986 that 'we will never negotiate wages and conditions with a union and we discourage our staff from joining' (Vidal, 1997).

The *sophisticated human relations* style, on the other hand, would be used by those organizations whose objective was to develop policies and practices that made it unnecessary or unattractive for staff to join trade unions. One company often identified as falling into this category is Marks & Spencer (M&S), although even with this relatively 'good fit' model organization, outside of the UK a different employment relations style has emerged (see below).

Purcell and Ahlstrand (1994) further refined this model, describing management approaches along three continuums. First, the tendency to view employees as either a commodity or a resource, resulting in the employee being treated as a factor of production – implying an emphasis on labour control (the *traditional* organization), or seen as a resource to be invested in (particularly through training and development) to maximize the commitment, performance and contribution of the employee (either as an individual or as part of a team – the *sophisticated HR* type). In between these two extremes sits the *paternalistic* employer, who exercises a benign welfarist employment regime. Companies pursuing this style would be found in long-established service and distribution firms such as insurance companies and department stores. Purcell and Ahlstrand suggest that, while the TV series *Are you being served?* captured this type perfectly, this style was being squeezed out as the old, predictable and stable order was changing.

The second continuum refers to the extent to which the collective representation of employee interests is accepted as legitimate; this axis ranges from the unitaristic *traditional* organization which does not accept as legitimate any degree of collective representation, to the *cooperative* organization which might not only recognize one or more trade unions, but might also tend to consult with employee representatives on a wide range of important issues (the *sophisticated consultative* ideal type). The third axis assesses the quality of the employment relationship, ranging from perceiving employees as having a subordinate role in the running of an organization through to accepting that employees' operational expertise and commitment need to be tapped-into systematically through a social partnership arrangement (the *sophisticated integrated* model) (see Salamon, 2000).

These conceptual models have proved useful in explaining to students of industrial and employment relations principles underpinning management approaches, but they offer only limited insights into the complex nature of contemporary workplaces. First, there are, a priori, large grey areas overlapping each type. For example, it is not clear how we can differentiate between an organization characterized as 'sophisticated consultative', and one fitting into the 'sophisticated integrated' box. In other words, how do we recognize that management has conceded the notion of 'managerial prerogative' (a characteristic of the *sophisticated consultative* type) and values a more genuine union participation in strategic decisions (the *sophisticated integrative* type). We would point to the case of Northumbrian Water in this respect, whose management style is particularly difficult to pin down, partly because of a company merger. It had previously de-recognized its unions for its 2,000 + workforce, but found itself back in the unionized sector after merging with North East Water in 1996, at which point employee forums were introduced. The forums comprise employee and union representation together with management and they are the basis for discussion and consultation on issues such as pay, terms and conditions and health and safety (reported in Terry, 1999). In discussion with the company's external communication adviser there appears to be a fairly relaxed attitude towards trade unions, where no one is discouraged from joining and there is membership of a range of different unions, including UNISON and GMB. However, the company was unable to provide details of union membership and also stated that the figures would not be representative since some individuals chose not to have union subscription fees deducted from their salary or wages.[2]

Second, it is likely that some organizations may contain parallel management strategies, either within the same establishment or across its operations geographically. Whilst we note above that M&S has a long-established *sophisticated HR* style in the UK, in Ireland it is 97 per cent unionized and collective agreements exist with both MANDATE and SIPTU. This high degree of unionization and the earlier predominance of UK managers resulted in an industrial relations climate that was confrontational and lacking in trust. This climate was exacerbated by a strike in the mid-1990s and led to all parties reconsidering the overall employment relationship (IBEC and ICTU, 2000). One of the factors influencing the decision by M&S to recognize trade unions in Ireland was the experience the company had when opening its first store in France. M&S faced difficulties as a result of imposing operating arrangements that were not tailored to fit with French custom and practice in relation to weekend working. As a result, management decided that in future, overseas operations would need to recognize host country practice. Consequently, because trade unions had an established presence amongst larger retailers in Ireland, M&S opted for a collective form of employment relations.[3]

A more profound difficulty encountered with these 'managerial style' conceptualizations is that they tend to lead to the conclusion that employers or the senior management of organizations have a relatively clear 'strategy' towards the employment relationship. Whilst it is possible to point to some organizations with an identifiable 'style', strategy per se is often, to use Mintzberg's (1978) term, 'emergent'. In other words, organizations are likely to acquire and develop employment relations strategy not so much as a consequence of a conscious and rational planning process, but rather as emerging in response to time and events, often within the context of competing pressures. For instance, senior managers may well wish to enhance commitment amongst the workforce in order to maximize operational expertise, whilst at the same time dealing with diminishing resources leading *inter alia* to job cuts. The emergent nature of employment relations strategies, therefore, produces diverse outcomes, even where organizations share similar contextual features and strive for ostensibly similar objectives.

Teague has argued that we need to look beyond the binary thinking behind the unitarist/pluralist divide, suggesting that management–employee interactions involve 'an overlapping combination of cooperation and rivalry' and to understand the implications of this the 'theory of the firm' might be usefully employed (Teague, undated). From this viewpoint, the management typologies outlined above are manifestations not so much of a top-down management strategy, but of experimentalism, opportunism and U-turns. Teague emphasizes two aspects here: first, the *resource-based* view of the firm; and second, *transaction cost* (or *new institutional*) analysis. The *resource-based* view of the firm emphasizes the importance of investing in skills formation and human capital as the key to gaining a competitive advantage; workplace social partnerships, for example, are a potential mechanism for the effective 'internal alignment of intangible, hard-to-transfer competencies'. However, it does not necessarily follow that managements will take the risks necessary to realize the benefits of tapping-into employees' operational expertise. *Transaction costs* analysis, focusing on governance aspects of the firm and institutional rules and procedures to reduce opportunistic behaviour, view partnerships as emerging from a complex bargaining process between the parties, suggesting that 'the interests of managers and employees are not automatically contiguous but have to be negotiated'. Hence the outcomes of partnership will differ across organizations, even where there is a high degree of contextual similarity.

For example, in two unionized health service trusts we have studied over several years, both in the same city, attempts at developing social partnership agreements between management and trade unions representing ancillary staff have had very different outcomes. In one trust, despite internal inconsistencies in the approach of both management and trade unions, a sustainable long-term strategy emerged, based on the principle that 'a quality service can only be delivered by a cooperative, high skilled staff, and that's impossible to achieve when the workforce is resentful of their situation and employer'.[4] This offered the potential reconfiguration of employment and industrial relations on a more consensual, mutual gains basis, perhaps edging towards a state of 'transitional' change, involving the implementation of new strategies and the rearranging or dismantling of old operational methods. To date, it is generally agreed that industrial relations in this trust have been significantly improved; for example, there has been an absence of industrial action in recent years, and a more coherent team-based work system has been introduced. Most tangibly, the lowest-paid ancillary staff were guaranteed a minimum rate of £5 per hour, in return for reductions in overtime working.

In the partnership strategy in the second trust, in contrast, the emergent strategy failed to move beyond a short-term 'survivability' approach, reflected in a tendency towards non-sustainable incremental change. The differentiated experiences of the two trusts can be seen as a reflection of different approaches towards the management of the organization and its key constituencies, in the context of gaining and retaining control over shifting human resource policies encouraged by the government through Department of Health guidelines. In the more successful trust, the central human resources, facilities and finance directorates attempted to drive the changes in employment and industrial relations with relatively centralized trade union representatives. In contrast, the management of the less successful trust pursued its agenda at a highly decentralized departmental level, which did not facilitate the creation of a higher-level social partnership strategy. This partly stemmed from a management wariness of creating a multilateral forum that might facilitate a cohesive trade union strategy towards the partnership agenda. Moreover, management in this trust tended to retreat to a cost-cutting approach when it faced difficulties in pursuing partnership, and in general did not see ancillary workers as a scarce strategic resource. Overall, the risks involved for the management in the second trust outweighed the perceived advantages of a workplace social partnership (for details of these cases see Heaton, Mason and Morgan, 2002, 2000).

In summary, even where the context is similar, such as in the highly unionized public sector, managerial employment relations styles are diverse and emerge in a complex and often contradictory process. Given this, we can expect to find similar complexities in management styles in the diverse non-union sector.

NON-UNION EMPLOYEE RELATIONS

As indicated in the WERS data detailed earlier, non-unionism has become increasingly common. However, while it is relatively easy to provide a statistical picture of non-union workplaces, it has proved less straightforward to come to a conclusion about the management of employees in these institutions. Some writers have portrayed non-union establishments as the locus of best practice and the most likely context for the flowering of a potentially positive form of HRM (Guest, 1989). Others have more recently argued that, compared with those that are unionized, non-union establishments provide fewer rights and benefits to workers, fewer opportunities to give or receive information and less scope to voice either constructive suggestions or dissent (Millward, 1994). Terry (1999) has considered whether systems of employee representation in the non-union sector can provide effective substitutes for union-based channels and concludes that there is evidence of potentially 'unionizable' companies adopting structures that closely resemble those associated with recognized trade unions, such as Pizza Express (see below). While little is known about the detailed workings of such bodies or their effectiveness, the overall impression is that they appear to survive during periods of growth but come under strain during difficult economic circumstances. Certainly, in the absence of legally binding requirements, management can ignore such consultation procedures when they wish.

Another perspective comes from the findings from Cully *et al* (1999) which show that workplaces without a union presence were substantially less likely, rather than more, to have put in place alternative mechanisms such as joint consultative committees. In other words, union representation and indirect employee participation go hand-in-hand rather than being substitutes for one another. Where there was a union presence but no recognition, the route to a place on a consultative committee tended to be by management appointment or volunteering.

We also need to bear in mind that there may be many reasons why organizations have either no union members or no recognized trade union. They may be anti-union, having either de-recognized trade unions or having pursued a policy of union suppression. Or they may be non-union through policies of substitution, where typically 'management recognizes the need to manage employee relations as if the workplace has divergent interests so that management is able to identify concerns, allay fears, satisfy workers' aspirations and stay non-union' (Blyton and Turnbull, 1998). Moreover, some organizations may have drifted into non-unionism more by chance or opportunism than by strategy, perhaps reflecting a withering away of interest in trade unions on the part of both the employer and employee. This was the case in a multinational company manufacturing medical equipment and employing around 500 people. Whilst formally having a union agreement with the GMB (membership of a second union for skilled workers had withered away in previous years), the company's approach to partnership was informal and formed around the introduction of cellular production systems, with a psychological contract exhorting employee commitment and high-trust relations. Competencies and work organization were identified and discussed through a management–employee works council, with trade union activity marginalized, in an attempt by management to align individual behaviour with the strategic goals of the enterprise.

In the remainder of this chapter, therefore, we examine the explanations for non-unionism and management styles in non-union organizations.

Explanations for non-unionism

McLoughlin and Gourlay (1994) argue that attention has been drawn to the issue of non-unionism by experience in the United States, where the non-union firm is the dominant feature of employment relations. Deep-seated managerial values opposed to unions, increased opportunities and incentives to avoid unions resulting from changing competitive and cost conditions, and critically the development of the 'HRM' approach in new and growing sectors have, it is claimed, provided an alternative model for managing without trade unions (Kochan, Katz and McKersie, 1986).

McLoughlin and Gourlay point out that while some commentators see the US experience as the future for Britain, others view the context and experience of the United States as unique and therefore of little or no value as a guide to developments in the British context. Certainly, trade unions have achieved much higher levels of organization and density in Britain than in the United States. Also, there has not been in Britain the widespread and deep-seated opposition from employers and managers to trade unions (Towers, 1997). However, surveys such as WERS show us that there is considerable variation in employer attitudes to trade unions both within and between industries. Thus, McLoughlin and Gourlay argue that the important issue is not so much the desire of British employers to de-unionize as their capacity to do so. In this regard, while employers were encouraged to marginalize trade unions during the 1980s and early 1990s, employers have been constrained by the post-1997 institutional reforms outlined above.

Some industries have, however, proved more resistant to unions than others. For example, unionization has always been low in the private hotel and catering sector, with estimates of union density placed at 10 per cent in 1993 and 4 per cent in 1998 (Labour Research, 1995). Wood (1997) offers four main reasons for the predominance of non-unionism in this sector: isolation and the ethos of hotel and catering work; the structure of the workforce; management and employer attitudes to trade unions; and the activities of trade unions.

Isolation and the ethos of hotel and catering work. Historically, the development of UK hotels followed travel patterns with the consequence that 'tourist' areas provided the focus for industry growth and, because of this, hotel workers were isolated from the mainstream of the urban working class and the subsequent development of industrial unionism. Both Riley (1985) and Wood (1997) argue that this geographical separation was reinforced by cultural separation, with the persistence of a domestic service ethos in which workers are dependent on management for preferment and where the negotiation of individual rewards militates against opposition to management values.

Structure of the workforce. The part-time, seasonal and casual nature of the workforce within the private hotel and catering industries presents unions with considerable problems of organization. A further issue is that of labour turnover. Wood argues that: 'Recognition of the union to participate in collective bargaining is frequently made conditional upon it maintaining a specific number of members within a company or unit. The high rates of turnover that prevail in the industry can make maintenance of a core membership difficult' (Wood, 1997).

Manager and employer attitudes to trade unions. A number of studies have found general managerial hostility to trade unions in the hospitality industry, providing evidence of managerial strategies of 'peaceable competition' and 'forcible opposition' to discourage employees from joining a union. Moreover, union presence has been viewed as evidence of managerial 'failure' and managers' rhetoric was firmly rooted in an explicit politically Conservative world-view (Aslan and Wood, 1993; Wood and Pedlar, 1978).

The activities of trade unions. Wood (1997) argues that trade unions in the hotel and catering industry have not acquitted themselves well regarding the problems of hospitality industry workers, and that, in many ways, trade unions are ill-equipped for effective action in that industry. He concludes that unions need to consider very carefully the resources that need to be committed to the hospitality industry if they are to make any inroads into membership.

Non-union management styles

Whilst the above may go some way towards explaining the features of the non-union organization, what of management styles per se? In one of the few dedicated studies of non-union organizations, McLoughlin and Gourlay (1994) proposed a classification based on the high-tech sector, and structured around two dimensions: the degree of strategic integration between personnel policies and overall business strategy, and the balance between individual and collective methods of regulating the employment relationship. The rationale for this approach was that, in a non-union setting, the concept of HRM has particular significance and that one of its defining characteristics is a high level of strategic integration. McLoughlin and Gourlay (1994) found a clustering of management styles around four categories:

- traditional HRM (high strategic integration/high individualization);
- benevolent autocracy (low strategic integration/high individualization);
- opportunistic (low strategic integration/high collectivization);
- strategic HRM (high strategic HRM/high collectivization).

Traditional HRM is not explicitly anti-union, but assumes that trade unions are irrelevant to employees who are being managed effectively as individuals. Thus, policies would include profit-sharing and share ownership schemes, performance-related pay and a strong emphasis within the appraisal system on training and development. A *benevolent autocracy* might be found typically in a small business, where the employer's position of power is clearly established in relation to employees, but employees, by virtue of their skills, are not entirely dependent upon the employer. Management, as a result, seek a close identification with employees. The absence of unions will probably not be a result of overtly expressed anti-union values, but rather it is likely that no formal stance towards trade unions has ever been formulated.

Within the category labelled *opportunists* a higher level of collectivization might be found, with trade unions recognized for perhaps part of the workforce. Alternatively, trade unions may be de-recognized, with management substituting a works council in an attempt to satisfy at least some of the functions a union might perform. Overall, this type might be characterized by fragmented personnel policies that lack formalization. The final category, *strategic HRM*, sees a management approach contingent upon the best fit with business objectives so that high levels of collectivization, including recognition of trade unions, might be tolerated so long as the trade unions are perceived as making a positive contribution. Equally, increased individualization and de-recognition may be seen as appropriate in changed circumstances. While these are convenient labels, 'on the ground' it may be difficult to split the *opportunists* and the *strategic HRM* organizations.

A rather different way of classifying non-union establishments is provided by Guest and Hoque who argue that

> we should get away from studying non-union establishments in relation to unionism and propensity to become unionized. Indeed, the very term 'non-unionism' becomes a limiting definition of workplaces. Instead, we should be developing frameworks and dimensions which allow us to study aspects of employment relations and human resource management without distinctive reference to the union issue (Guest and Hoque, 1994).

They propose a classification of establishments on two dimensions. The first is whether or not they have a human resource strategy. The second is the nature of human resource policy and practice. They suggest three possible types of non-union establishment:

- Establishments which have a clear HRM strategy and make extensive use of a range of techniques associated with employee involvement and commitment. This can be labelled the 'full utilization, high involvement' model or the 'good' side of non-unionism.
- Establishments which have a clear strategy but make little use of HRM. They provide a minimum level of workers' rights and represent the 'bleak house' or 'ugly' side of non-unionism.
- Establishments which do not have a clear HRM strategy but which have adopted a large number of innovative HRM practices, perhaps by copying others or following personnel management 'fashion'. They represent the 'lucky' side of non-unionism.

Since Guest and Hoque ignore the collectivist–individualist dimension, their types cannot be fully compared with those of McLoughlin and Gourlay, though it is possible to equate the 'lucky' type roughly with the 'opportunists'. Guest and Hoque's typology has been criticized on the basis that it implicitly denies the possibility that collective employment relations can exist within a non-union context (Rose, 2001) (a point to which we return shortly), although both typologies can be regarded as complementary, rather than mutually exclusive.

Another way of understanding management styles is to consider these in the context of size of organization. This has intuitive appeal and some work has been conducted on both small and large firms. For example, Scase (1995) proposes three styles as typical of small firms:

- *Paternalism*, used by employers where there is stable demand for goods and where employees are unable to easily shift from one employer to another. Employers are therefore hiring on a long-term basis and a culture of high mutual trust can be fostered; examples would include craft-based industries in small-scale manufacturing.
- *Fraternalism*, where owner-managers tend to work alongside their employees, as may be the case with painting and decorating firms or hair-dressing.
- The *autocratic* style, found where employees are vulnerable, in a poor bargaining position; examples may be found in textiles, hotel and catering and retailing.

Scase suggests that while it is relatively unusual for employers to manage in an entirely autocratic way, paternalism and fraternalism are convenient, if crude, descriptions of employment relations in many small firms. Support for this comes from further analysis of the WERS 1998 data. The findings for small businesses (fewer than 100 employees) may be summarized as follows:

- Very few managers in small businesses were in favour of union membership at their workplace.

- Union recognition was found in only 12% of small businesses.
- Seventy-four per cent had no union recognition and no mechanism for formal consultation of employees.
- The most common way of setting pay was unilaterally by management.
- Overall, small businesses were characterized by informal procedures but a high level of job satisfaction.

Some empirical work has also been carried out into management style and HR practice in large non-union firms. Flood and Toner (1997) examined companies characterized by very good pay and conditions and a sophisticated HR policy (typical of Guest's 'good' type), in seeking to answer the question 'what precise advantage do large companies expect to achieve through policies designed to remove triggers for unionization?' They question whether it is rational for large companies to pursue a union substitution strategy, rather than acquiesce in union organization, arguing that companies may well find themselves in a 'Catch-22' situation, whereby if they take advantage of the absence of a union by offering less favourable pay and conditions than the union norm, this is likely to give the workers an incentive to join a union. Therefore Flood and Toner propose the following rationale for a union avoidance policy:

Large non-union companies:

(a) cannot hope to avoid these features of unionized companies:	(b) can hope, in the absence of unions, to:	(c) if successful in building a unitary culture, can hope to reduce the likelihood of:
• high wages and benefits • good complaints procedures • job security • good communications	• reduce platform for radicals • promote a 'unitary' culture • put individual reward systems in place • improve personal contact	• resistance to change • restrictions on production • work stoppages and strikes • inflexibility and excessive manning levels

Flood and Toner's research is validated by reference to a set of practices proposed by Kochan *et al* (1986) as designed to eliminate the triggers to unionism, which includes sophisticated systems of communications and information sharing as well as the customary individual appraisal and pay systems. However, as already noted, in some instances collective representation may be used as part of a union substitution policy, such as at Pizza Express. Founded in 1965 and now employing around 6,500 employees over 290 sites, Pizza Express has introduced a works council system called employee forums. There is no union presence and a recent statement from the Training and HR Director presents the company's stance on trade unions: 'I have no problem with unions, but it's a sad reflection on a company if employees feel that they have to call someone in to talk on their behalf.'

Managers in Pizza Express are adamant that the works council system is not a 'toothless body set up to give the impression of democracy', stressing how representatives are grassroots staff and the system reaches right down to individual restaurants where half an hour of their two-monthly meetings is dedicated to forum business. Restaurant representatives attend area forums that send representatives to regional councils. They, in turn, appoint someone to sit on the national forum which meets every six months. The works council system considers issues of pay, working hours and customer care. Pizza Express also funds training in a range of subjects, including law for those representatives who wish to avail themselves of it. Moreover, trained forum members are expected to represent individual members of staff in grievance and dispute situations (Cooper, 2001). Whilst non-union collective forms of representation may contain inherent weaknesses, such as a lack of 'oppositional' or alternative institutional resources, this company's approach is an example of the potential limitations of a purely individualized strategy towards effective employment relations.

CONCLUSION

In this chapter, we have suggested that in the past few years a new institutional basis has been put in place, which offers the potential for the reconfiguration of collective forms of employment relations. In particular, European Union legislation concerning the establishment of European Works Councils has had a direct influence on collective representation in many multinational companies. The EWC directive may have an even greater indirect influence, if organizations in both the private and public sector come to view this mechanism as an effective way of establishing social partnerships and creating a forum in which the strategic knowledge of senior management can be aligned to the operational expertise of the workforce.[5] Moreover, the Employment Relations Act 1999 has strengthened the basis of union representation by reintroducing a statutory procedure for union recognition. Even before this Act came into force, the trend towards de-recognizing unions appeared to have peaked in the early 1990s, and by the end of that decade, the number of new recognition agreements were exceeding those cases of de-recognition. Nevertheless, non-union and non-collective forms of employment relations have become a significant feature on the UK landscape. By the end of the 1990s, data from WERS showed that there were no union members in 47 per cent of British workplaces and no recognized union in 55 per cent of workplaces (Cully *et al*, 1999).

Against this institutional and structural background, we have overviewed the multiplicity of approaches and rationales towards employment relations in both the union and non-union sectors, drawing on case study evidence for illustrative purposes. We have argued that whilst, a priori, there is a growing need for employers to seek strategic alliances with employees to extract higher levels of performance and productivity, there is no direct link between this need and specific forms of employment relations, for three main reasons. First, there are a large number of grey areas between conceptually distinct models, and in practice it is often difficult to distinguish between types. Second, we have pointed out that some organizations will contain parallel management strategies, either within the same establishment or across its operations geographically. And third, we have questioned the assumption that management have a clearly delineated strategy towards employment relations. In this respect, we have highlighted the 'emergent' nature of strategy, arguing that whilst a resource-based view of the firm often underpins approaches towards the employment relationship, the transaction costs involved in developing new forms of organizational governance is a negotiated process, with social partnership being only one of a number of possible outcomes. It is equally likely that neither management nor trade unions will take the risks that developing genuine partnership entails, thus constraining the development of a strategic employment relationship in both union and non-union organizations. In the union sector, this might look like the 'regulated market' model; in the non-union sector, this might be the 'bleak house' scenario, where no forms of representation or strategic HRM exist.

Overall, we have suggested that old and new forms of employment relations are developing in a context of competing and often contradictory pressures. Whilst the new institutional environment has created a degree of stability in the structures of representation, trade unions need to be proactive in their relations with management and employers, in order to realize the potential that this might offer for the re-invigoration of collective employment relations.

Notes

1 We draw on two sources of case study evidence: first, previously published material, where we identify the organization; second, our own research (ongoing since the late 1990s) on a number of organizations developing varying forms of social partnerships – these cases are not identified by name for reasons of confidentiality.
2 From an interview conducted by the authors, April 2002.
3 Hourihan and Gunnigle (1996) cited by the Labour Relations Commission, http://www.lrc.ie/research_and_publications/competitive_strategies/19.htm.
4 Royal Hospitals Trust, Partnership Agreement, 1998.
5 This may be further strengthened in the workplace by the EU's Information and Consultation Directive.

References

Aslan, A and Wood, R (1993) Trade unions in the hotel and catering industry: the views of hotel managers, *Employee Relations*, **15** (2), pp 61–69

Blyton, P and Turnbull, P (1998) *The Dynamics of Employee Relations*, 2nd edn, Macmillan, London

Brook, K (2002) Trade Union Membership: An analysis of data from the autumn 2001 LFS, *Labour Market Trends*, **110** (7), pp 343–54

Cooper, C (2001) Talking Italian, *People Management*, 14 June

Cully, M, Woodland, S, O'Reilly, A and Dix, G (1999) *Britain at Work: as Depicted by the 1998 Workplace Employee Relations Survey*, Routledge, London and New York

Disney, R, Gosling, A and Machin, S (1995) British unions in decline: determinants of the 1980s fall in union recognition, *Industrial and Labor Relations Review*, **48** (3), pp 403–19

European Foundation for the Improvement of Living and Working Conditions (2000) *A Review of Negotiating European Works Councils: A Comparative Study of Article 6 and Article 13 Agreements*, EFILWC

Flood, P and Toner, B (1997) Large non-union companies: how do they avoid a catch 22?', *British Journal of Industrial Relations*, **35** (2), pp 257–77

Fox, A (1966) Industrial sociology and industrial relations, *Royal Commission on Trade Unions and Employers' Associations*, Research Paper 3, HMSO, London

Gall, G (2000) In place of strife, *People Management*, 14 September, p 26–30

Gall, G and McKay, S (1994) Trade union de-recognition in Britain 1988–94, *British Journal of Industrial Relations*, **32** (3), pp 433–48

Gall, G and McKay, S (1999) Developments in union recognition and de-recognition in Britain, 1994–98, *British Journal of Industrial Relations*, **37** (4), pp 601–14

Gall, G and McKay, S (2001) Facing fairness at work: union perception of employer opposition and response to union recognition, *Industrial Relations Journal*, **32** (2), pp 94–113

Goodrich, C (1920) *The Frontier of Control*, Bell, London

Guest, D (1989) Human resource management: its implications for industrial relations and trade unions, in *New Perspectives on Human Resource Management*, ed J Storey, Routledge, London

Guest, D and Hoque, K (1994) The Good, the Bad and the Ugly: Employment relations in new non-union workplaces, *Human Resource Management Journal*, **5** (1), pp 1–14

Heaton, N, Mason, B and Morgan, J (2002) Partnership and multi-unionism in the Health Service, *Industrial Relations Journal*, **33** (2), pp 112–26

Heaton, N, Mason, B and Morgan, J (2000) Trade unions and partnership in the Health Service', *Employee Relations*, **22** (4), pp 314–33

Hyman, R (1997) The future of employee representation', *British Journal of Industrial Relations*, **35** (3), pp 339–60

IBEC and ICTU (2000) Case study on Marks and Spencer: review of the effects of partnership arrangements on lifelong learning at enterprise level', http://www.etst.ie/downloads/marksspencers.pdf.

Incomes Data Report (2001) *Union recognition widens: the state of play on the first anniversary of the new law*, No. 836, July, pp 12–20

Kelly, J (1998) *Rethinking Industrial Relations: Mobilization, Collectivism and Long Waves*, LSE/Routledge, London

Kochan, T, Katz, H and McKersie, R (1986) *The Transformation of American Industrial Relations*, Basic Books, New York

Labour Research (1995) Work change takes toll on unions, *Labour Research*, May, p 15

Machin, S (2000) Union decline in Britain, *British Journal of Industrial Relations*, **38** (4), pp 631–45

McLoughlin, I and Gourlay, S (1994) *Enterprise without Unions: Industrial Relations in the Non-union Firm*, Open University Press, Buckingham

Millward, N (1994) *The New Industrial Relations?* Policy Studies Institute, London

Mintzberg, H (1978) Patterns in strategy formation, *Management Science*, **24** (9), pp 934–48

Purcell, J (1993) The end of institutional industrial relations', *Political Quarterly*, January–March, pp 6–23

Purcell, J and Sisson, K (1983) Strategies and practices in the management of industrial relations, in *Industrial Relations in Britain*, ed G S Bain, Blackwell, Oxford

Purcell, J and Ahlstrand, B (1994) *Human Resource Management in the Multi-Divisional Company*, Oxford University Press, Oxford

Riley, M (1985) Some social and historical perspectives on unionization in the UK hotel industry, *International Journal of Hospitality Management*, **4** (3), pp 99–104

Rose, E (2001) *Employment Relations*, Financial Times/Prentice Hall, Harlow

Salamon, M (2000) *Industrial Relations Theory and Practice*, 4th edn, Financial Times/Prentice Hall, Harlow, ch 7

Scase, R (1995) Employment relations in small firms, in *Industrial Relations: Theory and Practice in Britain*, ed P Edwards, Blackwell, Oxford

Sisson, K (1989) *Personnel Management in Britain*, Blackwell, Oxford

Smith, P and Morton, G (2001) New Labour's reform of Britain's employment law: the devil is not only in the detail but in the values and policy too, *British Journal of Industrial Relations*, **37** (2), pp 315–36

Streek, W (1992) National diversity, regime competition and institutional deadlock: Problems in forming European industrial relations system, *Journal of Public Policy*, **12** (4), pp 301–30

Teague, P (undated) *Social Partnership and the Enterprise: Lessons from the Irish Experience*, Working Paper from Policy Institute, Trinity College, Dublin

Terry, M (1999) Systems of collective employee representation in non-union firms in the UK, *Industrial Relations Journal*, **30** (1), pp 16–30

Towers, B (1997) *The Representation Gap: Change and Reform in the British and American Workplace*, Oxford University Press, Oxford

Vidal, J (1997) *McLibel: Burger Culture on Trial*, Macmillan, London, p 233

Weber, T, Foster, P and Egriboz, K L (2000) Costs and benefits of the European Works Council Directive, *Employment Relations Research Series No.9*, Department of Trade and Industry, London

Wood, R (1997) Working in hotels and catering, 2nd edn, International Thomson Business Press, Oxford

Wood, S and Goddard, G (1999) The statutory union recognition procedure in the Employment Relations Bill: a comparative analysis, *British Journal of Industrial Relations*, **37** (2), pp 203–45

Wood, S and Pedlar, M (1978) On losing their virginity: the story of a strike at the Grosvenor Hotel, Sheffield, *Industrial Relations Journal*, **9** (2), pp 15–37

Wood, S, Moore, S and Willman, P (2002) Third time lucky for statutory recognition in the UK? *Industrial Relations Journal*, **33** (3), pp 215–33

14

Trade unions and the employment relationship

Roger Undy

INTRODUCTION

This chapter considers the key choices facing trade unions as they seek to develop the employment relationship from a position of relative weakness. First, the present union context – ie a marked decline in union membership and a concomitant reduction in influence – is described and explained; second, the unions' main approaches to recruiting and organizing employees are discussed; third, unions' leading strategic approaches to employers (including managers as agents of employers) are examined; and, in conclusion, unions' chances of staging a recovery are reviewed.

UNION CONTEXT

Between 1979 and 1998 union membership was in continual decline from 13 million in 1979 to 7.8 million in 1997 (down 40 per cent). Since 1998 union membership has marginally increased, but in 2000 it was still below 8 million (7,897,519).[1] Union membership, as a proportion of those employed (union density), stood at 29 per cent in 2000,[2] as against 57 per cent (McIlroy, 1992) in 1980. In the same period the number of trade unions was also falling. In 1980 there were 461 and in 2000 221 unions.[3] The Trade Union Congress (TUC), the principal body representing trade unions in Britain, experienced similar changes. In 1980 it represented 109 trade unions and 12,172,508 members. By 2000 the TUC had 73 affiliated unions and 6,772,118 members: a fall of 33 per cent in affiliated unions and 45 per cent in union members. Following a series of union mergers, the nine largest TUC affiliates accounted in 2000 for 65 per cent of the TUC's total membership.

Union membership in 2000 was not evenly spread across different sectors. Density was much higher in the public as against the private sector: 60 per cent in the public and 19 per cent in the private sector.[4] There were also marked differences within the private sector: the privatized utilities of electricity, gas and water supply were 53 per cent unionized, while in private sector hotels and restaurants only 4 per cent were in trade unions.[5]

At the start of the new millennium British trade unions were therefore showing the first signs of a possible resurgence in membership – even though union density had not increased. The likelihood of such a recovery – the end of almost 20 years of *annus horribilis* for trade unions – will be examined by setting out the causes of the decline in membership and influence, before considering what, in 2000–1, could give trade unions cause for optimism.

Three main types of explanation were offered as to why trade union membership declined so radically. First, there were the quantitative studies of aggregated data which focused, almost entirely, on external or structural factors (Mason and Bain, 1993). In this scheme of analysis unions were seen as doing little themselves to influence the level of union membership. Amongst such structuralist interpretations of events were those who claimed that in the 1980s the loss of members was almost entirely due to 'a cyclical phenomenon' associated with such macroeconomic factors as wage and price inflation and unemployment (Carruth and Disney, 1988). Yet other analysts, using similar quantitative techniques, claimed to show that the same loss of members was the result of unfavourable labour legislation (Freeman and Pelletier, 1990). In addition, several other structural adjustments were noted as reducing union membership. These included the shift of employment out of traditionally unionized sectors, adverse compositional changes in the spatial location of work (from north to south), the growth of part-time work and a reduction in the number of large workplaces. All were argued to militate against trade unionism in this period (see Waddington and Whitston, 1995, for a discussion of these factors).

Second, studies of individual trade unions' behaviour suggested that unions themselves played a significant part in determining union membership. Rather than being purely recipients of employees, moving in and out of unionization as determined by structural factors, unions were found to behave in ways that affected the recruitment and retention of members. For example, the Transport and General Workers Union (TGWU) recruited 944,891 new members in the four years between 1985 and 1988, yet its membership fell in the same period by 177,702 members (Undy *et al*, 1996).

Similarly, the Union of Shop Distributive & Allied Workers (USDAW) recruited 118,000 new members in 1988, but only added 10,000 to its stock of members (Upchurch and Donnelly, 1992). These large flows of members in and out of trade unions were common to all the major unions and were likely to be affected by unions' recruiting activities, their chosen means of collecting subscriptions (direct debit or deduction from wages) and members' satisfaction with the services provided. Further, unions' successful and unsuccessful strike action could affect recruitment and retention. For example, the failure of the miners' strike in 1984–5 served to demonstrate that unions were now less capable of protecting their members (Adeney and Lloyd, 1986), hence raising doubts about the efficacy of union membership. In such a context tailor-made deals to suit particular employers – including no-strike deals – also gave some unions access to new recruiting territories which they otherwise would not have penetrated (Taylor, 1994). It therefore seems reasonable to assume that employees and employers were not all indifferent to the kinds of trade unionism on offer. In consequence, unions' own behaviour, and the image they projected, also contributed to these changing levels of membership.

Third, it was argued that the changing attitudes of government and employers towards trade unions adversely influenced the level of union membership in the 1980s and 1990s. In particular, the previous political consensus regarding the positive role played by collective bargaining was broken by the successive Conservative governments of the 1980s and 1990s. The new market-orientated policy promoted unitarist and individualistic attitudes towards work relations and moved the social and political climate against the pluralist and collectivist values which had helped to sustain trade unions (see Brown, 1990, for a discussion of these changes). The intention was to reduce 'the propensity of employees to join and remain in trade unions' (see Kessler and Purcell, forthcoming) and to encourage them to pursue their work goals as individuals, rather than opt to contribute to a collective 'voice'. Employers also showed a preference for dealing with individual employees rather than trade unions. In 1998 managers in 72 per cent of workplaces reported (and only 13 per cent disagreed) that they would prefer to consult directly with employees rather than with unions (Cully *et al*, 1999). Moreover, in 1998 the presence in workplaces of managers with negative views of trade unions was highly correlated with no union presence or low union density (Kessler and Purcell, forthcoming). In an environment which enhanced the power of the employer this no doubt contributed to the resistance which trade unions found in trying to organize non-union workplaces.

It may be concluded, therefore, that the loss of union membership in the 1980s and 1990s was the result of a complex mix of interrelated factors. The structural conditions made it hard for trade unions to sustain their historically high levels of membership, particularly as the heartlands of unionization were decimated by change in the sectoral composition of employment. In a business, political and legislative climate that favoured the employer, managers in non-union territories who preferred to deal with individual employees thus had the power to resist unionization. Furthermore, the Conservative government's denigration of collectivism, the rise of human resource management and associated high-commitment techniques gave managers a rhetoric which could be used to justify greater individualization of both work and reward. Managers could claim, from a unitary perspective, that such developments were in the interests of both employer and employee, so helping them legitimize the decline in collective representation and collective agreements (see Legge, 1995).

In 2000–1 most of the above factors found to reduce trade union membership still existed. As regards structural factors, there were (in 2001) fears of an economic recession, which suggested that the cyclical phenomenon of the early 1980s and early 1990s could repeat itself. Also, employment in manufacturing industry was predicted to decline still further, and the proportion of employees in private services was forecast to increase (Institute of Employment Research, 2001). Much of the Conservative government's labour legislation restricting industrial action also remained in place. The economic and business environment had thus not become significantly more favourable to trade unions.

On the other hand, the election of two successive Labour governments (1997 and 2001) was a potentially significant change which could, by changing the political climate and introducing favourable legislation, improve trade unions' fortunes. However, this was a 'New Labour' government concerned with 'fairness not favours' as regards trade unions. But it still signed the European Social Chapter and introduced the Employment Relations Act (ERA) 1999 (see Chapters 5, 7 and 9), both of which strengthened employee and, to a lesser extent, collective rights. However, the ERA did not start to have a significant and direct effect on employment relations until 2000. Nevertheless, the critically important – for trade unions – clauses concerning union recognition (see Chapter 7) started to affect union recruitment almost immediately. In 2000–1 the Advisory Conciliation and Arbitration Service (ACAS) recorded an increase of over 80 per cent in the number of requests for assistance in resolving claims for union recognition. Moreover, of 264 cases settled in 2000–1, 66 per cent gave the union involved recognition (ACAS, 2001).The Labour government also supported the TUC's policy of social partnership. In 1999, at the TUC's Conference, the Prime Minister stated that he saw 'trade unions as a force for good, an essential part of our democracy, but as more than that, potentially, as a force for economic success. They are part of the solution to achieving business success and not an obstacle to it' (cited in Brown, 2000). This endorsement stood, of course, in contrast to Mrs Thatcher's previous view of trade unions as the 'enemy within' (Adeney and Lloyd, 1996: 210).

Trade unions seeking to influence employment relations at the start of the new millennium were therefore relatively weak. However, the environment was moving in their favour in two areas – political climate and labour legislation. Hence, there were some reasons for thinking that in 2000–1 trade unions could begin to reverse the trends of the previous 20 years. Assuming, as argued above, that trade unions can by their own actions help strengthen their position, the following discussion will examine unions' choices in employment relations in relation to, first, employees (and union members) and, second, employers.

UNIONS, EMPLOYEES AND UNION MEMBERS

In this section the characteristics of union members will be described before examining unions' two main approaches to the recruitment and organization of employees. These are frequently referred to as representing a choice between a servicing strategy and an organizing strategy (Incomes Data Services, 1999). In conclusion, the two strategies will be evaluated. It will be argued that both have their merits and that aspects of the two strategies may be employed in a complementary rather than conflicting manner.

In the early part of the 20th century unions organized primarily male full-time manual workers employed in skilled and semi-skilled jobs (Bell, 1960). By 2000 the characteristics of union members had changed radically. In terms of gender the level of unionization was broadly the same for men and women, ie 30 per cent men and 28 per cent women; non-manual workers (30 per cent) marginally exceeded manual workers (28 per cent) in the degree of unionization; service sector employees (31 per cent) were more likely to be unionized than employees in production (27 per cent); in terms of age it was the older employees, those over 40, who had the highest rate of unionization (those aged 40–49 years were 37 per cent unionized), while among employees aged 20 to 29 only 20 per cent were unionized; and, in respect of educational attainment, it was graduates (or equivalents) who had the highest rate of unionization at 37 per cent (only 24 per cent of those with no qualifications were unionized).[6]

Unions in 2000 had therefore recruited a higher proportion of professional staff than they had craft and related workers, or sales staff. This imbalance between occupational groups largely reflected the high density that unions reached in the public (60 per cent) as against the private sector (19 per cent). For example, '23 per cent of all public sector employees were professionals; of these 74 per cent were trade union members'.[7] However, unions still tended to recruit full-time employees (34 per cent unionized) rather than part-time workers (22 per cent unionized).[8]

In the 1990s, commentators sympathetic to trade unions were searching for means of reversing the above trends in union membership which, as the TUC put it in 1997, showed that 'union organization is weakest among those groups who need protection most, in both private and public sectors' (TUC,

1997). Given the above arguments regarding the negative effect on trade union membership of growing individualism and the claimed decline in collectivist values among the workforce, it was not surprising that a case was made for union regeneration by treating members more like individual consumers or clients, rather than as members of a collective and self-help organization (Bassett and Cave, 1993). This became known as the 'servicing model' or strategy.

The 'servicing strategy' fundamentally perceived unions as customer service organizations providing rather passive members with the kinds of services offered by the Automobile Association. For trade unions these services were of two kinds. The first involved the professional full-time official representing members in negotiations with the employer, and supporting them in individual disciplinary or grievance procedures. This was, of course, very much the existing position in a number of white-collar unions, such as the Institute of Professionals, Managers & Specialists (IPMS). Under this strategy the local branch official or lay workplace representative largely acted as a gatekeeper or post box through which the member would engage the professional skills of the full-time officer (see Ben Yehuda, 1997).

The second string of the servicing model involved an extension of union services or benefits outside of employee interest representation at work. In 1998 the TUC reported that some 40 such benefits were provided by different unions and that 25 benefits were provided by at least a fifth of trade unions (see TUC, 1998). Free legal help on employment issues and financial and tax advice figured high in the list. However, little of this was new. As was noted in 1970 in a discussion of white-collar union recruitment policies, 'the normal "friendly" benefits – accident pay, educational grants, funeral benefits, convalescent facilities, superannuation benefits, free legal advice, unemployment benefits and benevolent grants' were readily available (Bain, 1970). Less frequently, discount trading schemes, most types of insurance, free advice on income tax and home purchase, continental holiday schemes, and in one case an advice and service bureau for help with members' individual problems were provided (Bain, 1970). In the 1980s and 1990s, about the only additions of note were the telephone help line and the extension of financial services, including the union credit card.

The significance of the 'servicing strategy' in the 1990s was thus more as a symbolic shift in union values towards greater individualism and more professional servicing, than a wholesale change in union practices. However, even among unions with a strong record of servicing activities, its appeal was limited because it represented a high-cost strategy, at a time of diminishing financial resources. For, although unions could make some financial gains from selling new financial services and insurance policies, it required an expansion in the number of professional full-time officials if the membership was to be serviced in the proposed manner. In particular, the employer-sponsored decentralization of bargaining units in the 1980s and 1990s left unions with major resource problems. For example, the National Union of Civil and Public Servants (NUCPS) estimated that between 1980 and the mid-1990s it had moved from servicing two bargaining units to servicing 400 bargaining units and the IPMS had seen its bargaining units grow from 12 in 1980 to 253 in 1996 (Undy, 1999). The question of how such unions could afford to extend their usual small cadre of full-time officials (IPMS had just 26 full-time negotiating staff (Undy, 1999)) to service members professionally in the new bargaining units was clearly a major issue.

The alternative 'organizing strategy' was promoted in 1996 by the TUC in its 'New Unionism' campaign 'organizing for growth' (TUC, 1997). Its roots lay in the TUC's analysis of the latent demand amongst employees for union membership. It argued that some five million non-union employees wished to be represented by a trade union and that what prevented them joining was lack of a union presence in the relevant workplaces (TUC, 1997). In developing its organizing strategy the TUC drew on union experiences in the United States and Australia. The message from the United States was 'a simple one, rather than servicing a passive membership, unions had to ensure that organizing never stops' (Carter, 2000). As part of this initiative the TUC founded the Organizing Academy in 1998 to 'train a new generation of union organizers and foster a "culture of organizing" within trade unions' (Heery *et al*, 2000b).

The different elements of the organizing strategy were designed around members' active involvement in the union. It was self-help writ large, but with paid, lead organizers in non-unionized workplaces initiating and overseeing an organizing campaign while fostering activism amongst the target (newly recruited) workforce (much of this commentary on the different dimensions of the organizing model is taken from Heery *et al*, 2000a). The planning of campaigns was directed by the individual union which selected a particular target group for recruitment. In determining which groups to target, the strategic aim was not just to expand union membership in this area, but also to convert the union involved to a culture of union renewal based on the organizing model. Such a policy, if successful, would see unions both consolidating their existing territory and penetrating new areas of non-unionization. However, in terms of groups of new members actually recruited by this strategy the Organizing Academy found, with some exceptions, that in practice a higher priority was given to 'in-fill' recruiting, ie recruiting non-union employees working alongside existing members, rather than seeking to enter greenfield sites.

Again, as with the 'servicing strategy', the organizing strategy had some new elements, but it did not herald a revolutionary change in union behaviour. For example, in the 1970s, albeit in a different environment, the TGWU had transformed itself from an officer-dominated union into one which developed a strong shop steward and workplace-based organization, with positive results for its membership growth (Undy *et al*, 1981). However, what was new, in the 1990s, was the central role played by the TUC in

promoting the strategy and creating an Organizing Academy. Also, the organizing model, in combating the individualism inherent in the servicing
model, helped bolster the traditional collectivist ethos of trade unions which
was coming under attack from several sources. But the confrontational
elements of the organizing strategy, and the aggressive pursuit of grievances
as a recruiting tool, were not to the taste of all the TUC's unions. As a result, a
small number of unions withdrew their support for the Organizing Academy
after a year's membership (Heery *et al*, 2000a: 14–16).

In evaluating the two strategies, the work of Waddington (Waddington and
Whitston, 1997) in examining employees' motivations for joining, staying in
and leaving trade unions will be used to cast some light on their relative
merits. In terms of recruitment, in a survey of 10,787 union members spread
across 12 unions and conducted between 1991 and 1993, Waddington showed
that 41.2 per cent were recruited by some union-related means, whereas only
30.9 per cent took the initiative themselves in contacting the union. The local
union representative played the major role in recruiting new members: 30 per
cent of new members were recruited by shop stewards. On this basis the
emphasis placed in the organizing model on strong local activist organization
seems to be fully justified. Further, in responding to questions regarding
reasons for joining the union, Waddington found that it was the kind of
benefits secured by collective representation, and not those associated with
individual services, that resonated most strongly with new members. In
particular, support from the union if they had a problem at work (72.1 per
cent) and improved pay and conditions (36.4 per cent) easily topped the list of
six reasons for joining a union. The much-promoted financial services, associated with the consumer model of unions and central to the servicing
strategy, were highly rated by only 3.5 per cent of the new members and came
bottom of the list.

In another study, in the mid/late 1980s, of trade unionism in six localities
with different experiences of economic life, Gallie and colleagues (1996) also
examined union members' reasons for joining and staying in a trade union.
This research similarly found that protection from problems at work was the
single most important reason for staying in the union. However, in examining
why employees joined the union in the first place, Gallie *et al* asked to what
extent this was a condition of the job or the result of strong informal pressures, and 41 per cent of union members indicated that the latter was the
primary reason for joining the union. A later Waddington study (2000) of
membership recruitment and retention in UNISON also alluded to similar
peer pressure when it showed that 40.4 per cent of UNISON members
surveyed cited 'most people at work are members' as the second most
important reason for remaining in the union. Hence, it can be reasonably
suggested that the organizing model is again more likely than the servicing
model to help recruit and retain members by helping build such peer group
pressure in the workplace.

The above empirical findings suggest that the organizing strategy may have some advantages over the servicing strategy as a means of recruiting and retaining members. This does not necessarily mean, however, that all aspects of the organizing approach are superior to those of the servicing model. In particular, the organizing model's reliance on local lay officials – shop stewards or branch officers – for representing members is not always the preferred option of members, or indeed the lay officials. Most noticeably, white-collar and managerial unions have shown a strong preference for full-time officer representation. For example, in 1996 a civil service union, the IPMS, considered shifting the balance between its servicing and organizing activities in favour of less full-time officer servicing of members' needs and more reliance on lay representatives. A survey of the union's branches showed that 81 per cent of branches rated as very important (only 1.3 per cent not important) full-time officer involvement in collective negotiations, and 54.7 per cent of branches also rated full-time officer support as very important in processing individual cases (only 9.3 per cent not important) (Ben Yehuda, 1997). Obviously, in the IPMS there was little support for those aspects of the organizing model which threatened the reliance of lay officials – as well as members – on the union's professional full-time officials.

Both the organizing and servicing strategies therefore have their merits and unions employ elements of both in their attempts to recruit, retain and support their members in the most efficient manner. Decisions as to which strategy should be given most emphasis in unions' attempts to regenerate union–employee (and member) relations is contingent on a number of factors. First, there is the context in which the union seeks to operate and the issue at hand, ie recruitment or retention. If the union is seeking to recruit employees against the wishes of their employer, the organizing strategy seems to offer the best choice. On the other hand, if the employer is willing to cooperate with the union, an organizing approach, which is basically adversarial in its nature, could be counterproductive – not least because some competitor union could trump the initial union's approach by offering a more conciliatory deal. Second, if the issue is retention, not recruitment, the great majority of union members may be indifferent as between servicing by lay representatives and full-time officers – assuming the level of servicing is perceived as similar in standard. However, in some unions the preference is for servicing via a strong cadre of full-time officials. Nevertheless, as with much else in trade unions at the start of the new millennium, the attraction of the organizing model for many unions is that it promises a cheaper self-help form of regeneration, as compared to employing relatively more expensive full-time officials. It may well be this aspect of the organizing model that persuades unions that the balance should be moved in this direction.

UNIONS AND EMPLOYERS

The main processes and structures shaping the present relationship between unions and employers in the workplace will be described before turning to examine unions' strategic choices for dealing with employers. The two opposed strategies to be discussed are first, the adversarial approach and second, social partnership. In conclusion the factors influencing the choice of strategy will be summarized.

Unions seek to influence their members' employment relationship – or their effort–reward bargain – by a number of different processes. In the workplace the three main and traditional processes used by unions are collective bargaining, joint consultation and autonomous job regulation. Each may be used to create rules around the effort–reward bargain which enhance union members' terms and conditions of employment. Collective bargaining, or joint regulation, may be described as the trade unions' 'prime function' (Taylor, 1994). In comparison, joint consultation, which normally involves unions in two-way communication with managers, is for unions a 'second-best' option, while autonomous job regulation, once the *raison d'être* of craft unions (Clegg, Fox and Thompson, 1964), has declined in importance in the modern, more flexible workplace, although some unions still exercise influence over the organization of work (Millward, Bryson and Forth, 2000).

The structure of collective bargaining (Clegg, 1976) – in particular, the coverage of collective agreements; the level at which collective bargains are made (for example, national level and enterprise level); and the scope of bargaining (the number of issues subject to collective bargaining) – all moved, in the 1980s and 1990s, in ways which reflected a decline in union influence in the workplace. A further indicator of union strength, related closely to collective bargaining processes, ie the degree and nature of industrial action, also declined radically in this period. Each of these factors will now be briefly discussed.

A good indicator of change in bargaining coverage is the percentage of establishments (25 or more employees) with a union recognized for collective bargaining. In 1980 it was 64 per cent, but in 1998 it was 42 per cent (Machin, 2000). Over the same period the proportion of workplaces with a trade union representative, the person most likely to act for the union in the first stages of the grievance procedure, dropped from 54 per cent in 1980 (Millward *et al*, 1992) to 33 per cent in 1998 (Cully *et al*, 1999). In aggregate the percentage of employees whose pay was covered by collective bargaining was 33 per cent in 1998, including 61 per cent in the public sector and 24 per cent in the private sector (Brown *et al*, 2000).

The level at which collective bargains were made was much changed between 1984 and 1998. In particular, the determination of pay through multi-employer bargaining (the equivalent of national pay bargaining in a particular sector, say engineering) declined dramatically. It influenced pay in 41 per cent of workplaces (with 25 or more employees) in 1984, but only 13 per cent in 1998 (Millward *et al*, 2000). At the same time, multi-site, single-employer bargaining remained constant, affecting 12 per cent of such workplaces, while workplace bargaining showed a marginal decline from 5 per cent to 3 per cent of workplaces (Millward *et al*, 2000). These aggregate figures masked, however, a marked decentralization of pay bargaining in the public sector where multi-site, single-employer bargaining grew between 1984 and 1998 from 11 to 23 per cent of workplaces, while the influence of the multi-employer or national-level bargain declined from 82 to 39 per cent of workplaces (Millward *et al*, 2000). In private sector manufacturing there was a decline in bargaining in pay at all levels over this period. In 1998 workplace bargaining was the most prevalent form of pay bargaining, but it only determined pay in 12 per cent of workplaces (multi-site, single-employer bargaining affected pay in 5 per cent and multi-employer or national bargaining in 6 per cent of manufacturing workplaces). In contrast, in private sector services, multi-site, single-employer bargaining was the most common in 1998, even though it covered only 10 per cent of workplaces (Millward *et al*, 2000).

The scope of collective bargaining also declined between 1980 and 1984, but it remained reasonably constant between 1984 and 1998 in those workplaces which continued to recognize trade unions for bargaining purposes. In 1998, in over half those workplaces which recognized trade unions, bargaining occurred over such issues as physical working conditions, staffing levels, redeployment within the establishment, size of redundancy payments and reorganization of working hours (Millward *et al*, 2000: 168).

Finally, as an indicator of union power, industrial action, on all measures, declined very significantly between the mid-1980s and 2000, although in 2000 the number of working days lost (499,000) showed an increase compared to 1999 (242,000) and 1998 (282,000). But the days lost in 2000 were still 24 per cent lower than the average of 660,000 working days lost per year in the 1990s. Prior to this, an average of 7.2 million days per year were lost in the 1980s and 12.9 million in the 1970s. In 1998 the lowest number of stoppages on record (166) was registered. This compares with an annual average of 1,129 stoppages in the 1980s.[9]

In the 1990s and early 2000s trade unions therefore faced a major challenge in determining the most appropriate way of dealing with employers. Collective bargaining was restricted to a minority of workplaces and collective agreements only influenced a minority of employees' terms and conditions. Further, unions were in danger of being confined to the public sector and the newly privatized parts of the private sector. Moreover, in the public sector the decentralization of pay bargaining was making it difficult for unions to service the needs of members fragmented into a growing number of bargaining units.

The alternative to collective bargaining and union voice, offered by joint consultative committees and employer-sponsored employee representation, could also be seen as a threat to trade unions. However, there had been no increase in the incidence of functioning joint consultative committees in non-unionized workplaces between 1984 and 1998: 20 per cent of such workplaces had joint consultative committees in 1984 and this had fallen marginally to 18 per cent in 1998 (Millward *et al*, 2000). In contrast, there was an increase of some importance in the incidence of non-union representation in workplaces where there was no union representative. This had grown, at the lowest estimate, from 28 per cent of workplaces in 1980 to 41 per cent in 1998 (Millward *et al*, 2000).

In these circumstances, where employers were generally in a relatively powerful position *vis-à-vis* the unions they recognized, and capable of hindering or helping unions extend union recognition into new territories, the strategy adopted by unions had primarily to match this reality. Further, with the advent of a 'New Labour' (Undy, 1999) party and in 1997 a New Labour government, intent on building a strong and positive relationship with business, trade unions had to position themselves so as to accommodate this new political change in the environment. Last, the trade unions also had to try to reconcile these conditioning factors with their traditional role of protecting existing members' interests who, as shown above, still valued union representation and a collectivized voice at work.

The broad strategic choice presently facing unions can be categorized as lying on a continuum between the conventional adversarial approach and the more cooperative social partnership strategy. Obviously, faced by an obdurate employer a union generally committed to social partnership could respond in a more militant manner. Similarly, a union largely preferring an adversarial strategy could, if faced with an employer and an issue more amenable to cooperation, adopt a more conciliatory stance. But, despite the above caveats, the choice for trade unions nationally was on the continuum between strategies of adversarialism and social partnership.

Adversarialism, or militant trade unionism, required unions to pursue members' goals by mobilizing union membership in opposition to management. Industrial action was an integral part of such a strategy and readily used for achieving ambitious objectives. Concessions were frowned on and the ideological underpinning of assumed adversarialism made compromise difficult (Kelly, 1996). In negotiating terms, collective bargaining was viewed as a trial of strength and issues were resolved in a distributive or zero-sum manner (see the seminal work of Walton and McKershie, 1965).

Such a win–lose approach to management may, of course, be reliant for its successful implementation on a set of circumstances beyond trade unions' immediate influence. If employers prove to hold the balance of bargaining power, there may be little to be gained in pursuing such a militant win–lose policy. For example, in the case of the most important dispute of the period, ie the miner's strike in 1984–5, the employer's greater bargaining power, including, *inter alia*, its ability to find alternative sources of fuel (Wilshire,

McIntyre and Jones, 1985), helped negate such a strategy. Nevertheless, some unions led from the political left still adhered to this option in the 1990s. These included the National Union of Mineworkers (NUM), the Fire Brigades Union (FBU) and the National Union of Rail Maritime and Transport Works (RMT) (Darlington, 2001). Indeed, the RMT could claim a number of successes for its adversarial strategy in dealing with the management of London Underground in the context of a 'monopoly service, buoyant markets, increased volume of traffic and lack of compulsory redundancies (Darlington, 2001: 5–7).

Unions maintaining such an adversarial stance were, however, the exceptions to the general rule. For, as the TUC stated, 'The rhetoric of struggle, strikes and strife... has little resonance in today's world of work... Embracing partnership is therefore the right strategic choice for the trade union movement' (TUC, 1999). Social partnership, or as the TUC seems to prefer, partnership, may be defined, initially, as occupying the opposite end of the continuum of trade union–employer relations to adversarialism, and equated with moderate trade unionism (Kelly, 1996). This may be further refined by reference to the political complexion of the actors using or promoting the term. On the moderate left (the TUC's position), partnership is assumed to reflect pluralist relations at work, to be open to statutory regulations and given form through collective agreements made between employers and trade unions (Ackers and Payne, 1998). In the language of labour negotiations it involves integrative bargaining, or problem-solving behaviour, and ideally produces a mutually beneficial win–win solution.

The TUC in 1999, in 'Partners for Progress: New Unionism in the Workplace', spelt out its six principles of partnership as follows (TUC, 1999):

- commitment to success of the enterprise;
- recognizes legitimate interests (ie independent representation of employees' interests);
- commitment to employment security;
- focus on the quality of working life;
- transparency (consultation over business plans);
- adding value (improved employee contribution and motivation).

The above principles have much in common with the Involvement and Participation Association's (IPA) proposals for industrial partnership (Coupar and Stevens, 1998). In brief, the IPA proposed in the 1990s that, in combination, security of employment and job flexibility, employees sharing in the success of the organization, information, consultation and employee involvement, and representation of the workforce represented the partnership model in employment relations. The degree to which employers accepted these principles was examined in 1998 (Guest and Peccei, 1998). This study of over 80 employers affiliated to the IPA, and therefore presumably representing the high tide of partnership ideals, suggested that the TUC faced an uphill struggle in translating its partnership model from concept to practice. Of the 82 companies studied, only 28 per cent were recorded as making high progress towards the partnership model. Particularly disappointing for the TUC's aspirations was the finding that 40 per cent of participants either strongly disagreed (19 per cent) or disagreed (21 per cent) with the statement that an independent union was the best means of ensuring that employees' interests were effectively represented. Indeed 39 per cent either agreed (21 per cent) or strongly agreed (18 per cent) that in a successful partnership organization there should be no need for trade unions.

The ambiguous attitude displayed above by employers with some sympathy towards partnership, as defined by the TUC (and the IPA), was also noted by research into partnership agreements signed in the earlier 1990s (Bacon and Storey, 2000). This found that managers behaved in short-term, contradictory and opportunistic ways in making such agreements. Indeed a number of the managers involved contemplated de-recognizing the unions and individualizing relationships with their employees, prior to signing partnership agreements. In some cases the preference was for unions to 'wither on the vine' (Bacon and Storey, 2000). Subsequently, however, in the changing political climate of the late 1990s and 2000, two of the companies identified above as considering de-recognizing their unions in the early 1990s – the Co-operative Bank and Npower – were cited in the TUC's 'Partners for Progress' as examples of what partnership could achieve for all parties by such agreements. Clearly in 2000 the political tide was, at least in some areas, turning in the TUC's favour and giving a significant boost to industrial partnerships based on trade union involvement.

A further important politically driven stimulus to the TUC's campaign to engage employers more positively in industrial partnership was provided in 1999 by the DTI's Partnership Fund (£5 million) and the DfES's Union Learning Fund, initiated in 1998. The 2001 Employment Bill also offers more support as it promises to provide time off for trade union learning representatives: some 3,000 such representatives existed in 2001. Both the above funds offered a financial incentive for employers to join with trade unions in partnership schemes and provided trade unions with the opportunity to demonstrate their ability to help solve management's and employees' problems. For example, the banking union UNIFI approached the HSBC in 2000 in the Manchester area to develop a learning partnership which would deliver a key skills programme for HSBC's employees. This proved highly effective in improving labour relations between management and union and contributed to HSBC's decision to restore union representation rights for managers, which had been withdrawn in 1996 (Undy, 2001).

Unions' choice of strategy for dealing with employers was therefore much influenced by each union's ideological preferences, assessment of bargaining power and appreciation of the wider political and economic changes. Those on the left of the trade union movement, and particularly those organizing in a context which had not diminished their bargaining power, were not minded to accommodate New Labour and the associated economic pressures which had undermined trade unionism in the private sector. Instead they preferred to maintain their traditional adversarial strategy. On the other hand, the TUC, with its wider responsibilities to the labour movement and in cooperation with its allies amongst politically moderate union leaders, recognized the need to adjust to the changed environment and the resulting loss of union power and influence, particularly in the private sector. Partnership was their preferred strategy.

SUMMARY AND CONCLUSION: RECOVERY OR REGRESSION

Trade unions in Britain in 2001 were in a much weakened position, as compared to 1980. The continual loss of members between 1980 and 1998 resulted in collective bargaining determining the pay of only a third of all employees. Nationally, as a consequence, the TUC's ability to speak to government with an authoritative voice, representing all employees' interests, was much diminished. Locally, union representatives were limited to a minority of workplaces and trade unions' influence over employers was hence similarly restricted. Moreover, unions' traditional claim to be the only legitimate channel for an independent expression of employees' views at work was under threat. The growth of non-union representation, managers' wishes to treat employees as individuals and the expression of unitarist values (Provis, 1996) all served to question the relevance of trade unionism in the workplace.

In 1997 and in 2001, however, the election of two consecutive Labour governments signalled a marked change in the unions' political context. The growing influence of the EU's social policy and the introduction of a series of statutes strengthening both employees' and, albeit to a lesser extent, trade unions' rights also suggested that the legislative tide might have turned in the trade unions' interests. Against this, however, were ranged the continuing structural and attitudinal conditions noted above as detrimental to trade union membership and influence.

During the 1990s trade unions were actively searching for the most appropriate responses and strategies to suit the new environment. However, different unions had different experiences regarding the loss of members and consequently the pressures on individual unions to adopt new strategies varied. Also, not all unions held the same ideological positions and not all suffered the same financial problems. There was, therefore, no one common response amongst trade unions to their changing fortunes. Nevertheless, the TUC took the lead in promoting, and to some limited extent coordinating, the unions' responses. In particular, it moved to sponsor the organizing strategy towards employees for the recruitment and retention of members, and the partnership strategy for dealing with employers. 'Partnership' also seemed to meet the aspirations of the New Labour Party, and subsequently the New Labour governments, for more harmonious union–employer relations.

The jury, in 2002, is still out as it deliberates on the likely effectiveness of both strategies. There is, however, growing recognition of the potential conflict between the two preferred employee and employer strategies. As the TUC itself noted, 'it is clear that inevitable tensions can exist between the active promotion of partnership and the "anger, hope, action" mode of organizing members' (TUC, 1999). The policy of the TUC to find and promote strategies which suit all actors in all circumstances may therefore be subject to more critical review. In particular, it could be argued that the effectiveness of the two strategies will be conditional or contingent on the process, actors involved and the context. For example, if the process is one of recruitment, in the face of employer opposition and in the context of the Employment Relations Act 1999, an organizing strategy may be best suited to achieve the milestones set out in the recognition procedure (see Chapter 7). Subsequently, if recognition is secured, either an adversarial or partnership strategy may be most appropriate, depending on the employers' post-recognition policy towards the union.

A flexible union response, according to the different contingencies, would thus seem the most effective way for trade unions to determine their choice of strategies. This would, however, call for a degree of pragmatism which could come into conflict with the ideological preferences of some union leaders. But, as the initial choice of strategies itself appears to have been largely driven by recognition of the realities of trade union power – or lack of it – a more flexible contingent approach would appear to offer the best chance for a self-help model of union recovery. Moreover, if unions prove incapable of finding the correct balance between their key strategic choices, the continuing antipathetic structural and attitudinal developments could mean yet further union regression.

Notes

1 *Annual Report* of the Certification Officer 2000–2001.
2 See *Labour Market Trends*, September 2001, pp 433–44 for a discussion of trade union membership in 1999–2000.
3 See Annual Reports of the Certification Officer for 1981 and 2000–2001.
4 *Labour Market Trends*, September 2001, p 436.
5 Ibid, p 440.
6 *Labour Market Trends*, September 2001, pp 436–37.
7 Ibid, p 438.
8 Ibid, p 436.
9 *Labour Market Trends*, June 2001, pp 301–14.

References

ACAS (2001) *Annual Report* 2000–2001, ACAS, London

Ackers, P and Payne, J (1998) British trade unions and social partnership: rhetoric, reality and strategies, *The International Journal of Human Resource Management*, **9** (3), pp 529–50

Adeney, M and Lloyd, J (1986) *The Miners Strike 1984–85: Loss without Limit*, Routledge and Kegan Paul, London

Bacon, N and Storey, J (2000) New employee relations strategies in Britain: towards individualism or partnership? *British Journal of Industrial Relations*, **38** (3), pp 407–27

Bain, G S (1970) *The Growth of White Collar Unionism*, Oxford University Press, Oxford, p 96

Bassett, P and Cave, A (1993) *All for One: the Future of the Unions*, Fabian Society, London

Bell, J D M (1960) Trade Unions, in *The System of Industrial Relations in Great Britain*, Blackwell, Oxford, p 134

Ben Yehuda, E (1997) *Professional Unions and Trade Union Mergers: A Case of a Much Treasured Identity*, University of Oxford MSc Dissertation

Brown, H P (1990) The counter revolution of our time, *Industrial Relations*, **29** (1), pp 1–14

Brown, W (2000) Putting partnership into practice in Britain, *British Journal of Industrial Relations*, **38** (2), p 305

Brown, W, Deakin, S, Nash, N and Oxenbridge, S (2000) The employment contract: from collective process to individual rights, *British Journal of Industrial Relations*, **38** (4), pp 615–16

Carruth, A and Disney, R (1988) Where have two million trade union members gone? *Economica*, **55**, pp 1–19

Carter, B (2000) Adoption of the Organizing Model in British trade unions: some evidence from Manufacturing, Science & Finance (MSF), *Work Employment & Society*, **14** (1), p 121

Clegg, H A (1976) *Trade Unionism Under Collective Bargaining*, Blackwell, Oxford, pp 8–10

Clegg, H A, Fox, A and Thompson, A F (1964) *A History of British Trade Unions Since 1889* Vol 1 1889–1910, Oxford University Press, Oxford, pp 4–14

Coupar, W and Stevens, B (1998) Towards a new model of industrial partnership, in *Human Resource Management: The New Agenda*, ed P Sparrow and M Marchington, Financial Times Management, London, p 145

Cully, M, Woodland, S, O'Reilly, A and Dix, G (1999) *Britain at Work*, Routledge, London, pp 88–89

Darlington, R (2001) Union militancy and left-wing leadership on the London Underground, *Industrial Relations Journal*, **32** (1), pp 2–21

Disney, R (1990) Explanations of the decline in trade union density in Britain: an appraisal, *British Journal of Industrial Relations*, **28** (2), pp 165–77

Freeman, R and Pelletier, J (1990) The impact of industrial relations legislation on British union density, *British Journal of Industrial Relations*, **28** (2), pp 141–64

Gallie, D, Penn, R and Rose, M (eds) (1996) *Trade Unionism in Recession*, Oxford University Press, Oxford

Guest, D E and Peccei, R (1998) *The Partnership Company*, IPA, London

Heery, E, Delbridge, R, Salmon, J, Simms M and Simpson, D (2000a) *Report on the Organizing Academy*, Cardiff Business School, Cardiff

Heery, E, Simms, M, Delbridge, R, Salmon, J and Simpson, D (2000b) The TUFC's Organizing Academy: an assessment, *Industrial Relations Journal*, **31** (5), p 400

Incomes Data Services (1999) *New Unionism*, IDS Focus No 91, Autumn 1999

Institute of Employment Research: Projections of Occupations & Qualifications 2000–2001 (2001) University of Warwick and DfEE

Kelly, J (1996) Union militancy and social partnership, in *The New Workplace and Trade Unionism*, ed P Ackers, C Smith and P Smith, Routledge, London, pp 79–82

Kessler, I and Purcell, J (forthcoming) Individualism and collectivism in industrial relations, in *Industrial Relations: Theory and Practice in Britain*, ed P Edwards, Blackwell, Oxford

Legge, K (1995) *Human Resource Management: Rhetorics and Realities*, Macmillan, London, chs 3 and 6

Machin, S (2000) Union decline in Britain, *British Journal of Industrial Relations*, **38** (4), pp 631–45

Mason, B and Bain, P (1993) The determinants of trade union membership in Britain: a survey of the literature, *Industrial and Labour Relations Review*, **46** (2), pp 332–51

McIlroy, J (1992) *Trade Unions in Britain Today*, Manchester University Press, Manchester, p 25

Millward, N, Bryson, A and Forth, J (2000) *All Change at Work*, Routledge, London, pp 174–75

Millward, N, Stevens, M, Smart, D and Hawes, W R (1992) *Workplace Industrial Relations in Transition*, Dartmouth, London, p 110

Provis, C (1996) Unitarism, pluralism, interests and values, *British Journal of Industrial Relations*, **34** (4), pp 473–95

Taylor, R (1994) *The Future of the Trade Unions*, Andre Deutsch, London, p 120

TUC (1998) *Focus on Union Services*, TUC, London

TUC (1999) *General Council Report*, TUC, London, p 62

TUC (1999) *Partners for Progress: New Unionism in the Workplace*, TUC, London, p 8

Undy, R (1999) Annual Review Article: New Labour's 'Industrial Relations Settlement': The Third Way, *British Journal of Industrial Relations*, **37** (2), pp 315–36

Undy, R (1999) Negotiating amalgamations: territorial and political consolidation and administration reform in public-service sector unions in the UK, *British Journal of Industrial Relations*, **37** (3), pp 445–63

Undy, R (2001) *Learning Partnership for Key Skills*, Unpublished Report to Cabinet Office HSBC/UNIFI, London

Undy, R, Ellis, V, McCarthy, W E J and Halmos, A M (1981) *Change in Trade Unions*, Hutchinson, London, pp 138–48

Undy, R, Fosh, P, Morris, H, Smith, P and Martin, R (1996) *Managing the Unions*, Clarendon Press, London, pp 38–39

Upchurch, M and Donnelly, E (1992) Membership patterns in USDAW 1980–1992: survival as success? *Industrial Relations Journal*, **23** (1)

Waddington, J (2000) Towards an Organizing Model in UNISON, in *Redefining Public Sector Unionism: UNISON and the Future of Trade Unions*, ed M Terry, Routledge, London

Waddington, J and Whitston, C (1995) Trade unions: growth, structure and policy, in *Industrial Relations: Theory and Practice in Britain*, ed P Edwards, Blackwell, Oxford, pp 170–71

Waddington, J and Whitston, C (1997) Why do people join unions in a period of membership decline? *British Journal of Industrial Relations*, **35** (4), pp 515–46

Walton, R E and McKersie, R B (1965) *A Behavioural Theory of Labour Negotiations*, McGraw-Hill, London

Wilshire, P, McIntyre, D, and Jones, M (1985) *Strike*, pp 216–24

15

Employment relations in smaller firms

Tony Dundon and Adrian Wilkinson

INTRODUCTION

Small firms, though extraordinarily difficult to define, commonly enjoy the approval of governments and economists who see them as important sources of innovation, economic renewal and economic growth. As employers, however, they often attract criticism. For example, the European Foundation for the Improvement of Living and Working Conditions (2001) recently found that employees in small establishments, particularly those in *micro*-sized firms (fewer than 10 employees), are more likely to 'work unsociable hours, have less training and job security and be more exposed to heath risks' (EFILWC, 2001). Yet, despite their high ratings in economic terms, and often poor reputation as employers, most textbooks on employment relations are surprisingly silent about them.

In this chapter we review a broad range of developments in small firm employment relations. The general thrust of the chapter is to critique the view that small firms are somehow more flexible and enjoy a conflict-free employment relationship. Indeed, we suggest in the conclusion that regulation and legislation in the areas of employment protection can actually work to the advantage of small business owners. After considering the criteria for defining an SME, the chapter will examine a number of central components of the employment relationship, including the prevalence of informality, trade union membership, and pay in smaller firms, along with recruitment, training and development and the adoption of new management techniques (NMT). Finally, some conclusions and implications are presented.

WHAT IS AN SME?

David Storey (1994) notes that 'there is no single or acceptable definition of a small firm'. The American Small Business Administration once defined a small to medium-sized firm as one that employed fewer than 1,500 people! Earlier definitions, such as those by the Bolton Commission (Bolton Report, 1971) in the UK, defined a small manufacturing firm as one that employed fewer than 200 workers. These definitions have been frequently criticized, presenting a misguided and outdated picture of firm size. More recently, the European Commission has recommended to member states a (non-binding) single definition for SMEs (DTI, 2001). This groups together a *micro* firm (fewer than 10 employees), a *small* business (10–49 employees) and a *medium*-sized enterprise (50–249 employees) under the umbrella terms 'small to medium-sized enterprise' (Table 15.1). However, as a definition of small firms, the criterion of 'the numbers employed' can be difficult, especially in sectors that rely on a transient, casual or part-time workforce (Curran and Blackburn 2001).

Table 15.1 European Commission SME definitions

Criterion	Micro	Small	Medium
Max. number of employees	9	49	249
Max. annual turnover	n/a	€7m	€40m
Max. annual balance sheet total	n/a	€5m	€27m
Max. per cent owned by one, or jointly by several, enterprise(s) not satisfying the same criterion	n/a	25%	25%

Source: DTI, 2001

But it is not only size that matters. In most westernized economies, smaller firms account for a significant proportion of economic activity (Lane, 1995). In the UK the DTI has estimated, by adding together the *micro*, *small* and *medium*-sized firms under the heading 'SMEs', that they account for over 99 per cent of all companies, 37 per cent of financial turnover and 44 per cent of non-governmental employment (DTI, 2000). In contrast, the 7,000 largest businesses account for 45 per cent of non-governmental employment and 49 per cent of turnover. However, there are dangers in using these figures in a homogenous and deterministic way. About 70 per cent of small firms are not actually 'companies' but rather 'sole proprietorships or partnerships' (DTI, 2000). Many small firms are also more prominent in key sectors, such as high technology and business consultancy. Thus in reality SMEs are more likely to be characterized by high heterogeneity, complexity and have an unevenness about how they manage people, representing wide diversity in terms of the type of people employed (Curran and Blackburn, 2001; Ram, 1984; Goodman *et al*, 1998).

FROM 'BLEAK HOUSE' TO 'SMALL IS BEAUTIFUL'

Much of this unevenness tends to be viewed in one of two perspectives concerning employment relations (see Table 15.2). The first has been described as 'small is beautiful'. Informal communication channels between employees and owner-manager are often used to suggest that relations are harmonious, more flexible and accommodative than those found in larger organizations. The Bolton Commission suggested that SMEs provide a better [sic] environment than large firms. SMEs were believed to have better means of involving and motivating staff, accompanied by low levels of conflict. This can be seen in the well-quoted section of the Bolton Report:

> In many aspects a small firm provides a better environment for the employee than is possible in most large firms. Although physical working conditions can sometimes be inferior in small firms, most people prefer to work in a small group where communication presents fewer problems: the employee in a small firm can more easily see the relation between what he is doing and the objectives and performance of the firm as a whole. Where management is more direct and flexible, working rules can be varied to suit the individual. Each employee is also likely to have a more varied role with a chance to participate in several kinds of work... no doubt mainly as a result... turnover of staff in small firms is very low and strikes and other kinds of industrial dispute are relatively infrequent. The fact that small firms offer lower earnings than larger firms suggests that the convenience of location and generally the non-material satisfaction of working in them more than outweigh any financial sacrifice involved. (Bolton Report, 1971, cited in Storey, 1994: 186).

However, this view has been widely criticized. As Edwards (1995) argues, strikes are only one form of discontent, and while the 'infrequency' of workers in smaller firms to strike may indicate some level of trust or

Table 15.2   From small is beautiful to bleak house

Positive HR	Negative HR
Harmonious	Hidden conflict
Good HR	Bleak house
Little bureaucracy	More instability
Family style	Authoritarianism

Source: Wilkinson (1999), p 207

commitment, it may also show a fear of management or an abuse of managerial power. Given that many owners define the small firm as their own creation, it is perhaps not surprising that employees should be seen as subordinate to the owner's view of what is best for the firm. In the WERS survey, two-fifths of small businesses had a working owner present, and in three-quarters of all SMEs, managers said that 'those at the top are the best placed to make decisions about the workplace' (Cully *et al*, 1999). Recent research conducted at Manchester School of Management (UMIST) – in the sectors of hotel and catering, transport, communications and engineering – reported owner-managers' influence on how the firm is viewed: 'virtually all of the senior managers interviewed at these companies aspired to the same unitarist notion of a "happy ship", a loyal and co-operative team, and a workforce as committed as the senior managers/owners to the continued success of the business' (Goodman *et al*, 1998: 547).

The second perspective of employment practices paints a Dickensian bleak-house picture (Sisson, 1993). In this image, employees suffer poor working conditions, inadequate health and safety and have less access to union representation than employees in larger establishments (Millward *et al*, 1992). Conflict is not lacking but rather expressed through high levels of absenteeism and labour turnover, as well as a greater propensity for problematic 'interpersonal' relations to develop and ferment over time (Rainnie, 1989; Goss, 1991). Employment relations are in reality viewed as a 'bleak house or sweatshop', with the assumption made that since no one complains, employees are satisfied. 'Flexibility' is more akin to 'instability', with few procedures or systems within which to formally manage people. And the idea of a harmonious 'happy family' is in reality a form of authoritarianism as few employees are able to question or challenge the owner-manager (Ram and Holliday, 1993; Ram, 1994; Rainnie, 1991).

Yet theorizing about employment relations in such 'either/or' terms can simplify and gloss over practices that are much more complicated in reality (Wilkinson, 1999). As Curran argues, 'small firms do offer more varied work roles and greater opportunities for close face-to-face relations in a flexible social setting with less of the bureaucracy of the larger enterprises. But these conditions also offer greater opportunities for interpersonal conflicts' (as quoted by Roberts, Sawbridge and Bamber, 1992).

MANAGING THE EMPLOYMENT RELATIONSHIP IN SMEs

Given the view that both the 'small is beautiful' and the 'bleak-house' perspectives are likely to be too polarized, in this section we review some of the specific issues and trends in employment policy and practice among SMEs, broadly defined. In particular, we examine the contours of informality and assess what this means in practice, and review the methods of recruitment, training and union membership in smaller firms. We also consider the use of new management techniques among smaller firms, and assess what these mean in practice for both workers and owner-managers.

Informality and the small business owner

It is generally accepted that few small firms place a high priority on the management of people. As Ritchie (1993) comments, small firms hardly contemplate formalizing their working practices and even less consideration is given to integrating human resource strategies with operational plans. This is partly the result of a lack of resources and the absence of specialists, with 'informal routinization' playing a large part in the day-to-day running of the firm (Scott *et al*, 1989; Matlay, 1997). Indeed, one study in the United States found that the lack of human resource planning among many SMEs was one of the main reasons for business failure (McEvoy, 1984). Informality, however, does not imply a particular view of the substance of work relations: it could be associated with an autocratic as well as a harmonious workplace. This results in a situation where management policy and practice is 'unpredictable' and 'indifferent' to the human resource needs of the firm (Ritchie, 1993). Indeed, one of the main characteristics of a small firm is their use of a web of informal, personal and business links to such an extent that the distinctions between personal and employment relationships are often blurred. As Roberts *et al* (1992: 242–3) point out:

> Relations are not of the impersonal 'structured' type characteristic of many large firms. But neither are they merely a collection of individual interpersonal relationships involving a loosely structured distribution of power, as in ties of friendship. Rather the characteristic feature of small firms is the overlap between personal and employee relations... Most owner/managers assume that their firm's goals are rational; therefore, as long as employees do what is good for the firm, they are also doing what is best for themselves.

The advantages of informality to owner-managers are limited when a firm employs more than around 20 staff (Roberts *et al*, 1992: 255). Informal networks of recruitment dry up, informal systems of communication are stretched and ad hoc responses to personnel issues create problems. This fits with the view that once the organization is above a certain size, management needs to be professionalized (Loan-Clarke *et al*, 1999). As Roberts *et al* (1992) found, in most small firms 'an all too often harassed owner/manager has to handle all such aspects in any "spare time" left over from the other functions of business and management'. Hence, personnel and employment relations issues are often accorded a low priority.

The issue of informality as a feature of small firm employment practices has been examined in the most recent WERS, using four separate procedures:

performance appraisals, grievance procedures, disciplinary procedures and equal opportunities (see Table 15.3). Only one-third of SMEs had appraisals, and while most reported some procedure for dealing with grievance and discipline, in many firms this appeared to be conveyed by word of mouth (Cully *et al*, 1999: 263–4). Very few (19 per cent) had written policies on equal opportunities. Of course the existence of formal procedures does not guarantee their usage, but they can clearly have an effective cooling-down value, especially given the highly personalized nature of relations in many of these firms.

Table 15.3   Incidence of appraisals, formal procedures for dealing with individual disputes and equal opportunities policies, by small businesses

Method	% of small businesses
Formal appraisals for most (at least 60 per cent) of non-managerial employees	32
Formal individual grievance procedure	68
Formal disciplinary and dismissals procedure	70
Equal opportunities policy	19

Source: Cully et al (1999), p 263

In part, the lack of formalized procedures is because many owner-managers see them as burdensome. The owners' particular sensitivity to market pressures and the need for speedy operational decisions have been employed as arguments against formalized procedures, often couched in the view from the Institute of Directors that small businesses were perennially 'drowning in a sea of paperwork' (Thatcher, 1996). However, this interpretation is highly debatable. It is by no means obvious that an emphasis on rules and procedures is outdated. Indeed, a belief in consistency and fairness is central to gaining the commitment of employees in any organization, and is not in itself contrary to informal relations (Clark, 1993).

The problem is that what seems to appear as flexibility to owner-managers can easily be interpreted as arbitrary treatment among workers. The non-formal systems, which operate in many small firms, tend to take the form of the owner speaking to one employee (possibly a supervisor), who in turn is asked to speak to the 'problem' employee. Rarely is the employee addressed directly by the owner on the issue, and this can lead to emotions running high when the problems come to a head and the employee is ordered to leave (Roberts *et al*, 1992: 253). Indeed, small firms are disproportionately represented at employment tribunals for unfair dismissal claims and are more likely to lose cases (Roberts *et al*, 1992: 252). As Goodman *et al* (1998: 549) found in their research, most problems centre around a lack of understanding of procedural fairness: 'it was clear that recourse to formal procedures following initial informal approaches to a disciplinary problem carried more serious implications for employees in small businesses than in larger organizations'. Consequently, procedures on absence, timekeeping, standards of performance, use of company facilities etc could actually stabilize important areas of employment relations within the firm when 'things go sour' and could actually be beneficial to them (Scott *et al*, 1989: 97). This is particularly significant in the light of the Employment Relations Act 1999 for enhanced unfair dismissal awards and statutory union recognition. Thus whilst there is evidence that owner-managers tend to considerable hostility to formalized procedures, this conventional wisdom has now been overturned and some benefits are being seen in terms of clarifying roles, delegating authority, and indicating the processes and procedures to follow.

Trade union membership and union recognition in SMEs

Union membership and employer recognition of trade unions are less common in small firms. There is also some evidence of a link between size and non-unionism (Beaumont and Harris, 1989; Millward *et al*, 1992; Cully *et al*, 1998). For example, in firms employing fewer than 20 workers, union membership tends to be 'below 1 per cent' (IRS, 1998). In 1998, in firms employing between 25 and 49 workers, union density was around 23 per cent, rising to 27 per cent for firms employing between 50 and 99 people (Cully *et al*, 1998: 15). Cully *et al* also found that over 20 per cent of small businesses had some employees who were union members and, in a little over half of these, unions were recognized. Where unions were not recognized it was unusual to find worker representatives (Cully *et al*, 1998: 15). The unionization data is illustrated in Table 15.4.

Table 15.4   Union membership density in relation to workplace size (per cent)

Year	Number of employees				
	25–49	50–99	100–199	200–499	500 or more
(a) 1984[a]	26	30	39	47	66
(b) 1990[b]	19	25	33	49	53
(b) 1998[b]	23	27	32	38	48

[a] Calculated from Millward *et al* (1992), p 64; [b] Cully *et al* (1998), p 15.

There are several reasons for the low levels of union membership among workers in smaller firms. One key factor is the ideological opposition towards unionism among many owner-managers. Another explanation is that many unions find it difficult to mobilize unorganized workers. These are, arguably, better explanations for the low levels of unionization in smaller firms than the alleged claim that harmonious worker–management relations render collective agreements superfluous (Dundon, Grugulis and Wilkinson, 1999). Historically, unions have found it difficult to organize workers in SMEs and the problem is made worse by the fact that many smaller firms are exempt from the recently introduced union recognition legislation. One estimate suggests that this exemption could in effect disenfranchise 5 million workers employed in small firms (Winters, 1999), as businesses employing 20 workers or fewer are exempt from the recognition procedure.

In practice, owner-managers should have relatively little to fear from union recognition. Recent research commissioned by the CIPD found that such legislation tended to act as a conduit for managerial choice and creativity rather than a burden to employment policy and practice (Marchington *et al*, 2001). Moreover, unions can actually help design more efficient managerial systems by promoting fairness, workforce skills and structured communication channels (Dundon and Eva, 1998). As Roberts *et al* (1992) found from a survey of small firms conducted at Durham University: 'unions can play a positive role. They can provide an effective channel of communication [and] … full-time officials have in some cases proved to be effective and almost "independent" arbitrators in cases of discipline and grievance'.

Brown *et al* (2001) note that the statutory union recognition provisions contained in the Employment Relations Act has implications for small as well as large firms. They suggest that the law has more of a 'procedural' emphasis to advance 'social partnership' rather than coercing legally enforced 'rights' to bargain. Thus while the legislation has the provisions for compulsory recognition, it also contains a strong reflection that the idea of voluntary recognition is distinctly superior. The ACAS Annual Report (2000/2001) shows an 80 per cent increase in union recognition claims, with 66 per cent resolved satisfactorily by both employers and unions, leading to full recognition. This suggests that owner-managers of small firms need not fear recognition legislation. The existence of a legal 'floor of rights' appears to be promoting 'voluntary' rather than 'compulsory' arrangements between the parties

If anything, the employment practices of many smaller establishments would merit greater regulation, similar to the information and consultation Directive now on course in the European Union. As Atkinson & Storey (1994) point out, 'wages are lower and in view of their relatively low levels of unionization, effective job security for workers is likely to be lower than for workers in larger firms'.

Scott *et al* (1989: 97) found that workers in SMEs generally expressed positive attitudes toward unions, and legislation can promote a structured basis for managerial decision making: 'legislation encourages management discipline… and should stabilize important areas such as grievance, discipline and dismissal'. However, the same research also noted that there was an 'air of resignation that whatever their wishes [employees] would not be able to join unions' (Scott *et al*, 1989: 97). In other words, the hostility of owner-managers towards unions in general remains a powerful disincentive for workers to join for fear of managerial reprisals. This fits with the Cully *et al* (1998: 15) data of an association between workplace size, non-unionism and the attitudes of managers, suggesting that 'anti-union sentiments on the part of employers provide a considerable hurdle to overcome if unions are to win members and recognition'.

Pay among small firms

As already noted, pay tends to be lower in SMEs than in larger firms (Atkinson and Storey, 1994). Research commissioned by the Low Pay Commission found that, overall, small business had adapted well to the introduction of the National Minimum Wage (NMW), although with some sector variation. In the sectors of 'security and cleaning', the introduction of the NMW had actually improved competitiveness and protected employment: '[T]he National Minimum Wage has protected employment and encouraged companies to tender for contracts on the basis of the service they can provide rather than how little they pay their staff' (Low Pay Commission, 2000). A security firm employer commented that: 'With a level playing field, clients will opt for the best standards available for the money they pay... We welcome the sympathetic and supportive response from private sector clients which helped us manage the introduction of the minimum wage' (Low Pay Commission, 2000: 51).

One of the most affected sectors seems to be private care homes, with women having their pay increased most. It seems that the business impact is because many private firms have had limited scope to increase prices as local authorities refuse to meet rising costs. In response, many owner-managers focused on increasing the pay of the lowest workers with very little impact on the earnings of the better paid. One care home employer commented: 'the wages of other staff were increased by a token gesture only... Our nurses are paid £7.20, previously £7.00 an hour and a cleaner now £3.60, previously £3.00 an hour' (Low Pay Commission, 2000: 53).

More recent analysis of the national minimum wage in three sectors (clothing, hotels and catering, and printing) found that most small firms did not expect to implement major changes in work organization or competitiveness, and few expected to raise skills or introduce new technologies to compensate for wage increases. Generally, informal and ad hoc pay systems remained common in many SMEs, with employees not knowing what their colleagues earned and with a wide variation in the pay of employees doing similar work (Gilman *et al*, 2002). This might be seen to represent a form of individual pay based on performance, but in the absence of criteria and objectives, it is more than likely to reflect 'gut instinct' or 'prejudice' on the part of owner-managers about who is 'a good worker and who fits in'. In our own research (Dundon *et al*, 1999), one garage mechanic explained the procedure for a pay increase: 'I know when we get a rise. It's each Christmas. It's not automatic though, you only get a rise if they think you should have a pay rise

[and] ... that's based on not dropping a bollock in the year... It's a letter in the Christmas card saying we're getting a rise... it really pisses the lads off. I mean a little card, "all the best and all that", but nought about your money and so and so next to you gets something.'

Overall, pay remains lower for workers in small firms when compared to larger organizations, although much depends on occupation and sector variation. The introduction of the NMW has made a substantial improvement to the terms and conditions of thousands of employees in SMEs, especially women and those on part-time contracts who tend to be the lowest paid. For some owner-managers the NMW has led to an increased wage bill, although in most cases these seem to be one-off transitional costs. Improvements in work design and pay systems seem to be one of the main benefits of the NMW for many SMEs, rather than job losses (Gilman *et al*, 2002).

Recruitment

In smaller firms the difficulties of recruitment can be magnified in contrast to larger organizations. As noted, SMEs tend to have few resources with few personnel specialists. Pay and terms and conditions are often inferior in smaller firms which makes it difficult for owner-managers to attract quality and skilled workers (Millward *et al*, 1992; Rainnie, 1989). These factors often equate to a highly informal and ad hoc approach to recruitment, although actual methods and processes have been shown to vary from one industry to the next. Carrol *et al* (1999) found four separate types of recruitment method among SMEs – internal recruitment, closed searches, responsive methods and open searches (Table 15.5).

Internal recruitment methods show that in some sectors there is a vibrant internal labour market among SMEs. For example, Carrol *et al* (1999) found that there are more opportunities for promotion into supervisory roles, although this tends to be more common in hotels than other sectors examined in their study. However, it is also evident that internal labour market mobility is the exception rather than the norm. The bulk of recruitment in these firms focuses on internal, closed and responsive methods that rely on informal processes. For all the firms in Table 15.5, recruiting people through existing 'staff recommendations' was most common, while another third 'poached' workers from competitors. In another study, the closure of a competitor business 'would often be viewed with relish' among owner-managers given the immediate availability of labour, many with highly relevant or easily transferable skills (Holliday (1995).

However, these informal practices can also lead to discrimination. Direct discrimination is seen in managerial bias in recruitment based on gender, age, religion or race. In the Scott *et al* (1989) research, almost all owner-managers were 'ignorant of sex discrimination legislation', and few had knowledge of their responsibilities or obligations in the area of equal opportunities. In

Table 15.5   Methods of recruitment in SMEs

	N	(%)
Internal recruitment		
Existing staff	27	68
Offering permanent jobs to temps	3	8
Closed searches		
Recommendations from staff	40	100
Network of contacts	11	27
Poaching	13	33
Former employees	27	68
Contacts in education	16	40
Recruitment consultants	2	5
Responsive methods		
Former applicants	22	55
Casual callers	21	52
Register of interested applicants	28	70
Open searches		
Job centres	37	93
Other agencies	13	33
Notice in own bar/shop	6	15
Local press	35	88
National press	3	8
Specialist journals	12	30
Other open	5	13
		N = 40

Source: Carrol *et al* (1999), p 243

contrast, indirect discrimination is more difficult to identify, although issues can arise from recruiting employees predominantly from the same sex or race. For instance, in Ram's case study firms, workers were recruited from a predominantly Asian familial and social milieu (Ram, 1991; Ram and Holliday, 1993). In addition, the use of family and ethnic labour can be extremely gendered: women tend to occupy positions of subordination in smaller (especially ethnic and family-run) firms: 'roles are rewarded accordingly, influenced by the "male-breadwinner" and female "actual or potential wife and mother" ideology (Ram and Holliday, 1993: 644).

As with other employment issues, owner-managers tend to shy away from formalized recruitment methods in the (mistaken) belief that they hinder competitiveness. Word-of-mouth recruitment is often seen as a cost-effective way of gaining a detailed profile about prospective employees – the person being either directly known to the owner-manager or based on another employee's personal recommendation. Curran and Stanworth (1979) found that owner-managers' views about potential recruits as 'a person' were significant factors in the selection process. This accords with Holliday's (1995) assertion that in smaller firms the ability of workers to 'fit in' to the existing culture of a small firm, and its informal and highly flexible practices, are important considerations for the owner-manager. Carrol *et al* (1999: 24) recently concluded that: '[W]ord-of-mouth recruitment methods are potentially discriminatory. On the other hand, given the lack of in-house expertise in human resource management techniques and the nature of the labour market, it could be argued that these methods are the most appropriate. Hiring "known quantities" could be seen as a very effective way of reducing uncertainty in recruitment decisions.'

Overall, then, recruitment methods are mainly informal in smaller organizations, although there can be a wide variation in methods and processes used between sectors. One implication is that there are potential ethical and legal issues concerning the 'hiring of known quantities'. Owner-managers may seek to avoid the transaction and opportunity costs associated with a systematic recruitment process, yet at the same time reliance on informality can also lead to a transient workforce plagued with retention problems. Atkinson and Storey (1994) found that workers recruited through personal recommendations would often leave shortly after appointment as they did not fully appreciate the pressures demanded by owner-managers.

Training and development

As previously mentioned, owner-managers are often more concerned with 'getting the products out of the door' rather than integrating human resource and business plans. Hence, providing training opportunities for employees is often viewed as a non-productive activity (Curran *et al*, 1993; Curran *et al*, 1997; Storey, 1994). These issues point to three probable reasons why owner-managers tend to be more concerned with short-term production issues than workforce training: ignorance, market forces and structural barriers.

Owner-managers can be 'ignorant' of the possible benefits arising from training because they are preoccupied with 'getting the products out of the door' on a day-to-day basis. Many also view training initiatives in a negative light. Westhead and Storey (1997) found that around one-third of small business owners had no formal qualifications and equate formal employee training with their own negative experiences of schooling. Despite government schemes to promote training initiatives among SMEs, owner-managers remain reluctant to embrace training even when information is available (Abbott, 1994).

The second reason for the lack of workforce training is the 'market forces explanation' (Westhead and Storey, 1997). The competitive and flexibility-demanding environment of many small firms means that there are higher opportunity costs associated with releasing employees from the shop floor for training. Further, many external training providers do not design training programmes to meet company-specific needs if there are only a small number of potential participants. Abbott (1994) found that a demand for training among small manufacturing firms was entirely different from that for small service sector organizations. Consequently, owner-managers are sceptical about the possible benefits from training if there is no immediate relevance to the market for their business.

A third reason for the low training investment among SMEs can be 'structural' difficulties. Smaller firms do not generally have internal labour markets and as such there is little incentive for either employees or owner-managers to embrace training, given the absence of promotion. Wynarczyk *et al* (1993) found that many small business owners expected line managers to leave the company if they wanted to advance their career. One implication is that owner-managers fear the 'poaching' of well-trained workers by competitor firms. Another structural barrier is regional diversity. Curran *et al* (1997) report a wide variation in the incentive schemes for SMEs provided by different government agencies – for example, Training and Enterprise Councils (TECs), Business Links, the Welsh Development Agency or the Scottish Enterprise Board. Each of these tended to offer different financial packages for regeneration and business assistance. In some cases these can help overcome owner-manager 'ignorance' and even ameliorate the cost burden in the short term. However, such incentive schemes rarely take sector variations into account or seek to allow for market imperfections (Westhead and Storey, 1997). The end result is that many owner-managers find it difficult to release employees from the shop floor for training purposes.

In summary, SMEs are generally reluctant to invest in training. Informal or 'sitting with Nelly'-type schemes may be more prominent in small firms given their lower cost and owner-managers' desire to get the products out of the door. Equally, it is also worth noting there are quite specific barriers that limit the ability of many smaller firms to adopt a more systematic approach to training. In practice, these are likely to include a combination of ignorance, market forces and structural factors. Of these, there is convincing evidence that deregulated and neo-liberal markets are more of a hindrance than an advantage to many SMEs (Westhead and Storey, 1997).

NEW MANAGEMENT TECHNIQUES IN SMEs

One of the more contradictory images of employment practices in smaller firms is the apparent coexistence of 'informality' with new 'professionalized' management techniques. New management techniques (NMT) cover a range of practices often associated with the 'Best Practice HRM' of larger organizations (Pfeffer, 1998; Duberley and Whalley, 1995). Examples include devolved managerial responsibilities, cultural change programmes, team working and a range of employee involvement initiatives (Wilkinson, Dundon and Grugulis, 1999).

There is evidence to suggest that SMEs may not be that far behind their larger counterparts when it comes to NMT (see Table 15.6). According to Bacon *et a*l (1996), the use of 'new' management techniques among many SMEs is not necessarily 'new'. Initiatives such as team working, quality programmes and cultural change may have been present for as long if not longer than those in larger organizations. Downing-Burn and Cox (1999) report on small engineering firms using various high-commitment practices such as quality audits, team working, job rotation and communication. WERS found that 28 per cent of SMEs (10–99 staff) had five or more new management practices, and 23 per cent involved their staff in problem-solving groups (Cully *et al*, 1999). We also have some case study evidence that supports this and, indeed, shows where SMEs are actually providing best practice ideas which are then adopted by large firms (Grugulis, Dundon and Wilkinson, 2000).

Bacon *et al* (1996: 87) argue that owner-mangers are not merely picking NMT up as 'flavours of the month'. They suggest that 'the new management agenda has penetrated deep into the UK economy and that innovative and progressive employee relations practices are no longer restricted to large mainstream companies'. The IPD report on SMEs (1995) also found participating managers to be aware of modern HRM practices, with many rating them just as important to small businesses as to large ones. There was, however, some discrepancy between the importance being placed upon particular techniques and the extent to which they are implemented.

Table 15.6 Examples of new management initiatives in smaller firms

	% of workplaces
No 'new' management practices or employee involvement schemes	8
Five or more of these practices and schemes	28
Joint consultative committee at workplace	17
One or more equal treatment practices	24
Union presence	22
Union recognition	12
Worker representative at workplace	10
Employees with one or more flexible/family-friendly working arrangements	48
Employees with high or very high job satisfaction	61
Low paying workplaces (quarter or more earn below £3.50 per hour)	21
High productivity growth	33
Industrial Tribunal complaints (rate per employee)	2.4

Stand-alone private sector workplaces with 10–99 employees.
Figures are weighted and based on responses from 250 managers and 2,957 employees.

Source: Cully *et al* (1998), p 26

Yet, as in larger firms, it is unclear whether (or why) new techniques should be viewed as positive. Many managerial practices implicitly and explicitly rely on the existence of such initiatives to justify 'harder' employment outcomes (Keenoy, 1997). Indeed, it is often 'assumed' that communications in small firms are automatically good because of the flexibility and close proximity between employee and owner-manager. However, this may be 'one-way' communication and based upon a 'need to know' approach defined by the manager. There is always a danger that samples reporting such change are self-selecting, and therefore give a misleading impression of what is going on among SMEs as a whole (Curran et al, 1997). In other words, those undergoing change or implementing a new managerial practice may be more likely to agree to be part of the study.

Another added complication is that many SMEs are highly dependent on larger organizations for business survival (Rainnie, 1991). Hence owner-managers may feel obliged to conform to certain models of HRM deemed desirable by the larger firm (Blyton and Turnbull, 1998; Kinnie et al, 1999). MacMahon (1996) found that subcontracting translated to little more than a shift in 'risk' from larger to smaller enterprises. In other words, many smaller firms are restricted to supplying the products and services deemed non-essential by many larger organizations. Examples include catering, cleaning, security and transport in which a significant proportion of employees work part-time, experience casual and temporary contracts and are low-paid women workers.

Yet the image of the bleak-house SMEs is equally misleading, as reports from workers employed in smaller establishments have been surprisingly positive. Guest and Conway (1999) comment that there are discernible 'shades of grey and occasional shafts of light' emerging from the 'black hole' of SMEs. In their survey 29 per cent of employees said they were 'very satisfied' with their job and 31 per cent displayed 'a lot of loyalty' to their firm. Similarly, the WERS data shows that workers in both big and small firms display broadly similar (positive) patterns of workplace 'well-being' (Cully et al, 1999: 179, 271). In explaining these results Guest and Conway (1999) suggest that employees in smaller firms appear to experience several features related to the psychological contract, such as perceptions of fairness and trust that may be characteristic of a small social setting. Cully et al (1999), in contrast, note that though employees in small businesses report high rates of job satisfaction, they are more likely to find themselves on lower rates of pay and make more claims for unfair dismissal than their counterparts in a larger organizations.

The interpretation of these survey results can be difficult. The notion that small firms have harmonious employment relations because of their size is highly debatable. In the WERS survey, for example, while 65 per cent of all managers reported that most employees work in designated teams, only 3 per cent confirmed that such teams were fully autonomous (Cully et al, 1999).

Overall, employment relations tend to be based on systems of 'unbridled individualism' with informality the central *modus operandi* in the day-to-day management of people (Scott *et al*, 1989; Lucas, 1996). Furthermore, many employed in smaller firms experience work-related illness, and face dismissal and have less access to union representation than their counterparts in larger organizations (Millward *et al*, 1992; IRS, 1998; Cully *et al*, 1999: 272).

CONCLUSION

Given the numerical significance of SMEs to the British economy, they remain an important institution, attracting the attentions of policy makers, trade unions and academics. For the first time the WERS series includes specific data on smaller firms. It is clear that although research in SMEs has begun to re-emerge, there is still more that needs to be done. As Storey (1994: 160) says, 'any consideration of the small firm sector which overlooked employment issues would be like *Hamlet* without the prince'. The initial findings of WERS suggest that 'there are some distinct features of small business employment relations' (Cully *et al*, 1998: 27). The type of further research needed is that which shows how size interacts with other factors such as labour and product markets, ownership, management style, large firm dependency or technology and industrial subculture. Given that we clearly do understand that in large firms employment relations are not simply a function of their size, the task of unravelling the relationship between factors in small firms should not be beyond us. If what constitutes 'smallness' is contextual and possibly subjective and interpretational, then we need to examine what factors come together to explain patterns of employment relations rather than assume one particular type, be it 'small is beautiful' or 'bleak house'.

Any study of employment in SMEs invariably starts by reference to the issue of defining size. Smaller firms may manage their human resources differently from larger organizations, although in itself size measured by numbers employed is not a very good predictor as to 'why' they are different. In this chapter attention has been given to the prevalence of informality but also complexity. Moreover, too much reliance on a given size threshold can neglect important contextual factors. As Goss (1991) points out, 'whilst there may be very general incidents when it is appropriate to speak of a small firm sector, it is clearly dangerous to treat this as an empirical fact rather than a convenient generalization'. Similarly, whilst categorizing smaller firms can be useful to assess the range of employment practices, simplistic models that group *micro*, *small* and *medium*-sized enterprises together can also be problematic and misleading.

It is more important to reflect specific organizational contexts and assess how and why these shape the behaviour of owner-managers and employees. Gender, industry, sector variation, occupational class and management ideology, along with market and regulatory pressures, are more significant explanatory factors that help understand specific employment contexts from the perspectives of workers as well as owner-managers. It is in this context that many SMEs may be seen as discriminatory owing to a lack of systematic resourcing, employment relations or training policies. Yet reliance on informality can be a rational (even though inappropriate) course of action. Roberts *et al* concluded that a personnel management needed to be developed and that a systematic approach was necessary, even if the personal element of small firm employment was fostered (Roberts *et al*, 1992). We agree.

A more recent factor for this structured adoption of employment policy is that SMEs are now more embedded in supply chain relationships. With this is an added pressure for owner-managers to conform to HR practices that are deemed appropriate or desirable by larger firms (Kinnie *et al*, 1999). Cully *et al* (1999) suggest that 'small workplaces do not operate in a purely informal manner' and the 'differences are of degree – a relative rather than an absolute absence of structure'. It is this complex interplay of external and internal factors, informal and formal systems of management style and the nature of the employees' work which supports the view that theorizing about human resources in polarized perspectives (small is beautiful or bleak house) simplifies what are actually complicated processes. Further, reliance on self-reported surveys is problematic because this form of evidence does not necessarily demonstrate that employees are being treated as an asset. Until the processes of change management in small firms are explored more fully and greater complexity used to inform and shape current debates about employment relations, theoretical models can only ever be partial.

References

Abbott, B (1994) Training strategies in small service sector firms: employer and employee perspectives, *Human Resource Management Journal*, 4 (2) Winter

ACAS (2000/2001) *Annual Report*, ACAS, London (www.acas.org.uk/publications/pub_ar.html)

Atkinson, J B and Storey, D (1994) Small firms and employment, in *Employment, The Small Firm and the Labour Market*, ed J B Atkinson and D Storey, Routledge, London, p 11

Bacon, N, Ackers, P, Storey, J and Coates, D (1996) It's a small world: managing human resources in small businesses, *International Journal of Human Resource Management*, 7 (1), pp 83–100

Beaumont, P B and Harris, R I D (1989) Non-union establishments in Britain: the spatial pattern, *Employee Relations*, 10 (4) pp 13–16

Blyton, P and Turnbull, P (1998) *The Dynamics of Employee Relations*, Routledge, London

Bolton Report (1971) *Report of the Commission of Inquiry on Small Firms*, chaired by J E Bolton, Cmnd 4811, HMSO, London

Brown, W, Deakin, S, Hudson, M and Pratten, C (2001) The limits of statutory trade union recognition, *Industrial Relations Journal*, **32** (3), pp 180–194

Carrol, M, Marchington, M, Earnshaw, J and Taylor, S (1999) Recruitment in small firms: processes, methods, and problems, *Employee Relations*, **21** (3), pp 236–50

Clark, J (1993) Procedures and consistency versus flexibility and commitment: a comment on Storey, *Human Resource Management Journal*, **4** (I), pp 79–81

Cully, M, O'Reilly, A, Millward, N, Forth, J, Woodland, S, Dix, G and Bryson, A (1999) *Britain at Work: As depicted by the 1998 Workplace Employee Relations Survey*, Routledge, London, p 257

Cully, M, Woodland, S, O'Reilly, A, Dix, G, Millward, N, Bryson, A and Forth, J (1998) *The 1998 Workplace Employee Relations Survey: First Findings*, Department of Trade and Industry, London

Curran, J and Stanworth, J (1979) Worker Involvement and social relations in the small firm, *Sociological Review*, **27** (2), pp 317–42

Curran, J, Blackburn, R, Kitching, J and North, J (1997) Small firms and workforce training: some results, analysis and policy implications from a national survey, in *Small Firms: Enterprising Futures*, ed M Ram, D Deakins and D Smallbone, Paul Chapman Press, London

Curran, J, Kitching, J, Abbott, B and Mills, V (1993) *Employment and Employment Relations in the Small Service Sector Enterprise*, Small Business Research Centre, Kingston Business School, Kingston University

Curran, J and Blackburn, R (2001) *Researching the Small Enterprise*, Sage, London

Downing-Burn, V and Cox, A (1999) Does size make a difference?, *People Management*, **5** (2), pp 50–53

DTI (2000) *Small to Medium Sized Enterprise: Statistics for the UK*, Department of Trade and Industry, Small Business Service, London

DTI (2001) *Small to Medium Sized Enterprise (SME) – Definitions*, Department of Trade and Industry, Small Business Service, London (www.sbs.gov.uk/statistics/smedefs.asp)

Duberley, J and Whalley, P (1995) Adoption of HRM by small and medium sized manufacturing organizations, *International Journal of Human Resource Management*, **6** (4), pp 891–909

Dundon, T and Eva, D (1998) Trade unions and bargaining for skills, *Employee Relations*, **20** (1), pp 57–72

Dundon, T, Grugulis, I and Wilkinson, A (1999) Looking out of the black hole: non-union relations in an SME, *Employee Relations*, **21** (3), pp 251–66

Edwards, P (1995) Strikes and industrial conflict, in *Industrial Relations: Theory and Practice in Britain*, ed P Edwards, Blackwell, Oxford

European Foundation for the Improvement of Living and Working Conditions (2001) Jobs in small firms, *Communiqué*, May/June, No. 6/2001

Gilman, M, Edwards, P, Ram, M and Arrowsmith, J (2002) Pay determination in small firms in the UK: contours of constrained choice, *Industrial Relations Journal*, **33** (1), pp 52–67

Goodman, J, Earnshaw, J, Marchington, M and Harrison, R (1998) Unfair dismissal cases, disciplinary procedures, recruitment methods and management style, *Employee Relations*, **20** (6), pp 536–50

Goss, D (1991) *Small Business and Society*, Routledge, London

Grugulis, I, Dundon, T and Wilkinson, A (2000) Cultural control and the 'culture manager': employment practices in a consultancy, *Work, Employment and Society*, **14** (1), pp 97–116

Guest, D and Conway, N (1999) Peering into the black hole: the downside of the new employment relations in the UK, *British Journal of Industrial Relations*, **37** (3), p 397

Holliday, R (1995) *Investigating Small Firms: Nice Work?* Routledge, London

Institute of Personnel and Development (1995) *People Management in Small and Medium Size Enterprises*, Institute of Personnel and Development, London

IRS (1998) *Predicting Union Membership*: Employment Trends No 669, Industrial Relations Service, London, December

Keenoy, T (1997) Review article: HRMism and the language of re-presentation, *Journal of Management Studies*, **34** (5), pp 825–41

Kinnie, N, Purcell, J, Hutchinson, S, Terry, M, Collinson, M and Scarbrough, H (1999) Employment relations in SMEs: market-driven or customer shaped? *Employee Relations*, **21** (3), pp 218–35

Lane, C (1995) The small-business sector: source of economic regeneration or victim of economic transformation?, in *Industry and Society in Europe*, ed C Lane, Edward Elgar, Aldershot

Loan-Clarke, J, Boocock, G, Smith, A and Whittaker, J (1999) Investment in management training and development by small businesses, *Employee Relations*, **21** (3), p 296

Low Pay Commission (2000) *The National Minimum Wage: The Story So Far* (second report of the Low Pay Commission), Cm 4571, HMSO, London, p 49

Lucas, R (1996) Industrial relations in hotels and catering: neglect and paradox, *British Journal of Industrial Relations*, **34** (2), pp 267–86

MacMahon, J (1996) Employee relations in small firms in Ireland: an exploratory study of small manufacturing firms, *Employee Relations*, **18** (5), pp 66–80

Marchington, M, Wilkinson, A, Ackers, P and Dundon, T (2001) *Management Choice and Employee Voice*, Report for the Chartered Institute of Personnel and Development, London

Matlay, H (1997) The paradox of training in the small business sector of the British economy, *Journal of Vocational Education and Training*, **49** (4), pp 573–89

McEvoy, G (1984) Small business personnel practices, *Journal of Small Business*, October, pp 1–8

Millward, N, Stevens, M, Smart, D and Hawes, W R (1992) *Workplace Industrial Relations in Transition. The ED/ESRC/PSI/ACAS Surveys*, Dartmouth, Aldershot

Pfeffer, J (1998) *The Human Equation*, Harvard Business School Press, Boston, MA

Rainnie, A (1989) *Industrial Relations in Small Firms*, Routledge, London

Rainnie, A (1991) Small Firms: between the enterprise culture and new times, in *Deciphering the Enterprise Culture*, ed E Burrows, Routledge, London

Ram, M and Holliday, R (1993) Relative merits: family culture and kinship in small firms, *Sociology*, **27** (4), November, pp 629–48

Ram, M (1991) Control and autonomy in small firms: the case of the West Midlands clothing industry, *Work, Employment and Society*, **5** (4), pp 601–19

Ram, M (1994) *Managing to Survive: Working Lives in Small Firms*, Blackwell, Oxford

Ritchie, J (1993) Strategies for human resource management: challenges in smaller and entrepreneurial organizations, in *Human Resource Management*, ed R Harrison, Addison-Wesley, pp 111–35

Roberts, I, Sawbridge, D and Bamber, G (1992) Employee relations in smaller enterprises, in *Handbook of Industrial Relations Practice*, ed B Towers, Kogan Page, London, p 240–47

Scott, M, Roberts, I, Holroyd, G and Sawbridge, D (1989) *Management and Industrial Relations in Small Firms*, Department of Employment Research Paper, London, No. 70

Sisson, K (1993) In search of human resource management, *British Journal of Industrial Relations*, **31** (2), pp 201–10

Storey, D (1994) *Understanding the Small Business Sector*, Routledge, London, p 8

Thatcher, M (1996) The big challenge facing small firms, *People Management*, 25 July, pp 20–5

Tremlett, N and Banerji, N (1994) *The 1992 Survey of Industrial Tribunal Applications*, Employment Department Research Series No 22, London

Westhead, P and Storey, D (1997) *Training Provision and the Development of Small and Medium Sized Enterprises*, Department for Education and Employment, Research Report No 65, DfEE/HMSO, London

Wilkinson, A, Dundon, T and Grugulis, I (1999) Exploring employee involvement in SMEs, paper delivered at BUIRA HRM Conference, Cardiff University, January

Wilkinson, A (1999) Employment relations in SMEs, *Employee Relations*, **22** (3), pp 206–17

Winters, J (1999) The final frontier: trade unions and the small business sector, paper delivered at BUIRA, HRM Conference, Cardiff University, January

Wynarczyk, P, Watson, R, Storey, D, Short, H and Keasey, K (1993) *The Managerial Labour Market in Small and Medium Sized Enterprises*, Routledge, London

16

Employment relations procedures

David Bott

This chapter defines and explains the term 'procedure' in the context of the employment relationship, explores the reasons why procedures are important to both management and employees, examines some of the fundamental elements of the more commonly used procedures, illustrates some problematic issues in the application of procedures, contemplates some recent trends, including the legal position regarding employee relations grievances, and speculates on what the future holds.

THE MEANING AND EXTENT OF PROCEDURES

It is necessary to distinguish between employment relations *processes* and employment relations *procedures*. Processes, for the purposes of this debate, are those activities which occupy the employee relations manager, such as collective bargaining or handling discipline. Procedures are the means or method of conducting or managing the process or activity, setting out the stages, for example, in handling the collective bargaining and disciplinary processes.

Salamon describes an employee relations procedure as 'an operational mechanism on the part of management which defines, and may limit, the exercise of managerial authority and power through establishing a formal regulatory framework for handling specified issues' (Salamon, 1998).

Although this description implies a restriction on management's prerogative to manage the employment relationship in an unfettered manner, there are obvious advantages to both management and employees, which result in orderly employment relations and fairness and consistency in handling employee relations issues. However, many employers, particularly smaller organizations, see employment procedures as synonymous with red tape, imposed on management through a seemingly endless chain of additional regulation. Furthermore, the law has increasingly placed obligations on employers to install and implement employee relations procedures, particularly issues concerned with equal opportunities and when managing employee grievances, discipline and handling redundancies. Successive EU Directives, implemented into British domestic law since the Labour government's return to office in 1997, have, in many employers' eyes, increased the burden.

Procedures fall into three main categories:

● Those which are jointly entered into by management and employee representatives, often called 'procedural agreements'. Examples include negotiating procedures, recognition agreements and procedures designed to avoid or resolve collective disputes.

● Those created and imposed by management unilaterally. Examples may include equal opportunities, discipline and grievance handling and managing redundancies.

● Those prescribed by legislation, or guidance contained in Codes of Practice, and case law. Examples include statutory union recognition, disclosure of information and health and safety matters.

Of course, it is perfectly possible to find examples of all types of procedures which fall into any of these categories. For instance, disciplinary and grievance procedures might be jointly agreed or imposed unilaterally, but they are also influenced by the guidelines contained in the ACAS Code of Practice on Disciplinary and Grievance Procedures (2000) and under the Employment Act 2002[1].

Since the 1970s voluntary employment relations procedures have become increasingly the norm as a means of ensuring consistency and fairness in the managing of the employment relationship. The 1998 Workshop Employee Relations Survey (WERS 98) (Cully *et al*, 1998) indicated that the vast majority of workplaces employing more than 10 workers had employee relations procedures, usually grievance and disciplinary procedures. Even with the apparent decline of trade unionism, the survey found that, in all workplaces, 45 per cent of management recognized trade unions for collective bargaining purposes.

The prevalence of procedures is due to a number of factors. The Royal Commission of Trade Unions and Employers' Associations 1965 to 1968 (Donovan Commission) recommended extending the use of employee relations procedures.[2] Since the publication of the Donovan Commission's report, successive governments have sought to encourage the installation of procedures, sometimes through statute and sometimes through Codes of Practice. Professional bodies, such as the Chartered Institute of Personnel and Development (CIPD), have published their own Codes emphasizing good management practice. Finally, Employment Tribunals and the courts have emphasized the need for the application of the principles of natural justice in managing the employment relationship, which are best facilitated through the application of fair and consistent procedures. Thus, there are now established guidelines, set out in legislation, Codes of Practice and case law, which employers disregard at their peril. In particular, the requirement to operate, and the stages of, grievance, disciplinary and redundancy handling procedures are now largely prescribed by employment law.

WHY PROCEDURES ARE IMPORTANT

As well as the obvious vulnerability through litigation which employers face in not implementing a fair and consistent procedure, there are good employee relations reasons for having them. WERS 98 found, for example, that there was an unambiguous correlation between employee job satisfaction and effective employee consultation. Thus there are good employee relations reasons and, by implication, a good business case for having joint consultation procedures. The analogy can easily be extended to other employee relations procedures.

The merits of having employee relations procedures may be summarized as follows:

- They provide a means of avoiding or resolving conflict.
- They establish standards of conduct and behaviour at work.
- They reinforce the need for fairness and consistency in the management of the employment relationship.
- They improve the esteem and morale of employees.

Nevertheless, the mere existence of procedures does not, in itself, ensure their use and application in practice. A Department of Trade and Industry background paper, published in 2001 (DTI, 2001a), citing work by Genn (1999), suggested that there were between 500,000 and 900,000 justiciable employment rights disputes each year. Despite the prevalence of grievance and disciplinary procedures, it was estimated that fewer than half of the applicants making claims to employment tribunals had availed themselves of an employee relations procedure. Clearly the existence of procedures does not necessarily mean that management always operate them or that employees necessarily wish to use them.

The reasons for the non-use of procedures, apart from their non-existence in some, mainly small establishments, are various. Management may feel that the use of procedures limits their right to manage and either party may be reluctant to acknowledge the rights and interests of the other in a particular dispute. Relations between the parties may have deteriorated such that neither is willing to use or continue the procedure.

In contrast to the dramatic rise in individual disputes, as evidenced by a threefold increase in claims to employment tribunals from 1990 to 2000, there was a reduction in the volume of collective disputes, recorded stoppages at work and working days lost, over the same period. Naturally this was reflected in a corresponding reduction in collective disputes handled by ACAS. However, there was no evidence to show that the use of ACAS collective conciliation, mediation and arbitration, although declining in volume, was not being used where appropriate.

Linked to the rationale for employee relations procedures is the question of whether they should be written or oral. The ACAS Code of Practice on Disciplinary and Grievance Procedures is quite unequivocal in recommending that disciplinary and grievance procedures should be in writing, and generally the advantages of written procedures outweigh oral procedural arrangements. The Code has been given statutory reinforcement under Schedule 2 of the Employment Act 2002, which contains two new statutory dispute resolution procedures covering dismissal and discipline and grievances. Written procedures minimize ambiguity and misunderstanding. They are not intended to be legal documents and so do not need to be legalistic. They should be universally accessible to employees and management alike within the workplace. In contrast to oral procedures, written ones are not 'lost' when managers or employee representatives move on to other establishments.

On the other hand, oral arrangements, often established through custom and practice, may provide welcome flexibility, be quicker to operate by being less restrictive on the participants and be seen as less 'legalistic'. Oral arrangements enable procedures to be operated less formally, although some written procedures may, nonetheless, cater for informal stages, eg discipline and grievance handling. Where written procedures are produced, management may consolidate them into a company handbook, or include a summary of the main features of each in the handbook. If such is the case, employees should be informed of the location of the full procedures, which should be readily accessible. Separate copies of procedures should be given to employee representatives and first-line managers.

There has been debate about whether procedures should be combined or kept separate. In general, it seems preferable to have separate procedures. An exception would be a union recognition agreement, where in addition to setting out the scope, functions and duties of the participants, it is usual to incorporate an avoidance of disputes procedure.

The ACAS Code of Practice on Disciplinary and Grievance Procedures sets out separate guidelines for disciplinary and grievance procedures. It is not uncommon for procedures to contain a provision for external assistance, for example using industry conciliation and arbitration machinery specifically agreed for the purpose of resolving disputes or using ACAS conciliation, mediation and arbitration. Where the latter is the case, management and employee representatives should discuss the matter during the formative stages with ACAS, whose officers can provide expert advice and opinion.

EMPLOYEE PROCEDURES AND THE LAW

The law does not expressly require employers to install and operate employee relations procedures. Some may find that surprising, given the considerable amount of employment regulation implemented in the last third of the 20th century. Nevertheless, as previously stated, the law does, in some instances, require employers to notify employees of procedures which do exist and there are many instances, for example in Codes of Practice and case law, where Parliament and the judiciary encourage the operation of procedures. There have been clear recent signs that the courts expect management to operate employment procedures when managing the employment relationship. Parliament reinforced that judicial principle in respect of dismissals, discipline and grievances by incorporating statutory procedures in the Employment Act 2002. Such procedures are now implied into contracts of employment and tribunals have the power to vary any compensation award to reflect failure by employers or applicants to follow those procedures.

The following are the main instances where the law encourages or influences the use of employee relations procedures:

- *Grievances*. The Employment Rights Act 1996 requires all employees to issue to employees a written statement of particulars of employment, which must contain the name or description of the person to whom an employee can go if they have a grievance.[3] Furthermore, the Employment Relations Act 1999 gives employees the right to be accompanied by a work colleague or a trade union official of their choice in any grievance procedure, including an appeal hearing, they invoke,[4] while the ACAS Code of Practice (2000: Section 2) contains guidelines and the Employment Act 2002 contains a statutory grievance procedures. The Code of Practice also suggests that organizations may wish to have specific procedures for handling particularly sensitive complaints of unfair treatment, such as discrimination, bullying and harassment, and a separate 'whistle-blowing' procedure in the light of the Public Interest Disclosure Act 1998.
- *Disciplinary matters*. The Employment Act 2002 requires all employers to include in the written statement of particulars of employment a reference to *any* disciplinary procedures which are in existence. This is complemented by the earlier Employment Relations Act 1999, which gives

employees who are the subject of any disciplinary hearing, including appeals, the right to be accompanied by a work colleague or a trade union official of their choice.[5] Furthermore, as with grievances, the ACAS Code of Practice contains guidelines on the content and application of employee relations procedures relating to the handling of disciplinary issues (ACAS, 2000: Section 2, para 47) and the Employment Act 2002, Schedule 2, contains a statutory procedure on dismissal and discipline. ACAS has also issued an advisory booklet 'Discipline at work', which contains additional advice to employers on handling disciplinary issues. Employment tribunals are also empowered to decrease or increase awards of compensation in unfair dismissal cases where they consider there has been an unreasonable failure on the part of the applicant or respondent respectively to use a dismissal procedure.

- *Status of Codes of Practice.* The primary function of such Codes is to establish standards of best practice. By doing so the government hopes to encourage managers and workers to operate and abide by the content of procedures designed to promote good employment relations. The Trade Union and Labour Relations (Consolidation) Act 1992 empowers ACAS to issue Codes of Practice 'containing such practical guidance as it thinks fit for the purpose of promoting good industrial relations'. Although Codes of Practice are not, in themselves, legally enforceable, any failure to observe their provisions is taken into account in proceedings before tribunals, the courts and the Central Arbitration Committee (CAC). ACAS has produced two other Codes of Practice: Disclosure of Information for Collective Bargaining Purposes and Time Off for Trade Union Duties and Activities, and a draft Code on Union Learning Representatives.
- Other bodies have also produced Codes of Practice which influence procedures for handling employee relations issues. Principally these are: Equal Opportunities Commission – Codes on Equal Pay and Sex Discrimination; Commission for Racial Equality – Code on Racial Discrimination at Work; Department for Education and Skills – Code on Age Diversity; and the Department for Trade and Industry – Codes on Balloting and Picketing.
- *Redundancies and business transfers.* The law relating to collective redundancies and transfers of business ownership is contained in the Trade Union and Labour Relations (Consolidation) Act 1992, the Employment Rights Act 1996 and the Collective Redundancies and Transfers of Undertakings (Protection of Employment) (Amendment) Regulations 1999. They provide for advance information to, and consultation with, trade unions and employee representatives in the event of redundancies involving 20 or more workers. ACAS has also published an advisory booklet, number 12 Redundancy Handling, which includes advice on the main procedural steps in managing redundancies.
- *Union recognition.* The Employment Relations Act 1999 amended the Trade Union and Labour Relations (Consolidation) Act 1992 and introduced rules

relating to the statutory right of trade unions to recognition for collective bargaining purposes. The provisions are detailed and lengthy, but could, in the event of no agreement being reached subsequent to a (CAC) declaration of recognition, result in the imposition by the CAC of a legally enforceable contract between the parties, containing the procedural arrangements for collective bargaining on pay, hours of work and holidays.[6] Failure to observe the procedural arrangements could lead to an order of specific performance from the High Court.

- *Case law.* In the early years after the introduction of the law on unfair dismissals in 1972, courts and tribunals placed much emphasis on the need for procedural fairness in termination of employment cases. This requirement was diluted as a result of a number of cases in the late 1970s and into the 1980s. Until 1987 the courts continued to accept that dismissals could be fair in the absence of a proper hearing, if the employer could successfully argue that the employee would have been dismissed even if a procedure had been operated. In 1987 the House of Lords over-turned that principle in *Polkey v AE Dayton Services Ltd.*[7]
- *The Polkey case.* This decision might be considered to be the most important unfair dismissal decision and reinforced the principle of procedural fairness. It is worth quoting the words of one of the Appeal Judges, Lord Bridge. 'An employer, having prima facie grounds to dismiss, will, in the great majority of cases, not act reasonably in treating the reason as a suffi-cient reason for the dismissal, unless he has taken steps, conveniently clas-sified in most authorities as "procedural", which are necessary in the circumstances of the case to justify that course of action'. It is true that another of the Appeal Judges, Lord Mackay, qualified this by suggesting that failure to implement a procedure, where it was utterly futile to do so, would still not render the dismissal unfair. However, since that decision it has been universally accepted by practitioners and the courts that employers must, in all but exceptional circumstances, ensure procedural fairness. For how long this principle will remain unchallenged will depend on whether Parliament changes the law. In the DTI's consultation document 'Routes to Resolution: Improving Dispute Resolution in Britain', the government invited responses to a suggestion that the law be changed again to the immediate pre-Polkey position, permitting tribunals to disregard procedural mistakes if they made no difference to the outcome of the case (DTI, 2001b: para 3.21). The Employment Act 2002 effectively modifies *Polkey* by allowing tribunals to disregard minor proce-dural shortcomings. There will always be a requirement for employers to act fairly and reasonably, following the basic statutory procedures, but they will no longer be penalized for procedural errors which do not substantively render the dismissal unfair.
- *Compliance with Codes of Practice.* Another recent legal trend can be discerned in unfair dismissal decisions where courts and tribunals have

drawn attention to the existence of the ACAS Code of Practice on Disciplinary and Grievance Hearings and the need to ensure compliance in order to satisfy the procedural fairness principle.

- From time to time tribunals and courts will, in the absence of specific guidance in the primary legislation, themselves suggest guidelines to be followed by employers in handling employment relations issues. Examples include redundancy. In 1982 the EAT[8] laid down five principles of 'good industrial relations practice' to be followed by employers when handling redundancies, namely advance warning, consultation with employee representatives, adoption of objective selection criteria, to select in accordance with those criteria, after consultation, and the consideration of redeployment before dismissal.
- *Sickness absence.* Two important EAT decisions established guidelines for employers when contemplating dismissals in sickness absence cases. In long-term sickness absence the EAT has held that it is necessary for the employer always to consult the employee and discuss future prospects, including reviewing the possibility of alternative work, rather than relying solely on medical advice.[9] In short-term sickness absence, particularly where it is of a repetitive short-term nature, the EAT suggested that it would be more appropriate for an employer to invoke a disciplinary procedure and give the employee an opportunity to improve before considering the ultimate sanction of dismissal.[10]
- *Compliance with health and safety procedures.* The Health and Safety at Work Act 1974, various subsidiary Regulations, notably the Management of Health and Safety at Work Regulations 1992, the Health and Safety (Consultation with Employees) Regulations 1996 and Approved Codes of Practice (ACOP), together create numerous rights and obligations for and upon employers, trade union and other employee representatives and employees. Detailed explanation of the various procedures required in workplaces as a result of this specialized body of law is beyond the scope of this chapter. Suffice to say that the overall duty on employers to conduct their undertakings in such a way as to ensure that persons in their work-places are not exposed to health and safety risks obliges them to agree, with their workforce, procedures to ensure compliance with that duty. These procedures embrace the role and functions of safety committees, the provision of information, instruction and training to employees, and time off work for employee representatives to carry out health and safety duties. As with other Codes of Practice, the Health and Safety ACOPs contain advice and practical guidance, including advice on procedures. Failure to observe an ACOP is admissible in evidence in tribunals and courts and proof of failure to comply will be deemed by the courts to be a contravention of a statutory provision unless the court is satisfied that the provision is complied with in some other way.[11]

NEGOTIATING PROCEDURES

Negotiating procedures are usually the product of joint consultation and are therefore procedural agreements setting out a framework for collective bargaining and the resolution of collective disputes. As previously stated, there may be a separate agreement for resolving disputes, perhaps incorporated into a recognition agreement.

WERS 98 showed that 45 per cent of all management in all workplaces recognized trade unions for collective bargaining purposes. This must mean that these organizations had concluded, either orally or in writing, a procedural recognition agreement which, in turn, gave disclosure of information rights to the recognized union or unions.

Collective bargaining was encouraged in the early part of the 20th century as an appropriate means of determining pay and other conditions of employment. Recognition procedure agreements became fairly common. Many industries had their own national agreements with clearly defined stages, internal and external, for settling disputes. The decline of trade union membership and changing management attitudes from the 1980s saw a gradual reduction in recognition procedure agreements, which, if they exist at all, are now more likely to operate at local level only.

Main features of negotiating procedures

Bargaining units and bargaining agents

The agreement should clarify which employees are covered by the collective bargaining process and which representative body or bodies, whether they be unions or other employee representatives, should conduct the bargaining. The agreement should define the area within scope, be it a geographical area, a particular department or departments, or a group of workers. If more than one bargaining agent is involved the agreement should clarify their relative 'spheres of influence'.

Scope

The agreement should specify what subject matter may be negotiated between the parties. This may range from substantive issues, the terms and conditions of employment, including pay, hours of work, holidays and sick pay schemes, to ancillary matters such as training and development. Where a legally enforceable contract has been imposed on the parties by the CAC under the statutory recognition provisions, the subject matter will only extend to pay, hours of work and holidays.[12]

Procedural steps

The agreement will normally include stages in the collective bargaining procedure leading to an in-house agreement or, in the event of a failure to agree, provision for external assistance in resolving the dispute.

Internal stages

Depending on the size of the organization and circumstances, there might be two or three internal stages. Stage 1 would usually be a meeting between first-line management and employee representatives, whether union shop stewards or representatives of some other negotiating body such as a works council or staff association. If the issue cannot be resolved at this meeting it may proceed to stage 2, where more senior management and employee representatives become involved. In the case of union representation, this stage might involve the convener, branch representative, or a full-time officer from district level. If there is provision for a third stage the issue would be referred to a meeting between senior-level management and senior union officials.

External stage

Some negotiating agreements provide for a reference, where there is a failure to agree, to industry conciliation and/or arbitration, or, alternatively, to ACAS for conciliation, followed by mediation or arbitration if unsuccessful in conciliation. ACAS has a consistently good record in resolving collective disputes at the conciliation stage. In 2000/2001 ACAS was able to resolve 93 per cent of cases referred to it for collective conciliation.

General comments

Negotiating procedures are designed to resolve differences between employers and workers in an orderly manner with the preferable outcome of a collective agreement. The parties should not normally be tempted to bypass the separate procedural stages, although in exceptional circumstances the parties may agree to fast-track the dispute to the final stage. An important feature should be the commitment by all parties not to pursue industrial action before exhausting the procedure.

Collective agreements in Great Britain are, unlike in many other countries, not legally enforceable, unless there is an express provision. An exception to that would be a legally enforceable contract imposed by the CAC under the statutory recognition provisions.[13] This principle reflects the view that employee relations practitioners, whether employer or employee representatives, are the most appropriate people to conclude industrial agreements. Nevertheless, there is an unwritten convention that the parties to the agreement conform to the spirit and intention of the agreement. In practice, it is rare for either party to break this convention.

It may be appropriate at this stage to comment on external assistance. Industry conciliation and arbitration arrangements have declined in recent years, mirroring the decline in collective bargaining at national level. There are still some industry arrangements, but it is now almost universally accepted that ACAS is the most appropriate body to offer these facilities.

ACAS will attempt to resolve a dispute first by conciliation and, only if that fails, by mediation or arbitration. Conciliation is carried out by ACAS's own officers, who explore, through side meetings and joint meetings, under their chairmanship, common ground which could lead to a settlement. Any agreement reached is that of the parties; ACAS does not impose a settlement, merely facilitating an agreement. Only where conciliation fails are the parties offered either mediation or arbitration. Arbitration is the usual alternative. Normally an arbitrator, appointed from an external panel, hears submissions from both parties, and makes an award. Both parties have previously agreed to accept the outcome of the arbitration. Mediation is similar to arbitration, conducted by members of the external panel, but is distinguished from arbitration by the mediator making formal, but non-binding proposals for the parties to explore.

GRIEVANCE PROCEDURES

The purpose of a grievance procedure is to permit employees to express grievances. It provides a mechanism for these to be dealt with fairly and promptly, before they develop into more serious issues or collective disputes. According to the WERS 98, there is a wide-ranging list of grievances raised by employees at work (Table 16.1).

The ACAS Code of Practice on Disciplinary and Grievance Procedures states that it is management's responsibility to develop grievance procedures, but, because such procedures should be acceptable to all in the workplace, managers and workers alike, management should aim to involve employee representatives in the formulation and revision of procedures.

The nature of grievance procedures

They should be:

- uncomplicated;
- in writing;
- operated promptly and speedily;
- known to all – managers and workers.

Complainants have a statutory right to be accompanied at all stages of the grievance procedure, including appeals, by a work colleague or a trade union official of their choice.[14]

Table 16.1 Nature of grievances raised by individuals in the workplace

Type of grievance	% of all workplaces where grievances raised
Pay and conditions	42
Relations with supervisors, line managers	30
Promotion, career development, internal training	26
Work practices, work allocation, pace of work	26
Physical working conditions, health and safety	23
Working time, annual leave, time off work	23
Job grading, classification	23
Performance appraisal	13
Bullying at work	7
Sex, racial or other discrimination	5
Sexual harassment	5
Racial harassment	2
Other	2

Base: Workplaces with 10 or more employees where a grievance had been raised in the past year, whether through a procedure or not (n = 1,212).

Note: Respondents could specify more than one type of grievance (ie multiple response question).

Source: WERS 98

The procedural stages

Many, if not most, grievances can be resolved informally in discussion with the employee's line manager. The law requires employers to specify, by description or otherwise, the person to whom a worker can go in the first instance if they have a complaint.[15]

Where the grievance cannot be resolved informally, the formal procedure becomes operative. The ACAS Code of Practice recommends at least a two-stage procedure, although it acknowledges that, in small establishments, there may be only one stage. In such cases it is particularly important that the person handling the complaint and any appeal acts impartially. In larger establishments it may be appropriate to have three stages. However, the process of handling grievances provides more scope for negotiating and compromise than disciplinary handling.

Comprehensive confidential records need to be kept of the nature of the complaint, the employer's response, action taken and the reasons for that action. Copies of minutes of meetings should be made available to the aggrieved employee. Under the Data Protection Act 1998 employees are entitled to see information held by the organization about them.

The first stage

Complaints should be referred, preferably in writing, to the employee's first-line manager. Sometimes the complaint will be about the line manager, in which case the grievance should be referred to a more senior manager. If the grievance is contested by management, the complainant should be invited to a hearing, accompanied if they wish, to discuss the grievance. Following the hearing the decision of management should be conveyed promptly, and preferably within five days, in writing to the employee.

The second stage

If the problem is not resolved there should be provision for it to be referred, in writing, by the employee to a second, in effect appeal, stage, where a more senior manager will meet the (accompanied) employee for a further discussion. As with the first stage, management's decision should be notified promptly to the employee.

The third stage

In larger establishments there may be a need for reference to another senior management level, perhaps a director, the managing director, or chief executive. Some grievance procedures contain a provision for external assistance, either by ACAS or another independent external facilitator.

Special circumstances

It may be preferable to have separate specific procedures to handle complaints about unfair treatment, which might 'overlap' with disciplinary issues. These might include complaints against other employees, including managers, and complaints about bullying and harassment.

The Public Interest Disclosure Act 1998 protects employees who, in certain circumstances, disclose alleged malpractices in the organization. This protection is qualified and limited, in some cases, where employees have not used an internal procedure first. The ACAS Code of Practice suggests that a separate 'whistle-blowing' procedure might be more appropriate for dealing with these cases.

DISCIPLINARY PROCEDURES

The purpose of a disciplinary procedure is to provide a mechanism whereby employees who fall short of the organization's standards of behaviour and performance are given an opportunity to improve. Organizations are, therefore, entitled to set standards regulating behaviour, conduct, perfor-mance and attendance. These standards are often specified in rules contained in a company handbook. It is important that workers and managers know what the standards are and how the disciplinary procedure is applied. The law now requires all organizations, regardless of size, to provide employees with a written statement of particulars of employment, which should contain details of *any* disciplinary procedure, including the stages of that procedure and a person they can approach if they are dissatisfied with any disciplinary decision taken against them.

Although there is no express legal obligation on employers to have such a procedure, there is now an implied term in contracts of employment, incorporating the statutory procedure contained in Schedule 2 of the Employment Act 2002. In any unfair dismissal proceedings in employment tribunals, or before an ACAS-appointed arbitrator, the grounds for and manner of dismissal will be examined and the absence of a procedure or failure to operate one will almost certainly render the dismissal 'procedurally unfair', even where the substantive reason is fair.

A significant proportion of claims heard by employment tribunals are for alleged unfair dismissal. The onus in tribunal proceedings is on the employer to show the reason for dismissal. It will be unfair if the reason does not come under one of the five statutory fair reasons. In addition, the tribunal must be satisfied that the employer has acted reasonably in all the circumstances, which include the size and administrative resources of the employer. The five statutory fair reasons are conduct, capability and qualifications, redundancy, failure to comply with a statutory requirement, and some other substantial reason.

Disciplinary procedures are also used to deal with conduct and some capability issues, for example poor performance or repetitive absence. Dismissals for these reasons, although genuine, may still eventually result in a decision against the employer if a procedure has not been used or has not been fairly applied. Note that, for long-term sickness absence, although a capability matter, a separate sickness absence procedure should be used, not the disciplinary procedure.

There are several underlying principles in discipline handling which are of paramount importance. These include the consideration of concepts of reasonableness and fairness and the application of the rules of natural justice.

The ACAS Code of Practice on Discipline and Grievance Procedures encapsulates these principles and the tribunals and courts have long ago accepted the need for dismissals to be judged against these standards.

The Code emphasizes that management is responsible for setting the standards, maintaining discipline at work, ensuring there are appropriate disciplinary rules, and ensuring there are procedures to handle issues of conduct, capability and performance.

As with other types of procedure, it is important that they are accepted by all within the workplace. Thus it is preferable for management to involve employee representatives in the formulation and revision of both disciplinary rules and procedures.

Disciplinary rules

Rules should be set out, in writing, clearly and concisely, specifying the standards, explaining why, for efficiency, safety and good employee relations reasons, they are necessary and the consequences of breaking the rules or failing to conform to standards.

The rules cannot cover every eventuality, but should cover such issues as:

- misconduct, including some examples of gross misconduct, which might result in summary dismissal;
- poor performance;
- harassment;
- bullying;
- misuse of company facilities – eg telephones, e-mail, the Internet;
- unpunctuality;
- unauthorized absence.

It is the responsibility of management to ensure everyone in the workplace is aware of the rules and disciplinary procedures. This may be done by:

- giving everyone a personal copy during induction training;
- making available a handbook which is readily accessible to all, eg in each department and in the Human Resources section;
- supplying individual copies to employee representatives and first-line managers;
- publishing copies 'online' on the company intranet.

It may also be necessary to make special provision for workers whose first language is not English, or for workers with a disability, for example those who are visually impaired.

The main features of disciplinary procedures

The underlying principle is that the procedure should be designed to help and encourage those workers whose standards have fallen below those required by the organization to improve. Discipline is therefore a term used in the sense of 'instruction' and 'correction' rather than 'punishment'. Of course there will be circumstances where sanctions will need to be imposed, and ultimately dismissal will follow if there is no improvement. Equally there will be occasions where, after a fair investigation, the failure to conform to standards, for example gross misconduct, will lead to summary dismissal. But, in general, dismissal should not take place for a first 'offence'.

Other essential features are that the procedure is operated fairly and consistently and in accordance with the principles of natural justice. These are that:

- no person should be a judge in his or her own case;

- everyone should know, in advance of a hearing, the nature of the allegation made;
- an opportunity is given to the employee to state his or her case;
- employees are given the right of appeal against any decision against them.

The Code of Practice lists 14 essential features for the guidance of employers. Tribunals are required to take into account, when assessing whether an employer has acted reasonably in dismissing an employee, the size and administrative resources of an organization, but only in exceptional circumstances would a tribunal look favourably on an employer who did not operate a disciplinary procedure which conformed to this guidance. ACAS's 14 essential features of good disciplinary procedures are that they should:

- be in writing;
- specify to whom they apply;
- be non-discriminatory;
- provide for matters to be dealt with without undue delay;
- provide for meetings, witness statements and records to be kept confidential;
- indicate the disciplinary actions which may be taken;
- specify the levels of management which have the authority to take the various forms of disciplinary action;
- provide for workers to be informed of the complaints against them and, where possible, all relevant evidence before any hearing;
- provide workers with an opportunity to state their case before decisions are reached;
- provide workers with the right to be accompanied;
- ensure that, except for gross misconduct, no worker is dismissed for a first breach of discipline;
- ensure that disciplinary action is not taken until the case has been carefully investigated;
- ensure that workers are given an explanation before any penalty is imposed;
- provide a right of appeal – normally to a more senior manager – and specify the procedure to be followed.

Operating the disciplinary procedure

When a disciplinary matter arises, management should first conduct a full and unbiased investigation. This should be conducted promptly by a member of management not directly involved in the matter being investigated. The purpose of this investigation is to establish the facts while the events are still fresh in people's minds. It is important, therefore, to keep a written record.

In allegations of gross misconduct it may be appropriate to suspend the employee, on full pay, during the investigation. This suspension should only occur in exceptional circumstances, for example where there are risks to personnel or property, or relationships have broken down. The suspension should not be regarded as disciplinary action against the employee and thus should be as short as possible.

The investigation may lead management to conclude that there is no case to answer, in which case the employee should be informed and the matter closed. Where the investigation shows a *prima facie* case to answer, management must decide how to proceed.

The Code of Practice acknowledges that some disciplinary matters may be disposed of informally. Minor misdemeanours and many cases of poor performance may be effectively handled by giving informal oral warnings, supplemented by informal advice, coaching or counselling. However, in all cases where disciplinary action proceeds, whether informally or formally, the employee should be given written details of the alleged shortfall in standards.

The disciplinary hearing should conform to the principles of natural justice and the essential features of the Code of Practice as outlined above. It should be arranged at a mutually convenient time with advance notification to the employee of his or her rights under the procedure, including the statutory right to be accompanied.

Forms of disciplinary action

Where it is appropriate to take disciplinary action, following the investigation and hearing, warnings should be given, if there is no improvement, before the ultimate sanction of dismissal. At each stage of the procedure before the ultimate sanction of dismissal, workers should be informed of the reason for the action, what improvement is required, and the timescale for improvement. A copy of warnings given should be kept on file, but disregarded after a specified period, typically 12 months.

At all stages, including dismissal, workers should be informed of their right of appeal and to be accompanied if they wish. The Code of Practice recommends the following stages:

- first warning, which should be either oral, for minor infringements, or written, for more serious matters;
- final written warning;
- dismissal or other sanction. The alternatives to dismissal may include, where the contract of employment allows it, suspension without pay, demotion, loss of seniority or transfer to other work.

General comments

When operating any employee relations procedure, management must ensure that there is no infringement of a worker's human rights, including current statutory employment rights prohibiting discrimination on grounds of race, gender and disability. These statutory rights will be progressively extended to include protection against discrimination on grounds of religion, sexual orientation and age.

Where, in the course of a disciplinary investigation, the worker raises a grievance it may be appropriate to suspend disciplinary action and deal with the grievance first. Where the grievance relates to a complaint about a manager who is involved in the disciplinary investigation, the employer should consider asking another manager to handle the case.

As with grievances, appeals should, wherever possible, be heard by a manager not previously involved in the investigation or disciplinary hearing. External arbitration may be considered as an alternative to the internal appeal stage.

Finally, rules and procedures should be reviewed, and where appropriate revised, in the light of changes in legislation and developing good employee relations practices.

REDUNDANCY PROCEDURES

The purpose of a redundancy procedure is to provide a mechanism for the redeployment of surplus employees arising from a closure of a workplace, its relocation or reorganization. Because of the legal requirement for management to consult employee representatives in advance of collective redundancies (involving 20 or more employees), the procedure should, wherever possible, be jointly agreed. Negotiations on the content of such agreements should, ideally, take place at a time when there is no immediate prospect of redundancies. The procedure should allow for consultation, objective selection of staff for redundancy and assistance with finding alternative work. The advantages of a redundancy procedure are that it helps to ensure fair treatment, enables employee representatives to influence the process and helps to minimize conflict and misunderstanding. However, although there is no legal obligation on employers to have a redundancy procedure, it makes good employee relations sense to have one, as in recent years few workplaces have escaped the redundancy experience. There is no ACAS Code of Practice, but ACAS has published an advisory booklet, *Redundancy Handling*,[16] which contains the main features of a redundancy procedure. The CIPD has published its own Guide on redundancy.

The content of a redundancy procedure

Preamble

It is conventional for the procedure to start with a statement explaining that it is the organization's preference in all circumstances to try to avoid redundancies.

If circumstances do arise where fewer workers are required, management will do everything they can to explore alternatives.

Consultation

Management is legally required to consult trade union representatives or their elected representatives where 20 or more employees are involved. Consultation must take place in good time, but in any event at least 30 days before the earliest dismissal takes place, where there are fewer than 100 employees involved, and at least 90 days where 100 or more employees are involved. Failure to comply with this legal requirement may lead to a complaint to a tribunal and a protective award equivalent to up to 90 days' pay for each employee. In addition, there are legal precedents to show that there is a requirement to consult individually as well as collectively. The purpose of the consultation is to enable management and employees to explore alternatives to compulsory redundancies. These might include: suspending replacements for leavers; reducing hours of work, including overtime; early retirement; redeployment elsewhere in the organization; and volunteers for redundancy.

Selection for redundancy

Where the circumstances constituting the redundancy apply equally to more than one employee doing the same work and some of those employees are retained, it is important that objective criteria are used for selecting those who stay and those who go. These criteria should be precise and unambiguous so that they can be consistently applied. Employees alleging unfair dismissal on the grounds of unfair selection for redundancy may make claims to tribunal.

Dismissals will be unfair where:

- the selection is in breach of a customary arrangement or agreed procedure, unless there are special reasons to justify departure from it;
- the selection is for a trade union reason;
- the selection is on grounds of the employee's gender, race or disability;
- the selection is because of, or connected to, the employee's maternity;
- the selection is related to health and safety, or the assertion of a statutory right.

The procedure should specify the agreed criteria to be used in selecting employees for redundancy. These may include the following:

- skills, qualifications and capability to do the job;
- length of service, for example 'last in first out' (LIFO), which is easily understood and applied; however, management may wish to retain discretion to modify such an arrangement in order to avoid losing people with key skills;

- type of work to be done after the redundancy operation and the employees' suitability to do it;
- attendance, but care must be taken in applying this criterion where the reason for poor attendance is connected to the employee's disability;
- disciplinary record.

In agreeing and applying criteria the employer should bear in mind the need to retain a balanced workforce after the redundancy. Specific skills, flexibility and adaptability are relevant criteria for determining who is to remain in the organization. The method most used by organizations in selecting redundant employees is to assess each by allocating a score under various factors. By totalling the scores the employer is able to select those for redundancy. Thus the employer may give credit, where appropriate, for factors such as service, skills, length of service etc. An agreement with employee representatives of the criteria, scores and their objective application will minimize the prospect of any successful unfair dismissal claim.

Detailed records of the selection process, including individual employees' scores, and the reasons for selection should be retained by the employer. The ACAS advisory booklet also advises that there should be an appeals procedure to deal with complaints from employees who feel that they have been unfairly selected.

Assistance with finding alternative work

The ACAS booklet advises that consideration be given to redeploying redundant employees elsewhere within the organization or with an associated employer. Tribunals have held that it is the responsibility of employers to show that they have considered such an option. An employee has a legal right to a trial period of four weeks in any alternative job offered, during which the right to claim redundancy, should they decide the alternative is unsuitable, continues.

Employees also have a statutory right to reasonable time off, with pay, to look for alternative work outside the organization, or to arrange training. It is also good employee relations practice to provide assistance in the form of counselling, coaching for job interviews and other preparation for alternative work.

FUTURE TRENDS AND DEVELOPMENTS

Employee relations procedures became a feature of the 1970s, encouraged by the Donovan Commission Report. The 1970s also witnessed a dramatic increase in formal disciplinary and dismissal procedures across British industry. Additionally, grievance, redundancy and health and safety procedures became prevalent as it became clear that tribunals and courts were prepared to judge employers' actions against procedural standards of fairness and consistency. This growth in the use of procedures took place during an era when the employee relations environment was characterized by industrial strife.

In contrast, the employee relations climate of the 1980s and 1990s saw a shift in the balance of power, where management's interests in business efficiency, competitiveness, labour flexibility and employee commitment – the 'hard' side of human resource management – superseded the 'soft' side, with its foundation in compromise, pluralism, procedural rules and regulations.

Nevertheless, a case can just as easily be made for procedural fairness in managing the employment relationship, which is consistent with either 'hard' or 'soft' human resource management. In its consultative document *Routes to Resolution: Improving Dispute Resolution in Britain*, the government made clear its preference for the use of procedures, indeed went further by setting out a case for compulsory use of grievance and disciplinary procedures as a prerequisite to hearings of complaints in tribunal, subsequently enacted in the Employment Act 2002. Research showed that fewer than half of employees who had experienced a problem at work had used a procedure. It also stated that the small employer was less likely to have a procedure and much more likely to be taken to tribunal as a result. Consequently the government's preference was to encourage employees to pursue their grievances in the workplace rather than go straight to tribunal. The document also showed that unionized workplaces were 'better at managing individual employment disputes', although the document fell short of suggesting that procedures should be the product of joint negotiation and agreement with employee representatives.

Two further developments should be mentioned. The first is the introduction of an alternative system for dealing with unfair dismissals claims. In May 2001 the Employment Rights (Alternative Disputes) Act 1998 was belatedly introduced. This provided for a bilaterally agreed arbitration alternative arranged by ACAS. Amongst the claimed advantages of such a system are:

- reduced workload on employment tribunals;
- reduced costs for the State – ACAS arbitration is cheaper than a tribunal hearing;
- a private hearing with no publicity;
- limited, if any, legalism;
- earlier resolution of individual disputes.

The system has no provision for an appeal, which some claim is a weakness and a breach of the Human Rights Act 1998. The scheme had a slow birth, with only one claim submitted during the first six months, although by the end of 2002 the number of cases had passed 20. However, at the time of writing it is not possible to make any firm assessment of its effectiveness. But if the scheme proves to be successful, and in particular reduces the volume of employment tribunal cases, no doubt the government would be tempted to expand the scope to include cases other than claims for unfair dismissal.

There can be no doubt that employee relations procedures are necessary and desirable in the workplace and that those who do not use them should be encouraged to do so. In most, if not all, circumstances a business case can be made for the use of procedures. Management can operate more effectively if the workforce is persuaded that procedures are fair and being operated fairly and consistently. The government's new proposals omit any suggestion that procedures should be jointly agreed between management and employee representatives and whether minimum standards, underwritten by ACAS Codes of Practice, should be the norm, as is the case with their Code of Practice on Disciplinary and Grievance Procedures. But it seems clear that the government is keen to foster a culture which encourages the use of procedures and where claims to tribunal are regarded as a last resort. This philosophy is underpinned by the concept of social partnership in the workplace.

Notes

1 Employment Act 2002, Schedule 2.
2 Royal Commission on Trade Unions and Employers' Associations (1968) Report, Cmnd 3623.
3 Employment Rights Act 1996 s.1.
4 Employment Relations Act 1999 s.10.
5 Ibid.
6 Ibid.
7 *Polkey v Dayton services Ltd* [1987] All ER 984 [1987].
8 *Williams v Compare Maxam Ltd* [1982] ICR 156.
9 *East Lindsey District Council v Daubney* [1977] ICR 566.
10 *International Sports Co Ltd v Thompson* [1980] IRLR 340.
11 Health and Safety at Work Act 1974 s.17.
12 Employment Relations Act 1999 s.10.
13 Ibid.
14 Ibid.
15 Employment Rights Act 1996 s.1.
16 ACAS Advisory Booklet No. 12.

References

ACAS (2000) *Code of Practice on Disciplinary and Grievance Procedures*, ACAS, London
ACAS (2000/2001) *Annual report 2000/2001*, ACAS, London
Cully, M, Woodland, S, O'Reilly, A, Dix, G, Millward, N, Bryson, A and Forth, J (1998) *The 1998 Workplace Employee Relations Survey: First Findings*, Department of Trade and Industry, London

Department of Trade and Industry (2001a) *Dispute Resolution in Britain – a background paper*, DTI, London, June

Department of Trade and Industry (2001b) *Routes to Resolution: Improving Dispute Resolution in Britain*, Consultative Document, para 3.21

Genn, H (1999) *Paths to Justice: What People Do and Think about Going to Law*, Hart Publishing, Oxford

Salamon, M (1998) *Industrial Relations: Theory and Practice*, Financial Times/Prentice Hall, Harlow

17

Pay and performance

Ian Kessler

INTRODUCTION

Pay remains one of the most potent techniques for the management of employee performance available to practitioners. While acknowledging that pay is just one form of reward alongside non-monetary extrinsic rewards such as fringe benefits and intrinsic rewards in the form, for instance, of 'interesting' and 'fulfilling' work, it nonetheless remains a central concern of most employees and a key pillar of the employment relationship. It is, however, this very potency and centrality that renders the relationship between pay and performance particularly problematic and uncertain. Thus, the importance of pay to employees is liable to lend a considerable degree of risk to managerial attempts to alter accepted and established pay–performance relationships, with demoralization and other dysfunctional organizational effects a potential outcome.

The 'double-edged' nature of the link between pay and performance has a number of related consequences for debate, understanding and practice in this key policy area. First, it has encouraged an ongoing and restless search for 'new' and 'improved' approaches to pay and performance as management seeks to resolve the dilemmas associated with pay's implicit power. Indicative of this pursuit of the 'holy pay grail' was a survey of US firms in the late 1950s which found that while 96 per cent of respondents considered their incentive pay system successful, almost 80 per cent of them were still seeking to change or modify it (Crandall, 1962).

Second, this search has often been informed by a powerful prescriptive literature playing to pay's potency in managing employee performance and presenting a myriad of techniques by which it might do so in more efficient and effective ways.

A 'flavour' of this literature is provided by Ashton (2000), who notes:

> Many variables interplay when accounting for corporate success. But the way in which individuals, groups or work populations are motivated, rewarded, recognized, fulfilled and challenged to perform better, has become a differentiator of growing importance between superior people performance or plain mediocrity – or, at least, it is a strategic issue of growing urgency.

Third, and reflecting a possible wariness on the part of management in the context of pay's potentially more disruptive face, care has been needed in assuming that rhetoric is reflected in practice. Despite an espoused pursuit of change and a goading prescriptive rhetoric, the take-up of new practices may well reflect a more hesitant managerial approach. In this respect not only does the take-up of techniques need to be firmly established but so do the ways in which they have operated. Thus, there is a well-developed research literature highlighting the discrepancy between the stated managerial intentions underpinning formal performance pay techniques and the practice, which suggests that they have been subverted by various stakeholders – line managers, employees and unions – in support of their own distinctive interests.

Recent developments in the link between pay and performance have been characterized by this familiar and ongoing search for novel techniques accompanied by a supportive rhetoric but with some uncertainty over actual practice. The purpose of this chapter is to explore this emerging rhetoric, together with its associated techniques and their application or non-application. In so doing, the chapter is designed to provide technical insights into the design, implementation and operation of 'new' approaches to pay and performance. In focusing on the extent to which 'new' practices have been adopted, it also seeks to cast some light on the nature and process of change and, more specifically, on the factors that might facilitate, hinder and shape attempts to relate pay more meaningfully to performance.

The chapter is divided into four main parts. The first seeks to classify the ways in which pay has been linked to, and used, to manage performance. The second draws upon this classification to evaluate the emergence of a new pay rhetoric. The third assesses evidence on the development of pay and performance practices and the last draws some conclusions about the managerial strengths and weaknesses of new approaches to pay.

CLASSIFYING APPROACHES TO PAY

The relationship between pay and performance is principally institutionalized through the development of pay systems and structures. These systems and structures link pay determination in terms of level and progression to certain criteria as a means of encouraging and eliciting 'desired' attitudes and behaviours. 'Performance' is pivotal to attempts to classify such pay systems and structures in a dual sense. As a means, 'performance', variously defined, remains one amongst a number of criteria used to determine pay. As an end, the management of employee 'performance', again variously defined, is a central purpose of any pay scheme. This section seeks to classify pay systems and structures, drawing on notions of performance in both senses.

In general, the determination of pay is linked to the three enduring and often complementary contingencies (Mahoney, 1989):

- job;
- person;
- performance.

Job

The job, viewed as a stable configuration of organizational activities and responsibilities, has traditionally formed the building block for the development of pay and grading structures. Such structures have essentially been concerned with establishing job worth, drawing on notions of internal and external equity.

Internal equity is the starting point for the establishment of job worth, with job evaluation the mechanism often used to establish it. Job evaluation (Armstrong and Baron, 1995) is concerned with job size, not with the performance of the individual in the job. It seeks to evaluate job size not according to any absolute standards but in relation to other jobs within the organization. The process of evaluation can never be completely objective, with personal judgements and subjectivity inevitably creeping in. However, it is designed to be a structured and systematic process involving the consistent and transparent application of a given set of rules. Moreover, the degree of subjectivity will vary according to the particular job evaluation technique used. Non-analytical schemes such as job ranking, paired comparisons and job classification are founded on whole-job comparisons and tend to be less formal and less structured in their application than analytical schemes, including factor comparison and point factor rating plans involving the unpacking of jobs according to defined characteristics and their assessment against established scales. The use of these different techniques has broader implications. Thus, non-analytical schemes are unlikely to be an effective defence again claims of equal pay for work of equal value.

The clustering of similarly weighted jobs provides the basis for a hierarchy of grades and it is at this point that notions of external equity come into play. Organizations need to establish the actual rates of pay which different grades attract. This involves ascertaining external market rates, a process which can be simplified where proprietary consultant-designed job evaluation schemes have been used, allowing for comparison with similarly weighted jobs elsewhere, and making a decision as to how internal rates relate to them. Will the organization position itself as a high, average or low payer within the national, regional or occupational labour market?

This process of internally weighting and then externally comparing jobs is not without its tensions. Organizations may well be faced with a situation where jobs weighted similarly in internal terms are subject to very different external labour market pressures demanding different rates of pay to attract and retain them. In these circumstances a choice must be made between internal and external equity. It would be fair to suggest that organizations have often been tempted more to respond to external labour market need than internal considerations, despite the fact that internal comparisons often have a more powerful effect on employee attitudes and behaviours. As Brown and Walsh (1989) note: 'Individuals appear to take comparisons more seriously when they are with those close to them... Consequently, employees tend to be far more upset if pay differentials deteriorate between themselves and others in their own department than if a similar deterioration occurs with respect to their company directors, or another company altogether'.

Person and performance

Pay progression related to movement within grades and more general uprating of pay rates has usually been driven by the other two pay contingencies distinguished – person and performance. Pay has been linked to various personal characteristics, primarily in the form of inputs. In other words, pay has been based upon what the employee personally brings to the workplace and the job. Simple personal presence has been the foundation for traditionally the most common system – time-based pay. Pay linked to an hourly, daily, weekly or annual rate has rewarded employees for guaranteed presence for a given period of time. Naturally, such an approach necessitates the use of various other managerial techniques to incentivize and directly motivate staff, but time-based pay has the virtue of being easy to administer and comprehensible, with low maintenance and operating costs. Moreover, given employee sensitivity to the uncertainties associated with variable pay, time-based pay might be seen as the best way of providing stability and predictability which, if not directly motivating employees, is at the very least unlikely to cause discontent, disruption and demotivation. Pay can also be linked to presence across time, with progression being based upon age and length of service. These criteria overlap with job-based pay and indeed performance in that the employee is assumed to bring greater experience to the job role and by implication carry it out more efficiently and effectively.

Alongside time, other personal characteristics can and have been used for pay determination processes, including qualifications and skills as well as competence, attitudinal and behavioural traits.

The relationship between pay and performance is based more on outputs with the need to distinguish between individual and group outputs or performance. Pay can be related to individual outputs in the form of sales (commission), units of production (piecework) and objectives (individual performance-related pay (IPRP)). The relationship between pay and the group depends very much on the nature of the group. Thus the workgroup, whether in terms of production cell, section or department, can form the basis for team-based pay while the group in the broader sense of the enterprise or the company provides the foundation for profit sharing, gain sharing and some forms of employee share ownership scheme.

Pay systems and structures based upon person and performance can further be distinguished along two cross-cutting dimensions. The first relates to the nature of the link between pay and these contingencies and more specifically whether it is a mechanistic or an appraised link. Certain systems, most obviously those related to age and seniority, but also those based upon a number of the performance measures such as commission, piecework and profit and gain sharing, are driven by certain formulae which tend to trigger pay increases. This is not to deny that such measures are open to manipulation by various parties but, at least in a formal sense, they operate in a relatively autonomous and self-regulating manner. Other systems rely much more upon a less precise, more discretionary and, in some cases, negotiated process of appraisal. Such evaluation tends to inform the use of certain personal characteristics such as competence, behaviour and attitudes as well as many forms of individual performance-related pay.

The second cross-cutting dimension is associated with the form of payment. More specifically, schemes vary according to whether pay linked to person or performance is consolidated and therefore recurring or non-consolidated and therefore non-recurring. Non-consolidated increases are labelled as bonuses and naturally have very different implications for future pay bill costs in comparison with consolidated increases.

PRESSURES, ISSUES AND A NEW PAY AGENDA

Traditional approaches

The relationship between pay, job, person and performance has assumed a variety of forms over time and space, reflecting shifting societal and organizational needs and more entrenched differences in the structure and character of regions, industries and occupations. Any attempt to generalize about this relationship must therefore be approached with some care. However, it is possible to discern some broad patterns which suggest that a traditional range of pay principles and practices has been subjected to recent pressures giving rise to a new set of prescriptions.

Traditionally, the managerial aims underpinning pay systems and structures were captured by the familiar 'mantra' of recruit, retain and motivate. This fed through to influence the links between pay, job, person and performance in various ways. In terms of pay and job, considerable emphasis was placed on external equity, with payment of the 'going rate', particularly for blue-collar workers. For white-collar staff and especially for organizations seeking to develop internal labour markets, internal equity played a more important role, reflected in the use of job evaluation. Indeed, job evaluation was based on fairly narrow and detailed job descriptions and, mirroring hierarchical organizational structures, on a significant number of grades or levels providing promotion opportunities. The personal characteristics valued in this context were largely those related to seniority, experience and to some extent qualification. Thus, for staff workers in particular, annual grade increments up to the scale maximum were fairly common. Where performance entered the pay equation it was largely driven by the individual or output measures. For manual workers, this emphasis on outputs was seen in the extensive use of piecework systems across whole swathes of British manufacturing industry in the 1950s and '60s, while for white-collar staff individual performance-related pay based primarily on the achievement of individual objectives or targets assumed prominence in the mid-to-late 1980s.

Over the past decade or so, this traditional pattern or model has been confronted with a number of pressures challenging its ongoing value and viability. The first set of pressures has related to organizational developments. Changes in organizational design with the growth of 'flattened' or 'de-layered' structures has inevitably had implications for extended grading schemes and movement through and up them as a form of reward. In addition, however, changes in job design with the search for greater task flexibility, often in the context of team working, have raised questions about the viability of tight and detailed job descriptions as the basis for grades. The second range of pressures has been institutional and related, in particular, to changes in the industrial relations landscape. Trade unions have always been a force for the preservation of established grading structures based on notions of internal equity (Rubery, 1997). The general decline of union membership and the consequent reduction in the coverage of collective bargaining has rendered such structures much more vulnerable to unilateral management change. A final set of factors can be viewed as managerially driven. These have reflected the need for responses to increasing and intensified competition and the search for ways in which pay might be used to leverage employee skills, attitudes and behaviours as a response.

These pressures have given rise to a new set of prescriptions often presented under the heading of the 'New Pay'. Initially driven by US commentators (Lawler, 1995; Schuster and Zingheim, 1992) but increasingly reflected in UK debates on pay and performance (Ashton, 2000; Brown and Armstrong, 1999; Armstrong and Brown, 2001), this set of prescriptions has taken the form of both a general approach informed by certain principles and values, and a range of practices which reconfigure the relationship between pay, job, person and performance.

A strategic approach

The new approach to pay is based on a shift away from what might be viewed as the rather narrow pay aims of recruitment, retention and motivation to a concentration on the way in which pay can be used as a strategic lever. The nature of this approach and its implications for more traditional principles are reflected in Gomez-Mejia's (1993) observation that: 'The emerging paradigm of the field is based on a strategic orientation where issues of internal equity and external equity are viewed as secondary to the firm's need to use pay as an essential integrating and signalling mechanism to achieve overarching business objectives.'

The identification of pay as a key strategic lever begs questions about the ways in which it can be used in a strategic sense. Drawing upon the broader employment relations literature, two distinct approaches to the strategic use of pay can be distinguished. The first is based upon a *high-commitment approach*, which suggests that there are certain universalistic pay practices which alone, or more often in combination with a bundle of other specified human resources management practices, are likely to elicit improved employee and organizational performance. The pay practices most commonly cited in this context are those which link pay to company performance in the form of profit sharing, gain sharing or employee ownership (Cully *et al*, 1999; MacDuffie, 1995; Pfeffer, 1998; Walton, 1998). However, there is no general agreement on what constitutes a high-commitment pay practice (Wood, 1996), with some commentators and researchers including individual performance-related pay, team pay and skills-based pay (Roach, 1999; MacDuffie, 1995).

This difference of view may well derive from the uncertainties and debates surrounding the impact of various pay practices on individual and organizational performance. A number of studies have suggested that high-commitment practices, variously defined, are positively related to different measures of company performance. Moreover, research on the impact of specific pay systems such as profit and gain sharing schemes has similarly shown a beneficial relationship with corporate outputs (Kruse and Weitzman, 1990). Such research still, however, leaves scope for interpretation. Are high-performing companies best able and more willing to introduce profit and gain sharing or do these schemes help create high-performing companies?

This debate on the relationship between pay practices and employee attitude and behaviours in the context of the high-commitment approach has emerged in its fiercest form in relation to individual performance-related and merit pay schemes. Some commentators have argued that such schemes should be viewed as high-commitment practices, 'locking' the individual into the organization and ensuring a close relationship between personal and corporate objectives (Storey, 1992). Others have been more critical, suggesting that individual incentives are more likely to disrupt the employment–management relationship, encouraging a transactional or instrumental attachment rather than a relational or emotive one (Kohn, 1993).

Certainly, a range of studies have catalogued the operational difficulties associated with individual performance-related and merit pay schemes, highlighting, in particular, the problems faced in setting 'objective' targets, in avoiding subjectivity in appraisals and in relating performance ratings to meaningful pay increases. However, an authoritative overview or meta analysis (Jenkins et al, 1998) of some 50 US studies undertaken over the past 30 years, on the impact of individually based financial incentives on hard, as opposed to softer, self-report, outcomes, concludes that such incentives are positively related to performance in terms of quantity of output, although significantly they are not associated with performance quality.

Of course, these findings still leave open the issue of whether such improved performance derives from attitudinal restructuring, with the emergence of greater organizational commitment on the part of employees, or from more direct behavioural compliance encouraged by such incentives. In one of the few studies which has attempted to link forms of individual pay to organizational commitment, Gallie et al (1998) found that a control system based on performance management principles including individual appraisal, merit pay and internal career structures was more likely to establish such commitment than one based on short repetitive tasks and incentives. However, this relationship was found to hold only for employees in the 'commercial sector'. This suggests that such performance-based control systems may be more appropriate to some types of workers than others, implying a degree of contingency at odds with the universalistic prescriptions of the high-commitment model.

It is this notion of contingency that plays a central part in the second approach to the strategic use of pay. In line with a broader *'fit' approach* to strategic human resource management, the efficient and effective deployment of pay has been seen to lie in relating it to the different organizational needs and circumstances. In this context, there is a perceived requirement for pay to 'fit' in three important senses:

- *Vertical fit*: pay needs to align with the broader business strategy. The presentation of this type of fit has assumed its most influential form in Schuler and Jackson's (1987) behavioural model. This suggests that competitive strategies based on cost reduction, quality enhancement and innovation require different behaviours and, as a consequence, different pay practices to generate and nurture them.

- *Horizontal fit*: pay needs to be aligned with other human resource practices. In other words, pay needs be compatible with, and supportive of, other employment relations techniques in furthering business objectives.
- *Internal fit*: pay needs to be aligned with other rewards. Thus, pay needs to complement and operate in ways which are in tune with other forms of benefit.

This 'fit' approach to pay implicitly draws upon a well-established contingency approach developed by Lupton and Gowler (1969) more than 30 years ago. Much more broadly drawn than the strategic human resource management alignment model, this contingency framework proposes that the selection of a payment system needs to be based on responses to three basic questions:

- What are the organization's pay objectives?
- What payment system helps further those objectives?
- Is the payment system 'right' for the organization, given its character and circumstances?

As already implied, pay can be used to pursue a wide range of managerial objectives which relate more or less directly to employee performance. It can be used to foster certain attitudes, such as organizational loyalty, team spirit, motivation, pride, and entrepreneurialism. It can be mobilized to encourage a range of behaviours, including individual performance in terms of quantity and quality of output, creativity, task flexibility, and coming to as well as staying with the organization. It can be informed by certain procedural or administrative aims such as comprehensibility, predictability and fairness or justice. Finally, it might underpin organizational change goals associated with drives to develop new organizational cultures through the establishment of new values and beliefs.

Given this range of goals, management needs to be clear what it is seeking to achieve through pay. There is often a temptation to use pay to address too wide a range of goals, sometimes to the neglect of other equally or more effective personnel techniques. This is reflected in the fact that companies commonly use an array of pay practices to encourage different attitudes and behaviours: organizational commitment through profit sharing; team spirit through group bonuses; and individual performance through merit pay. Yet, the employees may become confused about these linkages or simply be unconcerned, looking more at the bottom line of their pay slip rather than at the elements that go to make it up. Partly related to the pursuit of too many aims is the danger that different goals informing a given company's pay approach may be in tension with one another. Management may, for example, be seeking to establish a strong corporate spirit while at the same undermining this by rewarding 'high flying' employees through its individual performance-related pay scheme.

Having identified the goals it is seeking to pursue through pay, the organization's next step is to consider the payment system best able to achieve them. It is certainly the case that any given payment system might be used to pursue very different objectives. For example, profit sharing could be used as a tax-efficient way of rewarding employees, given the tax benefits associated with certain approved schemes, or, more ambitiously, as a means of encouraging greater employee loyalty to the company. It is certainly the case, however, that particular payment systems have often been associated with specific goals. Thus, piecework is a way of increasing volume output, while commission has been regarded as a means of driving up sales. Employee share ownership and profit sharing schemes are ways of eliciting greater employee commitment, with group pay supporting team working.

The alignment between management goals and appropriate payment systems must finally confront the issue of whether the pay scheme is 'right' for the organization. The 'rightness' of a scheme can be linked to three related sets of factors. The first concerns the organization's technology. It would clearly be inappropriate to use a pay system based on individual performance if the employee had no control over production output, as would be the case, for instance, in a continuous process production industry like electricity generation. On the other hand, there are industries whose technology does appear to lend itself to a particular payment system. Thus, in the footwear and garment industry, piecework has continued as the predominant form of pay system over many years and up until the present (Undy, Kessler and Thompson, 1999).

The second set of contingent factors is associated with the nature of the work. More specifically, the viability of a given pay scheme may be linked to the type of workers employed. For example, individual performance-related pay has often been seen as problematic for those in caring occupations such as nurses and teachers where *meaningful* personal objectives are difficult to find. This is not to deny attempts to establish such schemes for these workers, as the British government's plans for the latter group confirm; it is, however, to question their wisdom.

The final set of circumstances relates to culture in a number of senses. It may well be that a particular payment system, while effectively supporting a given management goal, is simply unsuitable in a given organizational culture. In other words, it is at odds with established corporate or workplace beliefs and values. For instance, when individual performance-related pay was first introduced into the civil service, an organization with a strong collective ethos, those receiving merit payments would often pool them as a means of supporting group or office-based activities, say a 'night out on the town' for everybody. This sensitivity to organizational culture naturally presents management with a dilemma. To what extent should pay drive culture change or reflect the culture prevailing? There are examples of organizations using pay in both ways (Kessler, 1994), although, as we shall see, evidence suggests that management is more inclined towards the latter option.

A concern with national culture might also affect the viability of a particular payment system. Individual performance-related pay is often seen as in tune more with the Anglo-American individualist values than the collectivist values of many Asian countries. Although there have been some noteworthy moves towards individual pay in Japan, team bonuses have traditionally been the main form of variable pay in that country (Sako and Sato, 1997).

The 'New Pay' agenda has therefore been associated with a strategic approach to pay in a 'high commitment' or contingent sense. It has also been related to a number of more specific pay practices.

New pay practices

The recent prescriptive literature has increasingly highlighted three main pay practices:

- broad banding;
- skill and competency-based pay;
- team pay.

Each in turn represents a re-evaluation of the traditional relationship between pay and job, person and performance.

Broad banding involves collapsing a multitude of narrow grades to create a smaller number of extended scales naturally subsuming these previous grades and capturing a wider range of occupational groups and employees. These broad bands often function on the basis of simple minimum and maximum pay rates, sometimes with a single midpoint, replacing standard annual increments. While job evaluation often continues to underpin broad banded structures, ensuring some consistency in, and justification for, the new arrangement, this approach is seen to address some of the limitations associated with more traditional approaches to pay and job. The broader bands allocate individuals to jobs and roles on the basis of less detailed, more generic job descriptions, reducing related administration, but, more importantly, ensuring greater flexibility in the use of staff. Moreover, the higher pay ceilings of such bands provide more scope for employees to be rewarded as they develop or grow in their jobs without the need for promotion. Broad bands still have to position and progress individuals. In this respect, and more generally in relation to the development of pay systems, increasing attention has been paid to systems of reward which are based upon input-based performance. This type of performance is more closely linked to the person in the form of skills and/or competencies, at the expense of output-based individual performance-related schemes.

Skills focus on practical abilities and expertise, often associated with certain specialist bodies of knowledge. Competencies, in contrast, are underlying behavioural and attitudinal characteristics or traits required to carry out a particular job effectively. In the pay context, competencies and skills can be used in two main ways. First, they can be built into job evaluation, providing a new dimension to this process which measures *how* jobs are undertaken, so complementing the more traditional focus on *what* tasks and responsibilities they involve. Second, they can be used to determine, wholly or in part, individual pay increases. This is a more person-driven usage, with employee progression tied to the achievement or acquisition of certain skills and competencies.

The use of skills and competencies in this way allows individuals to be rewarded as they develop within the job in the absence of avenues of promotion. In other words, increased pay can be achieved through a deepening of skills and competencies within a job rather than by moving upwards in the organization to a 'larger' and perhaps different job. Moreover, in the context of rapidly changing work requirements and the emphasis on empowerment, a link between pay and ways of working may be more appropriate than a link between pay and the achievement of narrow and rigid performance targets.

The redefinition of the job, person and pay link in terms of competency and skill has been accompanied by calls for a pay–performance link with the group rather than individual outcomes. This has partly been reflected in the attention given to employee share ownership schemes, especially in the form of stock options and particularly as a means of attracting and retaining 'talent' in start-up companies. However, it has also been manifest in calls for pay to be linked to team performance, in tune more with developments in job design with the emergence of team working. Highlighting this interest, Armstrong (1996) states:

> The significant part that teamwork plays in achieving organizational success has directed attention towards how employee reward systems can contribute to team effectiveness. The focus is now shifting away from individual performance-related pay which has conspicuously failed to deliver results in many instances, and towards team pay and other methods of rewarding the whole team.

Certainly team-based pay has a number of attractions. It fosters cooperative behaviour within groups, while also acting as a mechanism for managerial control by encouraging peer pressures to ensure standard performance at a high level.

These new pay practices, therefore, have assumed prominence within the prescriptive literature on the basis of some fairly persuasive arguments. They seem to be in accord with, and sensitive to, contextual developments in organization and job design, the nature of competition and requisite employee attitudes and behaviours. In the face of such a powerful literature, attention now turns to corporate approaches and whether such prescriptions have actually been adopted.

PAY APPROACHES IN ACTION:
EXAMPLES, TRENDS AND LESSONS

Take-up of new approaches: the evidence

There are a number of high-profile examples of change in approaches to pay and performance along the lines suggested by the prescriptive literature. However, care is needed in assuming that such high-profile examples reflect a broader trend. Indeed, the general pattern is one of low take-up of the newer pay practices. This is not to deny change, but the evidence suggests that where this change is taking place it is more in terms of 'fine tuning' established systems and structures rather than in radically overhauling them. This section looks in greater detail at the evidence on new approaches to pay.

There are a number of instances where pay can be interpreted and has been seen by the organizational protagonists as being used in an explicitly strategic way. Drawing upon the distinctions made earlier, these case study examples have usually presented pay as strategic in terms of vertical fit; in other words, as supporting new business strategies or ways of competing more efficiently and effectively. Brown and Armstrong (1999) cite the example of dealers of a European car company who sought to move 'upmarket' and become more customer driven, and in so doing increase repeat business. As a means of encouraging the employee behaviours and attitudes needed to support such an approach, they moved from low base pay and high individual commission to high base pay linked to pay progression through the acquisition of competencies. In a more general sense, it is also interesting to note that many of the more radical developments in approaches to pay have been amongst companies in the finance sector (Lewis, 1998) forced by deregulation to compete in new ways by also becoming more customer focused.

It is debatable, however, whether this strategic approach is widespread. A recent Industrial Society survey (Industrial Society, 1997) of 300 UK organizations certainly found that almost three-quarters of the companies had formal written reward strategies, but under a half of these agreed that such strategies were efficiently linked to HR strategy and with just over a half feeling that they met business needs effectively. Most striking, however, was the fact that under half of the surveyed organizations felt their employees understood their company's reward strategy.

The take-up of new pay practices can also be illustrated by reference to a number of high-profile examples. Broad banding, for instance, was recently introduced at RoMec, the facilities services division of the Post Office (Industrial Relations Review and Report, 2000). Driven by the search for greater flexibility in rewarding employees and the need to facilitate a move to a flatter organization structure, RoMec managers moved from five incremental pay grades to four pay bands. These bands were tied to certain job roles – strategic management, tactical direction, tactical management and operational management – each band being based upon a minimum salary level and open-ended progression. This structure also overlaps with an interest in competencies. The bands were founded upon competency-based job descriptions, while progression within the band was linked to the acquisition and deployment of specified competencies.

An example of a pay scheme more directly linked to a competency-based approach was one introduced for store managers in Adams (IRRR, PBB, 1999), the children's wear retailer. Seeking to provide managers with a clearer understanding of their roles and a stronger link between reward and performance, the company developed two sets of competencies around personal effectiveness and business management. Pay increases between grade minima and maxima were directly tied to the achievement of a given level of competency.

Finally, there are instances of organizations seeking to introduce team pay. One such case focuses on store staff in Tesco Express (IDS Studies, 2001). Given the fact that these stores were somewhat smaller than the Tesco supermarkets, management felt there was an opportunity to use pay to develop a 'strong team culture'. The scheme links pay to targets, set by area managers in consultation with the store's site managers, related to four dimensions of store performance: shop sales, recorded costs, unrecorded stock loss and customer service. Each factor contributes 5 per cent to the total bonus pay-out, with actual bonus pay-out running at between 10 and 20 per cent of salary.

These examples of organizations adopting some of the newer pay practices provide useful information on how such practices might be developed and used. However, it remains important to place such cases in perspective. Evidence on broader developments suggests that these instances are exceptions rather than the rule. The incidence of broad banding is limited. A Wyatt survey of 346 organizations found that only 20 per cent had broad banding (quoted in Market Tracking International, 1996). An Industrial Society survey of pay structures (1997) suggested a higher figure of a third, but this is still well short of what might be viewed as extensive use.

The deployment of team and competency-based pay appears to be even less common. A number of surveys have highlighted the low take-up of both techniques. This trend is most forcefully reflected in the findings from the largest of such surveys conducted by the then Institute of Personnel and Development (now Chartered IPD) of 1,158 organizations with a combined workforce of around 1.5 million (IPD, 1998). Some of the findings are set out in Table 17.1.

This table is of interest in a number of respects. First, it cautions against overstating the presence of variable pay amongst British organizations. While individual performance-related pay and profit sharing are present in a significant minority of workplaces, the table indicates that even these systems are absent in around two-thirds of organizations. Second, it suggests that pay practices between managers and 'other' employees are fairly similar. Thus,

Table 17.1 Organizations that do not have performance pay·

	For managers (%)	For others (%)
Individual	60	75
Team	92	92
Skill/competency	94	89
Profit sharing	65	66
Shares	83	85

Source: IPD Survey (1998) quoted in IDS Focus, 1998

with the exception of IPRP, which is markedly more common for managers, other practices seem to be used or not used in similar ways across these two groups. More pertinent in the context of the current discussion on new pay practices, the IPD survey suggests that well under 10 per cent of organizations are using team-based or skill/competency-based pay for either managers or 'other' employees.

The doubts raised about the strategic use of pay and the stronger evidence suggesting a low take-up of the new pay practices highlighted in the prescriptive literature should not obscure the fact that important changes are taking place in organizational approaches to pay. However, as implied, these changes are incremental, involving a process of modification rather than a fundamental shift in direction.

This more gradualist approach to change is reflected in developments as they relate to the relationship between pay and job. For example, it is clear that many organizations are 'fine-tuning' their grading structures. An Industrial Relations Services survey (1998, quoted in IDS Focus, 1998) indicated that 55 per cent of the 80 organizations covered had altered their grading structure in the last five years. In most cases these alterations involved a simplification of the grading with a reduction in the number of grades. Examples of such simplification include Mercedes Benz (UK), Scottish Nuclear and Barclays Commercial Services. Incremental change is also apparent in relation to performance pay. Thus the IPD pay survey found that 40 per cent of the organizations it covered had modified their performance pay system, with almost three-quarters of these suggesting that the changes were 'moderate' and only a quarter that they were 'radical'. It is a finding confirmed in an Incomes Data Service survey (2000/2001) which found that just over a half of its organizations had modified the performance criteria used in their individual performance pay systems. This survey also found that the distribution of awards had been changing, with employers tending to be more selective, a consequence perhaps of the perceived need to target money on high performers in the context of tight pay budgets. It was also apparent that performance payments were increasingly taking the form of non-consolidated bonuses, thus limiting the organization's ongoing cost commitment.

Understanding developments

The developments in organizational approaches to pay and performance highlighted in this discussion, characterized by low take-up of new practices but considerable modification of established ones, beg important questions about the nature and process of change in relation to pay. What explains this pattern? Why have new practices been generally shunned? Why has change been incremental rather than radical? What lessons can be learned from the nature and process of change about the future design, implementation and operation of new approaches to pay?

The low take-up of new pay practices may well reflect design and operational difficulties. New approaches are often presented as a means of dealing with problems associated with prevailing systems and have superficial attraction as a consequence. Thus team pay has been seen as a way of dealing with the detrimental consequences of individual performance pay on work-group cooperation and cohesion, while competency-based pay has been viewed as a way of addressing the 'tunnel vision' effects of IPRP's focus on output targets. However, closer attention to the technical details associated with new practices reveals major complexities, which inhibit their use. Table 17.2 sets out some of these technical difficulties. Drawing selectively from this table, it is clear that team-based pay raises difficulties which relate to defining the team and identifying targets for, and standards of, team performance to be used for pay purposes. Competency pay poses challenges that revolve around distinguishing relevant competencies and then evaluating them. Broad banding generates problems linked to transparency and predictability in pay progression.

Table 17.2 Strengths and weaknesses of new pay techniques

New technique	Strengths	Weaknesses
Broad banding	flexibility higher ceilings absorbing market pressures	lack of transparency unpredictability criteria for progression
Team pay	in tune with job design encourages cooperation peer pressures fairness	finding performance standards temporary teams defining teams
Competence pay	rewards 'how', not just 'what' more transparent scope for development	defining a competence measuring a competence management skills

While the difficulties associated with the new pay practices relate to the substance of change, the incremental approach to change adopted by organizations more profoundly points to the complexities surrounding the process of change. Indeed, this gradualism emphasizes the fact that the decision-making process as it relates to pay is highly problematic. As suggested at the outset, pay strikes at the heart of the employment relationship and, partly as a consequence, the interests of a wide range of organizational actors are affected by any attempt to alter associated systems and structures. Clearly, most immediately affected are employees and there is evidence to suggest that the incremental pace of change reflects organizational concern about the possible consequence of unleashing employee discontent. On the basis of research into pay developments in a number of major industries, Arrowsmith and Sisson (1999) conclude that 'organizations had made simple and straight-forward changes (to their pay systems). The next step needed to put them into effect were of a different order of magnitude, making them especially daunting, and potentially involving costs in terms of employee commitment.'

Radical change to pay systems is difficult and, partly as a consequence, might be seen as undesirable in two further senses. First, such change may be seen as undesirable simply because established pay practices are seen to be working efficiently and effectively. There are strong grounds for suggesting that the success of a pay system depends on its becoming fully embedded in the organization which, by definition, takes many years. One of the payment systems commonly cited as a key organizational resource, the piecework system at Lincoln Electric, the manufacturer of arc welding products, was introduced almost a hundred years ago in 1914. The importance of continuity in the development of a successful pay system can readily be accounted for by the contribution made by longevity to the development of trust amongst employees in the operation of the system. It is only over time that employees come to accept a pay scheme. Only time will tell whether a scheme operates in ways that ensure fairness in both distributive and procedural terms.

Rapid change may also be difficult and undesirable because an established pay system becomes normatively enshrined. While the Lincoln Electric example highlights continuity on economically rational grounds, with the established pay scheme contributing to organizational profitability, a normative perspective suggests that pay practices may well be retained on less rational grounds associated with social and political considerations. For example, the continuation of a pay scheme may reflect the articulation or rein-forcement of certain political norms as it becomes associated with particular interest groups and used to pursue their sectional objectives. It may simply become a social norm, with inertia encouraging the establishment of pay practice as an 'organizational habit' long after the original rationale for such practice has been forgotten. Indeed, pay practice may also assume symbolic significance as pay comes to represent important organizational values or beliefs. Ahlstrand (1990) illustrates the power of these normative factors in his study of productivity pay agreements at Esso's oil refinery at Fawley. He finds that such agreements continued to be negotiated over the years not because they were contributing to the refinery's economic performance but because they had assumed symbolic significance, acting as a signalling device to various stakeholders that management was taking firm action to deal with broader organizational problems.

The complexities surrounding pay-related change highlight the need for organizations to give as much attention to process as to substance. Indeed, some commentators suggest that the effectiveness of any pay initiative lies less in what you do than how you do it. There is a considerable degree of consensus that the process of pay design and implementation should rest on two features: inclusiveness and communication. ACAS, for example, places considerable weight on involving and informing employees in its guidance on pay systems, appraisal-related pay and job evaluation (ACAS, 1988, 1990). In general guidance on the development of payment systems it notes:

> Where trade unions are recognized the final form of a new payment system is normally settled around the negotiating table. But management should not wait until that stage before involving employees and their representatives in the process of installing the new systems; the earlier they are informed of any management proposals and their views sought the better. (ACAS, 2000)

SUMMARY AND CONCLUSIONS

This chapter has argued that while pay remains a key lever for managing employee performance, it is a lever which needs to be handled with considerable care. Its centrality to the employment relationship encourages pay to be used to pursue a range of managerial objectives, but this very centrality also gives it the power to disrupt. It is the danger inherent in the use of pay which cautions against the ready acceptance of easy prescriptions. Certainly, there is a growing prescriptive pay literature calling for a more strategic approach to pay and for the take-up of practices which relate pay to job, person and performance in new ways. This literature is not without merit or empirical support. It seeks to develop approaches to pay that reflect very real changes in organization and job design as well as in competitive conditions. Research has shown that certain high-commitment pay practices are positively linked to aspects of employee and organizational performance. The 'fit' literature provides sound advice on the need for clarity in what organizations are seeking to achieve in pay terms and the circumstances in which these goals and their related pay schemes might be appropriate. Moreover, there are high-profile examples of organizations which have sought to adopt the new pay practices distinguished – broad banding, competency pay and team pay.

However, despite this evidence and these examples, the general pattern remains one of low take-up and incremental change. Such a pattern suggests technical problems with the new pay practices, but more profoundly process difficulties. Pay will always remain deeply embedded in a web of social and political rules developed by organizational stakeholders with a keen interest in how it operates. As a consequence, change, particularly of a rapid and radical kind, will always be difficult and problematic. Recognition of these complexities highlights the need for management to focus as much on how change is introduced as on what that change looks like. Indeed, given pay's ability to excite groups with competing interests, there are strong grounds for supporting calls for an inclusive approach to the design, implementation and operation of pay schemes.

References

ACAS (1988) *Job Evaluation*, Advisory Booklet 1, ACAS, London
ACAS (1990) *Appraisal Related pay*, Advisory Booklet 14, ACAS, London
ACAS (2000) *Introduction to Payment Systems*, Advisory Booklet No. 21, ACAS, London
Ahlstrand, B (1990) *The Quest for Productivity*, Cambridge University Press, Cambridge
Armstrong, M (1996) How group efforts pay dividends, *People Management*, **25**, January, pp 22–27
Armstrong, M and Baron, A (1995) *The Job Evaluation Handbook*, IPD, London
Armstrong, M and Brown, D (2001) *New Dimensions in Pay Management*, CIPD, London
Arrowsmith, J and Sisson, K (1999) Pay and working time: Towards organization based arrangements? *British Journal of Industrial Relations*, **37** (1), pp 51–75
Ashton, C (2000) *Strategic Compensation*, Business Intelligence, London
Brown, D and Armstrong, M (1999) *Pay for Contribution*, Kogan Page, London
Brown, W and Walsh, J (1989) Managing Remuneration, in *Personnel Management in Britain*, (ed) K Sisson, Blackwell, Oxford, p 253
Crandall, R (1962) De-emphasized wage incentives, *Harvard Business Review*, **4** (2), pp 110–15
Cully, M, Woodland, S, O'Reilly, A and Dix, G (1999) *Britain at Work*, Routledge, London
Gallie, D, White, M, Cheng, Y and Tomlinson, M (1998) *Restructuring the Employment Relationship*, Oxford University Press, Oxford
Gomez-Mejia, L (1993) *Compensation, Organization Strategy and Firm Performance*, Southwestern, San Francisco, p 121
IDS Focus (1998) *Pay: The Test of Time*, IDS, London, pp 3–14
IDS Focus (2000/2001) *Performance Pay*, Winter, IDS, London
IDS Studies (2000) *Job Evaluation*, Autumn
IDS Studies (2001) *Bonus Schemes*, IDS, London, pp 8–10
Industrial Relations Review and Report (IRRR), Pay and Benefits Bulletin (PBB), (2000) No 494 *Broadbanding Delivers Change at the Post Office*, IRS, pp 2–6

Industrial Society (1997) *Pay Structures*, Industrial Society, London
Industrial Society (1997) *Reward Strategies*, Industrial Society, London
IPD (1998) *Performance Pay Survey*, IPD, London
IRRR, Employment Trends (1996) No 600, *Reviewing and Revising Grading Structures*, IRS, pp 7–13
IRRR, PBB (1999) No. 480, *Retail Rewards: Competency based Pay at Adams*, IRS, pp 2–6
Jenkins, G, Gupta, N, Mitra, A and Shaw, J (1998) Are financial incentives related to performance? *Journal of Applied Psychology*, **83** (5), pp 777–87
Kessler, I (1994) Performance related pay: Contrasting approaches, *Industrial Relations Journal*, **25** (2), pp 22–35
Kohn, A (1993) Why incentive plans cannot work, *Harvard Business Review*, Sept–October, pp 54–63
Kruse, D and Weitzman, M (1990) Profit sharing and productivity, in *Pay for Productivity*, ed A Blinder, Brookings, Washington
Lawler, E (1995) The new pay: A strategic approach, *Compensation and Benefits Review*, July, pp 14–20
Lewis, P (1998) Managing performance related pay: Evidence from the Financial Services, *Human Resource Management Journal*, **8** (2), pp 66–77
Lupton, T and Gowler, D (1969) *Selecting a Wage Payment System*, EEF, London
MacDuffie, J (1995) Human Resource Bundles and Manufacturing Performance, *Industrial and Labour Relations Review*, **48** (2), pp 197–221
Mahoney, T (1989) Multiple pay contingencies: Strategic design of compensation, *Human Resource Management*, **28** (3), pp 337–47
Market Tracking International (1996) *Reward Strategies*, Haymarket, London
Pfeffer, J (1998) *The Human Equation*, HBS Press, Boston
Roach, W (1999) In searching of commitment oriented human resource management practices and conditions that sustain them, *Journal of Management Studies*, **36** (5), pp 653–71
Rubery, J (1997) Wages and the labour market, *British Journal of Industrial Relations*, **35** (3), pp 337–66
Sako, M and Sato, H (eds) (1997) *Japanese Labour and Management in Transition*, Routledge, London
Schuler, R and Jackson, S (1987) Linking competitive strategies with human resource management practices, *Academy of Management Review*, **1** (3), pp 129–213
Schuster, J and Zingheim, P (1992) *The New Pay*, Lexington, New York
Storey, J (1992) *Developments in the Management of Human Resources*, Blackwell, Oxford
Undy, R, Kessler, I and Thompson, M (1999) *The Impact of the National Minimum Wage on Clothing, Knitwear and Footwear*, Research Report, Low Pay Commission

Walton, R (1998) From control to commitment, *Harvard Business Review*, March–April, pp 77–84

Wood, S (1996) High commitment management and payment systems, *Journal of Management Studies*, **33** (1), pp 53–77

18

Managing sickness and absence

Lynette Harris

THE EMPLOYEE ABSENCE CONTEXT

Managing absence is a sensitive area of human resource management which raises potential conflicts between control and care for the individual. Paradoxically, employers can spend as much time dealing with issues concerning employees frequently absent from work as those with excellent attendance records. Whilst organizations are seeking to maximize productivity and minimize their labour costs, employees have growing expectations of the quality of organizational care that will be paid to their physical and mental well-being. Improving levels of attendance at work is of increasing topicality in both the United States and EU member states as international competition stimulates interest in reducing employment costs, particularly in countries with high sick pay expenditure as part of their social security system. The direct and indirect costs associated with employee absence are considerable. For example, a CBI survey (CBI and PPP Healthcare, 2000) calculated that, based on a 228-day working year, the absence rate was 3.4 per cent which, extrapolated to the whole of the UK workforce, suggested 187 million days were lost due to absence in the year 1999–2000.

As the pace and nature of work intensifies, there is also a growing awareness of the part stress can play in employee absence. Studies in both the UK and the United States have linked half of the annual total days off work to stress-related illness (Bailey, 1998). The following factors have particularly contributed to the growing emphasis on managing sickness and absence.

Legislation

UK and EU regulations place a general duty of care on employers for the health, safety and welfare of their employees. The landmark case of *Walker v Northumberland Council*[1] established the duty of employers to safeguard the mental as well as physical well-being of their employees. The growth in litigation in the UK, manifested in the growth of tribunal claims received by ACAS from a total of 52,071 in 1990 to 167,186 claims in 2000–1 (ACAS, 1990/2002), has led to greater awareness among employers of the importance of following the correct procedures in handling employee absence.

Staffing levels

As organizations have less spare capacity to cover for absence, it has become more critical to maximize employee attendance. In addition, EU regulations on the employment of part-time and temporary staff have reduced opportunities for 'low cost' temporary adjustments. Labour shortages in occupations such as nursing, teaching and engineering trades (Labour Market Quarterly Report, 2001) are exacerbated by employee absence. This is evidenced in closed hospital wards, increased class sizes and a reduction in the quality of services. In the private sector, employee absence can not only reduce profitability but even limit business growth.

Public sector absence levels

There is a particular focus on absence management in the public sector which consistently reports the highest levels of employee absence, with full-time public sector employees revealing an annual absence rate of 4.1 per cent compared to 3.4 per cent for full-time private sector employees (Barham and Leonard, 2002). In local government, competitive tendering and the 'best value' reviews undertaken as part of the 'modernization agenda' have changed attitudes towards absence management. The traditional 'laissez faire' culture that prevailed in much of the public sector is no longer acceptable as levels of absence become yet another indicator used to measure performance standards. There is a particular commitment to reduce average absence rates following a 1998 Cabinet Office report which identified absenteeism as 'a major source of preventable loss' and set targets for government bodies for its reduction. The Local Government Association (LGA) publishes benchmarking data about absence levels in local authorities to be used as a measurement of standards.

Statutory sick pay changes

Changes to the statutory sick pay regulations have increased the organizational costs of employee sickness. Since the Social Security Contributions and Benefits Act 1992, employers have had the responsibility for paying sick pay to their employees, and the Statutory Sick Pay Act 1994 removed the right of all but small businesses to reclaim the total amount of statutory sick payments from the government. These arrangements were replaced by the New Employers Relief Scheme in 1995 which introduced a new compensation scheme which provides for full reimbursement of an employer's costs in any month where the amount of statutory sick payments incurred have exceeded 13 per cent of the employer's gross National Insurance contributions.

More proactive HR policies

The advent of human resource management as a more proactive approach to employment relations than traditional personnel management (Sisson, 1995) has led to support for interventions aimed at reducing levels of absence previously regarded as unavoidable. Performance management systems designed to integrate employee contribution with the strategic objectives of the organization have encouraged the evaluation of individual performance, which may include attendance levels. Absence has thus become a criterion for assessing acceptable performance in a range of selection decisions.

One of the defining characteristics of human resource management (HRM) is the devolvement of personnel responsibilities to line managers (Guest, 1987). The 1992 Workplace Industrial Relations Survey (Millward and Stevens, 1992) reported that a general organizing principle of the time was to 'return as much responsibility as possible to the line manager', a trend again identified in the 1998 survey (Cully *et al*, 1999) which observed that the portfolio of employee relations responsibilities falling to line managers had continued to grow. As a result, managing absence tends to be the responsibility of general management, supported by centrally developed policies and procedures.

Changing employee expectations

Recent legislation is aimed at promoting more family-friendly policies and employee expectations about the contribution of employers to their well-being are changing. Employees have a greater awareness of health issues and the value of benefit packages that contain provisions that contribute to their personal health, such as annual medical check-ups, stress counselling, routine screening and private health insurance schemes. A number of companies, such as Shell UK, have gone further and developed 'work–life balance' policies identifying positive organizational benefits in helping employees to balance the demands of work and personal commitments. Without such provisions, employees may resort to claiming sickness as the only means of obtaining time off to cope with pressing domestic responsibilities.

EMPLOYEE ABSENCE IN THE UK

Absence levels

The major sources of government statistics on absence trends and statistics are provided by the Labour Force Survey (LFS) published by the Office for National Statistics. Other sources of absence data include the annual surveys conducted by the Chartered Institute of Personnel and Development (CIPD), the Industrial Society and the CBI. Government statistics and other studies reveal falling UK absence levels. A major factor in the reported reduction in government statistics is that employee absence is now only recorded for 'scheduled working days'. The CBI 2000 survey found that absence levels in the UK were continuing a downward trend, with an average of 7.8 days' absence per employee for the year compared to 8.5 days in the previous year, although with significant differences between occupations (CBI and PPP Healthcare, 2000). LFS data reports substantially lower absence levels for people in professional, managerial and administrative positions than for those in clerical and secretarial occupations.

Absence levels among non-manual employees is falling faster than for manual employees, although there is a narrowing of the gap. Absence levels have traditionally been higher for manual employees. There is not the scope within this chapter to analyse this difference in any depth but it is worth noting that opportunities for more flexible working and performance management processes have had more impact on non-manual workers and, potentially, their absence levels. Significant variations in absence rates exist between different sectors, with absence levels continuing to remain highest in the public sector. Table 18.1 illustrates the absence levels per sector in the UK reported in the CBI 2000 survey.

There is a strong correlation between absence levels and organizational size, with the lowest levels of absenteeism in small companies. Absence in companies with fewer than 50 employees is reported by the CBI as 2.1 per cent of working time compared to 4.0 per cent among the largest employers and higher in those organizations with recognized trade unions. This has previously been explained by the link between trade union recognition and larger employers, but the 2000 survey factored out size yet still found levels of absence likely to be higher where there are recognized trade unions. The explanation offered is that a trade union presence may actually discourage managers from tackling absence issues perceived as complex and difficult to handle.

Table 18.1 Attendance levels in the UK by sector

Sector	Number of days lost	% of working time
Public sector	9.9	4.3
Transport and communication	9.1	4.0
Retailing	8.6	3.8
Manufacturing	8.0	3.5
Energy and water	6.3	2.8
Distribution, hotels and restaurants	6.1	2.7
Other services	6.1	2.7
Banking, finance and insurance	6.0	2.6
Professional services (lawyers, medical etc)	4.9	2.1
IT and hi-tech services	4.7	2.1
Construction	4.4	1.9
Average	**7.8**	**3.4**

Source: 'Focus on absence, absence and labour turnover survey 2000', CBI/PPP Health care

The Chartered Institute of Personnel and Development surveys particularly explore policy and practice on managing absence. The 2001 survey, based on responses from HR professionals from 1,466 UK organizations employing in total just over two million people (CIPD survey report, 2001), reported the average rate of employee absence as 3.8 per cent of working time or 8.7 working days for each employee per year. Most employers identified absence levels as decreasing due to a tightening of review policies and methods of recording. One in five employers did not know the level of sickness absence within their organization and a fifth reported that absence levels had actually increased due to work pressures, for example within call centres, or due to workforce morale. As an occupational group, managers tend to have the lowest absence level (IRS Employment Review, 1998) but the CIPD survey found that a third of the employers believed managers under-reported their own absences. Opinion was divided as to whether the introduction of family-friendly initiatives had an impact on sickness absence.

Absence levels can be linked to the age profile of the workforce and the survey reported that those employers with lower than average absence levels in the South East and East Anglia had predominantly young workforces. This seems rather at odds with LFS statistics (Roberts, 2000) which reveal that the highest occurrence of sickness is for employees aged 16–34, although employees under 50 tend to take only one day off compared to those aged 50 or more who are more likely to take five days off or more. Put another way, younger workers are reported to have more frequent 'spells' of absence than older workers, whose absences are less frequent but of a longer duration. Women continue to have higher absence levels than men. As most studies find little or no differences in standards of health between the genders, the explanations must lie in factors which largely or only affect women's work attendance.

Costs

Estimating the cost of employee absence is complex as it not only has to take account of direct costs but also the indirect costs of reduced productivity. The annual average cost of sickness is calculated by the CBI and the CIPD as between £430 and £500 per employee, at an estimated cost of 12 billion to the UK economy. Nine out of ten employers identify absence as either a very significant or significant cost to their business, particularly in the public sector. Only four out of ten employers, however, report monitoring the cost of absence, and the elements included in any calculation of absence cost vary (CIPD survey report, 2001). An Industrial Society study (2000) conducted in 1999 similarly found that the financial impact of absence was calculated in only 43 per cent of the organizations surveyed. Less than half of employers included any resulting replacement of overtime costs and even fewer estimated the cost of lost productivity resulting from absence. In descending order of importance, the stated reasons for not calculating the cost of absence were:

- it consumed too much time;
- the absence of a computerized personnel system;
- absence was not a sufficient problem to justify measuring the cost.

Causes of sickness absence

The majority of employers who collect data on the causes of sickness absence find that minor ailments are by far the most frequent reason for sickness absence for all employees. In common with other recent surveys, the 2001 CIPD study revealed stress as the second most frequent cause of sickness absence for non-manual workers, with recurring medical conditions such as asthma or angina in third place, followed by back pain. Stress-related illness was identified as a cause of absence far more frequently by public sector organizations, where two-thirds of education and local government employers identify it as the leading cause of long-term absence for non-manual staff. It features far less frequently in the private sector. A TUC campaign in 1998 (Labour Research Department, 1999) identified workloads, long hours, shift work, job design and bullying as the main causes of stress-related illness.

Among manual workers, the same CIPD survey identified back pain as the second major reason for absence but the main cause of long-term absence, followed by musculo-skeletal injuries and then recurring medical conditions. Respondents believed that over a third of employee absence was not ill health related, but this varied significantly across occupational sectors, which suggests a need for further research. For example, in the public sector, where there are more family-friendly initiatives, 80 per cent of sickness absence was held to be as a result of illness. In comparison, respondents in mining and quarrying believed that as much as 75 per cent of absence was not due to ill health.

Patterns of absence

Patterns of absence are dominated by reported sickness of one day's duration. According to CBI surveys, long-term sickness was a major cause of absence for only 7 per cent of employers and LFS statistics reveal that this level of long-term sickness absence has remained fairly constant for the past 20 years. Short-term absence is particularly significant in smaller businesses and in the service sector where it accounts for 68 per cent of absence across finance, leisure, retailing and wholesale operations. This contrasts with the public sector where short-term absence is reported as accounting for only 46 per cent of absence. New questions in the LFS surveys were introduced in Spring 2000 which now make it possible to identify trends in the days of the week when absence occurs. Contrary to popular perception that Mondays and Fridays are the most common days, recent LFS data suggests no evidence of this, with absence levels being consistent from Monday to Friday with only a slight increase on Thursdays and Fridays.

A study undertaken by the European Foundation for the Improvement of Living and Working Conditions in 1997 considered patterns of absence across EU member states and Norway. It proved difficult to establish reliable figures on levels of employee absence for comparative purposes. The available statistics were based on the proportion of the workforce absent from work on a given day and revealed major differences in levels of absenteeism: for example, 3.5 per cent in Denmark compared to 8.3 per cent in the Netherlands. Sickness prevention activities were reported to be taking place only on a modest scale in most European countries, and with regional differences. There was more emphasis on the promotion of individual health and well-being in Northern Europe compared to Southern European countries, where measures are aimed at improving the physical working environment. The report singled out the vulnerability of SMEs to absenteeism, particularly in their handling of long-term sickness. It concluded that absenteeism and its causes needed to be placed much higher on the EU agenda, with national governments, employers' organizations and trade unions becoming far more aware of measures for reducing absence levels.

UNDERSTANDING ABSENCE

Managing absence tends to be viewed as a series of control interventions without which absenteeism would escalate. Traditionally the emphasis has centred on reducing absence, which encourages a negative rather than a positive approach promoting attendance. Process models for analysing the causes of absenteeism have tended to emphasize the centrality of the work-related factors rather than reflect the tensions in attendance between the demands of work and non-work responsibilities (Youngblood, 1984). According to an Institute of Employment Studies report (Bevan and Heyday, 1998), a more enlightened approach to absence management aimed at providing a working environment which encourages attendance is developing. To do this effectively, employers need to develop their understanding of those factors which influence attendance and are of particular relevance to their working environment. Rhodes and Steers (1990) provide a diagnostic model designed to assist managers in analysing absence, which essentially recognizes the three key influences as:

- organizational practices;
- the absence culture;
- employee attitudes, values and goals.

Whilst the model provides for a consideration of attendance barriers, in common with much of the literature, it rather underplays their significance. Yet, these are issues of growing relevance in the light of the increased participation of working mothers in the UK workforce and the growing debates about the work–life balance. This is particularly topical in the public sector where there has, arguably, been a greater predisposition, for reasons of ideology and public accountability, to have concerns for equality of opportunity (Harris, 2000). Leaving aside illness as the principal reason for absence, the IES report identifies the following as being particularly influential:

- **workplace factors** such as working patterns and hours, travelling to work time, and health and safety concerns;
- **attitudinal and stress factors** stemming from job satisfaction, career aspirations, levels of commitment and the organizational absenteeism culture;
- **domestic and kinship factors**, particularly those related to gender, children under the age of 16 and the lack of opportunities for flexible working;
- **health and lifestyle factors** influencing general health, which may be due to smoking, excessive use of alcohol, lack of exercise and body weight.

Workplace factors, attitudinal and stress factors

Evans and Palmer argue for a change in emphasis from managing absence to promoting attendance and suggest that the impact of the working environment on absenteeism means it can be viewed from a range of different perspectives (Evans and Palmer, 1997) which influence the approach taken. One-third of the managers in the Industrial Society research identified low morale and a monotonous job as major causes of absence. Studies by Rhodes and Steers (1990) and Huczynski and Fitzpatrick (1989) similarly concluded that there is a relationship between low job satisfaction and lack of involvement and higher levels of absence. But such factors cannot be considered in isolation. For example, an employee with a very routine job providing little job satisfaction may enjoy significant flexibility in working patterns to accommodate domestic responsibilities and, consequently, absenteeism is low. Studies have also found that levels of absenteeism are lower among part-time than full-time workers. Labour Force data survey data in 2002 identified a 3.5 per cent absence rate for full-time employees compared to 2.8 per cent for those working part-time (Barham and Leonard, 2002).

Increasingly, research suggests that absence can be a mechanism for avoiding work viewed as unpleasant or stressful. The influence of individual personality attributes plays a part in any propensity towards absenteeism and certain types of personality may be more prone to stress-related illnesses (Robbins, 1993). It is difficult to see what organizations can actually do to accommodate this in their policies other than screening for absence risk, which is far from straightforward in practice. The significance employees attribute to their organizational contribution has a bearing on attendance. If the perception is that their absence makes no difference or there are others to cover the work, then there are fewer intrinsic pressures to attend work than, for example, for those working in a small, highly interdependent team.

The absence culture of the organization is a major influence on attendance. It is shaped by the influence of workgroup norms on behaviours, the rigour with which absence rules have been applied in the past and the extent of organizational controls. Where custom and practice has established a certain level of absence as 'acceptable', it can become the norm for management, employees and trade unions alike. Attempts to reverse this unilaterally are likely to be met with considerable resistance. In that sense, an absence culture becomes part of an informally negotiated agreement between management and employees which is heavily influenced by the expectations of all the parties.

A rarely mentioned consideration in studies of attendance is that employees may be exercising a form of 'retributive justice' by taking time off. This may occur when an employee feels exploited due to poor pay, working conditions or an unacceptable style of management and absence is viewed as a means of redressing the balance in the employment relationship. Another under-researched impact on absenteeism is the effect of home-based working. Avoiding demanding journeys into work can be related to absenteeism and is a very positive benefit of home working, yet its impact on absence levels has hardly been considered. Monitoring absence levels of the distanced home worker introduces a whole new dimension to attendance measurement. How should attendance appropriately be measured for a distanced and essentially 'invisible' workforce where the concept of the working day may be related to outputs rather than attended hours?

Domestic, kinship and other external factors

The Industrial Society reported women's family responsibilities as the third most likely cause of absence. The higher absence levels for women are explained by the gender differences in domestic roles and the availability of childcare facilities (Hendrix, Spencer and Gibson, 1994). Female absence falls as the age of dependent children rises but, with an ageing population, a growing issue is employees' caring responsibilities for their elderly relatives and how these are distributed between the genders. One large textile company in the East Midlands, with a predominantly female workforce, recorded significant differences in absence levels in the mid-1990s among its production workers at three sites within a 40-mile radius. An investigation into the causes of absence revealed that where there was higher unemployment due to redundancies in the local mining industry, women's attendance levels were higher. The identified reasons were the increased availability of fathers for childcare and economic pressures to attend work. The overall influence of the economic climate is, however, unclear. For example, CBI survey data reveals that absence levels fell during the last period of recession but also continued to fall during recent years of economic prosperity.

Health and lifestyle factors

Studies of absenteeism reveal a link between lifestyle and attendance at work. If healthier lifestyles reduce sickness absence, employers can benefit from an investment in programmes promoting employee health.

ABSENCE POLICIES AND PRACTICE

Employee absence has been described as HR's common cold in the sense that it is widespread, taken for granted and no one has yet discovered a universal cure, but positive measures by employers can help. The elements of any strategy to encourage attendance lie in fostering an organizational culture of attendance and providing clarity about roles and procedures. Policies to manage absence and attendance can be classified into five main areas (IDS Study 702, 2001) but the combinations of these will vary, as will the emphasis. The suggested categories are:

- sanctions against behaviour deemed unacceptable;
- positive rewards for good attendance;
- screening out employees during selection in the light of previous attendance levels;
- increasing attendance through work design;
- programmes promoting employee health and well-being.

Written policies

The majority of large employers have written absence policies; this is particularly the case in the public sector which is the most proactive sector in
managing absence. A typical absence policy contains:

- definitions of types of absence;
- procedures for the notification of absence;
- a process for managing the return to work;
- procedures for managing short-term absence, which may include any
  'trigger points' used to start monitoring and review in individual cases;
- linkages to the disciplinary/grievance procedure;
- procedures for managing long-term sickness, the involvement of the occupational health service and guidance on legislative requirements;
- clarification on the responsibilities of line managers, the HR function and
  individual employers.

Absence management tools

According to the CIPD's survey evidence, the most common approaches to
absence management are disciplinary procedures, line management
involvement and return to work interviews. Details of the absence
management tools reported by UK employers are provided in Table 18.2.

Leaving aside the use of disciplinary procedures for unacceptable levels of
absence, this chapter provides only an overview of the most frequently used
measures, but there are a number of sources of information which provide
more detailed information (IDS Study 702, 2001; ACAS, 1999).

Absence measurement

Monitoring and analysing attendance records is the starting point for all
policies and for benchmarking levels against that of comparable employers.
The most common measure of absence is the lost time rate, which shows the
percentage of time lost during a particular period. This will not, however,
explain the absence level, which may be due to a large number of individuals
having short spells of absence or to a few employees away on long-term
sickness. A measure of the frequency rate will reveal this, calculated as follows:

$$\frac{\text{No of spells of absence}}{\text{No of employees}} \times 100 = \text{the frequency rate}$$

Computerized personnel systems have increased the ease with which
absence can be monitored, the quality of data provided to line managers and

Table 18.2 Absence management tools used by UK employers

Absence policies and practices	% of respondents using this approach ($n = 1{,}463$)
Disciplinary procedures for unacceptable absences	82
Providing sickness absence information to line managers	81
Line managers' involvement in absence management	78
Leave for family circumstances	71
Return to work interviews for absences	61
Occupational health involvement	59
Restricting sick pay	48
Training managers in absence handling	44
Attendance record as recruitment criterion	43
Stress counselling	32
Health promotion	28
Return to work interviews for longer-term absence only	20
Rehabilitation programme	18
Employee assistance programme	17
Attendance bonuses or incentives	14
Physiotherapy services	12
Disability leave not counted as sickness absence	10
Nominated absence case manager/team	7
Others, such as home visits	3

Source: Employee Absence: a survey of management policy and practice, Survey report, CIPD, June 2001, p 17

when absence thresholds, known as 'triggers', are exceeded by individual employees. One of the more sophisticated absence measurement systems is known as the Bradford formula. This highlights repeated short-term absence by giving extra weight to the number of absences in a given period. This provides an absence measure which can provide an indicator as a trigger point for action by using a formula of

Index (I) $= S^2 H$, where S = the number of absences and H = the total hours absent in any given period

Thus, an employee with four absences totalling ten days (80 hours) would provide an indicator of 1,280 by calculating as follows:

$I = 4 \times 4 \times 80 = 1{,}280$

For example, First Direct Bank measures absence using the Bradford index based on a combination of frequency and duration of absence in a given period but places the emphasis on frequency as the trigger point for action. To act fairly it is important that absence measures take proper account of both duration and frequency, otherwise the system can have unforeseen and dysfunctional consequences. This is illustrated by the large privatized utilities company which reduced absence levels from an annual average of just over 6 per cent to just over 3 per cent by using a trigger of three absences in four months to initiate an 'absence counselling' interview. Whilst this resulted in a dramatic and rapid drop in absence levels by changing the absenteeism culture, the policy was viewed as highly unjust by those at the receiving end. Long-serving employees with excellent sickness records suffering from a period of ill health found it was not worth attending for work if not absolutely fully recovered. The process encouraged fewer but longer absences as there was little inducement to return to work as quickly as possible.

Involving line management

Involving line management is central to effective absence management. Return to work interviews have been identified as an important means of encouraging a culture where it is known that attendance is regarded as important. Normal practice is for these to be conducted by line managers or supervisors who have the day-to-day contact with staff. One large unitary authority, with an absence policy that has been highly effective in improving attendance levels, emphasizes this clearly in its guide for the Council's Managers. This states:

> Line managers – not personnel officers – will in future hold a return to work interview with every member of staff when they return from a period of sickness absence... **Sickness absence is not an issue to be offloaded onto personnel to deal with but a welfare approach is still important to enable employees to maintain good attendance and to identify underlying reasons for absence**.

The second point is a critical one. Training which stresses the importance of a sensitive approach is essential. Return to work interviews will otherwise be perceived as part of a punitive warning process which is inappropriate in handling sickness absence. Relying upon line managers to decide when a review of attendance should be implemented is highly reliant on managerial discretion and widens the potential for inconsistencies between managers. This may be resolved by the use of specified trigger points but the IES study of attendance management policies found only a minority expressly mentioned the use of a sympathetic approach.

Absence as a selection criterion

Certain studies have shown past absence rates to be a predictor of future attendance levels (Warr and Yearta, 1995) and 'absence risk' is sometimes used as a factor in recruitment and redundancy selection. The use of such criteria has to be fair and consistently applied and is open to legal challenge if this is not the case. Rejecting a prospective employee on the grounds of an atten-dance record without sufficient understanding of the causes runs the risk of rejecting an applicant whose absences relate to a disability. It is now common practice for information about attendance levels to be sought in references from previous employers and in pre-employment health screening. There is greater caution in using absence criteria in redundancy selection and the IES survey found this to be the practice in only 39 of the 182 organizations surveyed.

Measures to promote attendance

In the past, attendance bonuses were often included as an element in collec-tively bargained agreements for manual employees; for example, the furniture maker, Wesley Barrell, pays a quarterly bonus to production employees with fewer than eight hours' absence in a quarter (Bevan and Heyday, 1998). This practice is, however, decreasing. The current view tends to be that such arrangements result in paying twice for what is contractually required and that most employees have good attendance records which are not influenced by financial inducement. A more positive approach, though rarely used, is to allow the carrying over of sick leave from one year to another. This not only conveys a message of trust but also provides employees with good attendance records with extra security should they ever suffer from long-term illness.

In recent years the focus has shifted away from financial recognition for good attendance to the role that sick pay schemes play in employee absence. Some sick pay schemes actually encourage longer periods of absence by not paying for initial days of absence or only retrospectively if the absence lasts for a longer period. The trend to harmonize terms and conditions of employment has addressed historical differences between the sick pay schemes of blue- and white-collar workers. The process has also provided opportunities to reduce higher absence levels among manual employees by offering the incentive of better sick pay terms as the reward for improved attendance levels.

Employers' absence policies are only just beginning to consider the impact of work intensification on employee health. Stress is now a major consider-ation in any approach to employee absence, but measures to tackle it are growing slowly. The provision of counselling services has increased, although this can be viewed with some cynicism by a workforce who perceive that prevention of the actual causes of work-related stress would be a better solution. Despite such criticisms, employers have to be aware of the impact of stress and take action to address it. When the Customs and Excise found that stress-related illness accounted for 20 per cent of all absence, it worked closely with the University of Manchester Institute for Science and Technology to tackle the issue. This resulted in a host of measures to help staff, which included stress management training, problem-solving groups based on a practice of 'health circles' developed in Germany, an internal counselling service and special paid leave for a range of circumstances.

LEGAL CONSIDERATIONS

The legal framework

In developing absence policies and procedures, employers need to be aware of relevant legislation and in particular the following:

- **Health and Safety law** and specifically the Health and Safety at Work Act 1974, the Management of Health and Safety at Work Regulations 1992 and the Health and Safety (Consultation with Employees Regulations) 1996.
- **Individual employment rights** relating to fair and unfair dismissal as defined by the Employment Rights Act 1996 (ERA) and the Employment Relations Act 1999.
- **Time off provisions for antenatal care, maternity, public duties, to look for work, parental leave and dependant care** as defined by the Employment Rights Act 1996 (ERA) and the Employment Relations Act 1999.
- **Time off for trade union duties** in accordance with the Trade Union and Labour Relations (Consolidation) Act 1992.
- **The Working Time Regulations 1998.**
- **Equal Treatment legislation** – in particular, the Sex Discrimination Act 1975, the Race Relations Act, the Disability Discrimination Act 1995, the Equal Pay Act 1970 and the Part Time Workers (Prevention of Less Favourable Treatment) Regulations 2000.
- **Information rights** under the Access to Medical Reports Act 1988, Access to Health Records Act 1990 and the Data Protection Act 1998.
- **Individual contracts of employment, collective agreements** and implied and express terms in common law.
- **Benefit rights** to Statutory Sick Pay and Statutory Maternity Pay.
- **The ACAS Code of Practice on Disciplinary and Grievance Procedures 2000.**
- **Rights to privacy** under the Human Rights Act 2000.

The three main areas of employment law employers need to be most aware of when dealing with absence and sickness are the unfair dismissal provisions, discrimination and contractual rights. The difficulty in handling such cases lies in the distinction between genuine sickness and instances where it is believed that an employee may be abusing a contractual or statutory right. As discussed earlier, this relates to the nature of the absence from work, which may classified as:

- persistent short-term absences of certificated sickness which may or may not be related;
- long-term sickness cases;
- uncertificated absences;
- pregnancy-related absences;
- mental health or stress-related problems.

Employers are increasingly introducing 'capability' procedures to deal with sickness absence to distinguish the process from cases of alleged misconduct. In cases of dismissal for levels of sickness, the most likely reason is one of capability assessed by reference to health. In comparison, if an employee is shown to be feigning ill health and falsely claiming from the organization's sick pay scheme, it would be regarded as misconduct. There are instances when an employer suspects malingering and feels further investigation is warranted, but employers do need to be mindful of breaching any individual rights to privacy under the Human Rights Act in considering surveillance.

Sickness absence dismissals are complex as no two situations are the same. This means that case law cannot provide definitive answers and there are a range of possible responses that a reasonable employer might take. What emerges from the case law on sickness absence is that following fair procedures is crucial. A number of general principles have emerged over the years on how tribunals expect employers to approach sickness dismissals. Decisions in Employment Appeals Tribunal cases such as *International Sports Co. Ltd v Thompson*[2] and *Lynock v Cereal Packaging Ltd*[3] have provided useful guidelines for employers. These include taking into account the nature of the illness, its likely duration and the chance of it reoccurring. Although there is no legal requirement to have a formal absence policy, employers are well advised to have one to demonstrate reasonableness and consistency in dealing with potential claims of unfair treatment arising from handling sickness absence. Once it is established that absence is due to sickness, the particular procedural considerations are:

- proper investigation of the employee's record;
- regular contact and consultation with the employee;
- informing the employee if employment is at risk;
- obtaining medical evidence;
- determining whether the employee is disabled within the meaning of the Disability Discrimination Act 1995;
- the possibility of alternative work.

Persistent short-term absenteeism

The ACAS handbook on 'Discipline at Work' offers the following guidance to employers on handling frequent and persistent short-term absence: 'Where there is no medical advice to support frequent self-certified absences employers are advised to ask the employee to consult a doctor to establish whether medical treatment is necessary and whether the absence is work related.'

A proper examination of the employee's absence record, its pattern, frequency and the explanations provided should be undertaken in the first instance. If it appears that there are no good reasons for the absences, the matter can be dealt with under the disciplinary procedure. Employees should always be made fully aware of the consequences of no improvement in attendance. The case of *Lynock v Cereal Packaging Ltd* illustrates the distinction to be made between warnings about absences within the control of an employee and those which are the consequences of genuine but disruptive intermittent sickness. In the latter circumstances, written communications need to be sympathetically worded. There should be evidence that any underlying problems have been properly addressed by the employer but also clarity when the stage is reached that 'with the best will in the world' it is not possible to continue with the employment if the level of absence does not improve.

A frequent difficulty in short-term absence cases is that an employee suffers from genuine illnesses which are unrelated and can individually be resolved quite quickly. Here the impact of the employee's general state of health on attendance is the issue. The Lynock case illustrates just such circumstances, where unrelated periods of sickness led to an extremely poor attendance record well below the average for the workforce. As no sustained improvement was achieved, it resulted in Mr Lynock's dismissal, but as he had been made fully aware of the position it was found to be fair.

Consultation

In all sickness cases, a failure to carry out a personal interview will almost certainly render the dismissal unfair if the employee has had no opportunity to put forward any explanation. In an unreported case the dismissal of a probationary postwoman for persistent absenteeism on the basis of written reports alone was held to be unfair. Discussion with the employee may bring to light information about the individual's health, personal circumstances or the work situation that the employer needs to address. It could emerge, for example, that an employee's stress-related illness stems from workplace bullying or harassment. Ideally an employee should be consulted after every absence, but managers need to be trained to conduct such interviews and be aware of the provisions of the Disability Discrimination Act 1995.

Medical evidence

Medical reports may prove to be of little value in dealing with intermittent unconnected periods of illness, as in the case of *International Sports Co Ltd v*

Thomson, but it is good practice for employers to check with the employee's doctor to determine whether absences are explained by any underlying health problems. In seeking information about an employee's health, employers must comply with the Access to Medical Reports Act 1988 and gain the employee's consent in writing if they are seeking a medical report. The 1990 Access to Health Records Act gives employers direct access to an employee's health records but again subject to the employee's consent.

An employee has the right to withhold consent, in which case the employer has to make a decision without the report and advise the employee that this will be the case. Employees have the right to see and amend any medical reports about themselves provided for employment purposes by a doctor who is or was responsible for their clinical care. This may include an independent doctor of the company's choice but it is unwise to have no contact with the employee's own doctor or consultant. The importance of deciding to dismiss without taking account of all available medical evidence was illustrated in the early but leading case on handling termination of employment on health grounds of *East Lindsey District Council v Daubney*.[4] In this instance the Council's decision to dismiss on grounds of ill-health retirement was found to be unfair without a consideration of a full report on the employee's state of health, the prognosis for a return to work or proper consultation with Mr Daubney.

In practice, an employer does not need a detailed diagnosis but information about the nature of the illness, its likely duration and impact on the ability to do the current job or alternative work. It is, therefore, sensible to provide the doctor or consultant with details of the job and the working conditions. Employers must be prepared to wait for medical reports before they take the decision to dismiss an employee for long-term sickness. In the case of *Lothian Regional Transport v Gray*,[5] the employers were held to have unfairly dismissed Mr Gray after nine months' absence due to a degenerative back condition on the grounds of his misconduct for refusing to return to work. They were found to have acted too hastily by reaching a decision before the results of an examination by a hospital specialist were known. This meant that alternatives, such as early retirement, were not considered in the light of the full medical evidence. Case law suggests that employers are well advised to consult with an employee again once the full medical evidence is available so that its implications can be discussed. For example, an employee may wish to obtain his or her own medical opinion in addition to that of the employer's medical adviser.

Alternative work

If an employee cannot return to a job in its original form on health grounds then employers need to consider the option of either amending the current job content or the availability of more suitable alternative work. The provisions of the DDA 1995 are relevant in considering modifications to an existing job in the light of temporary or longer-term disability. The Code of Practice on Disability also suggests giving an employee time to adjust to any alternative employment. In considering the suitability of a job upon the return to work after illness, employers need to be aware of their duty of care for an employee's mental as well as physical well-being. In the case of *Walker v Northumberland County Council*, the High Court held that the Council was in breach of its duty of care to Mr Walker when he experienced a second mental breakdown upon returning to his original job. It is worth noting that this case occurred before the DDA 1995 which now would also expect the employer to consider reasonable adjustment to the job if the mental breakdown amounted to a disability.

Pregnancy and ill health

Under Section 99 of the Employment Relations Act 1996, it is automatically unfair to dismiss a woman because she is pregnant or for any reasons related to pregnancy. There is no qualifying period for such claims. Where ill health is related to pregnancy, particular care and attention needs to be paid to the comparability of any alternative work. In the case of *British Airways (European Operations Gatwick) Ltd v Moore and Botterill*,[6] two pregnant cabin crew were put on ground duties in accordance with their contracts of employment but no longer received their flying allowances. The Employment Appeals Tribunal held that British Airways had failed in its duty to offer suitable alternative work as the terms and conditions of the alternative work were substantially less favourable.

Decision to dismiss

Whilst an employer must clarify the medical situation, ultimately the decision to dismiss remains an organizational not a medical one. The law recognizes that employers cannot hold open an absent employee's job indefinitely but dismissal must be carried out in accordance with the employee's employment contract and any company pensions provisions that relate to ill health. The questions that a tribunal will ask in sickness absence dismissals is whether the nature of the illness, the likelihood of any return and the impact of continuing absence on the business mean that it is reasonable not to wait any longer for a return to work. Once fair procedure is established, the effect on the business will be the critical factor in deciding reasonableness.

Right of appeal

Even where there is an extremely poor attendance record, it is essential that there is a right to appeal. In many procedures this is a contractual right, as it was in the case of *West Midlands Co-operative Society Ltd v Tipton*,[7] where the dismissal was found to be unfair as Mr Tipton was denied his right to appeal even though he had had an excessive level of absence.

CONCLUDING COMMENTS

Effective absence management begins with fair, well-understood and consistently applied policy. This should not only define absenteeism and clarify procedures but also provide support for employees absent due to sickness or disability. To develop appropriate approaches to absence management, employers should analyse their organizational absence levels to understand the patterns of absence and its underlying causes as well as the overall cost. Employees should be made aware of absence procedures and the consequences of not adhering to these as well as the impact of persistent absenteeism on the organization.

Employee absence is complex, multifaceted and explained by roles within and outside the workplace, and there is a lack of any one unifying theory that can be reflected in a model which embraces all the variables that influence attendance. Each case of absence is different and the factors causing absence do not have equivalent meaning for individuals (Martocchio and Judge, 1994). This presents a considerable challenge in managing absence and demands good judgement in the implementation of policies. All the available evidence points to line managers playing a crucial role in creating a positive culture of attendance. Policies are of little value unless their aims and objectives are shared by the managers who are required to apply them, and they provide vital role models through their own attendance patterns and in the sensitivity and fairness with which employee absence is handled. At the heart of creating a positive culture is the balance between demonstrating that absence is of organizational significance whilst exercising care and support for the employee's well-being. The importance of achieving a 'work–life balance' in providing flexible working patterns of work that can reduce levels of absence and improve motivation is beginning to be recognized by employers (Bean, 2001; CIPD, 1999).

Employers have a wide range of absence management tools at their disposal but these should be considered in the light of the majority of employees having good attendance records, which means that providing extra financial rewards to motivate attendance is likely to be inappropriate. The legal framework increasingly informs approaches to absence and employers have a responsibility to ensure that the working environment does not put at risk their employees' physical or mental well-being. Although legislation requires employers to demonstrate procedural justice in absence practices, what matters at the level of the individual employee is the quality of personal interactions in the handling of any absences. Whilst the suggested steps for effective absence management are those of education, monitoring, counselling, follow-up and taking corrective action, this will lead to an atmosphere of distrust and low employee commitment unless supported by sensitive and consistent managerial behaviours.

Notes

1 *Walker v Northumberland Council* (1995) IRLR 35.
2 *International Sports Co. Ltd v Thompson* (1980) IRLR 340.
3 *Lynock v Cereal Packaging Ltd* (1998) IRLR 510.
4 *East Lindsey District Council v Daubney* (1977) IRLR 181.
5 *Lothian Regional Transport v Gray* (1990) (EAT 139/90).
6 *British Airways (European Operations Gatwick) Ltd v (1) Moore and (2) Botterill* (2000) ICR 678.
7 *West Midlands Co-operative Society Ltd v Tipton* (1986) IRLR 112.

References

ACAS advisory booklet (1999) *Absence and labour turnover,* Advisory, Conciliation and Arbitration Service, London
ACAS (1990/2002) *ACAS Annual reports 1990 and* 2002, Advisory, Conciliation and Arbitration Service, London
Bailey, R (1998) Attendance allowance, *Occupational Health,* **50** (4), pp 23–25
Barham, C and Leonard, J (2002) Trends and sources of data on sickness absence, *Labour Market Trends,* **110** (4), pp 177–94
Bean, S (2001) Whose life is it anyway? *Employers' Law,* July–August, pp 10–12
Bevan, S and Heyday, S (1998) *Attendance Management: a Review of Good Practice,* Report 353, Institute for Employment Studies, Brighton
Cabinet Office (1998) *Working Well Together: Managing Attendance in the Public Sector,* Cabinet Office, July
CBI and PPP Healthcare (2000) *Focus on Absence and Labour Turnover Survey,* Confederation of British Industry, London
Chartered Institute of Personnel and Development (1999) Flexible working cuts sickness absence, *People Management,* **8** (1), p 13
CIPD survey report (2001) *Employee Absence; a survey of management policy and practice,* Chartered Institute of Personnel and Development, London
Cully, M, Woodland, S, O'Reilly, A and Dix, G (1999) *Britain at work as depicted by the 1998 Workplace Employee Relations Survey,* Routledge, London
European Foundation for the Improvement of Living and Working Conditions (1997) *Preventing absenteeism in the workplace: research summary,* Office for Official Publications of the European Communities
Evans, A and Palmer, S (1997) *From absence to attendance,* 3rd edn, Chartered Institute of Personnel and Development, London
Guest, D (1987) Human resource management and industrial relations, *Journal of Management Studies,* **24** (5), pp 503–21

Harris, L (2000) The pursuit of demonstrable fairness and 'felt fairness' in selection practice, *International Journal of Selection and Assessment*, **7** (4), pp 148–57

Hendrix, W, Spencer, B and Gibson, G (1994) Organizational and extra organizational factors effecting stress, employee well being and absenteeism for males and females, *Journal of Business and Psychology*, **9** (2), pp 103–28

Huczynski, A A and Fitzpatrick, M J (1989) *Managing employee absence for a competitive edge*, Pitman, London

IDS Study 702 (2001) *Absence Management*, Incomes Data Services Ltd, London

Industrial Society (2000) Maximising Attendance, Managing Best Practice No. 7, Industrial Society, London

IRS Employment Review (1998) Sickness and absence – a survey of 182 employers, *IRS Study No 665*, pp 2–20

Labour Market Quarterly Report (2001) *Labour Market Trends Skills and Enterprise Network Publications*, DfEE, 3 August

Labour Research Department (1999) *Sickness absence policy – trade unionists' guide*, Labour Research Department, London

Martocchio, J H and Judge, T A (1994) A policy capturing approach to Individuals' decisions to be absent, *Organizational Behaviour and Human Decision Processes*, **57**, pp 358–86

Millward, N and Stevens, M (1992) *British Workplace Industrial Relations in Transition*, The ED/ESRC/PSI/ACAS Surveys, Dartmouth Publishers, Aldershot

Rhodes, S R and Steers, R M (1990) *Managing employee absenteeism*, Addison-Wesley, Reading, MA, p 57

Robbins, S P (1993) *Organizational Behaviour*, Prentice Hall, Englewood Cliffs, NJ

Roberts, G (2000) Sickness absence, *Labour Market Trends*, **108** (1), pp 541–47

Sisson, K (1995) Human resource management and the personnel function, in *Human Resource Management: A Critical Text*, ed J Storey, Routledge, London, pp 87–109

Warr, P and Yearta, S (1995) Health and motivational factors in sickness absence, *Human Resource Management Journal*, **5** (5), pp 33–48

Youngblood, S A (1984) Work, non-work and withdrawal, *Journal of Applied Psychology*, **69**, pp 106–17

19

Managing health and safety

Ian Cunningham and Phil James

The subject of health and safety at work has tended to receive relatively little attention within the field of industrial relations. This lack of attention is surprising given that it is the only area where long-standing statutory provisions have existed in Britain in relation to workforce representation. It is also surprising given the fact that over one million workers suffer work-related injuries and ill health each year and that such harm imposes enormous costs on both industry and society. As a result, health and safety is clearly an issue that is of considerable importance to workers, trade unions, employers and government.

Against this background, the present chapter provides an overview of the issues central to the management of occupational health and safety. It proceeds as follows. Initially a review is provided of the existing data available on both the scale of work-related harm and the costs that it imposes on employers and the wider economy. Following this, the causes of such harm are discussed and four processes which are seen as central to the effective management of health and safety at work explored. First, the process of risk assessment, secondly, the types of preventative measures that can be taken, thirdly, the factors that influence the implementation of such measures and fourthly, the methods that can be used to evaluate and monitor health and safety performance. Finally, in recognition of the contribution it can make to each of these management processes, the role that worker involvement can play in enhancing workplace health and safety is discussed and attention paid to both the legal framework relating to such involvement and the factors that act to influence its effectiveness.

SCALE AND COSTS OF WORK-RELATED HARM

Official accident statistics show that during the year 1999–2000 295 workers died as a result of workplace accidents, 29,315 suffered major injuries and 136,113 experienced accidents that resulted in absences of over three-days (Health and Safety Commission, 2001). These figures, however, substantially underestimate the scale of injury-causing accidents since they not only fail to include injuries resulting in either no absence or absences of three or less, but, even on their own terms, lack comprehensiveness because of the failure of employers to report more than half of the accidents that should be reported. In fact, estimates based on Labour Survey (LFS) data suggest that in reality around one million workers suffer a non-fatal work-related injury annually (Health and Safety Commission, 1999). This last figure nevertheless still provides only a very partial indication of the scale of work-related harm arising from work activities since, by definition, no account is taken of the work-related illness suffered by workers.

In a recent HSE study, which also analysed LFS data, it was estimated that during 1998/99 around two million workers, amounting to approximately 4.5 per cent of all workers, considered that they had suffered a work-related illness caused or made worse by their work during the previous 12 months. Musculo-skeletal disorders followed by stress, depression and anxiety were the most commonly reported complaints. Musculo-skeletal disorders were more likely to be experienced by those aged between 45 and 54 years of age and employed in skilled manual occupations. Those suffering from stress, depression or anxiety were more likely to be employed within non-manual occupations such as education, public administration and health and social work. In relation to both types of disorder, higher rates occurred among people who worked more than 40 hours a week and who were employed in medium to large workplaces (HSE, 2000).

Overall, it has been officially estimated that some 23 million working days are lost per year as a result of absences stemming from workplace injuries and ill health (Health and Safety Commission/DETR, 2000). Such absence clearly has major cost implications for employers. However, these financial conse-quences constitute only a small proportion of the total costs arising from acci-dents and work-related ill health. For example, the HSE's Accident Prevention Advisory Unit scrutinized five organizations, a creamery, a construction site, a North Sea Oil platform, a transport company and an NHS hospital, to identify all of the costs associated with accidents, regardless of whether they caused injuries or not (Health and Safety Executive, 1997). In each of these cases, the HSE concluded that the costs incurred were of considerable significance to the organizations concerned. Thus, on an annualized basis, they were esti-mated to have represented 8.5 per cent of the tender price of the construction organization, 1.4 per cent of the creamery's operating costs, 37 per cent of the transport company's profits, 14.2 per cent of the potential output of the oil platform and 5 per cent of the annual running costs for the hospital.

More generally, the HSE has estimated that in 1995/96 workplace accidents and ill health cost employers nationally between £3.5 and £7.3 billion and that once account was taken of additional costs borne by society, such as through social security benefits and NHS treatment costs, this financial burden increased to between £9.9 and £14.1 billion (HSE, 1999). In the light of such findings the HSE has consequently gone on to argue that employers have a clear financial incentive to do more to improve standards of workplace health and safety. However, it should be noted that other commentators have raised serious doubts about the validity of this 'business case' argument (Cutler and James, 1996). For example, doubts have been expressed about the degree to which organizational decision making embodies an 'economic rationality' and reservations have been expressed about the willingness of organizations to invest in prevention measures in the face of uncertainties about longer-term 'pay backs'. In addition, it has been argued that, even if such investments do generate financial benefits, this does not mean that these benefits are as attractive as those that would be produced by spending the relevant money on some other activity.

CAUSES OF WORK-RELATED HARM

The causes of work-related ill health and injuries are inevitably very diverse. Dermatitis and other skin conditions may arise from contact with harmful substances. Stress-related conditions can stem from an array of factors, such as long working hours, work overload or underload, and role conflict and ambiguity (Cox, Griffiths and Rial-Gonzalez, 2000; Smith *et al*, 1999). Respiratory problems may be caused by exposure to harmful fumes and sprays, and musculo-skeletal conditions can be caused by engagement in repetitive manual activities, lifting excessive weights and, more generally, poorly designed work processes that do not accord with the physical capabilities of workers (Buckle and Devereux, 1999).

As a result, as will be discussed further below, the avoidance of work-related harm can require the carrying out of a wide variety of preventive actions. The existing research evidence relating to the causes of accidents serves to further illustrate this point and in doing so to highlight that the putting into place of an effective system for the management of health and safety requires actions at all levels of an organization.

That said, many, if not most, accidents do stem directly and immediately from the actions of individuals. There is consequently an obvious temptation to blame those who are responsible for those actions. In fact, for many years, following British research undertaken in munitions factories during the First World War which found that the bulk of accidents occurred related to a limited number of individuals (Greenwood and Woods, 1919), much effort went into identifying the personal characteristics of workers who were 'accident prone'. In general, this research failed to establish a clear and stable linkage between such characteristics and accident propensity, at least to the point where its findings could be used as a basis for 'selecting out' those who were more likely to suffer accidents (Lawton and Parker, 1998).

This is not to say that worker personality, cognitive capabilities and attitudes and motivation do not play a role in the occurrence of accidents. There is some evidence, for example, to suggest an association between accident experience and personality characteristics such as extroversion, aggression, anxiety, general social deviance, and a positive attitude to risk taking (Glendon and McKenna, 1995). Similarly, variations in worker attitudes have been found to be associated with inter-departmental and inter-company differences in accident rates, and younger and less experienced workers have been found to be more likely to suffer an accident.

It is also true that worker errors have been identified as a major cause of accidents. As a result, a number of attempts have been made to develop classifications of such errors. One of the most well known of these is the Generic Error Modelling System developed by Reason (1990). In this model three different types of error are distinguished:

- skill-based, encompassing unconscious automatic actions resulting in slips and lapses;
- rule-based, involving either the application of a bad rule to a situation or the application of a good rule wrongly; and
- knowledge-based, consisting of mistakes made during problem solving.

The fact that worker errors contribute to the occurrence of accidents does not, however, necessarily mean that they can unquestionably be held responsible for them. Thus, the reference to applying 'bad rules' in the context of rule-based errors highlights the fact that organizational factors may also play a role. For example, skill-based errors and the accidents arising from them may reflect both the provision of inadequate training and the utilization of work processes that are unnecessarily vulnerable to such slips and lapses, and knowledge-based ones may also stem from inadequate training in problem identification and resolution.

In fact, Reason has argued that rather than being the main instigators of an accident, operators tend to be the inheritors of system defects created by poor design, incorrect installation, faulty maintenance and bad management decisions (Reason, 1990). In other words, that the 'active errors' that are the immediate precursor of accidents frequently stem from broader 'latent failures' located in the broader working environment which are the responsibility of management. Reason has consequently further argued that the efforts of safety specialists could be directed more profitably towards the proactive identification and neutralization of latent failures, rather than at the prevention of active failures.

The upshot of existing research findings is therefore that the causes of accidents are often multidimensional and hence cannot be fully understood by merely examining the immediate actions that gave rise to them. This point is echoed in a number of accident causation models and theories (Dyer, 2001; W S Atkins Consultants Ltd, 2001). For example, Johnson's Management Oversight and Risk Tree (MORT) constitutes an attempt to operationalize a theory of accident causation that takes as its starting point the fact that the antecedents of accidents 'often develop in a number of sequences involving physical, procedural and personal elements' (Johnson, 1980). Consequently, their identification requires attention to be paid to such issues as management structures and the distribution of responsibilities within them, planning and design processes, the machinery and materials used, supervisory practices, task procedures, and the actions of workers and third parties.

MANAGEMENT OF HEALTH AND SAFETY

More generally, the models developed by Johnson and others, including Hale and Glendon (1987), can be seen to support the adoption of a systems approach to the management of workplace safety. That is an approach that is typically seen to encompass four main types of management processes:

- the assessment of risk;
- the development of strategies to control/remove the risks identified;
- the putting in place of arrangements, including the provision of adequate training and information and the creation of appropriate management structures and systems of accountability, to ensure that these strategies are implemented effectively; and
- the establishment of arrangements to monitor the adequacy of the control strategies themselves, as well as their operation, and the development of procedures which ensure that any weaknesses identified through these arrangements are addressed.

Given this, in the following subsections attention is paid to a number of issues concerning the design and operation of each of these processes.

Assessment of risk

A number of statutory duties are imposed on employers in respect of the carrying out of risk assessments, most notably under the Control of Substances Hazardous to Health Regulations 1999 and the Management of Health and Safety at Work Regulations 1999.[1] The Approved Code of Practice which accompanies these latter regulations makes clear that the nature and depth of the assessments required depend on the types of risks present at the workplace. For example, in paragraph 13 it notes that for 'small businesses presenting few or simple hazards a suitable and sufficient risk assessment can be a very straightforward process based on informed judgment and reference to appropriate guidance'. In contrast, it also observes that 'large and hazardous sites will require the most developed and sophisticated' assessments and goes on to point out that there may be 'some areas of assessment for which specialist advice is required'.

Organizations can, and do, adopt different approaches to regarding who carries out risk assessments. In addition, different approaches may be adopted within the same organization in relation to particular types and areas of activity. Nevertheless, five main choices with regard to the 'authorship' of assessments can be identified. These are:

- the utilization of internal health and safety specialists, such as safety advisers/managers, occupational health physicians and hygienists;
- outside health and safety consultants;
- line managers;
- workers engaged in the activities concerned, an approach, for example, sometimes utilized in relation to the evaluation of visual display equipment workstations; and
- joint assessments by internal specialists/line managers and workers or their representatives.

Each of these options has potential advantages and disadvantages. Outside consultants, for example, may bring in much-needed specialist expertise but be unable to sufficiently take into account the way in which work activities are actually carried out rather than how they are formally supposed to be conducted. In contrast, while line managers and workers and their representatives may have a greater awareness of actual work practices, they may lack the health and safety knowledge and expertise needed to carry out an effective risk assessment. That said, there is some evidence to suggest that provision for worker input into the assessment process can be potentially beneficial by providing a different perspective to that of managers concerning the nature and causes of workplace risks. For example, on the basis of a series of case studies conducted in the chemical industry, Dawson *et al* (1988) found that there 'was a clear relationship between positions in the hierarchy and perceptions of hazards across establishments'. In particular, they discovered that substantially larger proportions of senior and middle managers than first-line supervisors and safety representatives saw hazards as arising from weaknesses in attitudes, knowledge and behaviour rather than stemming from the chemicals produced, or the surrounding mechanical and material environment.

As to the relative use made of each of the above options, little evidence is at present available. However, it seems unlikely that the majority of employers utilize health and safety specialists, for the simple reason that most of them do not possess such staff – a situation that can be contrasted with the situation in other European countries where statutory requirements exist relating to their use (Walters, 1996). For example, the current membership of the Institution of Occupational Safety and Health (IOSH) stands at around 25,000, of which only 40 per cent consist of corporate members who are both professionally qualified and have three years' relevant work experience (James and Walters, 1999). In a similar vein, a 1993 HSE-funded study found that just 8 per cent of private sector establishments either employed, or had access to, occupational health specialists such as occupational physicians and nurses and hygienists (Bunt, 1993). Such a lack of specialist expertise inevitably raises concerns about not only the quality of many assessments but how far employers are even aware of their legal obligations regarding them and the protective and preventive actions that they need to take on the basis of the results obtained. These concerns are, moreover, given added weight by research findings which suggest that a significant proportion of organizations, particularly smaller ones, are unaware of relevant statutory requirements (Hanson *et al*, 1998).

Adoption of preventive and protective strategies

The earlier discussion of the causes of work-related accidents and ill health indicated that the effective management of risk can require consideration to be given to a range of different types of actions. These include the removal of hazards from the workplace, for example through ceasing to use certain substances and activities and the adoption of safer machinery and processes; the supply of protective equipment; and the design of work environments, equipment and processes that are compatible with the physical and psychological characteristics and capabilities of workers. They also encompass the establishment of adequate methods for assessing risks and identifying necessary remedial actions, the provision of appropriate information and training to workers, initiatives to change worker safety perceptions and attitudes, the putting into place of adequate mechanisms to ensure that organizational rules and procedures are complied with, and the employment of staff who have the expertise necessary to ensure that all of these activities are carried out adequately.

The fact that appropriate risk assessments have been conducted does not, however, necessarily mean that their findings will be translated into the taking of effective preventive actions. Indeed, there is ample evidence to suggest that either their findings may be ignored or that the measures put in place as a result of them are inadequate. Reason's observation that workers may be encouraged to circumvent laid-down safety procedures due to the fact that they are incompatible with work activities adds weight to this point (Reason, 1990). The same is true of the following extract from Lord Cullen's official report (Department of Transport, 1998) on the causes of the 1987 King's Cross fire:

Many of the shortcomings in the physical and human state of affairs at King's Cross on 18 November 1987 had in fact been identified before by internal inquiries into escalator fires... The many recommendations had not been adequately considered by senior managers... London Underground's failure to carry through the proposals resulting from earlier fires... was a failure which I believe contributed to the disaster at King's Cross.

Consequently, it is clearly important that adequate mechanisms are put in place to ensure that the findings of assessments do lead to the taking of effective remedial actions. It further needs to be borne in mind that, in considering what actions need to be taken, it is preferable to remove risks and combat them at source through, for example, the enclosure of dangerous machinery or the extraction of hazardous fumes, rather than place reliance on the provision of personal protective clothing and other equipment and the specification of rules and procedures designed to avoid workers engaging in practices that are potentially hazardous. Thus, it has been observed that: 'There is one form of defence that we know really does not work, that is the use of specific instructions and procedures in which errors are not allowed, but no further preventive measures are taken other than telling people not to do it' (Wagenaar and Hudson, 1998).

Implementation of preventive measures

Even if appropriate health and safety precautions are developed, it does not follow that they will be implemented effectively. Dawson *et al* have, for example, usefully drawn attention to the fact that the 'technical control of hazards' – a term seen to incorporate the processes of hazard identification and assessment, the prescription and implementation of control and the maintenance, monitoring and adaptation of control standards and procedures – is unlikely to be carried out adequately in the absence of a supportive wider organizational context (Dawson *et al*, 1988). In particular, they have argued that three aspects of this context exert a critical influence in this regard. These are the presence of a positive commitment to health and safety at all levels of the organization; the defining of responsibilities to clearly demonstrate that line managers bear direct responsibility for the health and safety of their subordinates; and the establishment of systems for monitoring performance and thereby maintaining individual and organizational accountability.

Between them the above three factors can be seen to highlight two related issues that are widely seen as central to the operation of an effective health and safety management system. First, the according within organizations of a high priority to the protection of worker health and safety. Secondly, a willingness to integrate the subject of health and safety into the wider and more general management of the organization. Or, to use the analogy put forward by Frick, to move beyond a situation whereby health and safety is treated as a 'side car' activity rather than one that is core to an organization's operation (Frick, 1990).

In practice, it is clear that neither of these features exist in many organizations. As a result, the implementation of well-intentioned health and safety arrangements can be highly problematic. Thus, in an environment where senior management is uncommitted to health and safety, not only may training and other resources not be available to support the implementation of health and safety reforms, but there is a clear danger that compliance with existing arrangements may suffer in the face of conflicting work pressures and a view that such compliance is of relatively little importance. For example, line managers may encourage workers to ignore safety rules in order to maintain production levels; or workers can be tempted to cut corners as a means of protecting or enhancing their earnings and may feel free to circumvent laid-down working methods in order to avoid the restrictions they impose on them (Nichols and Armstrong, 1973; Wrench and Lee, 1982; Reason, 1990).

In recent years, and in recognition of the way in which such attitudinal factors can adversely affect health and safety performance, increasing attention has been paid to the taking of actions to improve health and safety cultures or climates (HSE, 1989; Pidgeon, 1997). This growth of interest is understandable. It is also, to some extent, soundly based, since a number of studies have shown how actions to change workforce attitudes can yield beneficial safety outcomes (Donald and Young, 1996).

At the same time, it needs to be recognized that, somewhat ironically, such change programmes are likely to be less successful within a context of poor management support and commitment. Indeed, there is evidence from the wider human resource management literature to suggest that centrally driven culture change programmes may, by downplaying countervailing workforce views and values, actually generate conflict rather than consensus and hence ultimately be counterproductive (Harris and Ogbonna, 1998). Consequently, while programmes aimed at creating more positive attitudes to workplace health and safety may yield beneficial results, this is only likely where considerable care is taken with regard to their design and implementation.

Monitoring health and safety performance

In broad terms, health and safety performance can be monitored in two ways. First, through the use of various 'output' measures which provide an indication of the extent to which the existing health and safety system has been successful in preventing (or not) worker ill health and injury. Secondly, the utilization of 'process' methods aimed at assessing the adequacy and operation of the health and safety arrangements in place. Each of these different forms of monitoring are discussed, in turn, below.

'Output' measures

A number of different indices can be used to measure the scale of work-related harm caused by work activities. These include employee sickness absence records; occupational health records, including first-aid treatments and the results of health assessments; self-report data provided by workers; and accident statistics.

The compilation and analysis of accident statistics is almost certainly by far the most utilized of these measures. However, organizations differ considerably in terms of the types of statistics they collect. Thus, some may limit their collection to those that are reportable under the Reporting of Injuries, Diseases and Dangerous Occurrences Regulations 1995, namely those that cause 'major injuries', result in fatalities or give rise to absences from work of 'over three days'[2]. In contrast, others may also compile figures on accidents giving rise to first-aid treatments and/or absences of shorter duration, such as those resulting in an absence from work of a day/shift.

A further point to note is that it is common for the statistics so compiled to be used to calculate accident rates that (a) provide a means of tracking trends in accident performance that are not due to variations in hours worked or numbers employed and (b) enable an insight to be gained into variations in the severity of the injuries caused (International Labour Office, 1983). Three of the most commonly used of these are accident frequency rates, accident incident rates and accident severity rates. These are calculated on the following bases:

1 Accident frequency rate $= \dfrac{\text{Total number of accidents}}{\text{Total number of man hours worked}} \times 1{,}000{,}000$

   ie accidents per 1,000,000 hours worked

2 Accident incident rate $= \dfrac{\text{Total number of accidents}}{\text{Number of persons employed}} \times 1{,}000$

   ie accidents per 1,000 employees

3 Accident severity rate $= \dfrac{\text{Total number of days lost}}{\text{Total number of person-hours worked}} \times 1{,}000$

   ie the average number of days lost per 1,000 hours worked

Such accident rates can be used to track trends over time within a whole organization, particular workplaces and specific departments. They can also be used to benchmark accident performance against that of the relevant sector or comparable operations either within the same organization or elsewhere. In addition, rates of this type can be broken down in order to identify differences in them between, for example, males and females, workers of different ages, and those employed in different occupational groupings.

Accident statistics therefore not only provide a potentially valuable source of information on overall and comparative standards of safety performance, but also can be used to gain insights into areas of activity where remedial action is needed (Boyle, 1994). At the same time, a potentially important limitation of such data is that, by definition, they only relate to 'undesirable' events that have actually resulted in injury. As a result, they exclude from consideration other such events that, perhaps fortuitously, did not cause harm and in doing so can potentially give a misleading picture of health and safety performance (Health and Safety Executive, 1976).

This last point, in fact, receives wide acknowledgment in the literature on health and safety through the concept of accident triangles (Health and Safety Executive, 1997). Thus, such triangles have been used to show statistical relationships between different types of accident and to support the view that the effective control of the most rare types of accident, those causing fatal and serious injuries, requires attention to be also paid to the control of the more common types, which cause more minor injuries and involve 'near misses' and damage to plant and other property. For example, the HSE has utilized LFS and RIDDOR data to show nationally that for every fatal accident there are 207 leading to serious or minor injuries, 1402 resulting in absences of over three days and 2754 causing minor personal injury (HSE, 1999).

The logic of this 'accident triangle' argument has not, it should be noted, been universally accepted. In particular, it has been pointed out that the events giving rise to near misses vary in terms of their potential to cause injury, and to focus attention on them on an indiscriminate basis runs the danger of according insufficient priority to those involving greater risks to worker safety. Nevertheless, accident triangle analysis does highlight the fact that statistics on injury-causing accidents are likely to provide only a partial indicator of the standards of safety management in place and hence can usefully be supplemented by data on other events that have the potential to cause injuries. In addition, by drawing attention to the often fortuitous relationship between unplanned hazardous events and the occurrence of injuries, it can be seen to provide a strong rationale for organizations to put in place arrangements that seek to assess proactively the degree to which workplace risks are being managed. It is therefore to this issue that attention now turns.

'Process' measures

A number of different techniques can be employed to assess more proactively the adequacy and operation of the existing health and safety management system. For example, workforce 'safety climate' surveys can be conducted to provide information on current policies, practices and attitudes; and worker exposures to particular occupational health hazards, such as noise and fumes, can be measured through such means as health surveillance and the use of 'hardware' like noise meters; investigations can be conducted into accidents and dangerous occurrences; and inspections and audits can be carried out.

It is beyond the scope of this chapter to provide a detailed exposition of all of the above techniques. However, as regards the investigation of accidents and other incidents, reference should be made to the need (given the preceding discussion of the causes of accidents) that in such investigations attention is paid to the potential role of both 'active errors' and 'latent failures', as otherwise the conclusions reached may be misleading. Account also needs to be taken of the fact that internal 'political' considerations and interpersonal relationships can potentially act to influence their conclusions and hence objectivity (Mascini, 1998).

In addition, some brief discussion of audit systems is merited since it appears that an increasing number of organizations, or at least the larger ones, are adopting them. Systems of this type, which are now often supported by computer software aimed at facilitating their analysis, can serve several different purposes. In particular, they can assess whether organizationally required and/or 'acceptable' (in the sense of legally required or officially recommended) arrangements are in place; investigate the extent to which such arrangements are in practice implemented; and, more generally, identify actions where improvements need to be made. They can further differ in terms of their form, and hence the degree to which they embody these objectives, and also vary regarding their 'authorship' and who conducts them (James, 1994a, 1994b, 1995). For example, systems can be completely internally created; or a complete package can be purchased from a commercial supplier; or a 'software shell' can be bought which can subsequently be used to develop an organizationally specific format. Similarly, audits can be conducted by an outside organization; by internal health and safety specialists drawn from a workplace; or, in the case of multi-establishment undertakings, or the wider organization, by using line managers or by joint working parties consisting of managerial personnel and their representatives. Finally, systems can differ in the extent to which they generate quantitative numerical scores, which can be used to identify trends in performance, as opposed to qualitative observations.

Unfortunately, little, if any, detailed research exists concerning the actual effectiveness of audit systems in improving health and safety management. It is consequently not possible to say which among these various options, all of which are currently used, are to be preferred. However, it seems reasonable to say that in choosing between them, due account should be paid to their appropriateness to the organizational context within which they are to be used. It further seems reasonable to emphasize that the impact of any audit system will depend on the rigour with which it is applied and the degree to which any resulting recommendations are implemented.

THE ISSUE OF WORKFORCE INVOLVEMENT

It has long been argued that worker involvement can make an important contribution to the maintenance and improvement of health and safety standards through exerting a positive influence on each of the four management processes discussed above: the assessment of risk, the identification of appropriate preventive measures, the implementation of such measures, and the monitoring and review of their adequacy. This belief has, in turn, resulted in the introduction of a statutory framework for such involvement. Consequently, against this background, this section reviews the case for such involvement, briefly outlines the current legislative arrangements relating to it and examines the extent of its usage.

The case for worker involvement

The involvement of workers in health and safety can be seen to make a potentially positive contribution to standards of health and safety in three main ways. First, through providing a means of using the detailed knowledge of workers and their representatives to identify risks and the measures needed to reduce them. Secondly, by engendering a greater degree of worker ownership and hence support for any preventative arrangements put in place. Thirdly, through creating channels by which management priorities and views in respect of health and safety can be challenged.

Such involvement can occur through both direct and indirect methods that may, or may not, be concerned exclusively with the issue of health and safety. These include: participation in risk assessment processes; membership of safety improvement teams and other types of problem-solving groups; team briefings and toolbox meetings; as well as health and safety committees and more broadly based consultative bodies. The evidence available concerning the effectiveness and impact of these various forms of involvement remains rather limited. However, that which does exist tends to support the view that they can yield beneficial results, particularly if they incorporate trade union representation (James and Walters, 2003). For example, an analysis of data from the 1990 Workplace Industrial Relations Survey found injury rates to be significantly higher in manufacturing workplaces where management dealt with health and safety matters without any form of workforce consultation (Reilly, Paci and Holl, 1995). The study also found that while workplaces that possessed health and safety committees had lower injury rates, this was particularly the case in those workplaces where all employee members of them were chosen by unions.

At the same time, it is also clear that the effectiveness of worker involvement is very much influenced by both the structures and broader organizational environment within which it operates. Research findings which shed light on the factors that affect the operation of health and safety committees illustrate this point clearly (Beaumont et al, 1982; Kochan, Dyer and Lipsky, 1977; Bryce and Manga, 1985). For example, the evidence suggests that committees tend to be more effective where there is a high level of commitment from employers, particularly through the appointment of at least one senior corporate officer who is able to exercise real authority; members have the information and knowledge to contribute effectively; management–worker relationships are good and worker representation operates through trade union channels. In addition, the effectiveness of committees has been found to be influenced by such structural factors as the quality of communications that exist between them and the workforce; the regularity of their meetings; the degree of attendance at them; and the size of their membership.

The current regulatory framework

It was not until the late 1970s, following the introduction of the Health and Safety at Work Act 1974, that rights to worker representation in respect of health and safety became a significant part of UK law. The Act provided for regulations to be made under which (a) recognized trade unions could appoint safety representatives, (b) the workforce could elect such representatives, and (c) these representatives could request the establishment of health and safety committees. Subsequently, as a result of pressure from the trade union movement, the power to make regulations for the workforce election of safety representatives was removed through the repeal of Section 2(5). However, regulations in the form of the Safety Representatives and Safety Committees regulations (SRSC) 1977 were introduced to provide trade unions with the right to appoint such representatives.[3]

Under the SRSC regulations an independent union is entitled to appoint safety representatives from amongst the employees of an employer by whom it is recognized. Once appointed in accordance with the regulations, representatives are accorded a number of functions which entitle them to:

- investigate potential hazards and dangerous occurrences, and causes of accidents;
- investigate complaints relating to an employee's health, safety or welfare at work;
- make representations to employers on these and on general matters affecting health, safety and welfare of employees;
- carry out workplace inspections;
- represent employees in consultation with health and safety inspectors;
- receive information from such inspectors;
- attend safety committee meetings.

In addition, safety representatives are entitled to the paid time off that is necessary to enable them to carry out their functions and to undergo such training as is reasonable in the circumstances. Employers are also obliged to make available information within their knowledge that is similarly necessary and to establish a safety committee, if requested to do so by two or more safety representatives.

Employers have a general duty to consult safety representatives by virtue of 2(6) of the Health and Safety at Work Act 1974. It is made clear under the 1977 regulations that this duty extends to consulting representatives in 'good time' over the following matters:

- the introduction of any measures that may substantially affect the health and safety of employees;
- the appointment and nominating of competent persons in accordance with regulations 6(1) and 7(1)(b) of the Management of Health and Safety at Work Regulations 1999;
- any health and safety information that must be legally provided to employees;
- the planning and organization of any health and safety training that must be legally provided to employees;
- the health and safety consequences for employees of the introduction of new technologies in the workplace.

Since the coming into force of the 1977 regulations, two further significant sets of legislative developments have occurred. The first came in the wake of the Cullen inquiry into the Piper Alpha disaster and led to the Offshore Installations (Safety Representatives and Safety Committees) Regulations 1989 (Woolfson, Foster and Beck, 1997). These provided for safety representatives to be elected from all workers in a constituency system and accord those so elected a variety of rights which, broadly, equate with those laid down under the 1977 regulations. The second, involving the introduction of the Health and Safety (Consultation with Employees) Regulations 1996, came as a result of concerns that the SRSC regulations failed to comply with the requirements of Article 11 of the EU's safety framework directive – concerns linked to the fact that no provision was made for the representation of non-unionized workers.[4]

The duty of consultation under the 1996 regulations extends to encompass the same matters as those specified in the SRSC regulations. However, employers are given discretion as to whether they consult employees directly or via elected representatives, known as Representatives of Employee Safety (RES). If this representative route is chosen, employers are obliged to provide the RES with adequate information so that they can fully and effectively participate in consultations and carry out their functions of making representations and consulting with employers and inspectors. Representatives are also entitled to training, time off, and such other facilities and assistance as they may reasonably require for undertaking their functions. However, in contrast to union-appointed safety representatives, they have no rights relating to the carrying out of workplace inspections, the inspection of statutory health and safety documents and the investigation of employee complaints and notifiable accidents and dangerous occurrences. In addition, they are not able to require the establishment of a safety committee.

The coverage of employee involvement

No comprehensive data is available on the extent to which direct forms of worker involvement in health and safety are utilized. However, the four workplace industrial/employee relations surveys provide comparable data on three types of representative arrangements: health and safety committees; joint committees of managers and employees dealing with health, safety and other matters; and the existence of workforce health and safety representatives in establishments where no such committees exist. The surveys, taken together, reveal that, in broad terms, around two-thirds of workplaces had one of these three forms of employee representation on health and safety matters during the period 1980–98 (Millward, Bryson and Forth, 2000). However, their findings also reveal that the coverage of such arrangements has fluctuated during this period, with the proportion of workplaces with them increasing from 69 to 72 per cent from 1980 to 1984, falling to 57 per cent during the period 1984–90 and rising again to 68 per cent between the years 1990–98.

The WIRS and WERS series also contain some interesting findings regarding the role of unions in health and safety committees (Millward *et al*, 2000). Thus, they reveal a marked decline in the extent to which unions appointed employee representatives, with the result that by 1998 union-appointed representatives existed in just one-third of workplaces. This waning of union influence was found to be most evident where union density was low and where there were no on-site union representatives. For example, where union representatives did exist, unions were found to make appointments to health and safety committees in 83 per cent of cases in 1990 and 37 per cent in 1998. In contrast, where such representation was absent, the corresponding fall was from 78 to 4 per cent. This decline of union influence clearly is a cause for concern, given the evidence referred to above concerning the positive impact of union representation on levels of workplace injuries.

CONCLUSION

Levels of work-related injuries and ill health remain high and impose enormous costs on workers, employers and society as a whole, although doubts exist as to how far it is possible to validly argue that a 'business case' exists for organizations to expend more resources on actions designed to reduce the scale of such harm. There is nevertheless general agreement as to the basic processes that need to be adopted if health and safety are to be managed effectively. In broad terms, these processes encompass the carrying out of assessments to identify risks; the adoption of appropriate remedial measures to address any problems highlighted through such assessments; the taking of action to ensure that these measures are meaningfully implemented; and the establishment of mechanisms to ensure that the performance of the health and safety system is kept under review. In addition, the available evidence indicates that both direct and indirect forms of workforce involvement can make an important contribution to the maintenance and improvement of workplace health and safety standards.

The available evidence, however, also indicates that aspects of the wider organizational environment can exert a crucial influence over the degree to which such processes are utilized and the extent to which they are carried out effectively. In particular, it is clear that health and safety are likely to be most effectively managed where senior management accords the issue a high priority; management is seen to constitute an integral element in the more general operation of an organization; and action has been taken both to clarify the responsibilities of line managers and put in place arrangements to ensure that they are accountable for the way in which they carry them out.

Notes

1 Control of Substances Hazardous to Health Regulations 1999 (SI 1999/437); and Management of Health and Safety at Work Regulations 1999 (SI 1999/3242).
2 Reporting of Injuries, Diseases and Dangerous Occurrences Regulations 1995 (SI 1995/3163).
3 Safety Representatives and Safety Committees Regulations 1977 (SI 1977/500).
4 Health and Safety (Consultation with Employees) Regulations 1996 (SI 1996/1513); and James, P and Walters, D (1997) Non-union Rights of Involvement: The Case of Health and Safety at Work, *Industrial Law Journal*, **26** (1), pp 35–50.

References

Beaumont, P, Coyle, J, Leopold, J and Schuller, T (1982) *The Determinants of Effective Joint Health and Safety Committees*, Centre for Research into Industrial Democracy, University of Glasgow
Boyle, A (1994) Records and Statistics, in *Safety at Work*, ed J Ridley, 4th edn, Butterworth-Heinemann, Oxford
Bryce, G and Manga, P (1985) The Effectiveness of Health and Safety Committees, *Relations Industrielles*, **4** (2), pp 257–81
Buckle, P and Devereux, J (1999) *Work-related Neck and Upper Limb Musculoskeletal Disorders*, Office for Official Publications of the European Communities, Luxembourg
Bunt, K (1993) *Occupational Health Provision at Work*, HSE Contract Research Report 57/1993, Health and Safety Executive, London
Cox, T, Griffiths, A and Rial-Gonzalez, E (2000) *Research on Work-related Stress*, Office for Official Publication of the European Communities, Luxembourg

Cutler, T and James, P (1996) Does safety pay? A critical account of the Health and Safety Executive document: The Costs of Accidents, *Work, Employment and Society*, **10** (4), pp 755–65

Dawson, S, Willman, P, Bamford, M and Clinton, A (1988) *Safety at Work: The Limits of Self-Regulation*, Cambridge University Press, Cambridge

Department of Transport (1998) *Investigation into the King's Cross Underground Fire*, HMSO, London

Donald, I and Young, S (1996) Managing safety: an attitudinal-based approach to improving safety in organizations, *Leadership and Organization Development Journal*, **17** (4), pp 13–20

Dyer, C (2001) Accidents, near misses, and the analysis of their causes, *Health and Safety Bulletin*, No 300, July/August, pp 15–20

Frick, K (1990) Can management control health and safety? *Economic and Industrial Democracy*, **11**, pp 375–99

Glendon, A I and McKenna, E (1995) *Human Safety and Risk Management*, Chapman & Hall, London

Greenwood, M and Woods, H (1919) *A Report on the Incidence of Industrial Accidents with Special Reference to Multiple Accidents*, HMSO, London

Hale, A and Glendon, A I (1987) *Individual Behaviour in the Control of Danger*, Elsevier, Amsterdam

Hanson, M, Tesh, K, Groat, S, Donnan, P, Ritchie, P and Lancaster, R (1998) *Evaluation of the Six-Pack Regulations 1992*, HSE Contract Research Report 177/1998, HSE Books, Norwich

Harris, L and Ogbonna, E (1998) Employee responses to culture change efforts, *Human Resource Management Journal*, **8** (2), pp 78–92

Health and Safety Commission (1999) *Health and Safety Statistics 1998/99*, HSE Books, Norwich

Health and Safety Commission (2001) *New Health and Safety Statistics show Fatalities Up, Reported Non-Fatal Injuries Down*, HSC Press Release, 30 July

Health and Safety Commission/Department of the Environment, Transport and the Regions (2000) *Revitalising Health and Safety: Strategy Statement*, Department of the Environment, Transport and the Regions, London

Health and Safety Executive (1976) *Success and Failure in Accident Prevention*, HMSO, London

Health and Safety Executive (1989) *Human Factors in Industrial Safety*, HSE Books, Norwich

Health and Safety Executive (1997) *The Costs of Accidents at Work*, HSE Books, Norwich

Health and Safety Executive (1999) *The Costs to Britain of Workplace Accidents and Work-related Ill Health*, HSE Books, Norwich

Heinrich, H (1980) *Industrial Accident Prevention: A Safety Management Approach*, 5th edition, McGraw-Hill, London

International Labour Office (1993) *Encyclopedia of Occupational Health and Safety*, 3rd edn, International Labour Office, Geneva

James, P (1994a) Applying STOP at Searle Pharmaceuticals, *Health and Safety Bulletin*, No 217, January, pp 8–10

James, P (1994b) Auditing systems: Coursafe at Kodak, *Health and Safety Bulletin*, No 223, June, pp 12–14

James, P (1995) Auditing Systems: CHASE at British Waterways, *Health and Safety Bulletin*, No 230, February, pp 10–12

James, P and Walters, D (eds) (1999) *Regulating Health and Safety: The Way Forward*, Institute of Employment Rights, London

James, P and Walters, D (2003) Worker Representation in Health and Safety: A Review of the Regulatory Options, *Industrial Relations Journal*, **34** (3)

Johnson, W (1980) *MORT: Safety Assurance Systems*, National Safety Council, Chicago

Kochan, T, Dyer, L and Lipsky, D (1977) *The Effectiveness of Union–Management Safety and Health Committees*, W E Upjohn Institute for Employment Research, Kalamazoo

Lawton, R and Parker, D (1998) *Individual Differences in Accident Liability: A Review*, HSE Books, Norwich

Mascini, P (1998) Risky information: social limits to risk management, *Journal of Contingencies and Crises Management*, **6** (1), pp 35–44

Millward, N, Bryson, A and Forth, J (2000) *All Change at Work: British Employment Relations 1980–1998, as Portrayed by the Workplace Industrial Relations Survey Series*, Routledge, London

Nichols, T and Armstrong, P (1973), *Safety or Profit: Industrial Accidents and the Conventional Wisdom*, Falling Wall Press, Bristol

Pidgeon, N (1997) The limits to safety? Culture, politics, learning and man-made disasters, *Journal of Contingencies and Crises Management*, **5** (1), pp 1–14

Reason, J (1990) *Human Error*, Cambridge University Press, Cambridge

Reilly, B, Paci, P and Holl, P (1995) Unions, safety committees and workplace injuries, *British Journal of Industrial Relations*, **33** (2), pp 276–88

Smith, A, Johal, S, Wadsworth, E, Harvey, I, Smith, G and Peters, T (1999) Stress and health and work, part IV, *Occupational Health Review*, No 80, pp 28–31

W S Atkins Consultants Ltd (2001) *Root Causes Analysis: Literature Review, HSE Contract Research Report 325/2001*, HSE Books, Norwich

Wagenaar, W and Hudson, P (1998) Industrial safety, in *Handbook of Work and Organizational Psychology*, ed P Drenth, H Thierry and C de Wolff, Psychology Press, London, pp 65–88

Walters, D (1996) *Occupational Health and Safety Strategies in Europe, Vol 1 – The National Situations*, European Foundation for the Improvement of Living and Working Conditions, Office for Official Publications of the European Communities, Luxembourg

Woolfson, C, Foster, J and Beck, M (1997) *Paying for the Piper: Capital and Labour in Britain's Offshore Oil Industry*, Mansell, London

Wrench, J and Lee, G (1982) Piecework and industrial accidents: two contemporary case studies, *Sociology*, **16** (1)

20

Managing training and development

Jim Stewart

This chapter has two main components. The first draws on academic debates concerning terminology and the meanings that can be, and are, attached to a number of related concepts. These concepts all have some application to managing training and development in work organizations. The second component draws on recent empirical research conducted by a partnership of universities and research institutions across Europe. More detail on the design of the research will be provided later in the chapter. The two components are utilized to support the conclusions on managing training and development offered at the end of the chapter.

HUMAN RESOURCE DEVELOPMENT

An alternative title for this chapter is 'The management of Human Resource Development (HRD)'. HRD has become increasingly used to denote those activities concerned with promoting and facilitating the learning of employees in work organizations (Stewart and McGoldrick, 1996). Three characteristics of those activities are commonly argued to be significant in distinguishing HRD from what might be termed traditional approaches to training and development (Sambrook, 1998). First, HRD encompasses activities focused on the learning of 'non-employees' (Walton, 1999). With the claimed rise in flexible employment contracts and application of notions of 'core' and 'peripheral' workers, development of non-employees could be argued to be as significant to organization success as that of workers employed on standard and traditional contracts. If the term non-employees is taken to encompass employees of, for example, strategic partners, suppliers or customers, whether they are 'core' or 'peripheral' in the context of their own employers, then in some industries and for some companies, non-employee development might indeed be a critical success factor. The second characteristic has a similar rationale. It is simply that HRD has more direct links with, and more significance for, organization and business strategies (Harrison, 2000). This is a similar argument to that which led to the use of the term Human Resource Management (HRM) in place of personnel management (McGoldrick and Stewart, 1996). So, according to those analyses, HRD is associated with the view that employees and their knowledge learning, commitment and capability are the only sustainable source of competitive advantage. The development of human resources therefore becomes a 'competitive weapon' (Barham and Rassam, 1989), and thus HRD, unlike training and development, provides a strategic contribution to organization success. The third and final characteristic of HRD is a focus on organizational as well as individual learning. Such a focus is not without its problems since it assumes that organizations can be conceived of as learning entities, and theorizing the nature of organizational learning processes has proved difficult (Easterby-Smith *et al*, 1999). However, those difficulties are not so great that useful attempts have not been offered (Argyris, 1999), and so the focus remains a distinguishing characteristic of HRD.

Notwithstanding these defining characteristics, the term HRD itself is problematic. Some research suggests that it is a term of more interest to academics than to practitioners, and that its use is less common among practitioners and others in work organizations (see eg Sambrook, 2000; Sambrook and Stewart, 2001). Even among academics, there is a continuing debate on the nature and meaning of HRD (McGoldrick, Stewart and Watson, 2000). However, the concept has clear links with related and additional terms of contemporary interest, including lifelong learning and learning organizations (Tjepkema *et al*, 2002). The former has been, and is, applied in UK government and EU policies related to vocational education and training (DfEE, 1998), and the latter is now widely applied in organizations in the United States, the UK and across Europe in attempts to create strategic advantage (Tjepkema *et al*, 2001). The rest of this chapter will therefore briefly examine those related terms before proceeding to describe the purpose and nature of current HRD policies and practices.

LIFELONG LEARNING AND LEARNIN
ORGANIZATIONS

The notion of lifelong learning is not new. It originally emerged in the 1970s along with related concepts such as 'recurrent education'. However, the term came to the attention of policy makers in the 1990s, which led to the European Union declaring 1996 as the official European Year of Lifelong Learning. According to the Organization for Economic Cooperation and Development (OECD), promoting lifelong learning has the following objectives: 'to foster personal development, including the use of time outside work (including in retirement); to strengthen democratic values; to cultivate community life; to maintain social cohesion; and to promote innovation, productivity and economic growth' (OECD, 1996). These are ambitious and lofty goals. To some extent, they relate to promoting and developing a 'learning society' (Glass, 1996). A learning society provides the necessary infrastructure to support learning throughout the life span of individuals. Ensuring the existence of such an infrastructure requires contributions from employing organizations and individuals, as well as from education and training providers and public authorities (Pawlowsky and Bäumer, 1996). The need to develop a learning society through promoting lifelong learning is argued to arise from significant changes in social and economic conditions affecting countries across the world. These changes are summarized in the UK government's 1998 Green Paper on lifelong learning:

> We stand on the brink of a new age. Familiar certainties and old ways of doing things are disappearing. Jobs are changing and with them the skills needed for the world of tomorrow... Learning is the key to prosperity... To achieve stable and sustainable growth, we will need a well-educated, well-equipped and adaptable workforce... We cannot rely on a small elite: we will need the creativity, enterprise and scholarship of all people. (DfEE, 1998)

There are a number of problems with these policy-based conceptions of lifelong learning. Two are worth highlighting in the context of this chapter (see Sambrook and Stewart, 2001). First, there is an emphasis on formal learning opportunities. This can be illustrated by the key and significant role afforded by the UK government to the University for Industry/Learndirect in achieving its policy objectives in relation to lifelong learning. Second, the individual is defined as the significant learning unit. While this reflects the application of currently dominant theories of learning (Stewart, 1999), it does ignore recent developments in the understanding of learning as a social process which underpin and inform the notion of organizational learning. It can be argued that the concept of the learning organization overcomes both of these problems. Before moving on to that concept, the related notion of 'work-based learning' is worth mentioning. The Chartered Institute of Personnel and

velopment (CIPD) is nearing the end of a five-year research project examining the application of that concept (CIPD, 2000). With a focus on learning with colleagues through the experience of work itself, promoting work-based learning may be the most important contribution of employers to achieving the policy goals of lifelong learning, and the CIPD research may provide useful guidance on how that can be done. As mentioned earlier, the concept of the learning organization is not without its problems. It does, though, have a sound theoretical origin in the notions of single and double loop learning (Argyris and Schön, 1978). The work of Argyris and Schön on learning processes in organizations suggests a distinction between learning which occurs within an established frame of reference, referred to as single loop learning, and learning which questions and challenges the established frame of reference and so provides new understanding of the nature of organizational problems. This latter form of learning is referred to as double loop learning.

The notion of the learning organization also benefits from wide experience of practical application (see eg Pedler *et al*, 1996). In straightforward terms, a learning organization is one which promotes and achieves continuous and shared learning as the basis of deciding on mission and goals, and the means of their achievement. In that sense, becoming a learning organization means adopting a particular organizational form rather than pursuing a particular organization strategy. That said, adopting that particular form is argued to be the means of achieving organization success (Senge, 1993), and so there is a clear association with strategy. This association of organization form with strategy is one argument in favour of the view that the concept of the learning organization is the ultimate articulation of the philosophy and goals of organization development (Stewart, 1996).

There are many descriptions and prescriptions in the literature on the form of learning organizations. Most encompass four essential characteristics (Stewart, 1999). The first is that organization members are both committed to and skilled in managing their own learning and development. Second, the existence and effective application of processes which promote mutual learning. Third, the existence and effective application of processes which promote the dissemination and sharing of learning. The first of these characteristics has an obvious and straightforward focus on individual learning. The second and third have a focus on organizational learning, and on linking the two processes of individual and organizational learning (see Sambrook and Stewart, 2001; Nonaka and Takeuchi, 1995). The fourth and final characteristic is a necessary condition for the other three, though it is insufficient without them for creating a learning organization. It is simply a matter of management style. What is needed to engender the other three characteristics is a style which fosters and encourages experimentation, independence in thought and action and involvement in decision making: a style which emphasizes control, dependence and conformity will not be able to achieve this. However, the possibility of achieving such a management style, at least with the level of consistency required, provides further grounds for doubting the realization of learning organization principles (Coopey, 1996). This doubt arises from the operation of *power relationships* within work organizations. Despite the rise of alternative discourses such as those associated with empowerment, it is clear that managerial hierarchies remain a constant factor in organizational design. Thus, the implicit unitary assumptions and commonality of interests associated with conceptions of the learning organization cannot be said to have been realized in practice. However, a further common theme in the literature on learning organizations is an emphasis on *becoming* rather than *being*. In other words, the learning organization form is a journey rather than a destination and the ideal should not be expected to be realized (Swieringa and Wierdsma, 1992). Related to this view is the argument that organizations are never in any case 'steady state' entities and are in a constant state of flux (Chia, 1996).

This brief discussion of lifelong learning and learning organizations has shown the links between those terms and HRD. The latter has a concern with promoting informal and continuous learning, as well as with traditional approaches to training and development, and so supports a conception of lifelong learning wider than that associated with current policy interventions. It also focuses on organizational learning and the strategic potential of learning and development. There are therefore clear links with the concept of the learning organization. The chapter now turns attention to examining HRD in more detail.

HRD IN EUROPE

Recent research has investigated the role of HRD policy and practice across Europe in promoting lifelong learning in learning-orientated organizations (Tjepkema *et al*, 2001). The project was funded by the European Commission and was conducted by partner institutions in France, Italy, Finland, Germany, the Netherlands, Belgium and the UK. Four case study organizations were researched in each of the seven countries and an additional 30 organizations in each country responded to a postal survey. The results and findings therefore reflect HRD practice in over 230 work organizations across Europe. The project commenced in January 1998 and was completed in December 2000.

The term 'learning orientated' is applied to work organizations with an intent to work towards learning organization principles and characteristics. The research considered the context influencing the role of HRD, the role envisioned by HRD professionals, the strategies adopted to perform that role and factors which both inhibit and support achieving the intended role and contribution. The following sections adopt those headings and draw on the findings of the research to describe and illustrate current issues in managing HRD in work organizations.

Organization context

The challenges identified by organization decision makers have a remarkably high degree of commonality across Europe. Two in particular are consistent. The first is increasing competitiveness in product markets. This in part relates to processes of globalization. The second challenge, though, also has a connection with competitiveness. This is the impact of technology, especially information and communications technology (ICT). This is seen as both a threat and an opportunity in terms of competitive advantage. Responses to these challenges in terms of business strategy are also remarkably similar, and again, two are consistent. The first, perhaps unsurprisingly, is to develop a client or customer-centred focus throughout the organization. The second is to increase innovation in products and services. In some cases, both of these strategic responses are related to the opportunities provided by technological development. A number of additional strategies related to internal organizational processes, for example process re-engineering programmes and increasing flexibility, are also pursued by some companies. An example of this context is provided by Wolverhampton and Dudley Breweries (W&DB) in the UK. As the largest 'regional' brewer in the UK, the mission of W&DB is to remain independent by resisting takeover by one of the large brewing multinationals. The strategy to achieve that mission is based on satisfying shareholders through continuous improvements in performance, achieved in turn through continuous improvements in customer satisfaction.

The two main challenges and two leading strategic responses are consistently recognized to have implications for the management of human resources, and HRD in particular. Implementation of competency frameworks, use of personal development plans, developing new styles of managing and developing a learning culture are examples of commonly applied changes in approaches to HRD. The examples are also illustrative of the strategic contribution of HRD. For example, it is argued in many organizations that these HRD interventions are essential to achieve the desired strategic response of a customer orientation and/or innovation in products and services. Such an argument and position does, though, illustrate another consistent finding of the research. This is that HRD, and the management of human resources more generally, are considered to be subservient to business strategy. In other words, only in a very few organizations is HRD itself considered to constitute the business strategy. In the majority of organizations, HRD interventions are seen as support mechanisms in the implementation and achievement of business strategies.

Envisioned role of HRD

By and large, HRD practitioners accept and often embrace the supportive position and role of HRD in relation to business strategies. This can be seen in their declared ambitions for the role and contribution of HRD departments. This in turn can be defined in terms of the objectives set by practitioners for their specialist departments and the division of HRD tasks they seek to promote in achieving those objectives. The most common objective set and pursued by practitioners is that of 'supporting the business'. In some cases, this is specified in more detail as being related to a current strategy, such as improving customer and client focus. In others, it is a more generalized objective of supporting business strategy. Examples of these include companies where the primary HRD objective is articulated as 'helping the company meet current and future challenges', or 'ensuring training and development contributes to corporate strategy'. In other cases, objectives are expressed more in HRD terms and language, for example 'keeping the organizational skills base up to date' or 'defining key competences and organizational learning needs', but these too are objectives with a clear focus on supporting the achievement of business strategies.

A second set of common objectives relates to supporting individual learning which, in many cases, also has a specific focus on informal learning. Examples of more general learning include objectives related to competence development and the professionalization of employees. The use of the latter term has a broader meaning than the narrow focus on professional qualifications that it might have in the UK. In those organizations where the term is used, the meaning of the concept refers to enabling employees to perform their job to the highest standards. Other examples have more direct connections with promoting lifelong learning; 'increasing the learning capacity of employees' and 'creating the conditions for lifelong learning', for instance. Objectives with a specific focus on informal learning include creating a learning culture in the workplace and stimulating appreciation and use of on-the-job learning opportunities. They also include those related to more informal methods such as coaching and mentoring. All of the objectives related to individual learning have two further characteristics of interest. First, they are as concerned with stimulating motivation to learn as they are with the provision or exploitation of learning opportunities. Second, and particularly in the case of the last group of examples, the objectives are also intended to change established and traditional views of learning and development. The 'hidden agenda' is to change the perception of managers and employees that HRD is concerned exclusively with courses and didactic methods.

Three additional categories of objectives are identified in the research, although the consistency and commonality of these are more variable. The first is to do with knowledge sharing. Included here are examples which utilize directly related language such as 'stimulate knowledge transfer' and 'develop knowledge exchange networks'. Other examples which focus on supporting team learning and promoting organizational learning are also considered relevant to this category. A major reason for this is the differences in terminology and language used in different organizations to express similar objectives. The second category of objectives is concerned with more traditional approaches to training and development. Examples included here are objectives to do with an adequate supply of training courses and with coordinating training provision. The final category is concerned with changing the HRD function itself. Objectives in this category focus on, for example, becoming more proactive, adopting new approaches and methods and integrating the HRD function more closely with business operations.

As well as their functional objectives, HRD professionals also define their desired role by the division of HRD tasks they envisage in achieving the objectives. Three additional groups are identified as undertaking such tasks: line managers, individual employees and external institutions. The first of these, line managers, are seen as the most important of these groups. It is clear that in a significant number of organizations line managers have devolved any formal responsibility for the development of their staff. In some cases, this manifests itself in staff development being a factor which features in managers' own performance objectives and assessment. In others, the responsibility is a recognized and acknowledged shared expectation on the part of HRD specialists, line managers and other employees, but it is not formally specified in performance management systems. However, the research indicates that the formalization of the contribution and responsibility of line managers is likely to grow in the future. The kinds of tasks which managers are and will be responsible for include devising and agreeing personal development plans with their staff, identifying learning needs, competence assessment and evaluation of HRD activities. While being slightly less common, individual responsibility for learning and development on the part of employees is also found to be a widespread phenomenon. This responsibility might be best characterized as an expectation that individual employees will take an active part in planning and fulfilling their development. In part, this characteristic arises from the fact that there is a great deal less clarity on the tasks to be performed by employees compared to that of managers. The most clearly defined is active involvement in identifying personal and individual needs as part of the process of producing personal development plans. As with managers, it is also the case here that the responsibility and involvement of individual employees are expected to increase in the future. In some companies, the two are linked in that the responsibility would be shared with line managers. One interesting finding of the research is that the expected increase in individual responsibility did not vary significantly across industries. Both manufacturing and service-based companies report similar results. Activities undertaken by external institutions, as might be expected, are largely confined to providing training and development programmes. Advisory and specialist services such as provision of assessment centres are reported in a few cases. In contrast to the other groups, the contribution and responsibilities of external institutions are expected to decrease in the future.

HRD strategies

In summary, the research suggests that the primary role of HRD is seen as providing support to the achievement of business objectives by providing formal training and opportunities for informal learning and knowledge sharing, and that this requires the active involvement of line managers and individual employees. HRD then is seen as a three-way partnership rather than as the sole responsibility or domain of HRD departments and professionals. The next question that arises, and which was examined in the research, concerns the nature of HRD strategies devised to fulfil the envisioned role. These strategies can be related to the objectives identified in the previous section, the first of which is supporting the business.

In the case of generalized support for business strategy, HRD strategies themselves also tend to be expressed in general terms. For example, in Motorola in France, the strategy is to move away from a 'catalogue' or 'menu' approach to HRD to much closer relationships with operational managers which, in turn, is intended to ensure relevant and timely HRD interventions. In other cases, the strategy is to adopt a 'demand-driven way of operating' or 'to provide organization development'. Where HRD aims to support more specific business strategies, the HRD strategies themselves are formulated in more specific terms. Examples include the design and implementation of culture change programmes, competency frameworks and programmes to support the development of team working and associated skills. For example, in Barilla, an Italian food producer, HRD professionals provide both formal training and development and ongoing advice and consultancy to line managers and their teams to support the implementation of self-managed teams in a new organization structure. Additional specific strategies found in the research include some that focus on recruitment and selection. A Finnish steel-producing company, Outokumu Zinc, provides an interesting example. In that company, a willingness to learn is incorporated as a generic criterion in the recruitment and selection of new employees.

The second set of strategies is related to the objective of supporting informal learning. As with the previous strategies, there is variability in the consistency and commonality of these strategies, and in the degree of specificity in the language in which they are expressed. However, common examples include non-course-based methods such as coaching and mentoring as well as action-learning-type activities such as special project and problem-solving groups. An interesting example of the latter is that found in the UK Royal Mail. The programme is called 'Pathfinders' and involves groups of eight competitively selected individuals working as teams to address a problem identified and sponsored by a business manager. Another interesting UK example is that found in W&DB, the brewing company mentioned earlier. Termed 'three-in-car', this programme involves an HRD professional coaching sales managers by observing and providing feedback on their coaching a member of their sales team. Other strategies under this heading focus more on emphasizing individual responsibility for learning as well as encouraging the use of non-traditional or non-course-based methods. The use of personal development plans and open learning or learning resource centres are two common examples. Other examples include provision of secondments and organized visits. An example of the latter is that found in Valmet, a Finnish paper mill. Here, groups of employees from across the organization are sent on visits to German customers and are proscribed from speaking Finnish during the whole trip. This not only improves their language skills but also provides a more international outlook and customer focus in their role and tasks in the mill. The cross-functional groups also facilitate organizational learning which carries on after the trips. A final example relates to this and other sets of objectives. The Belgian telecommunications company, Alcatell Bell, introduced a minimum number of training hours for all employees. The total hours are broken down into both formal and off-the-job training, and more informal and on-the-job training.

Objectives related to knowledge sharing also have supporting HRD strategies. Many of these are technology based in the form of intranets and computer-supported knowledge exchanges. However, while not specifically identified by the respondents as related to knowledge sharing, many of the types of strategies mentioned above would also be relevant under this heading. An example is provided by the UK financial services company, Royal Scottish Assurance. HRD professionals attend regional sales meetings where ideas and suggestions from financial advisers are discussed. The HRD professionals pass on those adopted by their region to their HRD colleagues who then introduce them at their own regional sales meetings. This clearly supports knowledge sharing even though the identified purpose is to support informal learning. The respondents in the research companies may have been inclined to associate knowledge sharing with only technology-based initiatives or programmes because of the general association of the two in the academic and professional literature (Scarbrough et al, 1999).

Two other types of strategies are identified in the research. The first are identified by the companies themselves as being concerned with the provision of traditional training and development. These include both off-the-job and on-the-job courses related to 'technical' or 'functional' training. However, even some of these strategies have, in some cases, non-traditional components. For example, some companies utilize intranets in the delivery of the courses, while others refer to the use of other modern media techniques such as 'video networking' or 'virtual classes'. The second are strategies concerned with changing HRD practices in the organization. This cluster of strategies includes those intended to support the decentralization of HRD responsibilities and activities. Examples here include the provision of tools and techniques, including processes and formats for producing personal development plans, to support both managers and employees in fulfilling new responsibilities. In some cases, these strategies also focus on developing HRD skills and abilities in managers through management development programmes. An example where this occurred is the Italian software company, Datalogic. In this company, managers are assessed and developed on their ability and motivation to support the learning of employees. Interestingly though, development for HRD professionals themselves is much less common. Decentralization of HRD activities is related to those professionals adopting new and different advisory and consultancy roles in place of the traditional training provider role (Stewart, 1999). However, few examples of deliberate and planned development for HRD professionals are apparent in the companies researched.

One final finding of the research is worth noting. Evaluation of HRD policy and practice has long been recognized as being neglected (Harrison, 2000). The research specifically investigated the existence of evaluation strategies, especially in relation to success in achieving the envisioned role and the effectiveness of the chosen strategies in achieving that role. While most companies engage in some evaluation activities, these cannot be said to be strategic in the sense of measuring the impact of HRD strategies on business objectives, or even on changing attitudes and roles among managers and employees in relation to HRD. It seems therefore that evaluation continues to be neglected.

It is clear from this research that HRD professionals formulate and adopt specific and deliberate strategies to support a change in their intended role. These strategies focus on directly supporting the achievement of business strategies and objectives; promoting informal learning; facilitating mutual learning and knowledge sharing; utilizing advances in ICT; and changing beliefs about and attitudes towards HRD within the organization. The latter is concerned with promoting ideas such as the learning organization to develop the notion of learning through work and working through learning to achieve continuous improvement in both. It is, though, important to realize that the provision of traditional training and development through formal courses remains a significant component of HRD policy and practice. However, this too can support other strategies and purposes through, for example, the use of ICT as a delivery mechanism. In some cases, this can also be true without the use of news media and techniques. For example, certificates of achievement are issued to all employees who complete a defined amount of formal training by ISS, a Belgian cleaning company. The purpose is to develop self-confidence and positive attitudes towards learning and development. Both of these are seen by the ISS HRD professionals as necessary conditions for success in promoting informal and self-managed learning. This approach has similarities with the employee development schemes promoted in the UK, where individual employees control a personal budget to spend on their own development (DfEE, 1998). It seems, therefore, that even strategies related to traditional training and development can be useful in creating a learning culture of the type associated with the concept of the learning organization.

Some individual and organizational factors will, though, facilitate the development of such a culture, and others will inhibit its development. Identifying those factors, and how HRD professionals respond to them, provided an additional focus for the research project.

Influencing factors

The results of the attempt to identify facilitating and inhibiting factors are mixed in that in many cases the same factor operated in both directions. In other words, the same factor can work to facilitate achievement of a new role for HRD in some companies while working to inhibit the change in other companies or, in some cases, do both at the same time in the same organization. A clear example is that of motivation to learn on the part of employees. A second example is the willingness of managers to accept and fulfil HRD responsibilities in relation to their staff. The following paragraphs therefore should be read in the context of the findings being very generalized and the existence of significant variability both across and within the organizations included in the study.

The two examples just given are the most commonly cited and significant inhibiting factors. Reasons for the lack of motivation on the part of employees and resistance to new responsibilities on the part of managers were not investigated and so, based on this research at least, are open to speculation. It is also likely that there will be great variability across organizations and indeed individuals. However, a further set of factors may provide some clues as to some of the reasons. These are to do with what might be termed pragmatic factors. Examples of these include increasing and intensifying workloads and associated lack of time for learning and development activities. This set of factors is again commonly cited as being significant. They also applied to HRD professionals and HRD departments, as well as to line managers and employees. Here, lack of HRD resources is the specifically identified inhibiting factor. Resources could mean either professional staff and/or the size of HRD budgets. Related to this also is the workload of HRD staff in relation to traditional activities rather than activities intended to support managers and employees in their new roles and responsibilities. An additional and related inhibiting factor is lack of clarity on the role of HRD professionals and the HRD department. In general, the lack of clarity is on the part of managers and employees, though in some cases it also applies to HRD professionals themselves. The final significant inhibiting factor is a general resistance to change. Taken all together, these inhibiting factors lead to a lack of the desired learning culture necessary for achieving the envisioned role of HRD.

As already indicated, many of the factors identified also work to facilitate and support achievement of a new role for HRD. High employee motivation and acceptance of involvement in HRD by managers in particular are commonly cited supportive factors. In addition, the use of new approaches and methods within HRD strategies and positive results being achieved by these are identified as being significant supportive factors. The same is true of new organizational structures and redesigned jobs. Two examples come from Germany. The chemicals producer Agr Evo and the consultancy firm GTZ both report structures and jobs based on teams as being supportive of a new role for HRD.

A number of strategies designed and intended to overcome the inhibiting factors and/or to exploit the facilitating factors are also identified across the seven European countries. The most common and significant of these, perhaps unsurprisingly, are based on creating effective communications. The initiators are HRD professionals, supported by senior managers in some cases, and the targets are line managers and employees. The content focuses on both the new envisioned role of HRD and the importance of continuous and informal learning and development. Some of these strategies also focus on involving managers and employees in devising and implementing HRD strategies and activities. Additional coping strategies include producing clear specifications of HRD roles and responsibilities, internal and external networking, demonstrating the added value of HRD and continuously updating HRD products and services.

A EUROPEAN MODEL OF HRD

The research results reported so far suggest that HRD departments across Europe are initiating and, to some extent at least, achieving significant changes in their role. There is a focus on a partnership approach to responsibilities with line managers and employees, and /or building learning cultures consistent with the principles of learning organizations in order to support both lifelong learning and the achievement of the economic goals of work organizations. New approaches and methods are being adopted in HRD strategies to achieve this new role, and to respond to the range of factors which influence the success of the envisioned role. Two further questions were addressed in the research, the first of which concerned differences across economic sectors.

Cross-organizational comparisons

As already stated, the research design included 28 case study companies and a postal survey of a further 200+ organizations. Companies in the former were classified as either manufacturing or service sector, and as either mass production or customer orientated in the delivery of their products or services. In the case of the survey, the effects of different organizational structures were investigated. The categories assigned to these were 'divisionalized', 'functional' and 'networked'.

Differences in economic sector and orientation were subject to analysis in the case study results. This indicated that any differences in goals, objectives or strategies cannot be accounted for by the two variables of economic sector and production or customer orientation. The results in general are surprisingly consistent; that is certainly the case in the UK case study organizations. The same also seems to be true of the case study organizations in the other six European countries. Overall therefore, the conclusion is drawn that differences across companies are not influenced significantly by either economic sector or a mass production or customer orientation. This result suggests that organization-specific variables such as history and tradition, recent and current performance, and the personalities involved are likely to be more significant in shaping HRD policy and practice. However, the sample of 28 cases in seven countries provides a limited basis for the conclusion.

The survey results were subject to detailed and sophisticated statistical analysis. While still small in number, the larger sample size adds to the confidence that can be placed in the results. The survey, though, did have a weakness that was not true in the case of the case studies, and that was that responses were provided only by HRD professionals. So, these results also need to be treated with some caution. The results of the main focus of the research such as organization context, role of HRD, HRD strategies and influencing factors were statistically analysed against the variable of organization structure and design. The results themselves present a homogenous picture with few significant differences. Where differences do exist, the further analysis suggests that these are not associated with organization structure. In other words, the differences that are found are not consistently related to whether the organization adopts a 'divisionalized', 'functional' or 'network' structure. This again suggests that organization-specific variables such as history and tradition and current personalities are likely to be more significant. However, one further set of variables, those to do with the country of operation, might be significant and so this too was investigated.

Cross-country comparisons

When subject to statistical analysis, there are more noticeable and clear differences in the results from each of the seven countries. This suggests that national as well as organizational variables may be significant in explaining differences in HRD policy and practice. However, the nature and content of those variables was not part of the investigation and so cannot be identified here. It is, though, possible at least that variation in national vocational educational and training policies adopted by the various national governments will be one significant variable. Even without possible explanations, it is useful to illustrate some of the differences.

The Netherlands seems to have companies with a greater focus on mergers and creating cost advantages as organization challenges than other European countries included in the study. There is also a greater use of open learning in HRD strategies. In Belgium, HRD seems to be less involved in supporting business strategies, and in initiatives such as knowledge management. Belgian companies, though, do seem to attach greater importance than those in other countries to the employee benefits of HRD policy and practice. In contrast, Finnish companies appear to have strong involvement of HRD in realizing business strategies, including significant change programmes. German companies identify a much more positive impact from the influencing factors such as clarity on the role of HRD and resources allocated to HRD. They also seem to report a higher degree of use of innovative learning methods than the other countries. The opposite is the case in France where traditional training and development approaches such as off-job courses seem to be more widely utilized. It also seems to be the case that the concept of the learning organization is less widely applied by French companies. In Italy, benchmarking as an HRD strategy is utilized more frequently than in other countries, and all of the influencing factors are rated as having a positive impact. The situation in the UK will be examined shortly.

A European model?

As well as relying on the results summarized above, a literature review was undertaken by the research team to compare HRD policy and practice in Europe with that in the United States and in Japan. The results above suggest that there is in fact no European model of HRD. It is the case that the differences found in the cross-country analysis are relatively small in number and significance. However, they are sufficient to conclude that variability in policy and practice across difference countries could not justify the formulation of a single European model. Based on the literature review, the same seems to be true of the United States and Japan; it is not possible to describe a single model for each of those countries. A limiting factor does, though, need to be acknowledged. The majority of the literature is based on policy and practice in large firms, so significant parts of the economy are largely excluded from the reported analyses.

Within the constraints of all of those caveats, a small number of interesting differences can be suggested. First, responsibility for HRD lies much more commonly and firmly with managers in Japan when compared with policy and practice in the United States and in Europe. The existence of separate HRD departments seems to be less common in Japan. Second, more responsibility is placed on the individual in the United States than in either Japan or Europe. Finally, the role of the HRD professional is that of a traditional training provider in Japan, that of an organization consultant in the United States and something of both in Europe. All of these points are of course very broad generalizations. They do suggest, though, that European policy and practice seems to be moving in a direction which encompasses elements of both US and Japanese policy and practice.

The UK situation

Turning now to the UK as compared with the other European countries included in the study, three observations are of potential interest and significance. Each of these will be discussed, with potential explanations. The explanations, though, are purely speculative as establishing reasons for differences was not part of the research design.

The first item is that UK companies report much less emphasis on internationalization as a strategic challenge than is the case in other European countries. This is the case both in terms of the current situation and expected future challenges. It would be wrong to conclude from this that international trade is less important to UK companies, or that the UK is somehow less affected by global competition. It is probably arguable that the reverse is in fact the case since the UK has a longer tradition and a higher incidence of international trade and global competition than some of the other countries in the study (Hollinshead and Leat, 1995). It is possible therefore to suggest that greater experience of internationalization in the UK explains the observation. Companies in the UK may have more confidence in their ability to operate internationally than those in the other countries, and so are less likely to rate internationalization highly as a strategic challenge when compared with alternative challenges.

UK companies also appear to emphasize the effects on and for employees as a justification for developing learning-organization-type cultures than do those in some of the other countries. This observation is supported by the absolute and comparative ratings given by UK respondents to items concerned with improving the quality of working life, improving employee retention and increasing employee commitment. There are of course many possible reasons for this being the case. Perhaps some of these will be associated with the wider application of models of HRM within the UK. A related reason which may be significant is the greater emphasis in recent years by both UK governments and employers on promoting and creating flexible labour markets. It is arguable that the UK has been the leading proponent of this policy objective in Europe, and that it has achieved a higher degree of success than other European countries (Bryson, 1999). A possible consequence of this is 'success' in bringing about a change of attitude to the employment contract on the part of employees as well as employers (IPD, 2000). Thus, individual employees deliver less commitment and loyalty to companies in response to decreasing levels of job and employment security. Over time, this may have resulted in companies needing to respond in turn by developing new and alternative ways of gaining employee commitment and retention. Emphasizing HRD and developing the characteristics of a learning organization is one of these new approaches. Therefore, UK companies may show interest in HRD and the concept of the learning organization as a means of dealing with some of the 'unexpected' or 'unintended' consequences of increasing flexibility in labour markets. There is little empirical evidence against which this assertion can be tested. The assertion does, though, provide a logic to explain the survey results.

The third and final observation that arises from the survey is that UK companies utilize ICT in HRD practice less than most of those in the other countries. No reasons to explain this result present themselves. However, it is a result that should be of concern to HRD practitioners in the UK. The role and use of e-learning is now firmly on the agenda (IPD, 2000), and its utilization is on the increase in the UK (Stewart and Tansley, 2002). The results of this research, though, suggest that UK HRD policy and practice is in danger of falling behind the rest of Europe in the application and use of e-learning.

SUMMARY AND CONCLUSIONS

This chapter has demonstrated a changing role and contribution for human resource development in work organizations. Traditional approaches to training and development are decreasing in popularity and new approaches associated with the term HRD are increasing. This requires a partnership approach on the part of practitioners, with line managers and individual employees having active responsibility and involvement in managing learning and development. It also requires closer integration of learning and development with business strategies. These points imply a need to focus on both informal and organizational learning processes. Use of new technologies can support the achievement of the changing role, as can application of the concepts of lifelong learning and the learning organization.

A new role for HRD does, though, have implications for work organizations (Stewart and Tansley, 2002). It demands a change in beliefs about and attitudes towards learning and development on the part of organization members. Relatedly, it also requires new competences and abilities in relation to HRD on the part of managers, and in relation to learning skills on the part of all employees. HRD professionals also require new competences to fulfil their new role as learning and development advisers and consultants. A final implication arises from this changing role. Work intensification inhibits learning and development, as do traditional structures based on managerial hierarchies. The potential benefits therefore are unlikely to be realized without significant changes in the organization and structure of work.

There are three additional potential implications for UK employers arising from the research reported in this chapter. First, HRD practitioners may be a little complacent about the significance of internationalization as a strategic challenge facing work organizations. They may also be out of step with the attention given to this issue by their senior management colleagues. Second, the same may be true in relation to the potential offered by emerging technologies. While some progress in their application is being achieved, UK practitioners seem to be lagging behind their European counterparts. Finally, the benefits claimed for flexible labour markets may have to be tempered by increasing understanding of some of the unintended consequences. From one perspective, this may be argued to create opportunities for HRD in that investment in development is one way of increasing employee retention and commitment. However, it is unlikely to be a sole or permanent solution and so practitioners need to be aware of the problem and to be anticipating the longer-term implications for their practice in relation to their new role.

References

Argyris, C (1999) *On Organizational Learning*, Blackwell Business, Oxford

Argyris, C and Schön, D A (1978) *Organizational learning: A Theory of Action Perspective*, Addison-Wesley, Reading, MA

Barham, K and Rassam, C (1989) *Shaping the Corporate Future: Leading Executives Share Their Vision and Strategies*, Unwin Hyman, London

Bryson, C (1999) Managing uncertainty or managing uncertainly, in *Strategic Human Resourcing: Principles, Perspectives and Practices in HRM*, ed J Leopold *et al*, FT Pitman Publishing, London

Chia, R (1996) *Organizational Analysis as Deconstructive Practice*, De Gruyter, Berlin

CIPD (2000) *Success through Learning: The Argument for Strengthening Workplace Learning*, CIPD, London

Coopey, J (1996) The learning organization, power, politics and ideology, *Management Learning*, **26** (2), pp 193–214

Department for Education and Employment (1996) *Employee Development Schemes: What Impact Do They Have?* DfEE, London

DfEE (1998) *The Learning Age: A Renaissance for a New Britain*, London: The Stationery Office

Easterby-Smith, M *et al* (1999) (eds) *Organization Learning and the Learning Organization*, Sage Publications, London

Glass, R (1996) *The Goals, Architecture and Means of Lifelong Learning: European Year of Lifelong Learning*, Office for Official Publications of the European Commission, Luxembourg

Harrison, R (2000) *Employee Development*, 2nd edn, CIPD, London

Hirschey, M *et al* (1995) *Managerial Economics: European Edition*, The Dryden Press, London

Hollinshead, G and Leat, M (1995) *Human Resource Management: An International and Comparative Perspective*, Pitman Publishing, London

Institute of Personnel and Development (2000) *Training and Development in Britain 2000*, CIPD, London

McGoldrick, J and Stewart, J (1996) The HRM–HRD nexus, in *Understanding HRD: A Research Based Approach*, ed J Stewart *et al*, Routledge, London

McGoldrick, J, Stewart, J and Watson, S (2000) Researching HRD: Philosophy, process and practice, in *Understanding HRD: A Research Based Approach*, ed J Stewart *et al*, Routledge, London

Nonaka, I and Takeuchi, H (1995) *The Knowledge Creating Company: How Japanese Companies Create the Dynamics of Innovation*, Oxford University Press, New York

OECD (1996) *Lifelong Learning for All*, OECD, Paris, p 15

Pawlowsky, P and Bäumer, J (1996) *Further Personal Development within Corporations: Management of Qualifications and Knowledge*, Beck, Munich

Pedler, M *et al* (1996) *The Learning Company*, 2nd edn, McGraw Hill, Maidenhead

Sambrook, S (1998) *Models and Concepts of Human Resource Development: Academic and Practitioner Perspectives*, PhD thesis (unpublished), Nottingham: Nottingham Business School

Sambrook, S (2000) Talking of HRD, *Human Resource Development International*, **3** (2), pp 159–78

Sambrook, S and Stewart, J (2001) Reflections and discussion, in *Towards Learning Organizations in Europe: Challenges for HRD Professionals*, ed S Tjepkema *et al*, Routledge, London

Scarbrough, H *et al* (1999) *Knowledge Management and the Learning Organization: The CIPD Report*, CIPD, London

Senge, P M (1993) *The Fifth Discipline: The Art and Practice of the Learning Organization*, 2nd edn, Century Business, London

Stewart, J (1996) *Managing Change through Training and Development*, 2nd edn, Kogan Page, London

Stewart, J (1999) *Employee Development Practice*, Financial Times Pitman Publishing, London, p 18

Stewart, J and McGoldrick, J (eds) (1996) *Human Resource Development: Perspectives, Strategies and Practice*, Financial Times Pitman Publishing, London

Stewart, J and Tansley, C (2002) *Training in the Knowledge Economy*, CIPD, London

Swieringa, J and Wierdsma, A (1992) *Becoming a Learning Organization: Beyond the Learning Curve*, Addison-Wesley, Reading MA

Tjepkema, S, Stewart, J, Sambrook, S, Mulder, M, Horst, H and Scheerens, J (2002) *HRD and Learning Organisations in Europe*, Routledge, London

Walton, J (1999) *Strategic Human Resource Development*, Financial Times Prentice Hall, London

Acknowledgement

This chapter draws upon research funded by the European Commission. The financial support of the Commission is gratefully acknowledged.

21

Managing change in the employment relationship

Allan P O Williams

INTRODUCTION

In the late 1960s and early 1970s the major clearing banks found themselves having to deal with new forces in their environment. Increasing competition meant there was a need for greater efficiency. Greater efficiency in turn meant that more flexibility was needed in dealing with their human resources. They were faced with the strategic choice of either continuing to operate on the assumption that their employees had a job for life, or to introduce the notion that a job for life was no longer tenable and that a new 'psychological contract' had to be implemented. A fundamental change in the employment relationship was in the making.

The banks realized that in this new relationship they had a lot to learn from other industries with regard to developing a more professional approach to industrial relations and to human resource management. Learning to deal with the unions, and learning to recruit, train and retain key staff moved up the list of priorities. Several banks recruited experienced industrial relations managers from manufacturing industry, and all started to initiate formal courses for their staff managers (who were mainly qualified bankers) in an effort to turn them into more professional human resource managers (Williams, 1980). Such fundamental changes in the employment relationship can readily be discerned in more recent developments. Examples include the implementation of more flexible patterns of employment in the sense of time (full time or part time), location (home or teleworker), and autonomy (employee or consultant).

In the process of adapting to environmental change, organizations will face a range of choices. How they arrive at their decisions and how they implement them will affect the outcomes that they are trying to achieve, whether these are expressed in terms of such criteria as profitability, productivity, market share, corporate image etc. In this chapter we shall be exploring some of the guidelines that can be found in the academic literature for managing these processes of change. Figure 21.1 will be the framework for our discussion.

The bold aspects of Figure 21.1 capture the very visible and objective aspects of change in terms of the environment, organization and outcomes. Management devise coping and enhancing strategies in the pursuit of given objectives. As part of this process feedback mechanisms will enable them to exert a certain amount of control over these processes. In trying to understand why some organizations manage to achieve more successful outcomes than others, organizational theorists have created a rich pool of knowledge. The application of this knowledge is not a mechanical and standardized process, hence the importance of good quality information feedback so that managers can successfully adapt the application of this knowledge to suit their particular situation. It is to exploring some aspects of this knowledge in the context of changing the employment relationship that we now turn, with the help of Figure 21.1.

THE PSYCHOLOGICAL CONTRACT

One of the lessons that we quickly learn in studying organizations (or any social system for that matter) is that behaviour is determined as much by informal as formal factors. The individual/organizational interactions that individuals share in relation to their company help them to shape, and to be shaped by, organizational culture. Organizational culture is a concept being used to refer to those basic collective beliefs that individuals and groups learn and apply in the process of carrying out their jobs (Schein, 1985; Williams, 2001). The psychological contract is a term that has come to be used to define the relationship between an individual and the employing organization (Argyris, 1960). It refers to the individual's perception of this reciprocal relationship, that is, his or her beliefs as to what they will be doing for the organization and what the organization will be doing for them. Some of those beliefs will be shared across individuals and thus reflect an aspect of the culture of the organization; others will be unique to the individual. The psychological contract is therefore more subjective and covert than the legal contract of employment. The informal nature of the psychological contract means that its effective functioning has to be based on trust. The justification for this view

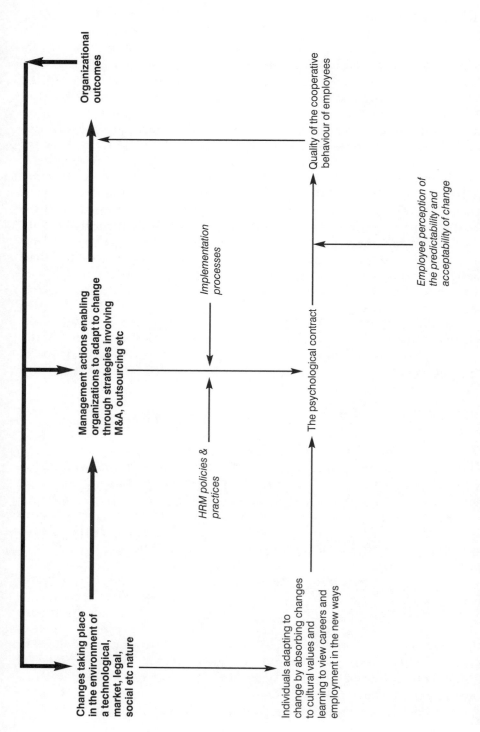

Figure 21.1 Managing change in the employment relationship

comes from the work of Rousseau and colleagues (Rousseau and Parks, 1993) who distinguish between two forms of psychological contract: the transactional, which is related to exchange theory (ie transactions between parties are independent events and not ongoing); and the relational, which is associated with social exchange theory (may involve unspecified obligations, the fulfilment of which is voluntary but highly likely to occur in a relationship of trust).

Thus employees may build up sets of beliefs relating to the sort of career that their employer has in store for them. Secure and lifelong employment were rewards that many organizations held out to staff a generation or two ago. This was not a written guarantee but it was equally as good – as long as you fulfilled the requirements of your job the company would look after your career interests. At one time this benevolent climate was very strong in the banking industry, and to a lesser extent still exists in parts of the Civil Service.

The nature of the psychological contract will change as employers seek more flexibility in adapting to changes in the market. What are the consequences if the employer violates the psychological contract? How can an organization 'manage' change in the psychological contract in order to minimize adverse effects?

QUALITY OF THE COOPERATIVE BEHAVIOUR OF EMPLOYEES

In return for the opportunity to work in an organization for given rewards, employees give something in return – they implicitly agree to cooperate in ways that they feel fulfil their legal and psychological contracts. From the point of view of management, the quality of this cooperative behaviour can vary widely. At one end of the scale there are those who show commitment, loyalty and put great effort into their jobs (the 'good citizens'). At the other end are those who cooperate only as far as is necessary in order not to lose their jobs (and thus reflect a transactional rather than relational psychological contract). Quality criteria extend beyond motivation to encompass standard of performance, ie the level of skill displayed in performing one's job.

Another way of exploring the criteria of cooperative behaviour is to follow the model of Katz and Kahn (1978) and to pose the question: What behaviours do employees need to display in order for organizations to survive in a changing and competitive environment? The authors specify the following:

- to join and remain employees;
- to consistently produce and maintain high standards of performance with respect to quantity and quality;
- to perform beyond role requirements, in other words to be creative and innovative according to needs and opportunities.

The important point to make here is that the 'quality of cooperative behaviour of employees' (ie the extent to which the above criteria are met) will moderate the effects that 'management actions' have on 'organizational outcomes'. (See Shore and Tetrick, 1994, for references to studies justifying this relationship in the context of the psychological contract.)

HRM POLICIES AND PRACTICES AND IMPLEMENTATION PROCESSES

In the process of adapting to change, management must recognize that they may be affecting the psychological contract and understand the implications of this for the quality of cooperative behaviour. There is also the need to recognize that the main problems encountered will arise in relation to existing rather than new employees. The expectations of new employees can readily be influenced at the recruitment and induction stages. However, the learning that takes place at these stages may be nullified over time if the culture of the organization is reinforcing the 'old' psychological contract. The socialization of new members takes place through interactions with existing employees and not only through the formal processes used in the recruitment and induction procedures (Wanous, 1992; Williams, Dobson and Walters, 1993).

The first step, then, in any planned attempt to change the employment relationship is to review the existing culture and identify those HRM policies and practices that are no longer appropriate for the new developing relationship. The second step is to generate sufficient momentum for making the changes. The third step is to implement the changes in a way that will create the minimum of resistance. Concomitant with these steps will be a continuous process of evaluation to monitor progress, and to revise action plans in the light of developing events. Of course in reality organizational change does not follow such logical and tidy steps in which management direct and control events as they would in the command structure of an army in battle. They have to take into account the interests of a range of stakeholders such as shareholders, the industry, unions, professional and trade bodies, the countries involved (as would be the case in multinational companies), and the individual employees themselves. Also, because of the power of certain interest groups, the 'choices' they make are largely predetermined. Thus IT professionals may be attracted to a company not because of the promise of a progressive career within the company, but because the experience will increase the range of their expertise and their market value. After three years they may feel that the technical challenges and the financial opportunities lie elsewhere. In such a situation the offer of job security and a slow but progressive career is unlikely to recruit and retain IT professionals.

One needs to be cautious not to over-generalize the changes taking place in the psychological contract. Nevertheless, there are many groups of employees who no longer expect to have a career within a single company. The cooperation they are prepared to extend to their employer may be limited. Thus, high-achieving managers may be motivated to display a high level of cooperative behaviour only so long as they find their jobs interesting, and financial rewards and promotion are perceived to be related to performance. A unionized workforce may display a high level of cooperative behaviour only so far as they feel that they are being dealt with fairly by management and that their unions are properly consulted on major changes, particularly those involving job changes and redundancy.

Changing aspects of an organization's culture with respect to the employment relationship (eg the length of their membership, opportunities for development, performance-related rewards) needs to be carefully managed if the level of cooperative behaviour is to be maintained and enhanced. Research that has been done so far on career-oriented groups indicate that there are three areas that companies need to focus on. First, there is the employability of the individual. Second, there is the perceived fairness and support extended to individuals whose membership is being terminated. Third, there is the leadership provided by management. The first two fall primarily under the wing of HR managers, and the last is primarily the responsibility of line managers. Let us look briefly at each of these in turn.

Employability

This is a concept that has rightly become popular in recent years. There are several aspects to it, but they all stem from the observation that individuals will have several different jobs during their working life because of environmental changes brought about by new technologies (eg the microchip), new competition, and the global labour market (eg cheap labour in developing countries). Employability means that if one employer no longer needs you, this is not the end of the road. Lifelong learning enhances the probability that your knowledge and skills will be updated and compatible with employment needs, and transferable to jobs that are expanding rather than contracting in number. Given the nature of the employment market for managers, employability is also increased for those who are prepared to be mobile and have at least one second language.

Employability therefore is facilitated by formal education and social norms as well as political factors. One of the basic ingredients of employability is the ability and willingness to take responsibility for managing one's own career. This contrasts with the 'traditional career' in which the paternalistic employer looks after your career in return for loyalty and commitment. Building for oneself a career out of a portfolio of jobs is a novel situation for many. As Bloch and Bates put it: ;You need to think of yourself as an intellectual nomad, rooted in knowledge rather than in one organization – and of the world as your marketplace.' (Bloch and Bates, 1995).

It is now recognized that it is good HR practice to run workshops in which individual employees can become more aware of their strengths and weaknesses in relation to given tasks. This knowledge or insight will enable them to plan appropriate actions to overcome their weaknesses and to build on their strengths. These planned developmental experiences will normally help them in their current job and make them more aware of alternative jobs that match their profile of competencies (Williams and Dobson, 1993; Stickland, 1996).

Fairness and support for those whose membership is being terminated or renewed

Being made redundant is a traumatic experience for many. Individuals need to know why redundancy is necessary and why they, as opposed to other colleagues, are being made redundant. Appropriate consultation and effective communications are essential for the sharing of this knowledge with employees. Those made redundant will need support, and possibly career guidance and counselling, to help them to re-establish themselves in alternative work. Again these support structures are already a feature of good HR practice.

An interesting, and somewhat surprising research finding is that there is also a need for organizations to provide support for those who remain. Survivors are not only likely to feel guilty in remaining employed while others are forced to go, but a major redundancy programme will almost certainly require them to change their role. Such 'internal' role transitions can be as stressful as the 'external' role transitions experienced by those made redundant. Studies suggest that HR managers need to be aware of this and to take steps to provide appropriate support and counselling. Research in this area is still yielding interesting findings. An example comes from a combined study of a case study of BT and a survey within the financial services sector. Few organizations appear to provide survivors with the help required in establishing a new psychological contract. The case study suggests that a redundancy programme is likely to result in a large drop in the loyalty felt toward the organization as a whole, but may have little effect on the loyalty felt at the level of the team (Doherty, Bank and Vinnicombe, 1996).

One of the unfortunate consequences of mergers and acquisitions is that they are almost always accompanied by redundancy programmes, and by 'unplanned' if not 'planned' cultural change programmes. This is often experienced as a 'violation' of the psychological contract. For those who remain employed it can have an adverse effect on the level of trust that may have developed as a feature of the psychological contract – the feeling of a fair deal between employer and employees. A relationship of trust takes time to develop but it can be destroyed overnight, and the consequences for the psychological contract and the quality of cooperative behaviour can be serious and long lasting (Herriot, Hirsh and Reilly, 1998).

Leadership in management

In the context of careers, particularly managerial careers, we have been witnessing a change in the psychological contract from one based on a relationship of trust to one driven by a 'bargaining relationship'. This latter relationship is no stranger to employees on the shop floor. In the case of managers and professional groups, they may have sufficient individual power (derived from their expertise and the criticality of their organizational role) to bargain directly with their employer rather than through a trade union. This individual bargaining power may take place explicitly, as when managers make out a case for a salary rise or promotion in the light of their market value; or implicitly, as when their cooperative behaviour shows signs of deteriorating, ie there is a decrease in their 'beyond role requirements' contributions (Katz and Kahn, 1978). This latter behaviour can be said to correspond to the work-to-rule behaviour of employees lower down the hierarchy.

Much has been written about leadership and what differentiates the leader from the manager. Our stance is that every manager is also a potential leader by virtue of the position that they occupy in the organization. However, those that we traditionally recognize as displaying leadership qualities are those who are never content with the status quo, but are constantly seeking to improve the performance of their teams and thereby of the larger organization. Where a psychological contract is characterized by a relationship of trust, or by a mutually satisfactory bargaining relationship, then there is likely to be sufficient commitment and loyalty for leadership qualities to be stimulated (ie to perform beyond the role requirements rather than imitate the 'free wheeling' manager). Where these conditions are not present the consequences can be expensive in many different ways. This is obvious where going on strike is part of the culture. In other situations low levels of cooperative behaviour may be less visible but equally damaging. Take for example the case of Railtrack in the UK where many managers have invested most of their life savings in the shares of their company (on the understanding that it is one of the safer investments, given the heavy involvement of the State), then to be told by government that the company has been put into administration. Such a violation of the psychological contract is hardly likely to motivate managers to show the leadership qualities desperately needed by their company.

While the characteristics of the systems that the HR function introduces to enhance employability and provide support are important, at the end of the day it is the implementation and operation of these systems that will impact on the quality of employees' cooperation and on organizational outcomes. It is therefore vital for all employees to understand the reasons and implications for changes in the employment relationship, and why and how the organization is coping with these changes. Line managers, from the most senior to the most junior, have a special responsibility here. The HR function can be instrumental in advising and designing appropriate structures and in training managers to operate them. But then it is up to managers to 'take the lead' by putting into practice the new learning and by helping others to do the same through modelling (Bandura, 1986) – the learning process that occurs when others imitate the behaviour of a model individual in the expectation that they will perform as well and experience the same rewards. This responsibility of line managers cannot be taken for granted, and needs to be dealt with explicitly on appropriate management development or leadership programmes.

EMPLOYEE PERCEPTION OF THE PREDICTABILITY AND ACCEPTABILITY OF CHANGE

There are two concepts that will help us to understand the conditions that are likely to affect the quality of cooperative behaviour. These are 'predictability' and 'acceptability'. Uncertainty, particularly in the context of job security, will generate stress in most employees (Lazarus and Folkman, 1984). Those who feel in control of their jobs, and the conditions surrounding their jobs, are less likely to experience uncertainty. This is partly why a participative culture in appropriate situations can be an attractive style of management. Employees feel more informed as to what is happening, and they feel that they can have an influence on decision making (Likert, 1967). Such a situation clearly favours 'predictability'.

Where participative management culture does not exist or is inappropriate (eg because of the autocratic culture of the society in which the company is located), then effective formal communications becomes critical (ie two-way so that misunderstandings can be minimized). Participative management is unlikely to exist where a redundancy programme is introduced (turkeys don't vote for Christmas!). Employees will want to know why the expectations they have come to share (the psychological contract) no longer hold, and what their employer is prepared to do by way of compensation and support to facilitate their coming role transition. As we have already pointed out, this information is as important for the survivors as for those made redundant.

The concept of acceptability in this context refers to the extent to which the employees' perceptions concerning the content and process of change are congruent with their expectations and their needs. In reality this is never an either/or situation – acceptable or not acceptable. In a restructuring situation many survivors will be offered a changed job. If this draws on their particular competencies and motivation, and adequate support and incentives are provided to facilitate the role transition, it is possible that the change will become more acceptable even though it may not have been at the outset.

However, for reasons that we have already indicated, in order to move from an unacceptable to an acceptable orientation, the expertise of the HRM function and the leadership qualities of line managers will be taxed.

The only circumstance that is likely to make redundancy acceptable to the less fortunate is if it is voluntary. The individual circumstance for some employees may be such as to make redundancy an attractive option. Following a takeover they may not want to work for their new employer; or they may see this as an opportunity to give vent to their entrepreneurial needs and to launch out into their own business. For those who do not welcome redundancy, little can be done apart from career counselling, paying for a consultation with a placement agency, and ensuring that there is enough financial support to provide a cushion until a suitable job is found. It is worth remembering that the overall package that is provided should be perceived as a fair one in order to minimize the adverse effects on leavers *and* on the survivors.

There is some evidence to suggest that the adverse effects of violation of the psychological contract can be lessened if there is enough information available to employees to show that the employer's breaking of the contract was involuntary, and that steps were taken to partially fulfil the psychological contract, eg voluntary retirement instead of redundancy (Bies, 1987).

As others have pointed out, the psychological contract serves a useful function in reducing uncertainty or increasing predictability (Shore and Tetrick, 1994). A formal contract can only cover so much; the psychological contract helps to fill the gap and to make the employee more informed, influential and confident about the conditions of employment. Predictability and control of the work environment are important ingredients in motivation theories. Thus expectancy theory states that beliefs that attractive rewards will follow good performance, combined with self-efficacy beliefs that predict one will achieve good performance, will create a powerful motivational force (Porter and Lawler, 1968; Bandura, 1997).

CONCLUSIONS

We are now in a position to return to Figure 21.1, and to summarize certain guiding principles for managing change in the employment relationship. These are very general principles that apply to managing change where the quality of employee cooperation is critical.

An organization is a system of interdependent elements, and any change in one element will have repercussions on others. A change in strategy, structure or technology will impact on organizational culture and the psychological contract. As Shore and Tetrick point out:

> Drawing on cognitive psychology, it has been proposed that people form schema and scripts which are highly structured, pre-existing knowledge systems to interpret their organizational world and generate appropriate behaviours. These schemas and

scripts can be thought of as individuals' belief structure of what is expected to occur in the organization and what is expected of them... As schemas, psychological contracts provide the employee with order and continuity in a complex employment relationship, allowing for predictability and control.' (Shore and Tetrick, 1994: 94)

It is because of these characteristics of employees that it is so important to predict what effects change will have on the employment relationship, and what planned steps need to be taken to minimize negative outcomes in terms of the quality of employee cooperation.

The literature on organizational culture change is relevant here since stable beliefs about the employment relationship are an aspect of organizational culture (and indeed national culture). Changing basic and shared beliefs is not an easy task, and it takes time (Williams, 2001). The self-reinforcing nature of organizational culture makes the task that much more difficult. Lewin's three-step model of change as unfreeze/change/refreeze is a useful framework (Lewin, 1951). Policies and practices that are part of the traditional culture need to be reviewed in order to identify those that are reinforcing movement in the desired direction and those that are working against these forces. Important elements here will include the content of induction training and management and career development workshops. If the strategy is to create a climate of trust in order to enhance the quality of cooperative behaviour, then line managers must be made aware of their role in achieving such an objective and provided with appropriate support structures (eg performance appraisal schemes that are 'developmental' rather than 'policing').

Unilateral efforts on the part of the employer to change the psychological contract will adversely affect the quality of employee cooperation. As we have seen, even in situations of mergers and acquisitions there are some 'good practice' steps that an employer can take. At the very least, individuals made redundant need to be seen to be treated fairly. A supportive (eg career counselling) and informative approach (eg through effective communications) will be more than repaid by the cooperative behaviour of the survivors.

A useful way of highlighting the potentially adverse effect of changes to the employment relationship is to be sensitive to their repercussions on the 'predictability' and 'acceptability' perceptions of those affected. Implicit in the psychological contract experienced by most individuals in developed countries are the beliefs that employees will be treated fairly, kept informed (through consultation and/or involvement) on matters that may affect their job and how it is performed and, as far as possible, be treated as an individual with a unique set of abilities and needs. These beliefs reflect the values of many democratic cultures; individuals bring these values as part of their 'baggage' into the organization. Employees who perceive that they have some control over their job (or at least work in an open climate where information is freely shared) will live in a more predictable world than those who do not. The former are less likely to suffer insecurity and stress. Acceptability is allied to predictability (changes that are expected as a result of planned, as opposed to informal learning experiences, are less likely to be emotionally arousing). But acceptability harbours an additional behavioural response. That is, whether the changes involved are likely to leave the employee worse off than before with respect to valued rewards (Porter and Lawler, 1968). Changes to the psychological contract are more likely to be tolerated (even if not welcomed) where certain conditions are perceived to be present.

Finally, organizations are complex social systems continually having to adapt to environmental change. Three key implications follow. First, as with individuals, they are more likely 'to learn from experience' when appropriate feedback mechanisms are in place (as suggested by the feedback loops in Figure 21.1). Attitude surveys are potentially useful tools in auditing the effectiveness of existing structures and procedures (Williams, 1998). Second, each organization is a unique entity (as are individuals) and therefore a response that has proved successful for one organization may not be the right solution for another. Third, guidelines are an attempt to make theories more applicable and as such they are intended to be helpful rather than prescriptive in influencing decision making and action. The guidelines discussed in this chapter are no exception.

References

Argyris, C (1960) *Understanding Organizational Behaviour*, Dorsey Press, Homewood, IL

Bandura, A (1986) *Social Foundations of Thought and Action: A Social Cognitive Theory*, Prentice Hall, Englewood Cliffs, NJ

Bandura, A (1997) *Self-efficacy*, Freeman & Co, New York

Bies, R J (1987) The predicament of injustice: the management of moral outrage, *Research in Organizational Behaviour*, **9**, pp 289–319

Bloch, S and Bates, T (1995) *Employability: Your Way to Career Success*, Kogan Page, London

Doherty, N, Bank, J and Vinnicombe, S (1996) Managing survivors: the experience of survivors in British Telecom and the British financial services sector, *Journal of Managerial Psychology*, **11** (7), pp 51–60

Herriot, P, Hirsh, W and Reilly, P (1998) *Trust and Transition: Managing the Employment Relationship*, Wiley, London

Katz, D and Kahn, R L (1978) *The Social Psychology of Organizations*, 2nd edn, Wiley, New York

Lazarus, R S and Folkman, S (1984) *Stress, appraisal and coping*, Springer, New York

Lewin, K (1951) *Field Theory in Social Science*, Harper and Row, New York

Likert, R (1967) *The Human Organization*, McGraw-Hill, New York

Porter, L and Lawler, E (1968) *Managerial Attitudes and Performance*, Dorsey-Irwin, Homewood, IL

Rousseau, D M and Parks, J M (1993) The contracts of individuals and organizations, *Research in Organizational Behaviour*, **15**, pp 1–43

Schein, E (1985) *Organizational Culture and Leadership*, Jossey-Bass, San Francisco

Shore, L M and Tetrick, L E (1994) The psychological contract as an explanatory framework in the employment relationship, in *Trends in Organizational Behaviour*, ed C Cooper and D M Rousseau, Wiley, Chichester, pp 91–109

Stickland, R (1996) Self-development in a business organization, *Journal of Managerial Psychology*, **11** (7), pp 30–39

Wanous, J P (1992) *Recruitment, Selection, Orientation and Socialization of Newcomers*, Addison-Wesley, New York

Williams, A P O (1980) Integrating individual and organizational learning: a model and a case study, *Management Education and Development*, **11**(1), pp 7–20

Williams, A P O (1998) Organizational learning and the role of attitude surveys, *Human Resource Management Journal*, **8** (4), pp 51–65

Williams, A P O (2001) A belief-focused model of organizational learning, *Journal of Management Studies*, **38** (1), pp 67–85

Williams, A P O and Dobson, P (1993) Developmental assessment centres on MBA programmes, *International Journal of Assessment and Development*, **1** (4), pp 233–40

Williams, A P O, Dobson, P and Walters, M (1993) *Changing Culture: New Organizational Approaches*, 2nd edn, Institute of Personnel and Development, London

Index